The Fire-Eaters

The Fire-Eaters

Eric H. Walther

Louisiana State University Press
Baton Rouge and London

Designer: Amanda McDonald Key
Typeface: Baskerville
Typesetter: G&S Typesetters, Inc.
Printer and binder: Thomson–Shore, Inc.

Library of Congress Cataloging-in-Publication Data

Walther, Eric H., 1960–
     The fire-eaters / Eric H. Walther.
          p.   cm.
     Includes bibliographical references (p.   ) and index.
     ISBN 0-8071-1731-5 (alk. paper). ISBN 0-8071-1775-7 (pbk.: alk. paper).
     1. Secession.   I. Title.
     E459.W25   1992
     973.7'13—dc20   91–38321
                                                                     CIP

The paper in this book meets the guidelines for permanence and durability of the Committee
on Production Guidelines for Book Longevity of the Council on Library Resources. ∞

Louisiana Paperback Edition, 1992
01   00   99   98   97   96   5   4

For Helen

And this is the fourth of July—a day in which we have talked so much in the past of liberty & independence, George Washington Etc, with all Yankee land [now] pressing upon our vitals & exhausting that substance which we so much begrudged old George 3 & Lord North. Independence indeed! In what has it at last culminated? Have ancient or modern times furnished a despotism more absolute & irresponsible than the one which left its head at the capital of the old republic & tramples underfoot with impunity every vestige of liberty. And yet the Creatures who denounce monarchy & claim the cognomen of Republicans par excellance, fling up their hats & shout hozzanah's to the despot who has his feet upon their neck. I am in despair! The course of republicanism seems to be the same in all ages & what hope have even we who are now staking our lives & fortunes in protection of its stronghold of a better fate as history advances? The evil day may be averted but how long. If this law is to be perpetual better at once acknowledge our error, repeal the declaration of Independence & return to the household of the Tudors, the Stuarts & the Guelphes! At all events any of these or even the house of Hapsburg rather than the vulgar & besotted & drunken rule of the Lincolns, Greelys & Sewards! Whilst there is a Southern sword to be drawn this last fate can never be ours!
        —James D. B. De Bow to Charles Gayarré, July 4, 1861

Contents

Contents

Illustrations

Acknowledgments

When I began this project, I knew that I would need the help of many others. Nevertheless, it is a source of constant amazement to me how many extraordinarily talented and nice people I have come into contact with, and it is a pleasure to thank some of them now. The librarians and staff at my base of operations, the Louisiana State University Libraries, were extremely helpful, especially Lynn Roundtree in the Louisiana and Lower Mississippi Valley Collections and Debbie Atchison in the microforms department. I am fortunate that their assistance and professionalism were matched throughout my travels to and correspondence with the Alabama Department of Archives and History, the Alderman Library at the University of Virginia, the Barker Texas History Center at the University of Texas, the Earl Gregg Swem Library at the College of William and Mary, the Huntington Library, the Historic New Orleans Collection, the Historical Society of Pennsylvania, the Howard-Tilton Library at Tulane University, the Library of Congress, the Mississippi Department of Archives and History, the North Carolina Department of Archives and History, the Robert W. Woodruff Library at Emory University, the South Caroliniana Library at the University of South Carolina, the South Carolina Historical Society in Charleston, the Southern Historical Collection at the University of North Carolina, the Virginia Historical Society, Washington and Lee College, and the William R. Perkins Library, Duke University. I hope that my special thanks to the following people will serve as partial repayment for their indispensable aid: Ellen Gartrell at Duke, Margaret Cook at William and Mary, Frances Pollard, Nelson Lankford, and Sarah B. Bearss at the Virginia Historical Society, and John White at the Southern Historical Collection.

Robert Johannsen provided me with my first opportunity to test ideas about some of these fire-eaters many years ago, and his insight and constructive criticisms provided me with a critically needed perspective. Robert Becker took on the unenviable task of sifting the worst of the chaff in the first draft of this book. His enthusiasm and unrelenting sarcasm were valued sources of support. He also provided several interesting suggestions for the title, all of which contained some form of the word *traitor*. Charles Royster, Burl Noggle, and Sam Hilliard each provided valuable suggestions, sound advice, and an abundance of encouragement in the early stages of writing. John B. Boles and members of Houston Area Southern Historians offered important ideas for revisions of the first chapter. William K. Scarborough pointed out an embarrassing number of factual errors and challenged me to rethink many of my interpretations. John Inscoe and Walter Buenger allowed me to exploit their friendship and time, and they deserve special thanks for careful readings of the manuscript showing me where and how to make significant changes.

Peggy Seale, Marlene LeBlanc, JoAnne McMullen, and Caroline Walker at Louisiana State University are the kind of people who make institutions run. Their friendship, good humor, and ability to cut through paperwork enabled me to finish this book without going crazy. My chairman at Texas A & M University, Larry Hill, provided me with student guinea pigs and valuable institutional support during two terrific years in College Station. Dale Baum and Joseph G. Dawson gave both critical and friendly comments on various portions of the manuscript.

Descendants of several of my subjects have shared with me knowledge of their respective relatives. Elizabeth Ruffin and her family at Evelynton Plantation opened their home to me and my wife; their hospitality and refreshments made a hot summer day into a delight. Equally gracious and informative was Tilghman Broaddus of Marlbourne, another Ruffin descendant. Dr. Janet Kimbrough of Williamsburg welcomed me into her historic home and shared many insightful thoughts about her great-grandfather, Beverley Tucker. Mary Walters, one of my students at Texas A & M University and a descendant of Barnwell Rhett, set me straight about the circumstances surrounding Rhett's death.

My undergraduate adviser, Ronald D. Rietveld, at California State University, Fullerton, transformed my interest in history into a passion, and his continued support and interest in my work have been invaluable. It was with fear and trembling that I sent each chapter to my dissertation director, William J. Cooper, Jr., and a matter of great relief and some pride that he left substantial portions intact. There are few people whose opinions or advice I find more important, none I know who express them better, and no one under whom I would rather have studied. My gratitude for his guidance in graduate school is matched by my good fortune to count him now as a friend.

The people of LSU Press have made working on this book enjoyable and have helped improve it tremendously, especially Margaret Fisher Dalrymple, Catherine Landry, and John Easterly. My editor, Trudie Calvert, has been a pleasure to work with and gave me a much-needed boost of confidence at the end of this long project.

The boundless love, support, and understanding of my family have kept me going through the very long process involved in producing this book; I could not have done it without them, nor would I have wanted to. My wife has lived with fire-eaters for more years than either of us like to count and has gently warned me when I started to take on some of their traits. She has helped substantially with every aspect of this book, from the initial research through the final revisions. Throughout, she has usually had a much clearer idea than I about what this all means and was always more confident than I was that everything would come together. This book is immeasurably better for her help, was more pleasurable a task with her support, and on her account is more satisfying now that it is done. Finally, Frosty would have helped, but she's only a puppy.

Abbreviations

ADAH	Alabama Department of Archives and History
AL	Alderman Library, University of Virginia, Charlottesville
BTHC	Barker Texas History Center, University of Texas, Austin
DBR	*De Bow's Review*
ESL	Earl Gregg Swem Library, William and Mary College, Williamsburg, Virginia
HL	Huntington Library, San Marino, California
HNOC	The Historic New Orleans Collection
HSP	Historical Society of Pennsylvania, Philadelphia
HTL	Howard-Tilton Library, Tulane University, New Orleans
LC	Division of Manuscripts, Library of Congress
LSU	Louisiana and Lower Mississippi Valley Collections, Louisiana State University Libraries
MDAH	Mississippi Department of Archives and History, Jackson
NCDAH	North Carolina Department of Archives and History, Raleigh
RWL	Robert W. Woodruff Library, Emory University, Atlanta
SCHS	South Carolina Historical Society, Charleston
SCL	South Caroliniana Library, University of South Carolina, Columbia
SHC	Southern Historical Collection, University of North Carolina, Chapel Hill
SLM	*Southern Literary Messenger*
SQR	*Southern Quarterly Review*

Abbreviations

VHS	Virginia Historical Society, Richmond
WL	Washington and Lee College, Lexington, Virginia
WPL	William R. Perkins Library, Duke University, Durham, North Carolina

Introduction

Patrick Henry thought he "smelt a rat" at the Constitutional Convention of 1787. Since then there have always been Americans who, like Henry, worried that the government of the United States had too much power, constantly acquired more, and in the process menaced the liberty of its citizens. Whether they called themselves anti-Federalists, Tertium Quids, or simply states'-rights men, in each generation before secession some feared that through one usurpation of power after another, naive or even sinister forces encouraged the growth of federal power. As the nineteenth century progressed, a small but vocal group of southerners emerged who identifed northerners as the source of this attack on liberty. By 1861, thousands of southerners agreed with fire-eater Robert Barnwell Rhett that northerners "like Frankenstein . . . have raised a monster which they cannot quell."[1] In a desperate effort to preserve their peculiar form of liberty in a slave society, most southerners finally listened to these warnings and chose secession.

Although secessionists helped plunge the United States into civil war, in all the literature concerning that conflict surprisingly little has been written about the leaders of secession. Inexplicably, Dwight Dumond's study of the secession movement barely mentions the men who led it for over a decade. Similarly, in some studies that focus on the secession of particular states, individual people are almost entirely absent, victims of historians' painstaking analyses of group behavior. Examinations of the disintegration and rise of political parties help put aspects of the secession movement in a national perspective but necessarily fail to demonstrate the influence of southerners who insisted that no political party could preserve southern rights or liberty. Other studies amply illustrate the determination of northern political leaders to preserve the Union and have carefully delineated the positions and values of radical

---

1. Jesse Carpenter, *The South as a Conscious Minority, 1789–1861* (New York, 1930); William J. Cooper, Jr., *Liberty and Slavery: Southern Politics to 1860* (New York, 1983); Charleston *Mercury*, March 4, 1861.

political groups in the North. Recent biographies have shed light on certain fire-eaters as individuals, but there are no adequate studies on secessionists as a group, on their values and ideologies, or on why so many southerners followed them out of the Union. Most historians, if they discuss the secessionists at all, tend to oversimplify and dismiss the fire-eaters as angry, disgruntled troublemakers out to deceive or manipulate their section of the country and subvert the integrity of the Union. Some older studies, by contrast, have treated them as heroes of a lost cause.[2]

Even the term *fire-eater* is shrouded in mystery. It was used as early as 1851 indiscriminately by both northerners and southerners to condemn anyone believed to be too far out of the political mainstream. Many historians have used the terms *southern radicals* and *fire-eaters* interchangeably. Almost fifty years ago, Ulrich B. Phillips, in an attempt to clarify, wrote that fire-eaters were those who engaged in a "persistent advocacy of Southern independence." I consider this definition accurate and useful in drawing a distinction between fire-eaters and southern radicals. The latter vigorously promoted southern interests but did not necessarily advocate secession. All fire-eaters, therefore, were radicals, but not all southern radicals were fire-eaters. And as both Phillips and the epithet itself implied, fire-eating carried connotations of violence and bitterness, if not also of showmanship.[3]

2. Dwight Lowell Dumond, *The Secession Movement, 1860–1861* (New York, 1931); William L. Barney, *The Secessionist Impulse: Alabama and Mississippi in 1860* (Princeton, 1974); Roy F. Nichols, *The Disruption of the American Democracy* (New York, 1948); Eric Foner, *Free Soil, Free Labor, Free Men: The Ideology of the Republican Party Before the Civil War* (Oxford, 1977); David M. Potter, *Lincoln and His Party During the Secession Crisis* (New Haven, 1942); Hans Trefousse, *The Radical Republicans: Lincoln's Vanguard for Racial Justice* (Baton Rouge, 1968); Ronald Walters, *The Antislavery Appeal: American Abolitionism After 1830* (Baltimore, 1976); Louis Filler, *The Crusade Against Slavery, 1830–1860* (New York, 1960); Peter F. Walker, *Moral Choices: Memory, Desire, and Imagination in Nineteenth-Century American Abolitionism* (Baton Rouge, 1978). Among the best recent biographies are Robert E. May, *John A. Quitman: Old South Crusader* (Baton Rouge, 1985), and Robert J. Brugger, *Beverley Tucker: Heart over Head in the Old South* (Baltimore, 1978). For the fire-eaters as troublemakers or heroes see William L. Barney, *The Road to Secession: A New Perspective on the Old South* (New York, 1972); David S. Heidler, "Fire-Eaters: The Radical Secessionists in Antebellum Politics" (Ph.D. dissertation, Auburn University, 1985); John Witherspoon DuBose, *The Life and Times of William Lowndes Yancey* (2 vols.; 1892; rpr. New York, 1942); Avery O. Craven, *Edmund Ruffin, Southerner: A Study in Secession* (1932; rpr. Baton Rouge, 1982).

3. Ulrich Bonnell Phillips, *The Course of the South to Secession* (New York, 1939), 128.

Introduction

A congressman from South Carolina once proclaimed, "*I have been a disunionist from the time I could think.*" Few others made it as easy for historians to classify them as fire-eaters. Historically the term was always a pejorative one; no fire-eater embraced it. Typically the fire-eaters tried to portray themselves as conservative, not radical, politicians who struggled to save fundamental American values. A fire-eater from Alabama once inadvertently applied the term to himself. During a speech in which he attacked opponents for claiming that "fire-eaters" denounced the Democratic party platform of 1856, this speaker clumsily bellowed, "When and where, I ask, did I ever denounce it?" Another fire-eater also applied the term to himself occasionally, but only in an abortive attempt to diminish the powerful negative impact of this epithet.[4]

Historians have attempted periodically to compile rosters of fire-eaters, but because of a lack of precise definition, no two lists were identical. U. B. Phillips named over a dozen, David Potter and William Barney mentioned fewer. A scholar of antebellum rhetoric, H. Hardy Perritt settled on fourteen and included several the three historians did not. More recently, in *The Encyclopedia of Southern History*, Alvy King mentioned seven in his entry that defined fire-eaters as those who most actively defended slavery and turned to secession only in reaction to antislavery agitation. Only three fire-eaters appear on all five of these lists: Robert Barnwell Rhett of South Carolina, Edmund Ruffin of Virginia, and William Lowndes Yancey of Alabama.[5]

The reaction of southerners to Abraham Lincoln contributed to this divergence of opinion among historians. Many politically active southerners waited to join the secession bandwagon until late in 1860, when Lincoln's election seemed likely, and most advocated secession only after the election was over. After several states had seceded, many veteran fire-eaters, like Edmund Ruffin, grumbled that "eleventh hour laborers" and recent "submissionists" had displaced some of the earliest and most staunch supporters of dis-

4. Preston Brooks quoted *ibid.*, 142; Nashville *Weekly Union*, October 26, 1860, in William L. Yancey Papers, ADAH. See Chapter 6 herein, text preceding n. 47, on James De Bow.

5. Barney, *Road to Secession;* Phillips, *Course of the South;* David Potter, *The Impending Crisis, 1848–1861,* completed and edited by Don Fehrenbacher (New York, 1976); H. Hardy Perritt, "The Fire-Eaters," in *Oratory in the Old South, 1828–1860,* ed. Waldo W. Braden (Baton Rouge, 1970), chap. 8; Alvy L. King, "Fire-Eaters," in *Encyclopedia of Southern History,* ed. David C. Roller and Robert W. Twyman (Baton Rouge, 1979), 434–35.

union in the service of the Confederacy. Recollecting the battle of Fort Sumter a quarter-century later, another fire-eater drew sharp distinctions between "political dudes, who sought prominence and did nothing in peace or war," and bona fide secessionists.[6]

The ambiguity surrounding fire-eaters is not limited to problems of definition. For instance, Robert May has concluded that fire-eaters' lives were as complex as those of their contemporaries in both the North and South and suggests that these radicals had much in common with their mainstream counterparts.[7] Furthermore, the few extant studies of fire-eaters reveal clearly that these were men with vastly different personalities and backgrounds and that, beyond their devotion to southern independence, they had markedly different political agendas and outlooks. Indeed, the fire-eaters joined the secession movement at various times and for various reasons, and the most prominent ones developed distinctive messages and political styles in their efforts to gain support. Their cohesion as a group has not yet received careful study, and the reasons for their ultimate success remain speculative.

Adding another layer to the riddle of secession is the array of provocative but often contradictory state studies of disunion. Virtually all agree that southerners were shocked into action when Lincoln emerged victorious in 1860, but rarely do they agree on anything else. J. Mills Thornton III presented the story of secession in Alabama as the culmination of Jacksonian democracy, a revolt by the common white people against established power—especially a federal government intent on telling them what to do with their slave property—and equally determined to preserve their own equality and independence. Similarly James M. Woods argued that secession in Arkansas resulted from a political realignment caused by a rebellion of yeomen against the state's aristocratic family dynasty. Michael Johnson assigned precisely the opposite reasons for the secession of Georgia. After revolting against the victorious Republican party, according to Johnson, the slaveholding elite used the issue of secession to preserve their hegemony in state politics. Steven Channing claimed that South Carolinians seceded because of their intense fear over losing absolute control over their slave

6. William Kauffman Scarborough, ed., *The Diary of Edmund Ruffin* (3 vols.; Baton Rouge, 1972–89), II, 229; Robert Barnwell Rhett, Jr., to E. C. Wharton, August 2, 1886, in Edward Clifton Wharton and Family Papers, LSU.

7. Robert E. May, "Psychobiography and Secession: The Southern Radical as Maladjusted 'Outsider,'" *Civil War History*, XXXIV (1988), 46–69.

population; Marc Kruman argued that North Carolina seceded as a result of interstate party bickering over who could best preserve slavery and white democracy. In Texas, according to Walter Buenger, disunion resulted from a multitude of local ethnic, political, and economic issues. David Goldfield suggested that urban growth and the regional economic ties of Virginia's cities influenced the secession debate in the Old Dominion. After reviewing these diverse and often contradictory studies, James T. Moore suggested that secession "stemmed, in large measure, from a broad-based and multifacted 'psychic crisis.'"[8]

The musings of a frustrated South Carolina Unionist lend credence to Moore's observation. After reading yet another speech arguing for secession early in 1861, Francis Lieber wrote in his scrapbook: "But what a story this speech tells! Everyone hates the Union, but no two for the same reason!" The various state studies on secession and the conclusions of Moore and Lieber point to an obvious though often overlooked fact: neither the Old South nor its constituent states were monolithic. Although a commitment to perpetuating African slavery and a fear of the Republican party were widespread, a multitude of other issues existed on local levels. Many of these issues had no direct relationship to the sectional crisis but reached critical proportions in the decade before secession.[9]

I began my research on the fire-eaters by seeking to discover the forces that brought them together and shaped the secession movement. I quickly discovered, however, that there were surprising and important variations. Certainly the fire-eaters were concerned with the growing power of the federal government and the coincident dilution of states' rights; all truly believed African slavery was

8. J. Mills Thornton III, *Politics and Power in a Slave Society: Alabama, 1800–1860* (Baton Rouge, 1978); James M. Woods, *Rebellion and Realignment: Arkansas's Road to Secession* (Fayetteville, 1987); Michael P. Johnson, *Towards a Patriarchal Republic: The Secession of Georgia* (Baton Rouge, 1977); Steven Channing, *Crisis of Fear: Secession in South Carolina* (New York, 1970); Walter Buenger, *Secession and the Union in Texas* (Austin, 1984); David Goldfield, *Urban Growth in the Age of Sectionalism: Virginia, 1847–1861* (Baton Rouge, 1977). See James Tice Moore, "Secession and the States: A Review Essay," *Virginia Magazine of History and Biography*, XCIV (1986), 60–76, for a detailed discussion of many of these monographs; quote on page 76.

9. Notes and press clippings on secession, January 6, 1861, in Francis Lieber Papers, HL. Lieber's note was on the speech of Judge Wither in the *National Intelligencer*, January 3, 1861. See Lacy K. Ford, Jr., *Origins of Southern Radicalism: The South Carolina Upcountry, 1800–1860* (Oxford, 1988), 279–80 and notes, and Michael F. Holt, *The Political Crisis of the 1850s* (New York, 1978).

essential to the maintenance of a republican society; all came to believe that their ideal government could exist only in a southern republic. Here they differed from most other southerners only in degree, for a working majority of southerners became secessionists by 1861. These fire-eaters had other concerns that reflected those of their fellow southerners, but they were convinced that only disunion promised a solution. Over the years, as an increasing number of southerners became frustrated or angry with the status quo and worried about apparently menacing political developments, the fire-eaters bolstered the spirit of resistance and offered a solution. It was their diversity that made the fire-eaters important and the secession movement successful. Because each emphasized different issues, ideas, and goals, they drew other southerners to the secession movement as the mushrooming sectional crisis made the fire-eaters seem prophetic instead of extreme.[10] Fire-eaters, then, did not cause secession, but they hastened it by capitalizing on a multitude of events and ideas.

This book attempts to clarify these issues. I have chosen nine men who illustrate simultaneously the unity and diversity of people and ideas encompassed within the secession movement. The sketches of their lives illustrate the range of backgrounds, personalities, and experiences from which fire-eaters emerged and the various directions they intended to go. Nathaniel Beverley Tucker, an early disunionist frustrated by his inability to rouse the multitude, found partial recompense in the classroom by refining secession theory and successfully teaching the ideals of conservative liberty to the next generation. The life of William L. Yancey stands in sharp contrast to that of Tucker. Though more successful than Tucker in putting theory into action, Yancey, the quintessential agitator, was so intent on rocking the political system that he was often able to do little else. Northern-born John A. Quitman, another early fire-eater, demands attention because of a string of accomplishments in his adopted South that just barely lagged behind his tremendous ambition. Devious, crafty, and manipulative, Robert Barnwell Rhett, "the father of secession," was a driven and vastly influential disunionist who stopped at nothing to achieve his prize. Laurence Keitt and Louis Wigfall are studied in the same chapter both because of the relative dearth of source materials for each and to en-

10. See John McCardell, *The Idea of a Southern Nation: Southern Nationalists and Southern Nationalism, 1830–1860* (New York, 1979).

hance comparative study; their similar backgrounds and identical beliefs alternately support and refute the hypothesis that status anxiety motivated some to join the proslavery crusade. James D. B. De Bow's commitment to economic modernization belies the assertion that secession was a flight from modernism, yet De Bow was as susceptible to youthful, romantic ideals of honor as any other fire-eater. Edmund Ruffin's all-absorbing fanaticism and delight in defying the norms of his society run counter to the introspective personality of William Porcher Miles. The latter—as moderate a fire-eater as any extremist could be, a nonslaveholder thoroughly committed to slavery, and more successful and prosperous after the Civil War than before—further illustrates the breadth of the secession movement and thereby provides additional challenges to past scholarship.[11]

Although these nine men interacted infrequently if at all, they forcefully and eloquently advocated secession years before Lincoln's election and were unwaveringly committed to southern independence. They spent decades refining a political philosophy as old as the Union, keeping conservative, republican ideals relevant to a slave society, adapting their message to a changing political world, and gathering converts. Because they participated actively in virtually every level of government and often received tremendous and sustained political support, these fire-eaters effectively refute those who insist the fire-eaters were political "outsiders."[12] Finally, their lack of cohesion, antipathy to organized political parties, various visions of a southern republic, and ultimate perception of secession as a panacea illustrate how the fire-eaters inadvertently contributed to the collapse of the nation they labored so long to conserve.

11. The most eloquent argument for the relationship of status anxiety to the proslavery cause is Drew G. Faust, *A Sacred Circle: The Dilemma of the Intellectual in the Old South* (Baltimore, 1977), esp. 112–14; for a recent assertion of secession as a reaction against modernization, see Thornton, *Politics and Power,* 267–342.

12. Assertions of "outsider" status are most forcefully argued in Barney, *Road to Secession,* 85–100, supported in McCardell, *Idea of a Southern Nation,* 317, and attacked in May, "Psychobiography and Secession."

To Make His Mind the Mind of Other Men

Nathaniel Beverley Tucker

Secession was not a spontaneous reaction to the election of Abraham Lincoln. Nor was it a popular movement taken over by radical politicians at the last moment. By the time the first state seceded in 1860 many southerners in and out of politics had spent over thirty years preparing their people to deal with the sectional crisis and lead them out of the Union. They indoctrinated the people with arguments for state sovereignty, issued warnings about hostile sectional majorities, and argued for the necessity of perpetuating and protecting slavery. These southerners acted as educators whose task was to teach the southern people the principles and necessity of secession.

Nathaniel Beverley Tucker was a teacher. As a professor of law at the College of William and Mary, an essayist, and author of a textbook on government, Tucker devoted his academic career to teaching his students a particular understanding of republican ideals and the nature of the Union formed by those ideals. But Tucker did not confine his teaching to the classroom. He became a close friend and political confidant of the important South Carolina politician James Henry Hammond. He reached for a mass audience by writing a novel intended to popularize secession. He tried to lecture presidents, both in person and through newspaper articles. In all these efforts Tucker strove to correct what he saw as flaws in the fabric of the Union or to prepare the southern mind for secession.

Tucker had a twofold purpose when he lectured to his college students about law and government. The first, and the one he professed to be more important, was to "subdue the mind of the student to a sense of the difficulty of the task before him. . . . To impress the student with a sense of the vastness and importance of the subject." Because so many young men entered college with the notion that they already had a vast storehouse of knowledge, Tucker believed he must "tame down the mind of the student to a teachable temper." He claimed that he had no intent to "infect" his students with his own opinions and concerns. When he began his teaching career, Tucker announced, "I shall be more gratified to find you prepared to 'give a reason for the faith that is in you,' whatever that faith may be, than to hear you rehearse, by rote, any political catechism that I could devise."[1]

In reality Tucker's second goal was far more important to him. Because his political philosophy placed him outside the political mainstream, Tucker worried that his ideas would not reach the southern people. "My only chance to impart my ideas to the world," he once wrote to a friend, "is by impressing them into the minds of my pupils." Although he denied that he was offering a political catechism, Tucker very much wanted to produce a generation of young, politically inclined men to propagate his political gospel throughout the South. He wanted to enlighten his students and open their minds to new ideas, but, he confessed to Hammond, "My ulterior motive is to make him a States-Right man." Tucker's students surely were aware of their teacher's plans, for occasionally Tucker revealed his desires in the classroom. In his first lecture at William and Mary, Tucker explained his belief that "correct constitutional opinions and sound maxims should be implanted" in his students' minds. Many years later he admitted to his students that he tried to use them to secure southern interests and that through his lectures he "sought to enlist" his pupils in a crusade for southern rights. As sectional tensions increased, Tucker asked Hammond for help in educating the South about "the evils of Union" and "the advantages which a Southern Confederacy must enjoy." Although exasperated whenever his students had trouble grasping his ideas, Tucker boasted to Hammond, "My plan has worked well."[2]

Many of the lessons Tucker passed along were ones that he had learned in his youth. His father, St. George Tucker, and his half-brother John Randolph of Roanoke had the greatest influences on him. He venerated his father's accomplishments as a revolutionary war hero, a jurist, and a scholar. He found a model of political in-

1. Nathaniel Beverley Tucker, *A Series of Lectures on the Science of Government, Intended to Prepare the Student for the Study of the Constitution of the United States* (Philadelphia, 1845), 3, 460; Nathaniel Beverley Tucker to James H. Hammond, April 24, 1847, in James H. Hammond Papers, LC; Nathaniel Beverley Tucker, "A Lecture on the Study of Law," *SLM*, I (December, 1834), 148.

2. Tucker to Hammond, March 13, April 24, 1847, April 18, 1850, in Hammond Papers, LC; Tucker, "Lecture on the Study of Law," 150; Tucker, *Lectures*, 450.

tegrity and boldness in Randolph, as well as an emotional bond that filled one of his most persistent longings. Yet Tucker held ambivalent attitudes toward both men. At times, he feared he could never surpass or even equal his father's deeds, yet he felt compelled to try. He envied his brother's oratorical skills and position in the political spotlight. But Tucker credited both of these men with teaching him his most important values, as well as his concepts of law, government, and the nature of the Union.

The Tucker family had resided in the British colony of Bermuda for over one hundred years when St. George sailed to the North American continent in 1771. He went to college at William and Mary, and when the revolutionary war began, he ran supplies from the West Indies to Charleston. He fought with distinction later in the war and rose to the rank of major. He became acquainted with George Washington and the Marquis de Lafayette and joined them at Yorktown in October, 1781, to witness the surrender of Lord Cornwallis. St. George married Frances Bland Randolph in 1778. Widowed in 1775, Frances had been left with three boys, Richard, Theodorick, and two-year-old John. She had inherited her husband's three plantations, Matoax in Chesterfield County and Bizarre and Roanoke to the west. Frances gave birth to Tucker children in 1780 and 1782, and on September 6, 1784, Nathaniel Beverley was born. He was named for his father's brother and for Colonel Beverley Randolph, who fought alongside his father during the Revolution. In 1786, St. George attended the Annapolis Convention, which met to discuss problems of interstate trade that arose from the Articles of Confederation. At the time of the Philadelphia Constitutional Convention in 1787, St. George was in Richmond attending to his law practice. He opposed the new document on the grounds that the Articles of Confederation better guaranteed state autonomy and were therefore the lesser of two evils. In 1789 he took a seat in the state judiciary on the general court circuit and the next year replaced his former mentor, George Wythe, in the Chair of Law and Police at William and Mary.[3]

During the 1790s, St. George lectured to his students about two of the most controversial issues of the day. In 1796 he published his lecture proposing emancipation of slaves in Virginia; he made the

3. Unless otherwise noted, the discussion of St. George Tucker is based on Robert J. Brugger, *Beverley Tucker: Heart over Head in the Old South* (Baltimore, 1978), 1–25.

same proposal to the general assembly later that year. Slavery, he believed, was incompatible with the revolutionary ideal that all men are created equal. His plan called for a gradual end to slavery; it allowed as long as one hundred years to implement emancipation fully. Toward the end of the decade, St. George warned his students that the Alien and Sedition Acts, passed under John Adams' administration, threatened personal liberties and foreshadowed consolidation of power in the federal government.

The study and practice of law soon took St. George away from his academic post. In 1802, he began editing Sir William Blackstone's *Commentaries on the Laws of England,* for half a century the most influential work devoted to the study of common law. Besides editing the text, St. George added notes to make the *Commentaries* more relevant for the United States. His became the standard American edition and the one his son would use in his law classes a generation later. St. George's legal studies culminated with his election to the highest court in Virginia, the Court of Appeals, in 1804.

St. George's impressive career and his personality left indelible impressions on young Beverley. As one of his biographers noted, his father's household was marked by a heritage of suspicion of government, idealization of public virtue, and debates on the merits of slavery. Beverley spent most of his life grappling with the issues he encountered in his earliest days. Eager for personal success and recognition, he often undermined the value of his own accomplishments by comparing them with his father's. Many of his deeds were motivated by the desire to impress St. George. "I have hardly a wish but to shew myself worthy of your affection," he once wrote to his father. But no matter how hard Tucker tried, his father reacted, at best, with indifference. His father's apparent aloofness caused Beverley no end of depression. He complained to John Randolph that he could not foresee any improvement in his relationship with his father and that his heart "sickens when I endeavor to look forward to a period when it will be ameliorated, and look in vain." Nevertheless, Beverley always viewed his father as "noble" and described his love for him as "the master passion of my heart."[4]

Beverley Tucker turned to his half-brother John Randolph for the emotional support his parents failed to provide. Besides feeling

---

4. Beverley Tucker to St. George Tucker, September 15, 1805, to John Randolph, March 20, 26, 1808, in Tucker-Coleman Collection, ESL; Beverley Tucker to Daniel Call, March 14, 1835, in Tucker Family Papers, SHC.

alienated from his father, Tucker lamented the untimely death of his mother on January 18, 1788, when he was not yet four. Randolph supplied him with stories and memories about her, as well as an almost maternal affection. The half-brothers grew close, and their meetings at Randolph's Bizarre plantation never seemed long enough for Tucker. He not only fell under the spell of Randolph's fraternal affection but also admired his sibling's political success and ideology. Tucker rapidly became a political disciple and pledged to his brother, "I would go with you to the end of the world." Late in his life, Tucker claimed that he learned more about politics from the "eloquent lips" of his brother than "all the men with whom I have ever conversed, and all the books I ever read." Intellectually and ideologically Randolph exerted greater influence on Tucker than did St. George.[5]

The lessons Tucker learned from Randolph came from the special role Randolph played in national politics. As a representative from Virginia, he displayed his dazzling speaking abilities in Congress. Originally a Jeffersonian Republican and loyal floor leader for the third president, Randolph believed he saw signs by 1805 that Thomas Jefferson had lost sight of the principles that had brought him into office. Under Randolph's leadership, a handful of congressmen formed a group they called the Tertium Quids. They maintained allegiance to no political party but tried instead to preserve old Jeffersonian principles of small government, local power, and strict construction of the Constitution. Eager to learn the lessons offered by Randolph, Tucker immediately began to interpret national politics through the Quid perspective and urged his brother to continue in his lonely political course. Halfway through Jefferson's second administration, Tucker wrote to Randolph, "The time I trust is at hand when it will be in the power of your 'Spartan Band' to display their firmness and decision, the happiest contrast to the imbecility & distraction of their opponents."[6]

When Tucker compared the ideals he learned from Randolph with political developments in the first quarter of the nineteenth

5. For Randolph as sort of a surrogate mother to Tucker, see Tucker to Randolph, February 19, 1806, in Tucker-Coleman Collection, ESL. On Tucker's devotion to his brother, see Tucker to Randolph, April 21, 1807, *ibid.*, and Tucker, *Lectures*, 28. Robert Brugger claims that St. George exerted the greater influence on Tucker (Brugger, *Tucker*, 26–28).

6. Tucker to Randolph, January 31, 1807, in Tucker-Coleman Collection, ESL; Brugger, *Tucker*, 26–28.

century, he concluded that the United States had "wandered far from principles formerly professed." He considered the "stark-naked ultra-federalism of John Q[uincy] Adams" the logical result of a generation of executive usurpation and the relentless assault of "power and villainy against liberty and truth." Like his brother and other "Old Republicans," Tucker reserved some of his harshest remarks for Thomas Jefferson, whom he condemned for augmenting federal power at the expense of state and local government. He shared his brother's indignation at the possibility that Jefferson might plunge the young nation into another war with Great Britain. He branded many of the laws passed under Jefferson's administrations unconstitutional, even if they had not been so ruled by the Supreme Court. By the end of 1807, Tucker believed Jefferson had acquired so much power that he began to refer to him as "his majesty." His disgust with "the absurd and ruinous policy of this self-willed administration" and his hatred of the president grew so intense that he now wished Jefferson would precipitate a war, "if it be only that it may burst upon his head, and expose him to a nation smarting under the lash which his own folly has prepared."[7]

As Tucker matured, he continued to link his political views to those of his brother. While reviewing various excesses of John Quincy Adams' administration almost two decades after Jefferson's presidency, he told Randolph, "I have never seen any reason to doubt the soundness of our principles, or the wisdom of our policy." He had long considered himself and his brother among the "few honest and independent individuals" in the country, and he promised that history would vindicate their bold stance, even if their own society did not seem to appreciate them. Whenever he perceived an assault on his brother's integrity or political ideology, Tucker felt personally outraged. He tagged a group of Randolph's opponents in western Virginia "sovereign Yahoos," who would be surprised to find that Randolph had neither horns nor tail. Once when Randolph became embroiled in a bitter controversy in Congress, his faithful brother assured him that no "union of Jacobins & federalists" could diminish his qualities of "Integrity fidelity independence courage and magnimity [sic]." In the years after Randolph's death, Tucker became more relentless in his defense. Hor-

---

7. Tucker to Randolph, January 19, February 16, 1808, February 13, 1827, July 19, December 23, 30, 1807, in Tucker-Coleman Collection, ESL; Norman K. Risjord, *The Old Republicans: Southern Conservatism in the Age of Jefferson* (New York, 1965).

rified at an 1851 biography of Randolph, Tucker treated its author to a "savage scalping" in a book review, which even the editor of Tucker's piece considered a "terrible & scathing" attack.[8]

Tucker's memories of his brother helped shape and guide his own political thought. Tucker considered himself the political heir of his brother, as well as a virtual copy of Randolph's independence and integrity. He considered his brother a prophet for anticipating the shattering of constitutional restraints during the War of 1812 and conveniently overlooked any differences of opinion between the two. Tucker once told his friend Hammond that he and Randolph did not agree about men or issues only when "we had not . . . the same data. But in other matters, having learned from him to think freely, I have no doubt that, had I been near him, it would have been said that all my opinions were taken from him."[9]

The dismal beginning of Tucker's career increased his reliance on Randolph. After attending William and Mary in 1801, he chose to emulate his father by pursuing a legal career. But when father and son clashed over where Beverley should locate his practice, his feelings of filial piety led him to yield, "as they always have done," to his father's choice, Fredericksburg. Perhaps no location would have been good. His practice in Virginia was always a financial nightmare. Tucker inadvertently compounded his monetary difficulties in 1807, when his marriage to Mary "Polly" Coalter so displeased his father that St. George threatened to cut him off financially. Tucker feared his father "means to be as good as his word in leaving me to shift for myself, or rather," he hinted to Randolph, "in leaving it to you." Randolph obligingly gave Tucker one hundred acres of land and sixteen slaves to support himself and his new bride. Despite this kindness and charity, Tucker's fortunes continued to plummet. Lack of income and mounting debts sent him into fits of depression. He complained to the sympathetic Randolph, "Can you wonder that in this state of things I am ever gloomy and despondent." He feared he would never attain a fraction of the eminence his father had achieved. "Of politics," he

8. Tucker to Randolph, November 4, 1807, March 22, 1826, April 12, 1809, February 26, 1827, in Tucker-Coleman Collection, ESL; William Gilmore Simms to Tucker, June 26, July 14, 1851, in Mary C. Simms Oliphant, Alfred Taylor Odell, and T. C. Duncan Eaves, eds., *The Letters of William Gilmore Simms* (5 vols.; Columbia, S.C., 1955), III, 132, 138.

9. Nathaniel Beverley Tucker, "South Carolina: Her Present Attitude and Future Action," *SQR*, IV (October, 1851), 285; Tucker to Hammond, April 24, 1847, in Hammond Papers, LC.

moaned, "I can not bring myself to think." The future looked dismal. He once hoped moving his practice to western Virginia might change his luck. Almost anything would be better than the "distress and horror" of his early years, which made him feel as though he "was growing old instead of maturing."[10]

The War of 1812 briefly promised a much-desired change. On February 20, 1812, Tucker received his commission as lieutenant in a Virginia militia unit. But the war brought few opportunities for him to earn distinction. He spent most of it on garrison duty, and his only chance for battle was thwarted in the summer of 1813, when an anticipated British attack on Norfolk never materialized.[11]

During the last year of the war, he confided to his brother-in-law, "I am no longer considered here as of the Bar—at least I am not consulted but for advice." At age twenty-nine, Tucker looked back on his life and decided he had done little but follow the advice of others "and with little profit." Deciding to strike out on his own, he first considered a military career but then decided to move to the West. Originally he considered Tennessee; he had heard that land around Nashville was cheap and plentiful. In 1815 he made an exploratory trip, traveling as far as Missouri Territory. He purchased land near St. Louis and returned to Virginia to prepare Polly, his two young children, and some of his slaves for their westward journey.[12]

Life in the West brought both tragedy and redemption. Late in the summer of 1816, his son Jack—named in honor of John Randolph—and his daughter Frances both died of fever. After recovering from these crushing losses, Tucker turned to farming and then late in 1817 was admitted to the bar in Missouri. This time success quickly followed. More polished and better educated than most of his competitors, Tucker attracted a large clientele and opened a law office in St. Louis. Before the end of the year, the territorial governor appointed him to the Northern Circuit Court of Missouri.[13]

10. Tucker to St. George Tucker, September 15, 1805, August 21, 1807, to Randolph, January 14, March 12, 26, April 6, 1808, to John Coalter, December 20, 1808, September 30, 1811, in Tucker-Coleman Collection, ESL.

11. Tucker's commission of February 20, 1812, is located in the Tucker-Coleman Collection, ESL. Also see Brugger, *Tucker*, 45.

12. Tucker to Coalter, February 8, 1814, in Tucker-Coleman Collection, ESL.; Brugger, *Tucker*, 45–49.

13. Tucker to St. George Tucker and to John Coalter, both on September 24, 1816, in Tucker-Coleman Collection, ESL; Brugger, *Tucker*, 45–49, 50–52.

While in St. Louis, Tucker perceived a surprising level of sophistication among the settlers of the territory. "We have some Yankees it is true but more Virginians," he boasted to Randolph. He rejoiced that most people he met "do not hold the doctrine of presidential infallibility" and found a happy contrast to "the wanton freaks of democratic despotism" he had recently observed in Kentucky. Excited with the possibilities of this situation, Tucker set out to find a place for a planned community based on his nostalgic impressions of Virginia and his belief that only a landed gentry could provide the basis for republican society. He moved his family to a six-thousand-acre site on Dardenne Creek in St. Charles. Coalter relatives from South Carolina and Kentucky soon joined them. Tucker envisioned a community in which slaves worked the fields while their masters devoted themselves to leisurely hours of reading, composing essays, refined conversation, and genteel visits. Initially his experiment succeeded, and several other southern families moved to Dardenne. Before the end of its first year, Tucker bragged to his father that he had created "a neighborhood hardly to be surpassed on the Continent. There is not one of our contemplated set who is not at least independent, none very rich, all intelligent, some highly cultivated, and almost all sincerely and eminently pious." [14]

When the people of Missouri prepared their territory for statehood, Tucker's newfound satisfaction ended abruptly. In Congress, Representative James Tallmadge of New York moved to eliminate slavery gradually from Missouri. Tucker was mortified. Under the pseudonym "Hampden" he wrote a series of editorials for the St. Louis *Missouri Gazette and Public Advertiser* entitled "To the People of Missouri Territory." He warned that the Tallmadge amendment threatened the gravest possible consequence for Missouri and the entire South. The people of each state and territory must be allowed to create their own constitutions. If the people of Missouri yielded the right to make any part of their constitution, Tucker declared, Congress could frame the entire document. Tucker warned further that if the people lost this right they would "become the veriest political slaves, divested of the only right which gives values

14. Tucker to Randolph, September 21, 1817, to St. George, September 26, 1819, in Tucker-Coleman Collection, ESL. For the persistence and impact of classical republicanism, see Risjord, *Old Republicans*, 4, and Lacy K. Ford, Jr., *Origins of Southern Radicalism: The South Carolina Upcountry, 1800–1860* (Oxford, 1988), 52n. More information on the Dardenne settlement is in Brugger, *Tucker*, 57–61, 70–71.

of citizenship—the right of governing themselves." Tucker claimed that if Congress acquired the power to legislate within states and territories, "after emancipating our slaves they may bring them to the hustings, and into the legislature, and into the judgment seat." If a hostile northern majority could implement such laws despite the objections of the people, Tucker cautioned, the integrity of the Union would be gone. "It is power alone which can enable one people to govern another without their consent, and power so exercised is *lawless domination.*" The Constitution would be "but waste paper," and the "bonds of Union," if drawn too tightly, "will burst asunder." [15]

Tucker at last found a sense of self-esteem in the role he played during the Missouri crisis. He reported to Randolph that "having been called to act an important and perilous part in the vindication of good principles . . . I find that sort of a *paternal* feeling toward that infant State has grown up in my mind." Especially when contrasted to his feelings of insignificance in Virginia, Tucker considered Missouri "my own Liliput." [16]

But the compromise reached in Congress in 1820 quickly soured Tucker's attitude toward Missouri, the West, and the Union. Congress defeated the Tallmadge amendment and allowed Missouri to retain slavery, but it prohibited future expansion of slavery above a boundary of 36°30′ north latitude. During a later sectional debate, Tucker looked back on the Missouri Compromise as a watershed. "Had it depended on me Missouri would not have come into the Union" under the terms of the compromise, he told Hammond. He explained to another friend that since 1820 he had considered the Union a curse and "vowed then, and have repeated the vow, *de die in diem,* that I will never give rest to my eyes nor slumber to my eyelids until it is shattered into pieces." [17]

Tucker's attitude toward the people of Missouri shifted quickly from respect to disgust. He now believed "Vanity and Cupidity are the master passions of the west" and was appalled to have to live

15. *Missouri Gazette and Public Advertiser* (St. Louis), April 21, May 5, June 16, 1819. For the relationship between slaveownership and white anxieties about their loss of liberty, see William J. Cooper, Jr., *Liberty and Slavery: Southern Politics to 1860* (New York, 1983), esp. 30–31.

16. Tucker to Randolph, May 16, 1825, in Tucker-Coleman Collection, ESL.

17. Tucker to William Gilmore Simms, n.d. [1851], in William P. Trent, *William Gilmore Simms* (1893; rpr. New York, 1969), 183; Tucker to Hammond, June 23, 1851, in Hammond Papers, LC.

under "the degrading domination of a set of miscreants whom every days experience teaches me more and more to despise and detest." Tucker told Randolph the "rabble" of the West could no doubt be bribed with federal money and promises of internal improvements and that the people knew nothing of states' rights or state sovereignty. He predicted that the West could be saved only by a protracted political conflict that would unite southerners and westerners "under one banner, until the cavalier spirit and devotion to principle which characterize the south may infect the west." [18]

Tucker did not have long to wait until the next crisis. In 1828 Congress passed a protective tariff with rates so high its opponents called it the Tariff of Abominations. Southerners objected strenuously. Many southerners considered all protective tariffs unconstitutional, and most believed the measure was strictly sectional, designed to promote northern industrial growth at the expense of higher prices for consumer goods in the South. John C. Calhoun, former South Carolina congressman and currently Andrew Jackson's vice-president, secretly wrote the *South Carolina Exposition and Protest* in response to the tariff in December, 1828. It contained his theory of state interposition and nullification. Like Beverley Tucker and a host of others, Calhoun believed that the ultimate source of power—sovereignty—belonged to the people of each individual state. According to Calhoun's theory, the federal government was merely the common agent of a collection of states and the Constitution a compact delineating the limits of federal activity. He reasoned that each state, as a sovereign unit, had the right to decide whether federal legislation was unconstitutional. He called this mechanism interposition: the people of a state could hold a convention and declare a federal law null and void within their state. Calhoun hoped this process would redress the grievances of states and keep them in the Union. If three-fourths of all states ratified a constitutional amendment embodying the law in question, however, the nullifying state had the options either of submitting to the national will or seceding.[19]

After four years of debate in Congress, a modified tariff became law in 1832. Dissatisfied with the adjustment, South Carolina held a

18. Tucker to Randolph, March 22, 1826, March 25, 1827, in Tucker-Coleman Collection, ESL.

19. For an excellent discussion of the nullification crisis and Calhoun's theory, see William W. Freehling, *Prelude to Civil War: The Nullification Controversy in South Carolina, 1816–1836* (New York, 1966).

convention in November and overwhelmingly passed an ordinance
of nullification that prohibited the collection of duties within the
state beginning February 1, 1833. A flurry of activity followed.
South Carolina radicals such as Robert Barnwell Rhett called for
secession. President Jackson asked Congress both to reconsider
the tariff and to pass a "force bill" enabling him to use the army
and navy, if necessary, to collect tariff revenue in South Carolina.
Under the leadership of Governor James Hamilton, Jr., the South
Carolina legislature passed laws authorizing the raising of a military force and appropriations for arms. Calhoun resigned the vice-
presidency and returned to his state.

Beverley Tucker observed these developments from the relative
quiet of the West. He was tempted to return to Virginia and rally
the Old Dominion in support of South Carolina. Then, late in
1832, Tucker received an urgent note from his brother. Randolph
was ill and pleaded, "Come to me." [20]

Tucker hesitated only a few weeks, but when he heard that the
Force Bill had passed, he concluded, "The die is cast—The Rubicon
is crossed." This was the occasion he had hoped for. He was sure
Missouri would join the South in any action that might be taken.
He foresaw an apocalyptic conflict. Before leaving Missouri, he
prophesied that, should the South acquiesce in this conflict, "there
is nothing left for any of us but to lie down and be trampled on, or
go away to some country where Liberty still exists, or was never
known. Any thing better than to be slaves where once we were
free." He expressed concern that nullification, secession, and rebellion would become confused with one another and that the confusion would aid the "Tariff party." He believed that because of his
participation in the Missouri crisis, "I shall be among those who
govern events" in Virginia.[21]

Before he left Missouri, Tucker began the self-imposed task of
clarifying issues and teaching southerners about the right of secession. "The views of the nullifier on this subject are manifestly
confused," he said. According to Tucker, nullification placed the
people of a state in a quandary. The president of the United States
must enforce its laws, but state governments must also "punish all
who impede their execution." The people, therefore, were placed

20. Randolph to Tucker, November 9, 1832, in Tucker-Coleman Collection,
ESL.

21. Tucker to General T. A. Smith, December 25, 1832, in Crump Family
Papers, VHS.

between two conflicting authorities, "commanding and prohibiting the same thing on pain of death." He asked rhetorically if a people could be accountable to both simultaneously. "Assuredly not," he said. How could the people of a state remedy such a situation? He answered, "BY CEASING TO BE ONE OF THE UNITED STATES." If a state attempted to remain in the Union after nullification, he claimed, its people must be considered "*rebellious citizens*," whom federal authorities must act against "*at all hazards, and to all extremities.*" [22]

After a joyous reunion with Randolph in Virginia, Tucker renewed and expanded his campaign. As his brother's health continued to deteriorate, Tucker began to look for someone to replace him in the struggle against the federal government. He first turned to Senator Thomas Hart Benton of Missouri, whom he had admired during his residence in that state. He asked the senator to carry the "banner of State Rights" that Randolph had unfurled and assured Benton that Randolph shared his own high estimation of him. He urged Benton to meet the issue of secession boldly and to avoid the "paradox of nullification." In editorials in the Richmond *Enquirer* he chastised Virginians for allowing South Carolina to suffer the burden of a federal confrontation unaided. He warned that unless a Virginian would take a leading role in the drama, "*Virginia* is not FIT TO BE LED, and there is nothing left, but to be *slaves in condition,* as sooner or later *all slaves in spirit are sure to be.*" Tucker offered, "on behalf of the whole planting and slave holding country," to say to "our oppressors . . . 'If this is the way the bargain is to be read, *we must be off;* and if YOU mean to continue the Union, the principles of that Proclamation [the Force Bill] must be DISTINCTLY AND FOREVER RENOUNCED.'" [23]

Through Randolph's "eloquent lips" Tucker found an opportunity to address the people of Virginia. He wrote a series of resolutions that his brother read at a Charlotte Court House meeting in February, 1833. The brothers pledged full support for South Carolina even "while we utterly reprobate the doctrine of nullification." They declared that Virginia was a "free, sovereign and independent State" and had never done anything to impair her sover-

22. Tucker's speech in St. Louis of April 24, 1832, in the Richmond *Enquirer,* February 7, 1833.
23. Tucker to Thomas H. Benton, February 6, 1833, in Tucker-Coleman Collection, ESL; Tucker's editorials were signed "A Friend of State Rights" and "A Friend of State Rights, *because* a Friend of the Union," in Richmond *Enquirer,* February 19, April 5, 1833.

eignty. The Union, they claimed, was merely a "strict league of amity and alliance," and they asserted that any state may secede "whensoever she shall find the benefits of Union exceeded by its evils." They castigated Jackson for turning his back on "his true friends and supporters"—states'-rights men—and succumbing to the influence of those who wanted power consolidated in the federal government. Governor James Hamilton, Jr., of South Carolina, who assumed that Randolph wrote the Charlotte Resolutions, asked Tucker to thank his brother for "his bold manly & glorious assertion of our rights." The governor even forgave the condemnation of nullification. He told Tucker that he considered the resolutions "dignified polished & elegant in the extreme" and that "they draw blood at every thrust."[24]

Pleased with his initial effort, Tucker next strove to correct the views of two of the principals in the nullification showdown, President Jackson and Governor Hamilton. In February, Tucker traveled to the White House and obtained an interview with the president. He warned Jackson that unless he rescinded the Force Bill the president would "provoke a *practical* trial of the right to secede." In a letter to Jackson a few weeks later, Tucker adopted a more conciliatory tone. He suggested that if Jackson rejected the Force Bill, "a door is open to you for correcting . . . all the misapprehensions of the Proclamation." Once the southern states regained "that sense of political security which has been alarmed by the proclamation," he might avoid a collision between state and federal authorities. But if Jackson forced a confrontation, the South would choose secession as "the only practical arbitrament." Calling nullification "superfluous," Tucker suggested to Governor Hamilton that South Carolina declare the tariff both null and unconstitutional "and invite the other aggrieved states to meet you in convention" within two years. Tucker thought the last chance to "save the Union and the States" would be for this convention to affirm the right of secession.[25]

The nullification crisis ended more rapidly than it began. In March, Congress worked out a compromise tariff acceptable both to Jackson and to most Carolinians. The latter reconvened on

24. Richmond *Enquirer*, February 9, 1833; James Hamilton, Jr., to Tucker, February 23, 1833, in Tucker-Coleman Collection, ESL.

25. Tucker to Andrew Jackson, March 1, 1833, to James Hamilton, Jr., March 22, 1833, in Tucker-Coleman Collection, ESL; Tucker's account of his meeting with Jackson is dated February 21, 1833, in Bryan Family Papers, AL.

March 11 to repeal their ordinance of nullification. Tucker's beloved brother died soon afterward. These developments left Tucker gloomy and despondent for many years. He thought Calhoun had acted boldly at first but quickly yielded to presidential ambitions, thereby sacrificing principle and integrity. Of the Quids, Tucker moaned, "Our little army is purged." He wondered what states' rights men like himself could do next, and in his depression answered: "Nothing. . . . The trial is past; the sentence is pronounced; our *earthly* doom is fixed, and we can only pray 'God have mercy on our souls'!!" [26]

The results of the nullification crisis did not extinguish Tucker's fiery spirit. In the summer of 1834, the Board of Visitors at William and Mary offered him the Chair of Law, the position once held by his father. Now fifty years old, Tucker saw it as a unique opportunity to pass along to a new generation the knowledge he had acquired and the principles he valued. He wanted to draw upon his interactions with Randolph and his experiences in the Missouri and the nullification crises to prepare the southern mind to handle any future crisis with unity and clarity of purpose. By this time Tucker also hoped to prevent northern influences from reaching southern youth. He thought it essential for southerners to teach southern students and wished more of them would write textbooks for their own schools. Tucker hoped his lectures and writings would "supply the materials for the reconstruction of the States Right party." More important, he wanted to show his students that if they could not preserve states' rights within the Union, they could do so through secession and the creation of a southern confederacy. As an intellectual, a man of letters, he believed he had a mission "To make his mind the mind of other men / The enlightener of nations." [27]

Tucker told his students that in every country the exclusive function of government was the preservation of liberty. He cautioned them that defining liberty, "and how far it may be enjoyed by all, are questions of acknowledged difficulty." Like most thinkers

26. Tucker to the editors of the Richmond *Whig*, February–April, 1838, Tucker to Richard C. Cralle, February 18, 1838, in Tucker-Coleman Collection, ESL. When Carolinians reconvened they nullified the Force Bill in one last act of defiance.

27. Notice of Tucker's appointment in *Southern Literary Messenger*, I (December, 1834), 145; William C. Preston to Tucker, September 22, 1835, in Tucker-Coleman Collection, ESL; Tucker to Hammond, December 29, 1846, in Hammond Papers, LC; Tucker, *Lectures*, 356.

since the Enlightenment, Tucker believed man was born in a natural state of freedom with no conditions or restraints. Thus isolated, however, individuals faced a variety of threats and therefore formed societies. Members of a society created an authority to enforce the rules of conduct all members had established. "Such authority is government, and such commission is the constitution establishing it." People created government out of their need for arbitration, to provide a means of adjusting differences, and to restrain "the vicious propensities of men." Because "the true idea of liberty" is "the enjoyment of every right," Tucker continued, governments must place restraints on some people so as to preserve the liberty of others. Thus, as he later explained to Hammond, liberty is "the most difficult problem in the world." [28]

The need for restraint occupied a central place in Tucker's theory of government because of his conception of power and adherence to the republican ideals of the Founding Fathers. In common with other Americans, especially the "Old Republicans" of the South, Tucker viewed power as the antithesis of liberty. He saw power as virtually a living thing that feeds upon itself if left unchecked. Because too much governmental power threatened liberty, Tucker emphasized the need to control federal power. He told his students that any government, "however weak, having power to assume more power, has already too much." Tucker reminded his students of Patrick Henry's belief that a lack of governmental power could always be filled, but an excess of power could not be checked. [29]

Tucker offered the same lesson to President John Tyler in 1841. Tucker recalled that every president from Jefferson to Jackson, although professing states' rights and "correcting federal abuses," found after taking office that it was impossible to resist the temptation to accumulate power. Just as he had lectured to his students,

28. Tucker, *Lectures*, 30–39, 53, 293, 144–45, 252; Tucker to Hammond, May 7, 1850, in Hammond Papers, LC.

29. Tucker, *Lectures*, 365–66. The literature on republicanism is vast and growing. The most important works remain Bernard Bailyn, *The Ideological Origins of the American Revolution* (Cambridge, Mass., 1967), and Gordon Wood, *The Creation of the American Republic, 1776–1787* (Chapel Hill, 1969). Among the best studies that show the persistence of republican ideals in the antebellum South are Ford, *Origins of Southern Radicalism;* Kenneth S. Greenberg, *Masters and Statesmen: The Political Culture of American Slavery* (Baltimore, 1985); Risjord, *Old Republicans;* Robert E. Shalhope, "Thomas Jefferson's Republicanism and Antebellum Southern Thought," *Journal of Southern History,* XLII (1976), 529–56.

Tucker told the president: "All Federal powers aid each other. Every usurpation facilitates other usurpations." He warned Tyler that those who supported the consolidation of federal power had worked systematically to achieve it for fifty years, resulting in a "corresponding depression and degradation of the State authorities." He promised Tyler that he would hold a place of distinction in the nation's history if he would refrain from continuing the aggrandizement of federal power. "The experiment is worth trying; for," he offered, "success would be a blessing to your country, and even failure must be glorious." If Tyler did not make the attempt, however, he would confirm himself as "a mere tool . . . for the accomplishment of their grand plan of consolidation, and the reestablishment of the abominations of 1828." [30]

Throughout his life, Tucker believed that unchecked power would have drastic consequences. During the Missouri crisis he had warned his fellow citizens that if they yielded any power to deal with slavery they would lose all power to control their peculiar institution. Tucker returned to this idea during the territorial controversy in the late 1840s. If the central government gained enough power, he warned Hammond, "What is to hinder the emancipation of our slaves?" His alarm over consolidation of power grew almost to paranoia by 1849. When he heard that the government contemplated the creation of a bureau of agriculture, Tucker feared it meant "the Federal Govt. is to assume a new jurisdiction, extending to the very soil of the states." He cautioned his students that if the federal government accumulated sufficient power, the states of the Union could "be obliterated and absorbed by it." [31]

Because of the great tendency for power to build upon itself, Tucker explained, means to control it had to be institutionalized and codified. Like many southerners, he considered all constitutions essentially negative in nature, designed to provide restraints, not grants of power. [32] In the American Constitution, he told his pupils, the Founding Fathers had diffused power as widely as pos-

30. "To John Tyler, President of the United States," signed "A State Rights Man," Richmond *Enquirer*, August 10, 13, 17, 31, 1841.

31. "To the people of Missouri Territory," *Missouri Gazette and Public Advertiser* (St. Louis), May 5, 1819; Tucker to Hammond, March 16, 1848, December 27, 1849, in Hammond Papers, LC; Tucker, *Lectures*, 429.

32. Don E. Fehrenbacher, *Constitutions and Constitutionalism in the Slaveholding South* (Athens, Ga., 1989), esp. 53; James Oakes, *The Ruling Race: A History of American Slaveholders* (New York, 1982), 194–96; Risjord, *Old Republicans*.

sible between various branches of the federal government "to afford a reasonable security against . . . an accumulation of power" in any one branch, thereby protecting "the liberty of the whole community." He emphasized that the Constitution set specific limits on what the federal government could do to the states, and he argued that the Bill of Rights was "mainly intended to guard the rights of the States." The "sole and avowed motive" for the adoption of the Constitution, he believed, was "to place the external relations of all the states on the same footing, and to unite the power of all for the common defense." Using an exceptionally strict interpretation, Tucker accused government officials of violating the spirit—if not the letter—of the Constitution when they used it for any ends besides those he had mentioned.[33] Tucker obviously favored the weak central government that his father had found under the Articles of Confederation.

Tucker pointed to the constitution of Virginia as closest to an ideal compact and illustrated his argument by comparing Jefferson's tenure as governor of Virginia, with the narrow limits its constitution placed upon him, and his record as president, armed by the federal Constitution with greater potential power. Tucker recalled, from the Quid perspective, that as president, Jefferson "has been seen to exercise a power over the thoughts, the affections, the will of his countrymen, without example before his time." But under the restraints placed upon him by the constitution of Virginia, Tucker asked, "what was he but an official drudge, bound down to the literal execution of his limited functions."[34] Clearly Tucker wanted his students to agree that the latter situation was preferable.

Although Tucker considered the checks and balances created by the Founders wise and prudent, he also believed that they could not possibly have prepared enough restraints for a future when "the maxims of consolidation are habitually received as the true interpretation of the Constitution." The Constitution was valuable in restraining power, but it was inert, lifeless. He therefore tried mightily to awaken southerners to the danger of "trusting too much to forms." In his lectures he spoke of the need for constant

33. Tucker, *Lectures*, 23, 361–62, 384; Tucker to Hammond, March 13, 1847, in Hammond Papers, LC; "To John Tyler, President of the United States," Richmond *Enquirer*, August 13, 1841. Tucker used similar arguments in "To the People of Missouri Territory," *Missouri Gazette and Public Advertiser* (St. Louis), May 5, 1819.

34. Tucker, *Lectures*, 363.

vigilance: "No people should ever permit themselves to feel secure in the enjoyment of their rights." Again drawing from revolutionary thought, Tucker warned that rights and liberties "are always in danger from some quarter." In a free, republican society every citizen had a duty to remain vigilant in defense of his rights: "We must not only be awake, and watch," he told his students, "but we must learn where to watch."[35]

Tucker emphasized these positions for over a generation. During the nullification crisis, he futilely tried to warn his fellow Virginians that "our sentinels are sleeping on their posts: our camp is assaulted." He once remarked that keeping watch on the federal treasury served as a better safeguard of liberty "than all our fine-spun theories about checks and balances." As early as Jefferson's administration Tucker had warned that if Americans did no more to preserve their rights than entrust their preservation to the Constitution, "the people may go to sleep with parchment under their heads and awaken with fetters on their hands."[36]

Along with a vigilant citizenry, Tucker believed a self-governing society required tremendous public virtue. When "ambition, and avarice, and the love of pleasure, and the love of display, have gained the mastery of the heart, freedom no longer exists, except by sufferance." He fervently believed liberty was "the reward of virtue" and conversely warned that if "the simplicity and plainness of our ancient manners" were replaced by "the dominion of passions," the country risked destruction and domination by "any master who will pamper them."[37]

Everywhere Tucker looked, however, he saw "a flood tide of corruption," not virtue. In the earliest years of the century he had complained of "prating youngsters who disgrace the halls of our assembly, and sometimes that of congress." In Tucker's mind, venality, not virtue, insubordination, and servility marked most politicians of the day. By the time he began teaching at William and Mary, Tucker found virtue completely lacking in the West and all but absent in Virginia. In 1851 he warned his fellow southerners that the North had come to count on southern "supineness, upon

35. Tucker to Thomas H. Benton, February 6, 1833, in Tucker-Coleman Collection, ESL; Tucker, *Lectures,* 21, 64, 93, 394.
36. Richmond *Enquirer,* February 19, 1833; Tucker to Daniel Call, March 14, 1835, in Tucker Family Papers, SHC; Tucker to Randolph, July 19, 1807, in Tucker-Coleman Collection, ESL.
37. Tucker, *Lectures,* 108, 237–38.

our cupidity and our cowardice," and added ominously, "They may be safe in doing so."[38]

The lack of virtue Tucker perceived among the most prominent southern politicians alarmed him the most. Calhoun, he told Hammond, "is the greatest riddle in the world to me." Tucker had often observed the Carolina politician adhering to principle and making personal sacrifices for the good of the South. Yet it seemed that "once in four years" Calhoun deserted his loftier ideals in an attempt to gain a presidential nomination. Before the nullification crisis, Tucker blamed the "ill weaved ambition of that restless aspirant" for diluting southern political cohesion and strength. He lumped Calhoun together with John Quincy Adams, Andrew Jackson, and Henry Clay of Kentucky as men "utterly destitute of principle." At the end of the 1830s, Tucker considered Calhoun morally dead and eulogized his "fallen greatness." Tucker admired Calhoun's talents as a politician but accused him of having an "overweening self-confidence" that led him to pursue personal interests and abandon those of the South.[39] Tucker wondered why Calhoun looked for personal glory within the Union instead of in the creation of a southern confederacy:

> Why does not Ambition look forward to the rewards which popular favour is eager to bestow, at the end of any revolutionary movement, on those who began it? Why can Mr. Calhoun never take his eye from that chain, which, in such event, would vanish into air? Why do those who expect to rise with him cherish more the shadowy prospect of future? and seats in the cabinet, than their own private interests, and all the honours that the Southern people have in store for him who shall be first to break the chain which fetters them, and crushes the very heart of hope and enterprize?[40]

Inheriting the Old Republican distaste and distrust of factions, Tucker saw no clearer sign of the lack of virtue in the South than in that region's adherence to political parties. Among Calhoun's other sins, Tucker accused him of buckling under to the dictates of

38. Tucker to Randolph, March 10, 1806, May 23, 1807, March 22, 1826, May 2, 1833, in Tucker-Coleman Collection, ESL; Tucker to Hammond, February 17, 1836, in Hammond Papers, LC; Tucker to Littleton W. Tazewell, June 26, 1826, in Nathaniel Beverley Tucker Letter, AL; Tucker, "South Carolina," 281.

39. Tucker to Hammond, October 11, 1848, February 6, 1847, in Hammond Papers, LC; Tucker to Randolph, March 22, 1826, March 25, 1827, to Richard Cralle, April 24, 1838, in Tucker-Coleman Collection, ESL.

40. Tucker to Hammond, December 27, 1849, in Hammond Papers, LC.

the Democratic party. He condemned Henry Clay for betraying, degrading, and compromising the rights of the South for the sake of his advancement in the Whig party. Tucker found his countrymen—especially Virginians—easily lured to supporting parties by the promise of federal patronage and money. Political parties, Tucker complained, presented party hacks as their presidential nominees, transforming elections from a "horse race" into an "ass race." He described Congress, racked by party squabbling, as "that synagogue of Satan," filled with men "whose valour oozes out of their fingers' ends" for the four brief months of each session. According to Tucker, the two major parties were "the curse of the Union," and he blamed them for "running down State sovereignty" since 1833. Tucker's relentless antiparty views struck a persistent and powerful chord in the southern mind, as other fire-eaters would soon discover and exploit.[41]

The greatest threat Tucker saw in political parties was in their appeal to the masses for support. The rapid expansion of suffrage during the early nineteenth century alarmed Tucker. He blamed contending parties for bringing more and more people into the political process, arming them with votes, and thereby increasing the power of the masses. Tucker maintained that the worst form of oppression was "the tyranny of numbers." He argued that power spread widely among a mass of people posed as great a threat to liberty as power concentrated in the federal government. Tucker said that advocates of democratic rule really preached "the divine right of numbers." He adamantly denied that majorities could do anything they chose without hindrance or restraint; this antecedent would inevitably lead to the trampling of the rights of minorities. In a representative government, Tucker could conceive of "no thraldom so hopeless as that of a fixed local minority." In his classroom he said that if representatives of a majority could do anything they pleased, they could ignore the rights of and oppress a minority even while acting within the forms of free government. With particular reference to the rise of abolitionism, Tucker predicted that a northern majority might soon try to pass legislation regarding slavery, even if doing so ignored the wishes and rights of the

41. Tucker to the editors of the Richmond *Whig*, February–April, 1838, in Tucker-Coleman Collection, ESL; "To John Tyler," Richmond *Enquirer*, August 24, 1841; Tucker, "South Carolina," 276, 292; Nathaniel Beverley Tucker, *Prescience: Speech Delivered by Hon. Beverley Tucker of Virginia, in the Southern Convention, Held at Nashville, Tennessee, April 13, 1850* (Richmond, 1862), 33. On the force of antiparty ideals in the Old South see Greenberg, *Masters and Statesmen*, 45–64.

southern minority. If such were free government, Tucker concluded, "then freedom is of little worth. If not, it shows well the
forms of freedom may coexist with the worst evils of slavery." As
with all other forms of power, "the Union between power and the
Democracy of Numbers" knew no limits. He described this bond as
similar to "the union of the sexes, and as *indissoluble*. Once joined it
is not for man to put them asunder."[42]

Tucker envisioned terrible consequences for liberty under this
union of power and numbers; a demagogue might appeal to the
passions of the "dumb brute voiceless multitude." He warned his
students that the skillful demagogue would use these passions to
manipulate the people:

> He corrupts them with the spoils of the treasury; he tempts them with
> the plunder of the rich; he engages them in the services of his profligate
> ambition; he gilds the fetters he prepares for them; and teaches them to
> wear them as badges of party, and the trappings of distinction, until,
> familiar with their weight, they permit them to be rivetted on their
> limbs. [This occurs during] the season of tumultary elections. . . . It is
> the season when leaders, drunk with ambition, and a rabble, drunk with
> flattery and alcohol, unite to plunder and oppress the middle classes,
> and shout the praises of parties and demagogues.[43]

The "meddling spirit of Democracy" threatened the entire fabric
of society. Property, which Tucker considered as valuable as liberty,
would become "the prey of the poor." The "low-bred insolence of
upstart ignorance intruding by unhallowed means into the throne
of legislation" would result in the violation of contracts, the printing of valueless paper money, and the loss of incentive for invest-
ment. In the final stage of democracy run rampant, he explained to
Hammond, the masses would invest their power in one man, "who
feels himself absolutely secure in the use of power."[44]

With himself and his country facing these possibilities, Tucker
sought a "controlling power over the brute force of the multitude"

42. Nathaniel Beverley Tucker, *Discourse on the Dangers That Threaten the Free In-
stitutions of the United States, Being an Address to the Literary Societies of Hampden Sidney
College, Virginia* (Richmond, 1841), 21; Tucker, "Lecture on the Study of Law," 151;
Tucker to Hammond, April 24, 1847, February 18, 1836, in Hammond Papers,
LC; Tucker, *Lectures*, 142–43; "To John Tyler," Richmond *Enquirer*, August 13,
1841; Tucker to Richard Cralle, February 18, 1838, in Tucker-Coleman Collection,
ESL.

43. Tucker, *Lectures*, 44.

44. Tucker, *Discourse on Free Institutions*, 14; Tucker, *Lectures*, 125, 329–30;
Tucker to St. George Tucker, January 20, 1822, in Tucker-Coleman Collection,
ESL; Tucker to Hammond, May 25, 1851, in Hammond Papers, LC.

so that "they who want will not take from they who have." He taught his students that the most basic step in this direction was to prevent universal suffrage and even to disfranchise many voters. The professor admitted that limits on suffrage seemed "an absurd and preposterous incongruity" to many who studied free government but pointed to the past to support his views. Tucker reminded his students that the founders of Virginia and the United States had institutionalized a freehold suffrage not because they felt "it ought to work" but because over one hundred years' experience had shown "the thing *had* worked well." Universal suffrage suited a society only if "the affairs of a people will be most discreetly administered by the ignorant; if the reign of virtue will be best secured by the authority of the most vicious." Until then, Tucker claimed, "the MIND of the community" must remain in control and refrain from yielding "the tasks of thought to the unthinking, and the authority of law to those who should be subjects of its corrective discipline." He argued that a natural order existed in every society and that the conservatism inherent in property owners uniquely qualified them to defend the personal rights and liberties of all.[45]

The basic principle behind Professor Tucker's advocacy of limiting the franchise was his denial of a universal capacity for self-government. The idea that "there is no best in government" permeated his lectures. He remarked that what was best for "a horde of poor and ignorant barbarians" would not suit "an enlightened, refined, rich and luxurious community," and the best form of government for one individual might not work well for another. He repeatedly argued that no government was good unless it allowed freedom, but he vehemently denied that any government could impose freedom on anyone. He once told Hammond that "compulsory Liberty is a solecism." He told his students, "The capacity for freedom is the capacity for *self-government.*" Without that capacity, Tucker thought a people given freedom "will but use it to seek a master."[46]

To qualify for participation in free government, Tucker insisted that an individual had to demonstrate certain capabilities. He regarded self-control as "the inseparable condition of political freedom." He emphasized the need for proper education and training because "in proportion as government is free, so is its structure in-

45. Tucker to Hammond, February 17, 1836, in Hammond Papers, LC; Tucker, *Lectures*, 262–63, 288, 344; Risjord, *Old Republicans*, 3.
46. Tucker to Hammond, January 27, 1850, in Hammond Papers, LC; Tucker, *Lectures*, 62, 64, 131, 144–45, 279.

tricate and delicate, and liable to derangement from the unskillful hand of meddling ignorance." He charged the statesman with the responsibility of checking "the expansive growth of the germ of evil" that exists within every government. No doubt his students understood when their teacher spoke of the "solemn and awful duty" of self-government. Tucker emphasized the difficulty of self-government at the conclusion of his first lecture, saying, "Whether we mount the hustings or go to the polls, we may well tremble to give or receive the power which is there conferred."[47]

Tucker found stark contrasts in the ways northerners and southerners dealt with the question of democracy. In discussing the issue with Hammond, Tucker asserted that northerners had "surrendered their authority to the mob on *compulsion*." In the South, however, no power existed "to extort the concession, because the great body of the disfranchised were slaves." Although he continued to fear the "epidemic" of democracy, he assured himself and Hammond that "slavery . . . is a perfect antidote." Throughout Tucker's teaching career he referred to African slavery as the South's "most sacred and fundamental institution, the only basis on which the temple of [white people's] freedom can stand firm and enduring."[48]

Tucker and all fire-eaters found one of their most important sources of unity in rejecting Thomas Jefferson's ideals of natural equality and making republican theory conform to the realities of a slave society. American republicans had long maintained that true freedom, for individuals as well as societies, required economic independence. And yet fire-eaters as well as Jefferson feared that even in America a poor, landless class might jeopardize both independence and social unity. By enslaving the poor, especially when that class was clearly separated by race, Tucker and other fire-eaters merely embraced a logical conclusion that Jefferson avoided: African slavery was necessary for American republicanism.[49]

In common with other advocates of slavery and secession, Tucker claimed that a fundamental inequality existed between blacks and

47. Tucker, *Lectures*, 14, 22, 236, 276–81; Tucker to Randolph, September 21, 1817, in Tucker-Coleman Collection, ESL; Tucker, "Lecture on the Study of Law," 152.

48. Tucker to Hammond, February 17, 1838, January 2, 1851, in Hammond Papers, LC; Nathaniel Beverley Tucker, "Slavery," reviews of J. K. Paulding, *Slavery in the United States*, and H. Manly, *The South Vindicated from the Treason and Fanaticism of Northern Abolitionists*, SLM, II (April, 1836), 377; Tucker, "South Carolina," 275.

49. Edmund S. Morgan, *American Slavery, American Freedom: The Ordeal of Colonial Virginia* (New York, 1978), esp. 376–87.

whites and, most important, that blacks lacked the capacity for self-government. Moreover, Tucker denied that blacks had the same "passions and wants and feelings and tempers" as whites. He said God had invested Anglo-Saxons with "moral and political truth" and created them as "a master race of unquestionable superiority." Africans, however, barely bore "the lineaments of humanity, in intellect scarcely superior to the brutes." Therefore, Tucker justified slavery on the grounds that it forced to labor those "who are unable to live honestly without labor."[50]

Tucker never meant to imply that whites could act capriciously toward slaves, no matter how great were the differences between them. In his lectures he said God must have mixed the two races in order to achieve some "moral good." Besides allowing the control of a supposedly shiftless people, slavery could be thought of as a "great school" through which blacks might eventually achieve full civilization. They had already learned much under the loving and benevolent tutelage of their white masters. Christianity, he said, had softened the Africans' fierceness, enlightened them, curbed their sensual appetites, and inspired feelings of self-respect, cleanliness, and manners. He claimed that slaveholders in America had reached more souls "than all the missionaries that philanthropy and religion have ever sent forth." Tucker argued that if a slave would but accept his fate, he would discover there are "none so free as those the world calls slaves." Motivated by kindness of heart, the slaveholder would make his slaves' lives secure, protect them from injustice and want, and care for the infirm and aged.[51]

Tucker hoped southerners would spread this benevolent and necessary institution everywhere they went. He had personally helped to implant and protect slavery in Missouri. When war raged against Mexico in 1847, he wished "the pupilage of the race of Ham" prolonged until whites had expanded African slavery from the western parts of the continent to the banks of the Amazon River. He even dreamed of taking slavery to the western shores of the Pacific.[52]

50. Tucker, "Slavery," 338; Tucker, Lectures, 298–302; Nathaniel Beverley Tucker, "Note to Blackstone's Commentaries, Being the Substance of Remarks on the Subject of Domestic Slavery," SLM, I (January, 1835), 230.

51. Tucker, Lectures, 298, 306–307; Tucker, Prescience, 30; Tucker, "Slavery," 338; Tucker, "Note to Blackstone's Commentaries," 227.

52. Tucker, Lectures, 303, 349; Tucker, "Note to Blackstone's Commentaries," 229; Tucker to Hammond, April 24, 1847, March 13, 1850, in Hammond Papers, LC.

Of more immediate concern, Tucker found African slavery essential to republican government. In his opinion domestic slavery created unity among whites and political and social stability for the entire slaveholding society. White southerners' observations of living examples of freedom and slavery fostered "a jealous passion for liberty in [even] the lowest class of those who are not slaves." In a slaveholding society, the color of a white person "is his certificate of freedom." All white southerners—even nonslaveholders—benefited from the institution: "Slave labor pre-occupies and fills the low and degrading stations of society. Menial offices are altogether discharged by it; and the tasks of mere brute strength are left to it. To the freeman belong those services which imply trust and confidence, or require skill; which therefore command higher wages than mere animal labor, and give a sense of respectability and a feeling of self-respect." By maintaining "a class lower than all, and more numerous than all, of a different race," white people would unite to control and manage them "in a common spirit and in perfect harmony." He promised that racial antagonism would prevent poor whites both from helping slaves launch insurrection and from enlisting the aid "of NEGRO *slaves*" in attempts to extort political power.[53]

Tucker's opinions about slavery changed rapidly during his tenure at William and Mary. When he arrived there, he believed slavery was "an evil in itself, and in all its modes." At that time he justified slavery as a necessary evil with which whites had to deal as best they could. As northern abolitionists grew in numbers and increased their campaign against slavery in the 1830s, Tucker, like many other southerners, quickly grew defensive about the institution and searched for ways to rationalize and justify it. Professor Thomas R. Dew, one of Tucker's colleagues, soon convinced him that slavery was not an evil but a blessing. Dew, one of the originators of a coherent proslavery argument, held that the institution violated neither human nor divine law. Tucker eagerly followed Dew's example and argued that a "manly discussion" of slavery would reveal that "the South will derive much more of good than of evil from this much abused and partially-considered institution." After his own lengthy consideration of slavery, Tucker concluded that it was a great, paternalistic institution that benefited slave and master alike. He told a later generation of students that the Found-

53. Tucker, *Lectures*, 331–35; Tucker, "Note to Blackstone's Commentaries," 230; Tucker to Hammond, February 17, 1836, in Hammond Papers, LC.

ing Fathers had sanctified slavery merely by refusing to abolish it. Tucker's proslavery zeal culminated in a letter he wrote to Hammond in 1848. If slavery were to be abolished, Tucker said, "I shall go to my grave thanking God that he was pleased to allot me my time on earth during its existence." [54]

No matter how enthusiastically Tucker supported African slavery, he knew "it was not easy for any one to sit down under the reproach of the world." In both England and the northern United States, Tucker observed growing numbers of abolitionists. He denied that these people had a right even to debate the merits of slavery. Such a right belonged only to slaveholders. Tucker urged his fellow southerners to discuss the issues pertaining to slavery. Thus confined, no one could condemn the institution "without standing self-condemned." He hoped the self-interest of slaveholders would prevent them from implementing schemes for emancipation. By applying so many restrictions, Tucker clearly separated his father's efforts toward emancipation from any association with later abolitionists. But he did encourage the study of slavery within the South. Whether or not others shared his conclusions, he warned prophetically, a thorough understanding of slavery "may become necessary to man our hearts and brave our nerves for the impending struggle." [55]

When the debate over slavery spread to the floor of Congress in 1836, Tucker campaigned to back his words with action. He wrote to Hammond—a congressman from South Carolina at the time— begging him to lead his state out of the Union. If sanctimonious northerners tried to impose their will on the South, secession would enable southerners to escape the "contagion" of abolitionism and leave them free "to regard as enemies those who hate us and whom we hate." Tucker believed that if South Carolina seceded all other slave states "would draw together in a new confederacy made wise by the experience of the past." [56]

The sovereignty of the states was Tucker's paramount concern in regulating slavery, suffrage, and every other state institution. State sovereignty was the cornerstone of his political philosophy, the key to his understanding of the nature of the Union, and his justification for secession.

54. Tucker, "Note to Blackstone's Commentaries," 228; Tucker, "Slavery," 339; Tucker, *Lectures*, 262; Tucker to Hammond, March 16, 1848, in Hammond Papers, LC.

55. Tucker, "Note to Blackstone's Commentaries," 228.

56. Tucker to Hammond, February 17, 18, 1836, in Hammond Papers, LC.

Tucker never provided a single, concise definition of sovereignty, but he did develop one in the course of his lectures. He taught that sovereignty included the rights to command, to be obeyed, to protect, to hold individuals responsible to the community, and to impose the collective responsibility of the community between the community and anyone external to it. The execution of sovereignty included enforcement of retribution, infliction of punishment, and the oversight of the life, liberty, and property of every member of the community. During the nullification controversy, he graphically summarized sovereignty as "the power of pit and gallows." The people of a state held all sovereign power. When the people met in a convention, there were no limits to their potential power except those they placed upon themselves. The people, not their governments, were sovereign; governments were the people's creatures, not creators, and elected officials their servants, not masters.[57]

Tucker tried to convince southerners that the people of each state retained sovereignty. He used Virginia as an example for his college students. Repeating his statement at Charlotte Court House, Tucker declared that Virginia had been "*a free, SOVEREIGN and independent state*" ever since her people declared her so on June 29, 1776. He told his students that the people of Virginia had assumed sovereignty and independence without making any obligation or alliance with other colonies and had done nothing since that date to dilute or alter their sovereignty. Tucker had used these same arguments during the debates over Missouri's statehood. Because he believed that only the consent of the people, freely given, made a constitution binding, he argued "that Missouri was already a Sovereign State" during the territorial period. The people of any territory or state perform a sovereign and independent act when they elect members to a constitutional convention; therefore, Tucker defined the creation of a constitution as "the highest act of Sovereignty." He called the territorial phase one of "pupilage and wardship" but one that left the sovereignty of its people untouched.[58]

The importance Tucker assigned to state sovereignty explained

57. Tucker, *Lectures*, 53, 73–74, 77, 362, 375–76, 387; Richmond *Enquirer*, February 7, 1833; Tucker, "South Carolina," 288.

58. Tucker, *Lectures*, 251, 374–76; Richmond *Enquirer*, February 9, 1833; "To the People of Missouri Territory," *Missouri Gazette and Public Advertiser* (St. Louis), April 21, 1819; Tucker to John C. Calhoun, November 13, 1844, in Chauncey S. Boucher and Robert P. Brooks, eds., *Correspondence Addressed to John C. Calhoun, 1837–1849* (Washington, D.C., 1930), 259.

his conception of state and federal relations. He described each state as a separate and distinct body politic, a society of men united to promote their common welfare and possessing the right, obtained by the consent of all members, to regulate their conduct. He told his students that when two or more states united to form a confederacy each retained its own government and the power to enforce its rules of conduct among its own people. Such a union, according to Tucker, had no effect on the bodies politic of its constituent parts and therefore resulted in "no loss of nationality" for member states. Re-formation of a body politic only occurred in a union that explicitly abrogated the sovereignty of each state. Tucker taught that sovereignty was indivisible; "*There can be but one Supreme.*" He viewed the American federal system as a confederation in which states delegated some of their authority to the central government but surrendered none of their sovereignty. The decision of the people of Virginia to join the United States was therefore an act of sovereignty, not a rejection of it. When it entered the Union, the state compelled its members to obey federal laws. Thus when the people of a state complied with federal laws, they did so only because their state commanded them to. "Virginia is your country," Tucker informed his students. "To her your allegiance is due. Her alone you are bound to obey." Conversely, as long as a person did not violate federal laws agreed upon by his state, "he may rob, and burn, and murder," and the federal government has no more authority over him "than the Emperor of China."[59]

Using this framework, Tucker tried to convince his students that the United States did not constitute a single body politic. Several bodies politic might unite to use their combined resources and authority to accomplish a common purpose, but they formed only a league of clearly divisible units. Such was the case with the United States. The "*people* of the United States," he said, was "an imaginary body politic. . . . There is no such body politic, and no such people," only a "mere multitude of men." As proof, Tucker asked his students to recall the Virginia constitutional convention of 1832. All acts of the convention represented the will of the people. The meeting "annihilated" the old constitution; "the government [was] abolished, but the people and commonwealth remain[ed]." He

59. Tucker, *Lectures*, 68, 77, 79, 380, 388–89; Richmond *Enquirer*, February 7, 1833. Tucker's absolute devotion to his state and extreme views of state sovereignty made him less a southern nationalist than the "Virginianissimus" described by Vernon L. Parrington in *Main Currents in American Thought* (3 vols.; New York, 1927–30), II, 35.

then asked his students to imagine taking away the Constitution of the United States: "The people of the United States vanish" and can never appear again without the consent of every separate state. If there were a single body politic that possessed sovereignty over all the states, why did the Constitution reserve certain rights to the individual states? If the words "We, the people of the United States" meant that the members of the Union constituted one people, it would be tantamount to "an absolute surrender of all power, by the fixed Southern minority, to the fixed Northern majority." If the United States represented a single body politic, Tucker believed it would transform each state into a mere municipal division, "liable at any moment, to be obliterated and absorbed by it." If states, as sovereign units, could delegate certain powers to the federal government, they could just as surely withdraw them. Like his father and other leaders of the Revolution, Tucker asserted that a people might choose to reform, alter, or abolish their government whenever they believed it failed to protect their rights. When parties to a constitutional compact disagreed over whether their government continued to serve its original purpose, final arbitration belonged to the people of each state. Because they originally entered the compact through the consent of the people as expressed in a state convention, the people meeting in another such convention had the right and authority to withdraw consent. No clause in the Constitution, no rule of government, could stop secession because "the great and essential rights of men are not to be sacrificed to technicalities and abstractions." A state might secede unilaterally and even against the expressed wishes of the remaining members of the Union because secession was an act of sovereignty. As Tucker put it, "On such matters, nations never consult the rest of the world."[60]

After a state seceded, it faced two choices. Referring specifically to the slave states, Tucker suggested that secession might be temporary. If the secession of one or more states led to changes that would place state sovereignty and states' rights "beyond dispute," Tucker claimed he would support a reunion. He said slave states might feel safe within the Union if other states passed certain constitutional amendments, and he proposed two particularly vital ones: two-thirds approval in Congress for all tariff legislation and a positive affirmation of a state's "right to secede for a good cause,

60. Tucker, *Lectures*, 380–82, 387, 429, 108–109, 270, 257; Tucker, "South Carolina," 280–82, 277–78, 288–89.

and their right to judge of the cause." Because he never expected the North to make these concessions, Tucker preferred the second option: permanent separation. If only one southern state would muster the courage and boldness to secede, Tucker believed it would form the nucleus for a southern confederacy. Tucker promised Hammond, "I . . . foresee a great destiny for the South, if . . . we take that step like men."[61]

By 1833, at the latest, Tucker longed for the creation of a southern nation. In letters to his intimate friends he gave form and substance to his dream. He thought a southern confederacy would command the trade of all industrial nations because of the importance of its staple crop production. Low tariffs would make this nation the "most flourishing and free on earth." The rest of the United States, he imagined, would "break to pieces" if they no longer had the slave states to plunder and oppress. He foresaw expansion of slavery to Cuba, Jamaica, and far into South America if only slaveholders would free themselves from northern domination. Tucker believed past mistakes would be corrected in this new nation if it would avoid democratic influences. As he explained to one friend, "Neither you nor I would have our Southern Confederacy swallow up the States, and we have had enough of the difficulty of guarding against misconstruction on this point." Tucker asked Hammond, "Have I written a world of nonsense; or is here matter on which a wise man might think a volume?" Tucker grew somber when he perceived a lack of popular support for his vision of southern glory. He knew the painful reality of a maxim he offered his students: "He, who in political life would act alone, must always act without effect." Tucker often felt the isolation of his small Williamsburg classroom, and his lack of oratorical skills prevented him from spreading his ideas to more than a handful of people at a time. He knew others looked upon isolated thinkers like him as "'abstractionists'—politicians of the absurd school of poor old Virginia, who, it seems, is one of these days, to *die of abstraction*." But after more thoughtful reflection, Tucker consoled himself with the thought that the classroom and his essays provided an adequate forum "to accustom the public mind to think of that which must come" and allow him to "act through others."[62]

61. Tucker to Hammond, December 4, 1849, June 23, 1851, in Hammond Papers, LC.

62. Tucker to Hammond, February 17, 18, 1836, May 29, 1849, March 13, April 18, May 7, 1850, March 15, 1836, December 27, 1849, *ibid.*; Tucker to Simms, n.d.

Tucker concluded his textbook on government by claiming partial credit for any successes his students might go on to achieve. He felt a great sense of accomplishment and pride in passing his political views along to his students. He once boasted that each of them entered his classroom "a staunch Whig or a rabid democrat" but left "a Southern man in feeling, and a States-right man in conviction." Tucker claimed that certain resolutions in the Virginia legislature "were my work—indirectly"; one of his former pupils had proposed them. Tucker's students came from some of the most prominent families in Virginia and included sons of state and national political leaders. The son of future president John Tyler studied under him in the 1830s. He looked with special favor on a son of Virginia Senator James M. Mason through whom, Tucker pledged, "I am resolved to try to act on the minds of those to whose hands the destiny of the South is now committed." He rejoiced when he found that a former student was the "private and confidential advisor" to the editor of the Richmond *Enquirer*. His graduates spread out from Virginia to North Carolina, Georgia, Tennessee, Mississippi, and Alabama. He once toyed with the idea of leading an expedition of fifty students to territorial California to make its laws and constitution. Tucker no doubt received his reward in a letter from former student John Murdaugh, who wrote in 1841 that several newspapers had reported a "Williamsburg influence; and from what I have read, I suspect such talk is not without truthfulness."[63] As other scholars have demonstrated, Tucker clearly felt isolated and alienated from southern society at large, but these studies underemphasize the sense of fulfillment he achieved in the classroom.[64] The fidelity of these students transcended Tucker's life. Walter D. Leake, William J. Nesbett, George W. Richardson, John M. Speed, and Robert Montague, all students of Tucker, cast their votes for secession while members of the Virginia secession convention in 1861; Montague even invoked the name of

---

[1851], in Trent, *William Gilmore Simms,* 183; Tucker, *Lectures,* 463; "To John Tyler," Richmond *Enquirer,* August 17, 1841.

63. Tucker, *Lectures,* 459; Tucker to Hammond, March 13, 1847, January 30, December 4, 1849, February 8, 1850, in Hammond Papers, LC; *The History of the College of William and Mary, from its Foundation, in 1660, to 1874* (Richmond, 1874), 124–43; John Murdaugh to Tucker, September 18, 1841, in Tucker-Coleman Collection, ESL.

64. Drew Gilpin Faust, *A Sacred Circle: The Dilemma of the Intellectual in the Old South, 1840–1860* (Baltimore, 1977); Robert Brugger, "The Mind of the Old South: New Views," *Virginia Quarterly Review,* LVI (1980), 294.

"my departed and venerated preceptor, the late Judge Tucker," to promote southern independence. Two other students became advocates of secession in other state secession conventions: William Clarke in Alabama and Richard Coke in Texas.[65]

Tucker's most important and influential student never set foot in his classroom and did not meet him until after the two had corresponded for fourteen years. Tucker's first letter to Congressman James H. Hammond in 1836 began a friendship that ended only with Tucker's death in 1851. The two immediately realized they held similar political values and goals. Tucker discovered that Hammond shared his "deepest convictions." He eagerly offered his thoughts on a variety of subjects and received joyful confirmation in Hammond's replies. The young Hammond came to admire the Virginia professor, "the cast of your mind, your historical, political & legal information, your long & close observation of our Government & of the men who have administered it." He asked Tucker to send him copies of everything he had ever written and told him, "I wish to become one of your pupils, & will be thankful for all the time you can bestow upon me." Encouraged by the Virginian's positive response, Hammond asked if his friend the writer William Gilmore Simms could also "enter . . . under your tuition." Simms, who found Tucker an "able thinker and a charming writer," used his influence to help Tucker publish some of his political essays in journals that circulated among the most influential men in the South. Tucker thanked God he had met friends "whose station gives them access to the public ear." The impressionable Hammond promised to yield his own judgment to that of his mentor. In times of confusion, Hammond told Tucker, "I see clearly, with your eyes."[66]

From the start Tucker and Hammond agreed that states' rights

65. William H. Gaines, Jr., ed., *Biographical Register of Members Virginia State Convention 1861* (Richmond, 1969), 52, 59, 61, 66–67, 70–71; *History of the College of William and Mary*, 124–47; George H. Reese, ed., *Proceedings of the Virginia State Convention of 1861, February 13–May 1* (4 vols.; Richmond, 1965), III, 12; *Dictionary of American Biography*, II, 278–79; Willis Brewer, *Alabama: Her History, Resources, War Record, and Public Men* (1872; rpr. Tuscaloosa, 1964), 378.

66. Tucker to Hammond, December 29, 1846, February 6, 1847, March 13, 1836, Hammond to William Gilmore Simms, April 1, 1847, in Hammond Papers, LC; Hammond to Tucker, January 24, March 2, May 12, 1847, December 26, 1848, January 23, 1850, in Tucker-Coleman Collection, ESL; Simms to Hammond, [*ca.* April 4, 1847], in Oliphant, Odell, and Eaves, eds., *Letters of Simms*, III, 300. Faust, in *Sacred Circle*, discusses in detail the friendship between these three and George Frederick Holmes and Edmund Ruffin.

would be safe only after secession and the formation of a southern confederacy. In 1836 Tucker sketched their strategy: "An opening must be watched for and struck at. If this be not the fit occasion, see what is wanting to make it so." Tucker explained to Hammond that the southern people feared secession carried some form of evil. The task of these men, therefore, was to show that this evil was imaginary "and then demonstrate the advantages which a Southern Confederacy must enjoy." If the two could "excite the South to something of what we feel" about the glory awaiting a southern nation, Tucker promised secession would rapidly ensue.[67]

Tucker exercised tremendous influence over Hammond. As early as 1836, Tucker suggested that southern congressmen, a minority, could accomplish nothing in Washington. He spent several years and many letters developing a strategy of "masterly inactivity," which he hoped a southern state might use if it balked at secession. "Has it ever occurred to you," he posed to Hammond, that by refusing to select presidential electors and withdrawing congressional delegations, a handful of states could practically "dissolve the [federal] government." Tucker said Hammond might find this idea appealing; indeed, in 1851 Hammond proposed just such a scheme for South Carolina.[68] For years Tucker lectured Hammond about the power of southern cotton in world trade; in 1858, Hammond announced "Cotton is King" in a landmark speech in the United States Senate. In the same speech, in his famous "mud-sill" theory, Hammond articulated Tucker's description of the role slaves played in uniting and elevating whites. So powerful was Tucker's influence that shortly before his death he informed Hammond, "I can easily feel as if I have a hand in all you do." So ambitious was Tucker for Hammond that the Carolinian once complained, "You seem to expect so much more from me than I can ever do."[69]

Despite his reliance on Hammond, Tucker never abandoned his

67. Tucker to Hammond, February 18, 1836, April 18, May 7, 1850, in Hammond Papers, LC.

68. Tucker to Hammond, February 18, 1836, April 24, October 13, 1847, January 30, December 4, 1849, December 18, 1850, in Hammond Papers, LC; Tucker, "South Carolina," 283, 288–90, 293; Drew Gilpin Faust, *James Henry Hammond and the Old South: A Design for Mastery* (Baton Rouge, 1982), 333; Charleston *Mercury*, May 2, 1851.

69. Tucker to Hammond, February 17, 1836, January 27, 1850, February 4, 1851, in Hammond Papers, LC; Faust, *Hammond*, 346–47; *Congressional Globe*, 35th Cong., 1st Sess., App., 69–71; Hammond to Tucker, October 1, 1850, in Tucker-Coleman Collection, ESL.

own efforts to convince southerners to secede. While he urged Hammond to lead South Carolina out of the Union in 1836 over the issue of northern abolition agitation, Tucker took quill to hand and wrote "the best exposition of the *advantages of dissolution* that I could give, presented in popular form." His efforts resulted in *The Partisan Leader,* a novel that Simms described as "a curious anticipative history." Published late in 1836, it bore the pseudonym Edward William Sydney and the false date of 1856. Designed to show the ghastly results of continued consolidation of federal power, Tucker's book described an effete and decadent Martin Van Buren serving in his fourth consecutive term as president, helping his party entrench itself in power and effectively destroying constitutional restraints. In a curious parallel to the actual secession crisis in 1860–1861, Tucker's novel had states of the lower South seceding first and being joined later by other slave states. *The Partisan Leader* showed Virginia racked with internal divisions, some supporting secession and some backing Van Buren's attempt to keep the commonwealth in the Union by force. Those already acquainted with Tucker's politics found many familiar ideas. One character explained that he fought to prevent Yankees from making blacks and whites do "*what we are not fit for.*" Another agreed, adding, "*the Yankees want to set the negroes free, and make me a slave.*" Virginians finally resisted after decades of submitting to federal usurpation of power, as though "the spirit of John Randolph had risen from the sleep of death." During the course of the war, free trade policies helped the southern nation grow more prosperous; at the same time, the loss of tariff revenue from the south crippled the northern financial structure.[70]

Duff Green, a publisher in Washington, D.C., gladly helped Tucker publish *The Partisan Leader.* He allowed almost no one to read the manuscript before publication and assured Tucker that "we will profit by the mystery" surrounding the future date and fictional author. Green prepared two thousand copies of the two-volume work, but his other duties forced him to postpone the first printing until September, after Congress adjourned. Green's only complaint about the arrangement concerned a "defect" in Tucker's

70. Tucker to Hammond, February 8, 1850, in Hammond Papers, LC; Simms to Evert Augustus Duycknick, December 6, 1854, in Oliphant, Odell, and Eaves, eds., *Letters of Simms,* III, 344–45; Nathaniel Beverley Tucker, *The Partisan Leader* ([1836]; rpr. New York, 1861), esp. 14, 40, 251, 320.

plot. Green wished Tucker had made slavery, not the tariff, "the basis of your supposed separation." Tucker complained that publication came too late "to produce the effect intended." He remained convinced, however, of the potential usefulness of his book. During the debates over secession in 1850 he urged Hammond and Simms to republish the novel, hoping it might sway the popular mood toward secession. Although Hammond remained unenthusiastic, Tucker continued to promote a new edition and wished he could afford to give away copies. Even though *The Partisan Leader* did not hasten secession, Tucker vowed, "I would rather be known, ten years hence, as the author of that book, than anything ever published on this continent."[71]

The sectional conflict of 1850 brought Tucker a greater opportunity for fame than anything he had written or said before. The acquisition of territory from Mexico in 1848 renewed a national debate over the expansion of slavery. Attempts in Congress to resolve the crisis eventually included several other national issues and resulted in the Compromise of 1850. Tucker complained that all past sectional compromises had caused the forfeiture of southern rights. Scheming politicians like Henry Clay and Lewis Cass of Michigan would gladly betray and bribe the South to advance their own careers. He considered all sectional compromises "bargains made with the Devil" and felt particularly offended that southern soldiers had spilled their blood "like water" on Mexican battlefields only to benefit "Northern harpies." When southerners decided to hold a regional convention in Nashville, Tennessee, in the summer of 1850, Tucker believed he faced a rendezvous with destiny. He des-

71. William C. Preston to Tucker, March 22, May 24, November 6, 1836, Duff Green to Tucker, May 2, September 13, 1836, in Tucker-Coleman Collection, ESL; Tucker to Hammond, December 29, 1846, February 8, July 17, 1850, in Hammond Papers, LC; Hammond to Tucker, February 15, 1850, in Tucker-Coleman Collection, ESL; Hammond to Simms, March 8, 1850, in Hammond Papers, LC. Ironically, both Union and Confederate presses republished *The Partisan Leader* in 1861, properly citing Tucker as author. In a preface to the northern edition (the one I used in this study), publishers offered the novel as proof that Tucker and other southern radicals had been working for decades to overthrow the government. Furthermore, they claimed that men such as Rhett and William L. Yancey "have done little else than servilely to follow out the programme sketched for them in this remarkable book" (v–vi). After reading Tucker's book in 1862, one southern reader commented, "Just such a rosewater revolution he imagines as we fancied we were to have—and now the reality is hideous and an agony" (C. Vann Woodward, ed., *Mary Chestnut's Civil War* [New Haven, 1981], 339).

perately sought an appointment to the Virginia delegation, feeling the "blood of my ancestors" stir within him at the thought of launching a southern revolution. If he could assume a leading role in the proceedings, future generations would remember that in the struggle for southern freedom "one of the first blows struck was mine." [72]

With eager anticipation Tucker prepared for the chance to go to Nashville. Hammond called on his mentor for "a trumpet blast." Tucker gathered his thoughts for a speech designed to "make men's nerves tingle." Besides being able to lecture to the entire South, he would finally meet Hammond, already chosen as a delegate from South Carolina, and could "trim and feather a shaft for that prince of humbugs charlatans and traitors *Henry Clay*." For once fate was kind to Tucker. Though he was originally bypassed as a delegate, the governor of Virginia asked the professor to be an alternate. [73]

In Nashville, Tucker found himself in the unaccustomed position of being the center of attention. His reputation at William and Mary and his essays led many of the assembled delegates to solicit his opinions and ask his help in writing resolutions. Tucker worked around the clock in the days preceding the convention. His ego swelled when people told him that he reminded them of John Randolph. Reporters asked if they could sit near him when he spoke. "There is my misfortune," Tucker remembered suddenly, "the want of voice." Nevertheless, he prepared himself as best he could for a moment he considered the culmination of his life's experience and work. [74]

"I have come here with my mind charged to bursting with thoughts that struggle for utterance," Tucker told the assembly. He announced his intention to make his fellow delegates aware of their rights and inspire them to defend those rights "at all hazards and to the last extremity." First, he tried to convince them that maintaining the Union could only result in the South suffering atrocities. The "fierce philanthropy and malignant love of our northern

72. Tucker to Hammond, December 4, 1849, January 27, February 8, April 18, July 30, September 21, October 9, 1850, in Hammond Papers, LC; Tucker, "South Carolina," 294. Also see Thelma Jennings, *The Nashville Convention: Southern Movement for Unity, 1848–1851* (Memphis, 1980).

73. Tucker to Hammond, January 27, February 2, May 7, 1850, in Hammond Papers, LC.

74. Tucker to Lucy S. Tucker, June 3, 8, 1850, in Tucker-Coleman Collection, ESL.

brethren" would soon result in the forcible abolition of slavery. If northerners destroyed this sacred and essential institution, southerners would lose the millions of dollars they had invested in slave property, land values would consequently topple, and whites would face "the necessity of destroying the negroes or of amalgamating with them, or of succumbing to them." He gave members of the convention the same lecture he offered to his students; they must chose "between Union, and all the rights and interests the Union was intended to protect." He begged his colleagues to throw off their idolatrous and blinding worship of political parties. He warned them that a sinister plot existed to rob them of their liberties. An evil triumvirate—Clay, Cass, and Daniel Webster of Massachusetts—had contrived the congressional compromise as a delusion. He announced that southerners would no longer listen to the scheming Clay. "They followed him in the Missouri Compromise, the root of all this present evil," and they followed him again in the compromise tariff of 1833, but Tucker swore that the South would follow him no longer. He dismissed Cass as a "claptrap charlatan," a tool of Clay and Webster, used "to fool us—to bamboozle us," to cheat southerners out of their rights.[75]

Having appealed to southern outrage, Tucker shifted his attention to solutions. In the most dramatic effort of his life, Tucker began, "I would speak of the magnificent future, and glorious destiny of a Southern Confederacy." If only South Carolina, Georgia, Florida, Alabama, and Mississippi would secede, they had all the resources necessary to form a powerful new country. Tucker warned of the "fatal consequences" that would befall any industrialized nation if these states stopped exporting cotton. After a single year without cotton, New Englanders would see "ships lie rotting at wharves; the factories tumbled into ruins." The social and political fabric of England would fall victim to Fourierism and communism. United by a "mere central agency for independent states" and supported by revenue from a modest tariff, this southern nation would soon draw other slave states out of the Union. Intoxicated with the thought of these anticipated glories, Tucker even argued that Pennsylvanians would see the advantage of becoming a workshop for the South and eventually secede. States along the Ohio River would see the advantages of slave labor; someday Ohio, Indiana, and Illinois would join the southern nation. The Mississippi River, "like an iron clamp," would bind these additions to a southern con-

75. Tucker, *Prescience*, 8, 9–14, 16, 28.

federacy. Tucker depicted an ideal society, a union "of congenial not conflicting interests," replacing the old union "between power and weakness." The "great school of domestic slavery" would continue and flourish. Tucker must have shocked his listeners when he elaborated a plan to make Haiti a colony for free blacks, "established under a provincial government, protected, regulated, and controlled by a Southern Confederacy." In some distant era, he predicted, blacks might learn enough from their paternal former masters to govern themselves. After stirring the imagination of the assembly, Tucker chided that only a "dull ass," a "coward cur," would now refuse to act. If southerners refused to act boldly to defend their liberty, Tucker vowed his life would have been lived in vain.[76]

The aftermath of Nashville left Tucker with great ambivalence. Pleased with his extraordinary speech, he wished only that he could have said more, "but my voice failed me." Hammond had hoped Tucker's speech would stir lethargic southerners but told Simms, "Such a philippic has not been seen lately." Another friend wrote to Hammond complaining about Tucker's "fire & brimstone" remarks about Clay, Cass, and Webster. "The easiest thing is to tear down," he pointed out; the South needed constructive solutions.[77] The convention adjourned without recommending secession or any other form of resistance to the compromise. Instead, delegates voted to reconvene in the fall. Exhausted by his efforts in Tennessee and weeks of travel, Tucker collapsed as soon as he returned to Williamsburg.

After regaining his strength, Tucker resumed his efforts to encourage secession. He set to work editing his Nashville address for publication. He bombarded Hammond with letters urging him to continue the fight and refused to accept Hammond's conclusion that the convention had been a failure. He even pledged to leave Virginia if South Carolina seceded alone and offered to command troops there. He anxiously observed the fate of Mississippi governor John Quitman, who Tucker believed had incurred the wrath of the federal government for his own disunion activities. He penned a long essay for the *Southern Quarterly Review* calling unequivocally for disruption of the Union, whether by secession or "masterly in-

76. *Ibid.*, 18–20, 22–26, 29–32, 38.

77. Tucker to Lucy S. Tucker, June 8, 1850, in Tucker-Coleman Collection, ESL; Hammond to Simms, June 27, 1850, W. W. Hodgson to Hammond, August 6, 1850, in Hammond Papers, LC.

activity." Even when his spirits fell and he realized that secession was not soon likely, Tucker found consolation. After his efforts of over twenty years, he concluded, "our cause has gained ground. The open discussion of the question of disunion, and the clear admission . . . that disunion is not the worst of possible evils, and that Union is a *means* not an *end,* place us far in advance of any position heretofore occupied." By the time of his death on August 26, 1851, Tucker felt confident that the South would never "fall back" from this position.[78]

Tucker never witnessed secession or the creation of a southern nation. In the South he never achieved the popularity or mystique of a John C. Calhoun. Few of his successors quoted Tucker in defense of states' rights or to justify secession. His political philosophy was not unique; his most original thoughts were his most fanciful. But his contribution to the secession movement should not be minimized. He constantly and consistently told his countrymen to take their destiny into their own hands. In his classroom and through his writings he left a legacy of resistance to federal power, defense of minority rights, and the promise of change. His message spanned two generations and reached thousands. His only regret was that he could not reach more. "Oh that I had the voice of J. Randolph," he cried, "to make myself heard by the assembled multitude!" He agreed with Hammond that only continued agitation would bring secession: "Yes; I would agitate. But how can I make my voice heard."[79] When Tucker died, his ideas remained for others to pass on. Fortunately for his cause, most of his successors had louder, more powerful voices.

78. Tucker to Hammond, February 4, March 15, June 6, 23, 27, July 17, October 9, 15, December 18, 1850, in Hammond Papers, LC.

79. Tucker to Hammond, December 27, 1849, February 8, 1850, *ibid.*

We Shall Fire the Southern Heart

William Lowndes Yancey

Williams Lowndes Yancey's brilliant oratory and violent temper left a profound impression on everyone who met him. Some believed him the greatest public speaker in the South since Patrick Henry or John Randolph. In 1860 a newspaper reporter dubbed him "the prince of the fire-eaters." The fire-eating editor of the Charleston *Mercury* acknowledged Yancey's prowess as an orator and debater but criticized him for "an evident want of leadership." A colleague in Alabama said, "He has great talent in some things, but his temper is impracticable." Some southerners saw Yancey as a Confederate Garibaldi; some eulogized him as a latter-day Moses. Unionists in a north Alabama town once burned him in effigy. Aware of his ability to provoke stormy reactions, Yancey actively cultivated his image as an agitator. He once jokingly described himself "as a disunionist, twenty seven feet high, weighing three thousand pounds and eating a little nigger broiled every morning for breakfast and a roasted Union man for dinner." [1]

Friends and associates saw a more human side of Yancey but nevertheless confirmed his public image. One of his earliest associ-

1. John Witherspoon DuBose to Robert Alonzo Brock, November 8, 1890, in Robert A. Brock Collection, HL; William Kauffman Scarborough, ed., *The Diary of Edmund Ruffin* (3 vols.; Baton Rouge, 1972–89), I, 479, 633–35; James P. Hambleton to William F. Samford, February 5, 1866, in William L. Yancey Papers, ADAH; William P. Hesseltine, *Three Against Lincoln: Murat Halstead Reports the Caucuses of 1860* (Baton Rouge, 1960), 8; Robert Barnwell Rhett, Jr., to William Porcher Miles, May 10, 1860, in William Porcher Miles Papers, SHC; J. Bragg to Genl. [McRae], January 21, 1861, in Colin J. McRae Papers, ADAH; Montgomery *Advertiser*, November 14, 1860; Atlanta *Intelligencer*, quoted in Montgomery *Advertiser*, August 5, 1863; Clarence P. Denman, *The Secession Movement in Alabama* (Montgomery, 1933), 149–50; Yancey quoted in Ollinger Crenshaw, *The Slave States in the Presidential Election of 1860* (Gloucester, Mass., 1969), 123–24. Yancey has provoked a similar reaction among some historians. Joseph Hergesheimer called him "The Pillar of Words," in *Swords and Roses* (New York, 1929), 35–64, and Clement Eaton compared him with Adolf Hitler in *The Mind of the Old South* (1964; rpr. Baton Rouge, 1976), 268.

ates, Benjamin Franklin Perry of South Carolina, described him as "a man of genius & talents, a man of impulse and feeling; but not a wise & sagacious man in politics." Perry found Yancey charming, cordial, and well-mannered but "too much devoted to politics & literature to make great progress in his legal studies" and too "susceptible to the charms of the other sex." Yancey could be cheerful and jocular in public, Perry remembered, but "in private he was subject to feelings of gloom & despondency." Thomas H. Watts, who at various times opposed and supported Yancey in legal and political contests, recalled, "There was a charm peculiar to him and his oratory." Watts said Yancey's mastery of facts and power of analysis were considerable, but the key to his success lay in "his sweet voice, and the enunciation of every word and every syllable . . . so that even in a conversational tone he was distinctly heard in any room and at a great distance when speaking in the open air." He always spoke earnestly, "from the innermost recesses of his heart," and exercised a "magnetic power" over his audiences. Watts also remembered Yancey's great flaw: his "fiery temper . . . sometimes permitted his passion to get the better of his judgment." Another colleague, William R. Smith, contrasted Yancey's speaking style to that of his longtime Whig opponent, Henry W. Hilliard. Smith claimed that Yancey "had a better knowledge of men, was a more perfect master of the passions." Hilliard, Smith said, excelled in "all that was soft and smooth and easy, graceful and persuasive." But "in all that was fierce, stormy, vituperative, denunciatory, impetuous, and scornful, Mr. Yancey excelled."[2]

Yancey's fiery spirit and impetuosity arose in his early years. He was born on August 10, 1814, at the Shoals of the Ogeechee River in Warren County, Georgia. His parents, Caroline Bird and Benjamin Cudworth Yancey, had reputations for tempestuousness. His father lived in South Carolina before his marriage to Caroline and shared a small law office with the young John C. Calhoun. Shortly after moving his family to Charleston and the birth of Benjamin C. Yancey, Jr., in 1815, the elder Yancey died of yellow fever. The family returned to Georgia. Caroline sent William to Mount Zion Academy, a Presbyterian school headed by the Reverend Nathan Sidney Smith Beman, who had moved from New England to Geor-

2. Benjamin F. Perry to William F. Samford, August 29, 1866; "Reminiscences of Thomas H. Watts," both in Folder 10, John Witherspoon DuBose Correspondence, ADAH; William R. Smith, *Reminiscences of a Long Life: Historical, Political, Personal and Literary* (1889; rpr. Louisville, 1961), 223.

gia in 1812. Caroline Yancey married him in 1821, and after Beman sold his wife's slaves, the family moved to Troy, New York, in June, 1823, where Beman became pastor of the First Presbyterian Church. Beman participated in the great religious revival in upstate New York in 1826 and zealously joined the movement to abolish slavery. In contrast to Beverley Tucker, who admired and strove to emulate his father, Yancey saw Beman as a vile personification of the abolitionist, a hypocrite who condemned all aspects of slavery even though he once owned and sold slaves. The young William also witnessed frequent arguments between Beman and his mother, which further alienated him from his stepfather. According to one of Yancey's biographers, he grew accustomed to a "blend of bitter argument and religious evangelism" in an "emotionally charged atmosphere of family feud and religious crusade."[3]

Beman provided Yancey with a good education. He attended the academies of Troy, Bennington, Chittenango, and Lenox and in 1830 entered Williams College in Massachusetts. The president of the college at the time was Edward Dorr Griffin, a friend of Beman's and another evangelist. Yancey developed his unique oratorical style under Griffin's guidance. His classroom attendance, however, was erratic, and he withdrew from the school in 1833. His family later claimed that he left out of a desire to save his stepfather some money. A contemporary rumor, however, said he was expelled after hurling a pickle barrel through the window of a nearby church.[4]

After briefly returning to Georgia, Yancey moved to Greenville, South Carolina, and studied law under the guidance of Benjamin Perry. He arrived just in time to take part in the resolution of the nullification crisis. His father and family had all been staunch Federalists. The elder Yancey had bitterly opposed Calhoun during his residence in South Carolina a generation before, and Perry was the leading Unionist in the Carolina up-country. Yancey naturally opposed the nullifiers and sided with the Unionists.

Although the confrontation between state and federal authority had just ended, the test-oath controversy forced Carolinians to continue debating many of the issues that arose during nullification.

3. Ralph B. Draughon, "William L. Yancey: From Unionist to Secessionist, 1814–1852" (Ph.D. dissertation, University of North Carolina, Chapel Hill, 1968), 1–29; and Draughon, "The Young Manhood of William L. Yancey," *Alabama Review*, XIX (1966), 28–37.

4. Draughon, "Yancey," 30–35.

Before the South Carolina Nullification Convention adjourned, its members recommended that all state officials take an oath of allegiance to their state, obliging them to disobey federal authority in case of any future conflict. Eager to jump into the fray, the nineteen-year-old Yancey addressed the people of Abbeville District in a Fourth of July oration that later events would prove ironic: "Listen, not then, my countrymen, to the voice which whispers . . . that Americans . . . can no longer be mutual worshippers at the shrine of Freedom—no longer can exist together, citizens of the same Republic. . . . Designing men have, indeed, effectually destroyed, in the minds of but too many in our State, the charm which has, until of late, invested our Federal Union. [Who can look at] the last few years, and not see the evident tendency of their proceedings to be, *disunion* and a *Southern Confederacy?*" That fall, Yancey became editor of a Unionist newspaper, the Greenville *Mountaineer,* and as Perry recalled, he "wielded a fierce & terrible pen against Nullification and disunion." Never afraid to challenge any foe, Yancey assailed Calhoun's theories of government as "the loathsome offspring of failed *Ambition.*"[5]

On August 13, 1835, Yancey married Sarah Caroline Earle, daughter of a wealthy Greenville family. The marriage instantly changed Yancey's fortune; his bride's thirty-five slaves suddenly elevated him to planter status. Yancey had grown accustomed to plantation living while residing with relatives at Rosemonte and Oak Wood Place near Greenville. His slaves provided him with a new means of support. He stopped his study of law in 1836 and moved west to Alabama, purchasing land near the town of Cahawba, close to an aunt and uncle. Yancey lived with his uncle Jesse Beene for a year and a half until his own home was completed. Beene was a prominent states'-rights leader in Alabama, and his influence on the young and impressionable Yancey soon supplanted that of Benjamin Perry.

On a trip back to Greenville in 1838, Yancey's quick temper and sense of honor resulted in an incident that would haunt him for years. While listening to congressional candidates debate, Yancey shouted out an abusive remark about one of the speakers. A nephew of the alleged "blackguard," Elias Earle, heard and took

5. *Ibid.,* 38–51; Perry to Samford, August 29, 1866, in DuBose Correspondence; William L. Yancey, "Address at Lodi, Abbeville District, July 4, 1834" (Typescript copy of speech in Greenville *Mountaineer,* July 12, 1834, in Yancey Papers, ADAH).

exception to the comment. Yancey and the young Earle, who was also Sarah's cousin, struck each other repeatedly but parted peacefully. After hearing his son's story, Dr. Robinson Earle, Sarah's uncle, became enraged and set off for Greenville, armed with a heavy walking stick and a small pocket knife, to find Yancey. Yancey hoped to reason with the elder and much larger Earle, but he also took a knife, a swordstick, and a pistol. After an abortive effort to talk calmly, Earle called Yancey a "g——d d——d liar." From his jail cell Yancey later recalled: "I then got my passions aroused. I told him to take back what he had said or take a shot." Earle refused to retract his words and advanced on Yancey, his cane raised menacingly over his head. The two scuffled. Yancey fired at close range, beat Earle on the head with his empty gun, and "was in the act of running him thro'" with a knife when the two were separated. Earle died later that night.

A month later Yancey was tried, found guilty of manslaughter, sentenced to a year in jail, and fined $1,500. Yancey showed no remorse. He boasted to his brother, "I have done my duty as a man, & he who grossly insulted me lies now, with the clod upon his bosom." The episode would serve as a warning "to others who feel like brow beating a Yancey." He was released after serving three months, and $1,000 of his fine was returned.[6]

Yancey returned to Alabama with his honor vindicated, but he soon faced new problems. In the Panic of 1837, he was dismayed when his cotton production flourished but prices and profits dropped steadily. In 1838 he bought control of the Cahawba *Southern Democrat* but had difficulty collecting from subscribers. After a year of frustration, he sold the *Democrat* and purchased the Wetumpka *Argus*. His energetic efforts at simultaneous plantation and newspaper management taxed his ability to deal with either. Then disaster struck in the summer of 1839; almost all of his slaves were accidentally poisoned, the unintended victims of two feuding over-

6. Draughon, "Yancey," 61–68, 71–76; William L. Yancey to Benjamin C. Yancey, September 8, 1838 (Typescript in Yancey Papers, ADAH). For a succinct and entertaining discussion of the violence associated with honor in the Old South, see Kenneth S. Greenberg, "The Nose, the Lie, and the Duel in the Antebellum South," *American Historical Review*, XCV (1990), 57–74; see also Steven M. Stowe, "The 'Touchiness' of the Gentleman Planter: The Sense of Esteem and Continuity in the Antebellum South," *Psychohistory Review*, VIII (Winter, 1979), 6–17; and Elliott J. Gorn, "'Gouge and Bite, Pull Hair and Scratch': The Social Significance of Fighting in the Southern Backcountry," *American Historical Review*, XC (1985), 18–43.

seers. Most died, and the survivors were too weak to work. Unable to harvest his cotton, Yancey was forced to sell all but six of his slaves to get enough money to survive the year. He returned to his legal studies and moved to Wetumpka in February, 1840, so he could better supervise the *Argus*. These crises led Yancey to review his outlook on local and national politics. He came to believe that the Bank of the United States was responsible for many of the nation's financial problems. Continued abolitionist attacks on slavery made him defensive about the peculiar institution. These issues tested his commitment to Unionism, and Yancey suddenly found John C. Calhoun and his states'-rights principles both admirable and useful against a menacing North.[7]

Yancey demonstrated his new commitment to states' rights and southern rights in the presidential campaign of 1840. In April he and his brother established the Wetumpka *Southern Crisis,* a weekly publication advocating the reelection of Martin Van Buren. As the newspaper's title suggested, the editors strove to prove to Alabamians that the election of Whig candidate William Henry Harrison would be catastrophic for the South. Yancey told his readers that a Whig administration would reenact alien and sedition laws, pass a higher protective tariff, recharter a national bank, tax southerners for northern internal improvements, tamper with slavery, and obliterate constitutional restraints on power, "making the President a King in all but *name*" and transforming Washington into "the centre of a vast, consolidated domain." He reminded his readers that "vigilance is the price of Liberty" and dutifully devoted his editorial attention to a relentless search for harbingers of evil. The Yancey brothers reprinted stories from other newspapers which claimed that Harrison had been a Federalist during the 1790s. They insisted that Harrison accepted political support from abolitionists. The Yanceys repeated a fantastic story in which they claimed that, while a state senator in Ohio in 1821, Harrison had voted for a bill allowing county sheriffs to sell men imprisoned for nonpayment of fines into bondage. Because the prisoner had to be sold to the highest bidder, so the story went, a white man could be "DRIVEN INTO SLAVERY BY A FREE NEGRO." As November drew closer, Yancey began the weekly publication of a short biography of Harrison. Designed solely to arouse indignation, it repeated every derogatory comment previously published and accused Harrison of cowardice during

7. Draughon, "Yancey," 80–100.

wartime, charged him with wishing to create a large standing army, and listed a string of his past electoral defeats.[8]

Yancey's vigorous participation in the campaign impressed many of his fellow Democrats and helped propel him to a term in the Alabama General Assembly. After his election he passed the bar exam, sold the *Argus,* and devoted his full attention to politics. As a legislator he was not preoccupied by national issues. Instead, like many other fire-eaters early in their careers, he promoted local reforms such as state-supported public education, the right of married women to own their own property, bank reform, and reform of the penal code and prisons. He also signaled his commitment to Jacksonian democracy by supporting the redistricting of Alabama based on white population only because the "federal basis" of representation, which included the slave population, favored a wealthy, aristocratic minority.[9]

In 1844 Yancey moved from state to national politics when he was elected to fill a vacant seat in the House of Representatives. Opposing protective tariffs and internal improvements, favoring the acquisition of both Texas and Oregon, he soon became one of the many southern Democrats who looked to John C. Calhoun for leadership. Yancey considered annexation of Texas the most vital issue facing the country. He sensed "a deeply seated hostility to the South" among northerners and a desire "to alter her fundamental system of government" by prohibiting slavery in the federal territories. Yancey claimed that the Missouri Compromise gave the North enough territory to create more than twenty new states but left the South only Florida. And yet, he charged, "a talk is kept up to frighten northern men out of their wits about the *enormous preponderance* which [Texas] annexation would give the *South!*"[10]

Using Texas as a political litmus test, Yancey condemned southern politicians he considered weak on the issue. In his maiden speech in Congress, he leveled his oratorical guns at Thomas L. Clingman, a Whig from North Carolina. Yancey gave the official Democratic response to Clingman's opposition to Texas annexation. Every year, Yancey said, southerners lost strength in Congress because of "the fatal Missouri compromise." Scheming New En-

8. Wetumpka *Southern Crisis,* esp. May 16, 23, October 24, 1840.

9. Draughon, "Yancey," 103, 119–20.

10. Yancey to J. R. Powell, J. A. Whetstone, B. L. Defreese, and B. L. Rye, June 6, 1844, Yancey to John D. Kellog *et al.,* January 25, 1845 (Typescript copies in Yancey Papers, ADAH).

glanders were in the vanguard of a general northern effort to circumscribe the growth and power of the slave states. The enormity of this sectional conflict was so great that it demanded the united action of all southerners, regardless of party divisions. Clingman, he noted, thought otherwise. "With him, the extension of our institutions . . . its effect upon the institution of slavery . . . have not sufficient interest or dignity to draw his intellect, or his passions." Yancey exclaimed that Clingman "had given a stab to the institutions of his own land, and wears the garb of its enemy." Clingman's position on Texas "merits the scorn and execration of every honest heart of the South." [11]

Yancey's zeal resulted in violent confrontation. Believing that Yancey's comments had tainted his honor, Clingman challenged the Alabamian to a duel. The two agreed to meet in Maryland even though that state had outlawed dueling years before. Local officials sent police to stop the encounter, but the two congressmen slipped away. On a cold winter day they faced each other on the field of honor, shot, and missed. Both felt vindicated, returned to Congress, and never exchanged hostile words again. [12]

Yancey's now famous temper manifested itself throughout his term in Congress, sometimes with little provocation. When someone objected to his motion to adjourn in honor of George Washington's birthday, Yancey angrily demanded that the objector show his face. Sometimes Yancey realized that he overreacted. After calling some colleagues "pretended Democrats" during a discussion of internal improvements, he apologized, explaining, "I regret that I too frequently, in the excitement of a general debate, use language that reflection convinces me were better left unused." [13]

During his congressional years, Yancey fully rejected his former Unionism. He called the United States a mere "cluster of Governments, each of which has yielded certain powers to a federal head

11. William L. Yancey, *Speech of Hon. Wm. Lowndes Yancey, of Alabama, on the Annexation of Texas to the United States* (N.p., n.d.), in Yancey Papers, ADAH; *Congressional Globe*, 28th Cong., 2nd Sess., 100–102.

12. William L. Yancey, *Memoranda of the Late Affair of Honor between T. L. Clingman, of North Carolina, and Hon. William L. Yancey, of Alabama* (N.p., n.d.), in Yancey Papers, ADAH; Draughon, "Yancey," 133–40. At least one southern Democrat, rooting along partisan lines, complained, "What a misfortune Yancey did not bore his man through" (George D. Phillips to Howell Cobb, February 21, 1845, in U. B. Phillips, ed., *The Correspondence of Robert Toombs, Alexander H. Stephens, and Howell Cobb* [Washington, D.C., 1913], 66).

13. *Congressional Globe*, 29th Cong., 1st Sess., 413, 499.

for purposes which are designated in the chart of union [the Constitution]." He believed all other powers belonged to the sovereign states. If the central government continued to enact sectional legislation such as protective tariffs, that action would stir "sectional divisions, jealousies, and hatreds" in both the North and the South. "Economy, low duties, a scrupulous regard for State rights, a nonexercise of doubtful powers, will preserve the Republic," Yancey said. His growing sensitivity to the plight of the South in its minority status changed his views of recent events. Yancey told the House of Representatives that "a band of more honorable men never existed" than the South Carolina nullifiers. He excused his former opposition to nullification as inability "to have had fixed opinions upon such grave matters when under age." During a tribute to Andrew Jackson, Yancey explained that the sole function of government was to provide for "the greatest good for the greatest number, consistent with the inalienable rights of the minority." [14]

Although he was reelected without opposition in 1845, Yancey had had enough of national politics within a year. He resigned from Congress, claiming that financial considerations demanded his departure from Washington. But his primary reason for leaving was his belief that representatives in Congress compromised principle for the sake of party unity. Yancey could not be satisfied. He had condemned politicians like Clingman for being overly partisan. He also blasted northern Democrats for abandoning their party to support sectional issues, "with one brilliant exception," David Wilmot of Pennsylvania. Ironically, only a few weeks after Yancey left Congress, Wilmot offered his famous proviso, which called for the prohibition of slavery in any territories the United States might acquire from Mexico. [15]

Yancey's experiences in Congress made him uncomfortable with the power of party organizations and disgusted with the corruption he perceived as endemic to the American party system. Like many other Alabamians he became increasingly devoted to having his state maintain an independent course and determined to keep it free from encumbrance from either national parties or federal power. His determination to continue his political career as an outside agitator cast him as the quintessential antebellum Alabama

14. *Ibid.*, 652, App., 85, 360, 626, 994; William L. Yancey, *An Oration on the Life and Character of Andrew Jackson* (Baltimore, 1846), 21.

15. *Congressional Globe*, 29th Cong., 1st Sess., 995–96; Draughon, "Yancey," 168–69.

politician described by historian J. Mills Thornton.[16] Upon his return to Alabama, Yancey moved to the capital, Montgomery, and
established a law firm with John A. Elmore, a relative of Robert
Barnwell Rhett. As a concerned citizen, Yancey remained active in
state politics and quickly gained the respect of Montgomery officials. When John A. Quitman, former governor of Mississippi and
more recently a hero of the Mexican War, traveled through the
capital late in 1847, city leaders chose Yancey to give the official reception oration. His most significant work at this time suddenly
brought him back into the national spotlight. With the aid of Mobile politician John A. Campbell and the support of Senator Dixon H.
Lewis, Yancey coauthored a series of resolutions known collectively
as the Alabama Platform. These resolutions, a direct response to
the Wilmot Proviso, were passed in the Alabama state Democratic
convention and expressly forbade Congress from preventing the
expansion of slavery into the territories. One plank bound Alabama delegates to the upcoming national party convention to withhold support from any presidential candidate who did not endorse
the platform.[17]

Elected delegate at large to the Baltimore convention, Yancey
spent the eartly months of 1848 preparing himself and his party for
a confrontation over the platform. He sent letters to the leading
Democratic candidates for the presidency, Lewis Cass, James
Buchanan, Levi Woodbury, and George M. Dallas, explaining the
platform and requesting a response so he could publish their an-
swers and help his delegation determine which man to support. He
warned these men that the territorial question was of the utmost
importance to southerners and that failure to endorse the platform
would jeopardize "the perpetuity of the union" and risk losing "the
equality of privileges, which that union was designed to confer
upon the people."[18]

16. J. Mills Thornton, *Politics and Power in a Slave Society: Alabama, 1800–1860*
(Baton Rouge, 1978), esp. xviii, 71–72, 127, 161, 211, 213–14, 236.

17. *Journal of the Democratic Convention, Held in the City of Montgomery on the 14th
and 15th of February, 1848* (Montgomery, 1848), 10–14; Thornton, in *Politics and
Power*, 173, credits Yancey with primary authorship of the platform. Ralph Draughon, in "Yancey," 182–90, shows that the influence of others was at least as important. Senator Lewis warned Yancey: "Attempts have been made to get up the impression that the Alabama Platform was made up by you—& to express your
individual opinions" (Lewis to Yancey, June 29, 1848, in Yancey Papers, ADAH).

18. See, for example, Yancey to James Buchanan, May 2, 1848, in James
Buchanan Papers, HSP.

When the convention met in May, delegates nominated Lewis Cass of Michigan and George M. Dallas of Pennsylvania for president and vice-president. They also soundly defeated the Alabama Platform by a vote of 216 to 36. Yancey and one other Alabama delegate, P. A. Wray, decided they had no more business in Baltimore and stormed out of the convention.

Yancey's actions created tremors throughout the South. A former North Carolina congressman found his course unduly provocative, the platform characterized by "hair-splitting distinctions," and the combined effect of the platform and Yancey's antics likely only to antagonize and abuse the friendship of northern Democrats. A prominent Georgia Democrat called the platform "a pack of nonsense" and was incredulous that all nine Georgia delegates voted for it. He suspected that Yancey, Calhoun, and the editors of the Charleston *Mercury* had formed a clique to gain control of the Democratic party. The Alabama delegates who remained at the convention condemned Yancey for leaving and labeled him a traitor to his party. Yancey answered his colleagues' accusations in a seventy-eight-page pamphlet. It was the rest of the delegation, he maintained, not William Yancey, who had acted treacherously; the thirteenth and fourteenth resolutions forbade them from supporting any candidate who did not unequivocally avow the principles of the platform. He accused them of remaining for petty political purposes such as trying to secure the vice-presidential nomination for an Alabamian, even though rejection of the platform meant "there was a real, palpable danger hanging over the South."[19]

Yancey was unable to persuade many Alabama Democrats not to support Cass. In June, Yancey and a handful of other extremists decided to adhere to the Alabama Platform even if the state would not. A self-appointed committee, which included Yancey, Campbell, and Elmore, looked beyond the organized political parties for an acceptable presidential candidate and settled on former Senator Littleton W. Tazewell of Virginia. They told Tazewell that Cass's failure to embrace the Alabama Platform proved that the Democrat was ideologically unsound on the questions of slave expansion,

19. James C. Dobbin to Howell Cobb, June 15, 1848, Henry R. Jackson to Cobb, June 21, 1848, in Phillips, eds., *Correspondence of Toombs, Stephens, and Cobb*, 108, 110–11; William L. Yancey, *An Address to the People of Alabama, by W. L. Yancey, Late a Delegate, at Large, for the State of Alabama, to the National Democratic Convention, Held at Baltimore, on the 22d May, A.D. 1848* (Montgomery, 1848), 3, 4, 23, 27, 33, 40–43, 50, 79.

southern equality, and the power of the federal government. They informed Tazewell, "We . . . have refused to recognize his nomination as binding on us, and we are resolved to war against his election." They chose Tazewell because of his vigilant defense of states' rights earlier in the century and asked the seventy-four-year-old Virginian to stand as a presidential candidate for their planned new party. Before Tazewell responded, Yancey wrote to Calhoun, whom he now looked to as a political adviser, both to complain of the problems involved in creating a new party and to discuss strategy. "I have labored incessantly, but I begin to despair," he told Calhoun. "I have hardly yet struck a spark from the flinty bosom of the [Democratic] party." His fellow citizens were "determined to vote for the regular ticket," a decision one could only reach out of "great ignorance of the political character of Cass." His faction needed to promote its cause through its own newspaper. Without one, he explained, "I greatly fear that we can not make even a start in Alabama." Yancey hoped at least to split the Democratic vote and secure the election of the Whig candidate, Zachary Taylor.[20]

Yancey admitted that his dream of a third party had little chance of success. Tazewell dealt the vision a fatal blow by refusing to run because of his advanced age. On the same day that Tazewell sent his letter, Senator Lewis of Alabama wrote Yancey to dissuade him from continuing to back a third-party movement. Lewis approved Yancey's actions at the Baltimore convention and expressed great confidence in his "power of carrying a crowd" but warned that he "had not even a half of a chance" of creating a viable new party in Alabama. The senator then offered Yancey advice that would later have a profound effect on his thinking: "But why talk of a 3rd Party? You have given me the names of several of the most respectable men in the State—I know none more so—They are now all Democrats— . . . with half the activity & zeal required to start a new Party—they might to any desirable extent . . . control the party to which they now belong. Cut off these gentlemen however, into a separate party—& how powerless—With all due respect to them & to you, I doubt if they could carry a single County in the State." Yancey learned many important lessons during the cam-

20. Henry C. Semple, William L. Yancey, S. Heydenfeldt, John A. Campbell, W. Harris, J. A. Elmore, and Thomas Mays to Littleton W. Tazewell, June 20, 1848, in Henry Churchill Semple Papers, ADAH; Yancey to John C. Calhoun, June 14, 1848, in Chauncey Boucher and Robert P. Brooks, eds., *Correspondence Addressed to John C. Calhoun* (Washington, D.C., 1930), 441.

paign of 1848, but ten years would pass before he would implement Lewis' strategy and move in and out of the Democratic party as it suited his needs.[21]

When Californians clamored for admission to the Union late in 1849, the debate over the expansion of slavery again dominated Congress and preoccupied the nation. While the Nashville Convention met to discuss possible southern responses to the situation, Yancey worked to bolster opposition to the Compromise of 1850 in Alabama and to convince all southerners of the necessity for secession in case southern rights were not vindicated. A month before the Nashville meeting, Yancey had participated in a nonpartisan gathering in Montgomery that resolved to support any positions recommended at that convention. Although delegates reached no consensus in Nashville, Yancey wholeheartedly endorsed Robert Barnwell Rhett's impassioned call for southern resistance to the compromise and marshaled his energies to rally the spirit of resistance in the Deep South.

On the Fourth of July, 1850, Yancey used the double occasion of Independence Day and the official observance in Montgomery of the death of John C. Calhoun to argue against the pending compromise. Yancey admitted that he had once opposed Calhoun's notions about state and federal relations but explained that he had "neither appreciated nor understood" the Carolinian's genius. Now, Yancey insisted, he did. He repeated Calhoun's plea to southerners "to crush the golden idol of party" and join in a common crusade to protect southern rights. He reminded his audience that as early as 1833 Calhoun had warned the South that the "spirit of Abolitionism" would relentlessly attack slavery. Since that date southerners had compromised and conceded so much that it was a wonder they had any spirit of resistance left. The next month Yancey participated in "an immense Southern meeting" in Montgomery that adopted "moderate yet firm ground" on the compromise and appointed two delegates—Yancey and John Cochran of Eufaula—to join Robert Barnwell Rhett at the "great Mass Meeting" planned for Macon, Georgia, the next week. There, in the first of only a few meetings of the two, one critic noted, "The godlike Rhett and his adjutant Yancey preached most eloquently in behalf of treason." Indeed, Rhett gave a long, inspired plea for disunion.

21. Littleton W. Tazewell to Semple, Yancey, *et al.*, June 29, 1848, in Semple Papers; Lewis to Yancey, June 29, 1848, in Yancey Papers, ADAH.

Yancey followed by repeating Rhett's assertion that the compromise would allow the North to trample on the rights of the South and called on Georgians to cease all discussion and prepare themselves for war. When Congress passed the compromise package in September, Yancey returned to Alabama to campaign for secession.[22]

During the autumn of 1850, Yancey encouraged the creation of southern rights associations throughout Alabama to promote secession. He inaugurated one himself in Montgomery and through it called for a statewide convention of such groups to assemble in the capital in February. Eighty-four delegates gathered, representing seventeen associations and eleven south Alabama counties. Yancey turned this small meeting into a personal forum. With the Compromise of 1850 a reality, he argued that there was no longer any "middle ground between *submission* and *secession*." He did not yet agree with Senator Lewis that creating a third party was futile; he called on his fellow delegates "to know no party but the great *Southern Party*." The resolutions adopted confirmed Yancey's position "that the question of secession of Alabama from this government is reduced to that of time and policy only." Anticipating the actions of a similar convention ten years later, the Southern Rights Convention issued a call to other slave states to secede, send representatives to Montgomery, "and use all proper efforts to the formation of a Southern Confederacy."[23]

Yancey and twelve others wrote an appeal to the people of Alabama that stressed protecting both slavery and the inalienable rights of white southerners. Before the convention presented the appeal, Yancey had one final resolution adopted: "That African slavery, as it exists in the Southern States of this Union, is both politically and morally right, and that the history of the world furnishes no proof that slavery is either evil or sinful." The appeal was based on this resolution. With the federal territories closed to the expansion of slavery, it stated, the South would soon be so overpopulated by blacks that slavery "will in time be looked upon as a curse." If circum-

22. William L. Yancey, *An Address on the Life and Character of John Caldwell Calhoun* (Montgomery, 1850), 7, 43–48, 56–58, 65; Yancey to Benjamin C. Yancey, August 17, 1850, in Benjamin Yancey Papers, SHC; James A. Meriwether to Howell Cobb, August 24, 1850, in Phillips, ed., *Correspondence of Toombs, Stephens, and Cobb*, 210; Draughon, "Yancey," 212–15; Allan Nevins, *Ordeal of the Union: Fruits of Manifest Destiny, 1847–1852* (New York, 1947), 354.

23. *Journal of the Southern Rights Convention Held in the City of Montgomery, February 10, 1851, and the Address of the Committee* (Montgomery, 1851), 3, 13–14.

scribed long enough, slave labor would become so cheap that it would drive out "free white labor of every description." With slavery shut out of the territories, the "dominant free soil power in the government" would continue to grow and render the South a permanent, powerless minority. Then the "great aim" of the free-soil North would manifest itself in "our political destruction and the emancipation of our slaves." Yancey and his colleagues told their fellow citizens that "absolute despotism" required them "to throw off such government and to provide new safeguards for their future safety," just as the Founding Fathers had done. To shrink from this obligation was to discard the Declaration of Independence. Though admitting that they were advocating rebellion, these men rejoined: "Washington was a rebel! LaFayette was a rebel—and so was Tell and so is Kossuth—rebels against abuse of power; and welcome to us be the appellation received in defense of our rights and liberties." [24]

After the convention adjourned, Yancey continued to promote secession by drawing ever sharper distinctions between supporters of resistance and Unionists. He declined a request from the Dallas County Southern Rights Association to run for governor; he refused to divert his attention from the "only issue" of importance in 1851: whether the South should quietly submit "to the unconstitutional action of Congress" or should resist "by separate State secession." He told his Dallas County supporters that the people of Alabama must align themselves with one of two groups: "In the ranks of the Advocates of submission will eventually be gathered whatever there is of federal and abolition tendencies in our midst, while . . . beneath banners of secession will as inevitably be rallied all that are true, to the institution of African slavery as a part of the fundamental basis of the social and political polity of the South, and all that shall prefer citizenship under separate State Sovereignty, to a servile acquiescence in the consolidation of the federal government upon the basis of free-soilism." Yancey predicted that the practice of "pandering to party prejudices" must soon end. He promised advocates of secession that perfecting their organization and continuing to explain the necessity of secession to the public would rapidly win enough converts to accomplish their goal. In a prophetic afterthought, Yancey said that even if southerners rejected secession, his tactics would ensure success the next time they

24. *Journal of the Southern Rights Convention*, 3–4, 8, 10, 13–14, 17, 34–39; Draughon, "Yancey," 220, 223–24.

felt "outraged and disregarded." Then, he stated, "we shall . . . not have again to await the slow process of the disintegration of those old parties which have heretofore preyed upon the vitals of the South."[25]

Yancey's campaign for secession began to falter during the summer. In debates with his Whig rival, Henry W. Hilliard, Yancey affirmed his commitment to secession, but he sensed that his cause was losing ground. The debates, therefore, were anticlimactic. Hilliard noticed that Yancey spoke passionately "but not with the vigor I had expected from him." Yancey split his attention between Alabama and South Carolina. Like many other secessionists, he had hoped the Palmetto State would secede first and act as a catalyst for other states. Yancey watched with frustration as both South Carolina and Alabama showed signs of rejecting secession and returning to national politics as usual. The Unionist *Alabama Journal* reported that "no one could have defended a bad cause better than did Mr. Yancey" but that in his last few outings his "heart did not seem in it." "He found himself," the *Journal* said, "in a position which he recently deprecated—that of tolerating expediency and milder remedies." By the year's end, Unionists had triumphed in Alabama, and South Carolina had balked at seceding alone. Yancey wrote bitterly to his brother that the southern rights cause had disintegrated in Alabama. Half of those who had once advocated resistance were "as much submissionists as the union men." He correctly predicted that the upcoming presidential election would "kill off all that remains of So. Rightsism" and witness a return to "old party colors."[26]

In despair, Yancey turned away from politics and busied himself with his law practice. He reconciled himself to lending tacit support to the Georgia Platform, in which that state both pledged to support the Compromise of 1850 (although it considered the measures unconstitutional) and vowed to resist future federal encroachments on southern rights, even to secession. Yancey thought that the Georgia Platform was as far as "Southern Rights men could hope now to advance" and that it would protect southern rights better

25. Yancey to Joel E. Matthews, C. C. Pegues, J. H. Campbell, C. H. Cleveland, and G. W. Gayle, May 10, 1851, in Yancey Papers, ADAH.

26. George F. Mellon, "Henry W. Hilliard and William L. Yancey," *Sewanee Review*, XVII (January, 1909), 44–47; Draughon, "Yancey," 225, 242–43, 247–48, 256–60; Yancey to Benjamin C. Yancey, November 7, 1851, in Benjamin Yancey Papers, SHC.

than the Democratic party could. Other state and national Democrats returned to the party fold, but Yancey still insisted that all national parties "deaden that active, inquiring and searching sectional spirit which alone could guard us against Northern aggression." Democratic leaders throughout the South rejoiced when Yancey decided to withdraw from party activity. In Louisiana, John Slidell exclaimed, "As to the Rhetts, Yanceys &c, the sooner we get rid of them the better." Two Georgia Democrats told Governor Howell Cobb that only "the most violent of the violent may follow the example of Yancey and others in Alabama, but the masses of the party will gladly return to their old standard." Yancey told a friend he would gladly vote for Democratic presidential nominee Franklin Pierce in the fall of 1852 to prevent the election of Whig candidate Winfield Scott, but he did not think Pierce's chance of election in jeopardy. Although the Southern Rights ticket (George M. Troup of Georgia and John Quitman) was more representative of his own views, he offered it only lukewarm support. That November, the disillusioned fire-eater did not vote.[27]

Compared with the tense sectional conflicts of the preceding years, the southern political scene in the early and middle 1850s was relatively calm. The lack of exciting sectional issues forced all fire-eaters, Yancey included, into political hibernation. But this quiet period was critically important for Yancey's personal and political maturation because he had an opportunity for introspection and time to revise his political strategy.

Yancey could not tolerate inactivity. In the summer of 1851, he took his family to coastal Alabama for a brief vacation. "The sea breeze, salt water bathing & excellent fishing constitute strong attractions," he told his brother, but added, "It is dull, very dull to me." As opportunities for political agitation diminished, he gave his energy and attention to his law practice. Yancey kept his docket full. Once when John Elmore, his partner, fell ill, Yancey worked many days from dawn to dusk without stopping for meals. Although he sometimes complained about his burden, Yancey thrived on his work. "I am almost overwhelmed in business," he told Ben,

27. Yancey to Benjamin C. Yancey, November 7, 1851, and newspaper clipping dated February 25, 1852, both in Benjamin Yancey Papers, SHC; John Slidell to Howell Cobb, January 28, 1852, John E. Ward and Henry R. Jackson to Howell Cobb, February 28, 1852, in Phillips, ed., *Correspondence of Toombs, Stephens, and Cobb*, 275–76, 286; John Witherspoon DuBose, *The Life and Times of William Lowndes Yancey: A History of Political Parties in the United States, from 1834 to 1864; Especially as to the Origin of the Confederate States* (2 vols., 1892; rpr. New York, 1942), I, 265, 269–70.

"but [am] working under it bravely." Thomas Watts remembered that Yancey relied on Elmore to do the bulk of the research for their court cases and Elmore relied on Yancey's oratorical magic to sway judges and juries. This strategy usually worked. He and Elmore had a large clientele and made money. Watts explained that the two charged reasonable fees and pointed out that Yancey "was rather a careful collector." Not afraid to tamper with success, Yancey wrote to his brother Ben in 1854 asking him to leave Georgia and come to Montgomery to practice law with him. "I will dissolve with Elmore & take you into partnership," he offered. Four years later, he did just that. The brothers practiced together for a year until Ben received a diplomatic mission to the Argentine Confederacy. In 1860, Yancey formed a new partnership with William Parrish Chilton and before the end of the year included his own son Benjamin and W. P. Chilton, Jr.[28]

National politics seldom distracted Yancey at this time. In 1852 and 1856, supporters advanced his name for a cabinet post, the second time seriously. Ben helped from Georgia by soliciting the aid of Congressman-elect Howell Cobb. Cobb was receptive if not enthusiastic and promised to use his influence to promote Yancey's cause. Yancey never expected to receive a post, but he was thrilled at the effect rumors of his possible appointment had on his political opponents in Montgomery. In 1856 Yancey toured South Carolina and was greeted as a hero. Various committees honored him for his bold advocacy of states' rights by presenting him and his wife with gifts of silverware, silver goblets, and a watch and chain. "Quite satisfactory exhibitions of popular favor," Yancey smugly reported to his brother. The next year he made a short visit to Washington, where he held a small reunion with some of his old congressional colleagues. While in the capital, he was successful in asking the secretary of state to press for a diplomatic appointment for his brother. Despite these brushes with political favor, Yancey resolved to return to Alabama and relative obscurity.[29]

Yancey's law practice did not absorb all his attention, however. It

28. Yancey to Benjamin Yancey, August 20, November 7, 1851, December 5, 1852, October 2, 1854, February 5, March 26, [April], 1855, Yancey to Caroline Beman, fragment, August 13, 1858, in Benjamin Yancey Papers, SHC; Watts, "Reminiscences," in DuBose Correspondence, ADAH; DuBose, *Yancey*, I, 406.

29. West Point (Georgia) *Advocate*, January 20, 1853; Yancey to Benjamin Yancey, January 12, December 4, 25, 1856, Howell Cobb to Benjamin Yancey, December 20, 1856, Yancey to Caroline Beman, April 5, [1857], all in Benjamin Yancey Papers, SHC. Ironically, the secretary of state was the despised Lewis Cass.

brought him back into professional contact with Benjamin Perry, and in spite of their political incompatibility, they reestablished their friendship. Planning a family vacation in Greenville, Yancey fondly wished "for the children of the two families to know much of each other." Although "Mrs. Y. and the children, have been ready (trunks packed) for two weeks," business considerations prevented him from joining them. Referring both to this misfortune and to the shooting of Dr. Earle, Yancey lamented to Perry, "I am fated, I fear, never to visit Greenville in peace."[30]

Being away from politics gave Yancey time to spend with his family. He took great pride in his children and loved them deeply. He named his eldest child Benjamin after his father and brother. Yancey bragged to Perry that Ben was "reflecting, amiable, and a fine student, beloved by teacher scholar & neighbor." He boasted that his daughter Mary was "tall, fine-looking—Yancey in all her features—very affectionate—very studious." His other children were boys: William, Goodloe Harper ("very much like me"), and Dalton Huger ("Yancey all over"). "Children should not have drilled into them the sedateness & gravity of age," he advised his brother. Instead, Yancey urged Ben to "let them romp . . . as much as they please."[31]

Yancey could offer advice on all domestic issues. He once counseled a friend who was about to marry: "You are entering upon a new sphere, a holier and happier one, than you have heretofore moved in." It was crucial for a husband to restrain his temper and never to swear, although he conceded, "I do not teach by example you will say, 'tis true." Drawing from his experiences with Sarah, Yancey promised his friend that if one worked hard to make a marriage strong, he would be rewarded with "a sweet confidence which the world can never disturb."[32]

Years after urging a friend to restrain his temper, Yancey began to show signs of doing the same. He had learned that uncontrolled emotion often undermined his best intentions when he spoke. As he explained to Ben, he now tried to avoid sarcastic remarks and provocative verbal attacks. "I endeavor to be entirely conciliatory," he said, "and while this detracts from the brilliancy and spice of

30. Yancey to Perry, December 2, 1852, July 25, 1853, May 20, 1854, July 17, September 19, December 25, 1855, in Benjamin F. Perry Papers, ADAH.

31. Yancey to Perry, September 19, 1854, in Perry Papers, ADAH; Yancey to Benjamin Yancey, December 12, 1851, in Benjamin Yancey Papers, SHC.

32. Yancey to W. O. Baldwin, November 24, 1843, in Yancey Papers, ADAH.

one's efforts, yet it gains the ears of the opposition and opens the way to their hearts." His political opponents greeted this change with alarm and told him "they would rather hear my abuse." Even when Yancey controlled his temper, his speeches provided plenty of "spice." An observer described one of them as "seasoned with the salt of argument, the vinegar of sarcasm, the pepper of wit, and the genuine champaigne [*sic*] of eloquence."[33] The "prince of the fire-eaters" would lose his temper occasionally, but seldom again would he hurl verbal pickle barrels through windows.

Yancey first used his new speaking style against a new foe, the American party. Also referred to as the Know-Nothings, this party emerged in the mid-1850s and campaigned to curb immigration and exclude Catholics and the foreign-born from public office. To Yancey these goals were so alarming that he ended his self-imposed political exile to oppose them. He never shared the xenophobia characteristic of the Know-Nothings. On the contrary, he rejoiced over the prospect of new waves of immigration. In 1845, Yancey had argued that immigrants "make up the sum of our national glory," and he opposed congressional legislation intended to restrict immigration. In direct opposition to the thinking of Beverley Tucker, Yancey believed that people with the least experience in self-government (blacks excluded) often made the best candidates for American citizens. In one debate he stated, "Honest poverty drilled in hatred of despotism by the long train of suffering under its deep rooted and relentless oppression of the poor, is the best material for our simple republican principles to operate upon." He pointed out that all Americans had immigrant backgrounds and hailed immigration as "the genius of our country." America was a "glorious temple to . . . religious equality," and when the American party sought to tamper with religious freedom, it attacked the First Amendment guarantees written by the Founding Fathers and, therefore, was "eminently anti-American." And if one party could legally proscribe Catholics, he warned his fellow southerners, another could as easily proscribe Baptists or Methodists.[34]

Though he sincerely feared that the American party would de-

33. Yancey to Benjamin Yancey, July 8, 1856, and W. B. Figures to Benjamin Yancey, September 8, 1856, in Benjamin Yancey Papers, SHC.

34. *Congressional Globe*, 29th Cong., 1st Sess., App., 43; Yancey to Benjamin Yancey, April 25, 1855, in Benjamin Yancey Papers, SHC; undated speech, in Folder 8, Yancey Papers, ADAH; Yancey to William H. Northington, June 23, 1855, in Du-Bose, *Yancey*, I, 294–97.

stroy fundamental rights, Yancey saw a greater threat in its positions on slavery and secession. Know-Nothingism originated in the North, where, he said, it was firmly allied with abolitionism. That the party's platform treated slavery "only as incidental" demonstrated its willingness to "sacrifice the South" to win votes. Yancey predicted that northerners would soon control every branch of the federal government, and southern interests would be threatened. Should any hostile sectional party prevail and attack slavery with the power of the federal government, the South would have no choice but to secede. And yet Know-Nothings stood for the Union "without qualification," even if it entailed the violation of southern rights. Therefore, Yancey concluded, "Know-Nothingism proposes to maintain the Union and crush secession, or any resistance to any kind [of] usurpation of power by the Union." Yancey's campaign against the Know-Nothings temporarily brought him back into cooperation with the Democratic party. He canvassed the state in support of Democrats in 1856 and worked energetically for the election of James Buchanan. Throughout the campaign he carried out his pledge to "speak respectfully, and with no feeling." Yancey refused the temptation to answer accusations his opponents leveled at Buchanan, choosing instead to "show up his virtues, his present position & that of our party." Yancey debated Know-Nothings in Alabama all summer, at one point confronting three at once in an effort "to weed out the whole thicket of KN orators." He ended the campaign with eight debates in eight different cities in thirteen days. The Democrats of Alabama rewarded him for his efforts by naming him a presidential elector for Buchanan.[35]

Beginning in 1858, Yancey's health became a threat to his renewed political activity. Neuralgia in his back, shoulders, and ribs weakened him, affected his digestion, made him cry out in pain at night, and almost prevented him from walking. His law practice suffered, and he considered traveling to water-cure hospitals in Arkansas and even in Europe for relief. Debilitated through the spring of 1859, he still had "a decided stoop in the shoulders" as late as June, 1860. His pain was so intense he turned to alcohol and morphine for relief. When Edmund Ruffin observed one of Yancey's speeches in 1858, the Virginian assumed that the Alabam-

35. Yancey to Benjamin Yancey, April 25, 1855, July 8, September 22, 1856, in Benjamin Yancey Papers, SHC; Yancey's speech at Columbus, Georgia, in DuBose, *Yancey*, I, 297–309; undated newspaper clipping, in Folder 22, Yancey Papers, ADAH.

ian required alcohol to brace himself for a public appearance, but there is no evidence that Yancey's use of alcohol ever became excessive.[36]

When the Montgomery Commercial Convention assembled in May, 1858, Yancey considered it so great an opportunity to renew sectional agitation that he participated despite his illness. Similar conventions met annually in various southern cities to promote commercial development. A year before, at the Knoxville convention, Yancey had been asked to participate in a debate over reopening the African slave trade at the next meeting. A month before the Montgomery convention opened, Yancey wrote to his old acquaintance Louis Wigfall and asked the Texas fire-eater to come to the convention. Although Wigfall did not attend, both Edmund Ruffin and Robert Barnwell Rhett did. In the greatest gathering of fire-eaters since the one at Nashville eight years before, Yancey, Rhett, and Ruffin politicized the convention and made it a forum to promote southern rights and secession.[37]

Yancey's debate with Roger A. Pryor of Virginia over the African slave trade dominated the convention. Yancey attacked the federal prohibition of the trade as a creature of abolitionism, an attempt to destroy southern honor by condemning one facet of an institution Yancey considered good and moral in all its manifestations. His intense emotions under control, Yancey concluded that the prohibition "was not only to check the prosperity of the South by cutting off the main artery of its prosperity, but to degrade us, and brand us in the estimation of what my friend from Virginia (Mr. Pryor) calls the opinion of Christendom. Rather the opinion of devildom." After the convention, Yancey continued to campaign for repeal of the law he found so odious. In letters to the editor of a local newspaper and to the editor of the influential De Bow's Review, Yancey said each state government, not the federal government, should decide for itself whether to engage in such trade. It was

36. Yancey to Caroline Beman, August 13, 1858, to Benjamin Yancey, November 7, 1858, to Dr. J. S. Hamilton, March 3, 1859, in Benjamin Yancey Papers, SHC; Yancey to Caroline Beman, March 5, 1859, in Benjamin Yancey Papers, WPL; Yancey to Reverend William H. Mitchell, September 3, 1859, in Yancey Papers, ADAH; Hesseltine, ed., Three Against Lincoln, 274–75; Scarborough, ed., Ruffin Diary, I, 188. Bertram Wyatt-Brown, in Southern Honor: Ethics and Behavior in the Old South (New York, 1982), 359, dismissed Yancey as an alcoholic without the slightest mention of the underlying medical problems he faced.

37. Yancey to Louis T. Wigfall, April 16, 1858, in Wigfall Family Papers, LC; DuBose, Yancey, I, 360.

"equally monstrous and unconstitutional" to punish as pirates those who currently engaged in the trade.[38]

Yancey did not expect to unite the South on this or any other solitary issue. He knew that for some southerners the slave trade was not an important enough issue to secede over. A better reason would be the election of a Republican president in 1860. Yancey objected that the legal, constitutional election of a president would be the worst conceivable reason for disunion. In that case, he said, "I am asked to put myself in the position of a traitor or a rebel," and if the federal government used armed force to "put down the revolution, [I would] be hung." But Yancey promised to support any excuse for secession because, in his mind, "the Union had already been dissolved" by the Compromise of 1850. As he explained to the convention, "All my aims and objects are to cast before the people of the South as great a mass of wrongs committed on them, injuries and insults that have been done, as I possibly can. One thing will catch our eye here and determine our hearts; another thing elsewhere; all united, may yet produce enough spirit to lead us forward, to call forth a Lexington, to fight a Bunker's Hill, to drive the foe from the city of our rights."[39]

Edmund Ruffin listened and watched with delight. He believed he had at last found the man to help him breathe life into one of his most cherished schemes, the League of United Southerners. The old Virginian approached Yancey after the convention and discussed his plan to create organizations throughout the South to promote secession. Ruffin had already written a concise "Declaration & League," showed it to Yancey, and gained his wholehearted approval. There was little subsequent collaboration, and the two remained in contact only until Yancey established a Montgomery chapter of the league that summer.[40]

Yancey had different expectations from the league than he did from the old southern rights associations. He finally took Senator Lewis' argument to heart and decided to work within the Democratic party instead of trying to overcome it. "If the Democracy

38. Newspaper clipping, May, 1858, in Folder 17, Yancey Papers, ADAH; Yancey to Thomas J. Orme, May 22, 1858, in DuBose, *Yancey*, I, 367; Yancey to the editors of the Montgomery *Advertiser*, June 13, 1859, in Charleston *Mercury*, July 9, 1859; Yancey to J. D. B. De Bow, March 25, [1858 or 1859], in James D. B. De Bow Papers, WPL.

39. Quoted in DuBose, *Yancey*, I, 361–63.

40. Scarborough, ed., *Ruffin Diary*, I, 195–96, 200.

were overthrown," he now believed, "it would result in giving place to a hungrier swarm of flies." Yancey discussed his plans for the league in a private letter that soon found its way into the nation's newspapers. He wrote to James S. Slaughter: "No National Party can save us; no Sectional Party can do it. But if we could do as our fathers did, organize committees of safety all over the cotton States . . . we shall fire the Southern heart—instruct the Southern mind—give courage to each other, and at the proper moment, by one organized, concerted action, we can precipitate the cotton States into a Revolution."[41] Yancey elaborated his plans later that summer in a local newspaper but in much milder language. League members would retain associations with their current political parties but work within them to support southern interests and "crush out the mere political tricksters, who now make the slavery question subordinate to the Parties." He envisioned an annual congress of southern leagues, which, freed from the contagion of national parties, would "vie with our Federal Congress in its influence on the public mind." Yancey claimed that the league would either save the Union, if its members could bring about guarantees for southern rights, or provide the vanguard for secession. He answered an editorial attack by Roger Pryor, who took exception to Yancey's call for southern revolution, by insisting that the Slaughter letter was private, was published without his consent, and was not a statement of policy. Because Yancey believed secession to be a legal right, he denied that the league would launch a revolution. "I am a secessionist, and not a revolutionist," he carefully explained, "and would not 'precipitate,' but carefully prepare to meet an inevitable dissolution."[42]

Despite all the commotion surrounding the league, it disintegrated by the end of the year. Its importance, however, did not. In 1860, Senator Stephen A. Douglas of Illinois accused Yancey of disrupting the Democratic national convention that spring in an attempt to precipitate a revolution that would be led by thousands of league members throughout the South. Early in 1861, a Kentucky secessionist told a friend that he had been "firing the Southern heart" to prepare his state for disunion. In introductory notes to an 1861 edition of Beverley Tucker's *Partisan Leader*, editors com-

41. Yancey to James S. Slaughter, June 15, 1858, in DuBose, *Yancey*, I, 376.

42. Montgomery *Advertiser*, July 28, 1858, in Folder 18, Yancey Papers, ADAH; Pryor's attack in Richmond *South*, September 14, 1858, and Yancey's reply in Montgomery *Confederation*, September 22, 1858, both in Folder 17, *ibid.*

mented that secessionists were prepared for direct resistance to federal authority "as soon as the 'Southern heart' could be 'fired' for that purpose."[43]

Although memories of the league and recollections of the Slaughter letter lingered, neither provided Yancey with the sustained agitation he had hoped for. The general elections of 1858, however, left him "content to abide [by] events." He believed that results of the elections "have opened the eyes of thousands in the South, and the foolish idea that the South is on rising ground is abandoned."[44] In adopting this attitude, Yancey demonstrated a newfound patience. Years of frustration caused him to plan more thoughtfully, and he now replaced boldness with caution, carefully beginning preparations for his next act of agitation, a contest at the national Democratic convention in Charleston.

The initial step in Yancey's design for the convention was to secure the cooperation of the most radical southern state, South Carolina. In 1859 he went to Columbia to present his strategy for the meeting in Charleston to the South Carolina legislature. Recalling Rhett's efforts at secession a generation before, Yancey asserted that Carolinians must not distract attention from the slavery issue by arguing for a reduced tariff. He compared southern interests to a ship: "That ship is slavery; the cargo may be the tariff; we must preserve the ship or all go down together." If any hope remained to secure southern rights without seceding, southerners had a duty to remain in the Union. "I have no such hope," he said, but expressed his willingness to work with those who did, under one condition. This was "to indoctrinate all parties in our midst with [southern] constituional views." Southern Democrats would have to "make a contest" at Charleston and vanquish the numerically superior faction headed by Stephen Douglas. Completely reversing his position of a year before, Yancey argued that the South must secede if a Republican won the next presidential election. Belatedly joining other fire-eaters, he discovered that the rise of the Republican party in the North made him a more credible speaker and made southern unity more likely and secession less frightening to others. In Columbia he asserted that southerners would find

43. Douglas' remarks in *Congressional Globe*, 36th Cong., 1st Sess., 2154, 2156; Blanton Duncan to William P. Miles, January 22, 1861, in Miles Papers, SHC; Beverley Tucker, *The Partisan Leader* ([1836]; rpr. New York, 1861), v.

44. Yancey to Benjamin Yancey, November 7, 1858, in Benjamin Yancey Papers, SHC.

greater physical danger in a Union dominated by Republicans than in a southern confederacy. He promised his listeners that southern arms would provide protection, cotton would guarantee foreign support, and their past experiences would enable them "to avoid the errors into which the [present] government has fallen."[45]

Yancey returned to Alabama to supervise the adoption of his views by the state Democratic convention. He repeated his belief that national parties would not protect southern rights and that the process of compromise forfeited constitutional principles. Yet, he admitted, "the South cannot get rid of these parties." Therefore, at Charleston, an effort ought to be made "to elevate and purify" the Democratic party and to persuade it to forgo all compromise "in dealing with Southern questions." Again, this necessitated a confrontation with the Douglas supporters. Mixing the rhetoric of conservative liberty and revolutionary rights, Yancey proclaimed that if intransigence on southern rights led to the destruction of either the Democratic party or the Union, "I am now, as I have ever been, ready to seize upon the Constitution in which those rights are guaranteed" and "form a new Union under that Constitution." If the North opposed secession by force of arms, Yancey vowed "to tread a pathway in blood to . . . secure and maintain us in our rights of person and property." He persuaded the convention to reaffirm the Alabama Platform of 1848. Secure in the backing of his state, Yancey headed for Charleston resolved either to conquer Douglas' forces or leave the party again.[46]

The Charleston Convention was ill-fated. Though the Democratic party was the only major one with a truly national following, it was rocked by internal divisions. Douglas' supporters matched Yancey in their determination to prevail at the meeting, with both their candidate and their platform, yet most southern Democrats agreed that Douglas was unacceptable. For the party's future, Charleston, selected at the 1856 party convention as a concession to southerners, was a most unfortunate site for the assembly. Recent events intensified the politically charged atmosphere in the city. John Brown's raid on Harpers Ferry the previous fall spurred se-

45. Charleston *Mercury*, July 14, 1859.
46. William L. Yancey, *Speech of the Hon. W. L. Yancey, Delivered in the Democratic State Convention, of the State of Alabama, Held at Montgomery, on the 11th, 12th, 13th, & 14th January, 1860* (Montgomery, 1860), 8, 11, 30, 31. Thornton, in *Politics and Power*, 382–83, claims that Yancey had no intention of disrupting the convention at Charleston. But it seems clear that Yancey was fully prepared to do so if his platform failed. He was prepared for domination or disruption but for no third alternative.

cessionists to renewed calls for disunion. Robert Barnwell Rhett, Jr., churned out an endless stream of propaganda in his newspaper, the Charleston *Mercury,* which condemned all southerners who favored compromise with the Douglas forces. Southern rights meetings, caucuses, and speeches were held for days before the convention.[47]

In this heated atmosphere, Yancey addressed the Charleston Convention on April 28, 1860, and argued for the adoption of his southern platform, which had been accepted by the majority of the platform committee. In a manner described by *Harper's Weekly* as "statesmanlike" and restrained, Yancey began by stating that his delegation had come to the convention to save the Union, not to disrupt it. The South, he explained, was a fixed minority. It could not protect itself within the Union without northern support. Yancey told the assembly that "the great and solemn fact faces you" that northerners must protect southern rights or force the South to secede; the North, not the South, would be responsible for secession. The South could not grant any concessions on the slave question. "Ours is the property invaded; ours are the institutions which are at stake; ours is the peace which is to be destroyed; ours is the honor at stake." Neither Republicans nor Democrats should limit slavery's expansion because to do so would deny the equality of southerners in the territories and stigmatize slaveholders as inferior. Northerners had no right to interfere with slavery in any form: "It does not belong to you to put your hands on it. You are aggressors when you injure it. You are not our brothers when you injure us." Yancey joked that northern delegates enjoyed the welcome they received in slaveholding Charleston, "even such hospitalities as you pay for so magnificently." He therefore asked them to allow southerners the full enjoyment of their property as they saw fit without outside interference or restrictions by nonslaveholders.[48] Yancey's speech drew thunderous applause from spectators in the galleries but did not sway Douglas' supporters. The majority platform was defeated. As soon as the voting ended, Yancey stormed out of the convention. In contrast to what hap-

47. Steven A. Channing, *Crisis of Fear: Secession in South Carolina* (New York, 1970), 195–208.

48. *Harper's Weekly,* IV (September, 1860), 580–81; William L. Yancey, *Speech of the Hon. William L. Yancey of Alabama Delivered in the National Democratic Convention, Charleston, April 28th, 1860. With the Protest of the Alabama Delegation* (Charleston, 1860), 2–4, 13, 15–16.

pened at Baltimore twelve years before, delegates from seven southern states followed him.

Yancey's bolt was dramatic, but it guaranteed neither a permanent dissolution of his party nor secession, as many southerners— including Yancey—knew. The night of his walkout, one observer reported, Yancey held a brief conference with Democratic leaders to discuss the possibility of returning to the convention. The editor of the Charleston *Mercury* must have heard of this meeting, for he observed "some want of nerve in the management of the seceders" by Yancey. Another Carolinian complained, "Yancey is by no means safe in the Saddle, and I protest against South Carolina being put upon the Gallop." Yet another South Carolina fire-eater, Laurence Keitt, even doubted Yancey's ability to continue leading events within Alabama.[49]

Yancey, however, was guardedly optimistic. A reporter observed him "smiling as a bridegroom" when the delegates in Charleston voted on the platform. Yancey's behavior, the reporter added, showed that he "was not perplexed by saucy doubts and fears" at this "solemn moment." Yancey then returned home to assure Alabamians that in a contest between a Republican, Douglas, and a southern Democrat no one man could attain an electoral majority. Once the election was thrown into the House of Representatives, the southern Democrat would prevail. At Richmond, where southern Democrats met after nominating John C. Breckinridge of Kentucky and Joseph Lane of Oregon for president and vice-president, Yancey conferred his blessings on the assembly. "The storm clouds of faction have drifted away," he intoned, "and the sunlight of principle . . . shines brightly upon the . . . Democracy."[50]

Still, Yancey worried about the election. He had entered the Charleston Convention determined to carry his platform or to disrupt the party. Now, he decided to work for the election of Breckinridge and the salvation of southern rights within the Union or, failing that, for secession. Hoping to unify the South and to

49. Richard Taylor, *Destruction and Reconstruction: Personal Experiences of the Late War* (New York, 1879), 12; Robert Barnwell Rhett, Jr., to William P. Miles, May 10, 1860, Alfred Huger to Miles, June 1, 1860, and Laurence Keitt to Miles, October 3, 1860, in Miles Papers, SHC.

50. Hesseltine, *Three Against Lincoln*, 80; William L. Yancey, *Substance of the Speech Made by Hon. Wm. L. Yancey, at the Democratic Meeting at Marion, Perry County, May 19, 1860* (N.p., n.d.), 22, in Yancey Papers, ADAH; Montgomery *Advertiser*, July 18, 1860.

issue a final warning to the North, Yancey embarked on an exhaustive national speaking tour.

Everywhere he went during the campaign of 1860 he made a vivid impression. One of his first speeches drew support from Alabamians who had once feared Yancey and his doctrines, "dreaded his rashness, and recklessness," but now agreed that his was the best course to protect southern rights. Yancey used both humor and controlled rage to gain the support of his listeners in Tennessee. In Knoxville, when someone taunted him by asking what he would do if Lincoln were elected, Yancey delighted his audience by saying, "I spent twelve years of my life in New England and there learned how to answer a question by asking another," and asked the heckler what he would do in the same situation. When Unionist leader William "Parson" Brownlow stepped forward and pledged to defend the United States against the likes of Yancey with a bayonet, Yancey offered to grab one as well and "plunge mine to the hilt through and through his heart, feel no compunctions for the act, but thank God my country has been freed from such a foe." At city hall in Atlanta a crowd of over twelve hundred turned out to hear Yancey speak; this number was several hundred greater than the voting population of the city.[51]

As Yancey headed north, his condemnation of the Republican party increased. In Washington, D.C., he warned his listeners that a Republican administration would lead to more raids against slavery like the recent attack by John Brown. The "flames of midnight arson" would light the southern sky while federal authorities looked the other way. In New York's Cooper Institution Yancey proclaimed that Abraham Lincoln, if elected, "will build up an abolition party in every Southern State." Abolitionist federal agents "will percolate between master [and] slave as between the crevices of rocks underground," spreading poison and fire and helping slaves escape from their masters. Yancey said Republicans intended to strip southerners of constitutional protection and make them "hewers of wood and drawers of water." But before that could happen, he told northerners, southerners would "take the banner of liberty and plant it on the mountains of Augusta, and there we will entrench ourselves as a body of freemen."[52]

51. Pratville (Ala.) *Southern Statesman,* July 14, 1860, and Atlanta *National American,* August 21, 1860, both in Folder 18, Yancey Papers, ADAH; DuBose, *Yancey,* I, 495.

52. Richmond *Enqurier,* September 25, 1860; New York *Herald,* October 11, 1860.

While Yancey attacked Republicans he also defended slavery. In Washington he cited Edmund Ruffin's essays to prove "Mr. Jefferson was wrong in his ideas about slavery" and that "the old fogies of that day" held beliefs about the institution "which we of this day are unanimously agreed were not sound." At Faneuil Hall in Boston, the citadel of abolitionist speakers, Yancey explained that blacks "sleep all day and prowl about all night. They make nothing themselves, and steal everything made by everybody else." He told Bostonians that white people constituted a "master race" and that the Founding Fathers intended the United States government to be a white government. In Syracuse, he explained that southerners treated slaves well and lovingly and that free northern factory workers faced greater hardship and deprivation than southern slaves.[53]

Yancey's tour ended in New Orleans in late October. A crowd estimated at twenty thousand, the largest ever gathered in the city's history, filled Canal Street to hear Yancey speak. The fire-eater repeated his charges that the Republican party was filled with "brave, sagacious, cool, determined and fanatic" assassins like John Brown and that Lincoln's policies would lead to the abolition of slavery. "But it will not be done," Yancey cried, "because before that time comes we shall take care of ourselves." He pointed to the thriving port of New Orleans as evidence that a southern confederacy could sustain itself and reminded southerners that cotton would command world trade. Even if the border states did not join other slave states in a new nation, they would never allow a hostile army to invade the South. Southerners, Yancey promised, had nothing to fear from secession.[54]

Although exhausted by his speaking tour, Yancey knew more work awaited him upon his return to Montgomery. After news of Lincoln's election became official, Yancey vowed to "trod the path before me fearlessly" and lead Alabama out of the Union and into a southern confederacy. Yancey assured some of his supporters in Georgia that no further compromises could delay secession. A new nation could be organized quickly by leaving the old Constitution fundamentally unaltered. "The great defect in the Union is the public conscience and education of the Northern masses upon the

53. Washington *States and Union*, October 19, 1860, in Yancey Papers, ADAH; Boston speech in Montgomery *Advertiser*, October 31, 1860; William L. Yancey, *Speech of the Hon. William L. Yancey of Alabama at Wieting Hall, Syracuse, N.Y.* (N.p., 1860), 8, 9, 12, 13.

54. New Orleans *Daily Delta*, October 30, 31, 1860; DuBose, *Yancey*, II, 531–34.

slavery question," and this problem, Yancey explained, would vanish forever in a southern confederacy. Prompt, decisive action would save the South.[55]

Yancey played a leading role in the Alabama secession convention, but after waiting ten years for disunion, he briefly lost control of himself on the eve of his success. When one delegate suggested that secession was too important to be decided by a simple majority vote, Yancey proclaimed that Alabama's ordinance of secession, "even if it be passed by the meagre majority of one," would represent the will of everyone in the state. Furthermore, the champion of minority rights bellowed, "Those who shall dare oppose the action of Alabama, when she assumes her independence out of the Union, will become traitors—rebels against its authority, and will be dealt with as such." His outburst caused such chaos that the meeting had to adjourn for the day.[56]

Yancey regained his composure by the time the convention resumed business. After the secession ordinance passed, he became conciliatory and called for a united, harmonious front. Under his leadership an invitation was issued to all seceding states to send delegates to Montgomery to form a new confederacy. In an effort to make secession peaceful, he offered a resolution to return all United States military installations in Alabama to federal control. In his final address to the convention, Yancey spoke of the "prosperity, so grand and so amazing," that awaited southerners in a new nation. With King Cotton to command world trade and threaten the North with ruin, with "a homogeneous people, accustomed to slavery, holding it in reverence for its origin and its effects," with "no domestic enemy to excite our vigilance," a southern nation must be "prosperous and powerful, for the purposes of peace or war."[57]

With secession accomplished, Yancey looked forward to a long rest. "I have no idea of ever again returning to public life," he confided to his brother Ben. Yancey was completely satisfied with the new Confederate government. He had admired the statesmanship of Jefferson Davis over the past year and heartily supported him as the nation's first president. As Yancey had wished, the Confederate

55. Yancey to John W. Forney, November 8, 1860, in Ferdinand J. Dreer Autograph Collection, HSP; Yancey to H. R. Jackson and J. M. Guerard, December 14, 1860, in Montgomery *Advertiser,* January 2, 1861.

56. William R. Smith, *History and Debates of the Convention of the People of Alabama* (1861; rpr. Spartanburg, S.C., 1975), 68–69.

57. *Ibid.,* 76, 116, 172, 250–52.

Constitution was a virtual copy of the United States Constitution. When he resigned his post in the Alabama convention, Yancey wrote a letter to the people of Montgomery County proclaiming that the citizens of Alabama had achieved a "complete triumph" and established "wise policy." Their triumph, he believed, would be supported and matched by the people in each of the Confederate states. The people of Montgomery asked Yancey as a final, honorary function to give the official introduction for President Davis. Overlooking the crowds that jammed the capitol grounds, the exhausted Yancey concluded his unusually brief remarks about Davis with the words: "The man and the hour have met. We may now hope that prosperity, honor and victory await his administration."[58]

Although the people of Alabama were ready to let Yancey retire from public service, President Davis was not. Davis shocked many by appointing Yancey to a special diplomatic mission to England and France aimed at securing recognition for the infant Confederacy. Although he was again almost crippled with neuralgia, Yancey accepted.[59]

Many southerners sensed that Yancey's appointment would end in failure. For a diplomatic assignment, one Carolinian asked, what good was Yancey's oratorical eloquence? Instead, she said, "We want someone who can hold his tongue." Robert Barnwell Rhett, now a member of the Provisional Confederate Congress, was astonished to learn that Davis had not granted Yancey any authority to make commercial treaties or concessions. Rhett implored Yancey to "take the counsel of a friend, do not accept the appointment. You will meet nothing but failure and mortification." Sharing Davis' conviction that King Cotton would provide all the negotiating power the South needed, Yancey spurned Rhett's advice and sailed for Europe. Although shortly after his arrival in London Yancey believed he saw signs that both England and France would soon grant recognition, he quickly learned that "important as cotton is, it is not King in Europe." He returned to the South in March, 1862, after a permanent commissioner replaced him. When

58. Yancey to Benjamin Yancey, January 28, 1861, in Benjamin Yancey Papers, SHC; Yancey to Clement C. Clay, May 4, 1860, in Clay Letters, WPL; Smith, *History and Debates*, 131–32; Yancey to H. R. Jackson and J. M. Guerard, December 14, 1860, in Montgomery *Advertiser*, January 2, 1861; Montgomery *Post*, February 20, March 5, 1861.

59. Benjamin C. Yancey to DuBose, February 8, 1887, in DuBose Correspondence, ADAH.

he disembarked in New Orleans, he told a somber crowd: "We cannot look for any sympathy or help from abroad. We must rely on ourselves alone." The legislature of Alabama chose Yancey to represent his state in the Confederate Senate. He arrived at the capital in Richmond a month later, still haunted by the failure of his mission. "Hopeless Despair was written on his face," a friend remembered. The failure affected him like "a personal execution. He seemed literally to have perished with his hopes."[60]

After a career of agitation, Yancey found the work of cooperation in the Confederate Senate unfamiliar. The emotion and obstinacy that had brought him into innumerable confrontations in the past resurfaced in his efforts to secure the revolution he had helped launch. Yancey soon became a bitter opponent of President Davis, whom he believed was building a centralized government almost as corrupt as the one the South has just abandoned. He also blamed Davis for southern military defeats. When Davis responded to Yancey's criticisms by denying a regular army commission to one of Yancey's sons, the senator tried again to soften his tone. "I have no interest apart from those of my country," he told the president. He explained that he had three sons in the army, two underage. Any differences he had with Davis were not personal but those "entertained by one who has his all at stake."[61] The rupture between the two never healed.

Only months before his death, Yancey again proved himself better at disruption than cooperation. On January 30, 1863, while debating the merits of creating a national judiciary with Senator Benjamin H. Hill of Georgia, the two exchanged several insulting personal remarks. On February 4, Senator Robert W. Barnwell of South Carolina suggested that Yancey should apologize for his language. Although Yancey vehemently denied uttering anything offensive, he said he wished he had done so. "You had better, then, do so now," Hill cried. Yancey stated calmly that he had already said everything a gentleman could say, and he started to sit down,

60. C. Vann Woodward, ed., *Mary Chesnut's Civil War* (New Haven, 1981), 171, 177; "Autobiography," 46, in Robert Barnwell Rhett Papers, SCHS; Yancey to Robert Toombs, May 21, June 1, 1861, to R. Chapman, July 3, 1861, to Samuel Reid, July 3, 1861, all in Yancey Papers, ADAH; V. C. Clay to John W. DuBose, October 13, 1887, in DuBose Correspondence, ADAH; M. J. Solomons Scrapbook, page 71, WPL.

61. Yancey to Clement C. Clay, May 13, 1863, in Clay Letters, WPL; Yancey to Benjamin C. Yancey, Jr., July 12, 1863, and to Jefferson Davis, June 26, 1863, in Yancey Papers, ADAH; DuBose, *Yancey*, II, 677–78, 682–84, 688.

"when I was shocked by a blow of great severity upon my cheek bone, just below the outer corner of my right eye and the temple, which immediately flooded my collar, neck and bosom with blood." As Yancey rose to attack the Georgian, Hill threw a second glass inkstand but missed. Their fellow senators forced them apart. Although no one recorded what Yancey had said in the secret session to provoke Hill, the Confederate Senate censured Yancey and not Hill for the incident.[62]

The facial wound Yancey received in February healed quickly, but his chronic medical problems worsened by summer. Afflicted with fever and a serious kidney ailment, Yancey remained in bed from July 2 until his death on July 27, 1863. Before he died he learned Vicksburg had fallen to the Yankees, and he blamed Davis for the crippling defeat. He asked his sons to get leaves from the army and hurry back to Montgomery before he weakened further. He knew that his namesake, Willie, had been wounded in the neck at Vicksburg and was due home soon to recover. His beloved wife, Sarah, was also terribly ill with fever. He watched her suffer for three days before death relieved him of his own agony.[63]

Even in death, Yancey's name was associated with the cause for which he had struggled so long. In 1858, the Mount Vernon Association had presented Yancey with George Washington's spyglass in gratitude for his efforts toward restoration of the first president's home. In an effort to heal his breach with Davis posthumously, Yancey willed this relic to the Confederate president. His sons Dalton and Benjamin joined hundreds of other southern refugees after the war in a flight to Brazil, where, in what became known as the Confederado colony of Americana, the Yancey name still survived in the 1980s.[64]

No one seriously questioned Yancey's devotion to the Confederacy, but the symbolic acts that followed his death could not erase the activities of a lifetime. After Yancey fractured the Democratic party in the spring of 1860, James Hammond wondered how the

62. Yancey's account of the story appears in DuBose, *Yancey*, II, 739–42. Also see Watts, "Reminiscences," and Benjamin Yancey to John W. DuBose, February 8, 1887, both in DuBose Correspondence, ADAH.

63. Yancey to Benjamin C. Yancey, Jr., July 12, 27, 1863, in Yancey Papers, ADAH.

64. Jefferson Davis to Mrs. W. L. Yancey, December 16, 1863, in Jefferson Davis Papers, HTL; Benjamin C. Yancey to John W. DuBose, February 8, 1887, in DuBose Correspondence, ADAH; Eugene C. Harter, *The Lost Colony of the Confederacy* (Jackson, Miss., 1986), 87–90.

American Revolution would have turned out if left to the agitators of that era such as Patrick Henry and Samuel Adams, instead of "the *silent men,* Washington Jefferson & Franklin." It would have been, he concluded, "a fizzle." As much as Henry and Adams, Yancey helped precipitate a revolution. But as Hammond feared, Yancey also contributed to its collapse. His brief career in the Confederacy paralleled those of the "Old Revolutionaries" following the Declaration of Independence; after a lifetime of agitation and challenging the political establishment, Yancey could not make a new career of compromise, consensus, and nation building.[65]

65. Hammond to William G. Simms, May 11, 1860, in Hammond Papers, LC; Pauline Maier, *The Old Revolutionaries: Political Lives in the Age of Samuel Adams* (New York, 1980), 294.

Honorable and Useful Ambition
John Anthony Quitman

S oon after establishing himself as a prominent new member of society in Natchez, Mississippi, John A. Quitman vowed to "devote the vigor and strength" of his life to "honorable and useful ambition." Quitman understood the hazards of his course, but he promised a friend that he would "not shrink from the labor and the struggle which that determination will cost." He pledged: "To raise the standard of independence, and boldly fling it in the face of any party; sink or swim, to stand by the interests of our country; to brave the shock of public opinion when required, shall be to me a pleasure." Throughout Quitman's multifaceted career, he searched for situations that would allow him to promote some principle and his own interests simultaneously. Quitman's commitment to the principle of southern rights indeed took on the characteristics of a crusade. His tremendous personal ambition was so overwhelming, however, that the opportunities various crusades presented him for personal distinction often supplanted the principle that originally drew him to the cause.[1]

Quitman was the only prominent fire-eater to be born and raised in the North. His father, a Lutheran minister, immigrated to the United States from the Duchy of Cleves, near the Netherlands, in 1795. John was born September 1, 1799, in Rhinebeck, New York. Although his father wanted him to enter the ministry and sent him to Hartwick Academy in 1817, the young Quitman quickly decided to pursue a more exciting life. After one year of teaching at Mount Airy College near Philadelphia, Quitman told his brother that he planned to "start West in search of fame and fortune." In 1819, the

1. John A. Quitman to J. F. H. Claiborne, July 31, 1831, in J. F. H. Claiborne, *The Life and Correspondence of John A. Quitman, Major-General, U.S.A., and Governor of the States of Mississippi* (2 vols.; New York, 1860), I, 106; Robert E. May, *John Anthony Quitman: Old South Crusader* (Baton Rouge, 1985). Although May addresses Quitman's crusading zeal, he does not give enough emphasis to the intensely personal motivation for Quitman's actions.

adventurous young northerner traveled to the frontier and settled in the town of Chillicothe, Ohio.[2]

After a few lonely months in frontier Ohio, Quitman briefly questioned "the wild ambition that induced me to wander so far from home." The limitless possibilities of life in the West, however, appealed to this very ambition. He thought he would become a lawyer or a soldier, or continue west to the Rocky Mountains and become a fur trader. While supporting himself by clerking at a local land office, he began to study law. "I will spare no pains to perfect myself in my profession, and to deserve the confidence of my clients," Quitman promised his father. He took great pride in the life he began to build in Ohio. To his sister he boasted: "I dress as well as any young man in town. I have attended the balls and parties; I have not gambled. I owe no man a cent." Quitman passed his bar examination in 1821 and joined a local militia company. As he began his law practice, Quitman found that clients often paid him with corn, wheat, pork, or lard. This was hardly acceptable to a young man with high aspirations, and he began to think of moving again. "The Southern States," he believed, "hold out golden prospects to men of integrity, application, and good acquirements." A woman he had met on his way to Ohio, Mrs. William Griffith, had urged Quitman to settle in Mississippi, where good attorneys were in great demand, money was plentiful, and a "gay and fashionable" society awaited. Mrs. Griffith had offered to introduce Quitman to her son William B. Griffith, who already had a practice in Natchez. "I mean to live by the practice of law, not be clerking in a land-office," he told his brother. After contemplating Mrs. Griffith's advice, Quitman stated, "My eyes are fixed on the South."[3]

Quitman arrived in Natchez in November, 1821, with only $15 in his pockets. He found cheap lodging and sought out William Griffith. Griffith loaned Quitman some money and let him use his office and books to prepare for the Mississippi bar exam. Quitman worked for Griffith after he passed his exam early in 1822 and the next year entered into a partnership with him. Their firm was successful, and Quitman's income and reputation grew rapidly. Late in

2. Quitman to his brother, August 18, 1819, in Claiborne, *Quitman*, I, 35; May, *Quitman*, 2–9.

3. Quitman to his brother, March 29, May 1, December 10, 1820, September 2, December 4, 1821, to Frederick H. Quitman, November 12, 1820, May 7, 1821, to his sister, June 26, 1820, and to F. R. Backus, February 28, 1821, in Claiborne, *Quitman*, I, 44–47, 49, 54, 56, 59, 61–65, 70.

1824, he married Eliza Turner, the daughter of a wealthy Mississippi planter. Sixteen months later, he bought Monmouth plantation, which included an impressive mansion and thirty-one acres of land, for $12,000. Quitman's list of achievements grew rapidly over the next few years. He won election to the Mississippi legislature in 1827. His work on the judiciary committee in 1828 earned him an appointment as chancellor of the state, the head of the state's court system, a position he held until 1835. During his tenure as chancellor, he also served on the judiciary committee in the state constitutional convention of 1832. Quitman did not limit himself to politics. By the time he was elected to the state senate in 1835, he was also president of antigambling, antidueling, and antiabolition societies in Natchez, president of a states'-rights association, director of the Planter's Bank, grand master of the local Masonic lodge, trustee of Jefferson College and the Natchez Academy, and captain of a militia unit called the Natchez Fencibles. He also continued to acquire land and slaves. In 1838 he owned at least 59 slaves and 2,000 acres of land; twelve years later, he owned more than 450 slaves on five plantations in two states, totaling more than 7,000 acres.[4]

After only a few years in Natchez, Quitman had totally rejected his northern origins and embraced the life-style of southern society. Quitman's acceptance of southern institutions came easily. When he left New York in 1817, slavery still existed there. Although New York had abolished slavery before the turn of the century, a generation had been allowed to phase it out gradually. Throughout Quitman's childhood, his family had black house servants, so he grew up with firsthand experience with slavery. In Natchez, he quickly accepted the belief that black slaves were "a happy, careless, unreflecting, good-natured race, who, left to themselves, would degenerate into drones or brutes, but, subjected to wholesome restraint and stimulus, become the best and most contented of laborers." Like all the other fire-eaters, Quitman considered slaves better off than free workers in the North; like the others, he came to believe that "domestic slavery is in harmony with, and almost indispensable to a constitutional republic." Early in his political career, Quitman called for legislation to prohibit the circulation of abolitionist literature in Mississippi. He condemned northerners for allowing abolitionists to impose their "fanatical doctrines" on

4. Quitman to his brother, October 17, 1835, *ibid.*, I, 138; May, *Quitman*, 20–21, 27–28, 32, 39–40, 42, 44, 63–64, 67, 111, 138.

southerners. While still in Ohio, Quitman had begun to find Yankees repugnant. "The farther they travel, the shrewder they become," he observed, remarking on "the proverbial keenness lurking about the mouth, and twinkling slyly and mischievously in the eyes." Through protective tariffs northerners taxed southerners "to build palaces in northern cities, and to support herds of lazy cattle." Quitman vowed that "such thralldom must not be submitted to." After ten years in Mississippi, he announced, "I am heartily tired of the North."[5]

From 1828 to 1832 Quitman satisfied his ambition in various capacities in Mississippi politics. He entered the legislature with an exaggerated sense of his own importance, but his vigorous work won him the respect of political leaders in the state. "My industry is in great demand," he reported to his wife. "I have much to do. My reputation requires that I should exert myself." His ego swelled after only a few weeks in the capital. He thought the state senate "one of the most stupid bodies I have ever known." He claimed credit for scoring key legislative victories while on the judiciary committee and told his new law partner, "I have great influence over many eastern members" of the assembly. As chancellor of the state court system, Quitman worked to reform the state prison system and penal code.[6]

Quitman believed that his influence was greatest during the constitutional convention in 1832. There, the thirty-three-year-old Quitman condemned younger delegates for promoting "extravagant & wild schemes" and for believing themselves "capable of legislating for all posterity." He chastised older delegates for their lack of leadership. Not surprisingly, Quitman found himself a solitary source of reason and guidance throughout the proceedings. As chairman of a committee, he told his wife, "I am . . . compelled to hear a great deal of absurdity." He sent Eliza copies of his own remarks and instructed her to publish them in Natchez newspapers, to show "that I have not taken an inferior station in this body."[7]

5. May, *Quitman,* 23–24, 31–32, 47, Quitman to Col. Brush, August 23, 1823, to Claiborne, October 18, 1830, July 31, 1831, to his brother, October 17, 1835, February 23, 1821, in Claiborne, *Quitman,* I, 84, 101–102, 57–58, 138–39, 108–109.

6. Quitman to Eliza Quitman, January 20, 1828, in Quitman Family Papers, SHC; Quitman to John T. McMurren, February 9, 1828, in J. F. H. Claiborne Collection, MDAH; Quitman to Claiborne, October 18, 1830, in Claiborne, *Quitman,* I, 101–102; Quitman to A. M. Scott, April 24, 1832, in John A. Quitman Papers, MDAH.

7. Quitman to Eliza Quitman, September 16, 23, October 2, 1832, in Quitman Family Papers, SHC.

Despite his best efforts, the resulting new constitution was, Quitman believed, "one of the greatest outrages ever committed on a
free people." Its great flaw was that it provided too many people
with too much power. He had complained about Ohio that it was
"not the place for a wealthy man to enjoy life; it is too democratic."
Now, he felt, this same democratic menace had invaded the South.
Although he had never rejected the notion of universal male suffrage, Quitman in the convention tried desperately to prevent the
electorate from voting on everything, especially for state court jus-
tices. Quitman, like many other Adams County planters, supported
John Quincy Adams and the National Republicans just as Andrew
Jackson began to gather tremendous popular support in the Southwest. Like Beverley Tucker, Quitman feared the specter of mass
participation in a republican government because he thought it
would imbue the people with too much political power and result
in mob rule. With disgust, Quitman predicted, "The *people's* doctrine will undoubtedly prevail" in the convention. This antecedent,
he warned, "is only one step removed from the rule and domination of lawless force and violence."[8]

Quitman's concern that the president of the United States was
accumulating dangerous powers soon overrode his anxieties about
popular power in Mississippi. During the nullification crisis, he
suddenly turned his attention to the concept of the Union and
states' rights. Quitman's recent biographer discovered no record of
his "conversion" to radical states-rights ideology, but by 1833 Quitman boldly supported both nullification and state interposition.
Perhaps anticipating that he could promote his own political career
by cooperating with other opponents of the president, Quitman
cautiously identified with the states'-rights faction of the new Whig
party. When Jackson issued his Force Bill proclamation, Quitman
hoped that "the sovereign state of Mississippi" would resist what
he considered a usurpation of power by the executive. Quitman
viewed the Force Bill as "vitally dangerous to the reserved rights of
the states." If states submitted to the bill, the president would "con-
solidate all powers in the National Government, and . . . erect upon
the ruins of the state governments, a supreme and arbitrary national power against which there will be no redress, no appeal but
to revolution." If southerners failed to rally behind the courageous

8. Quitman to his brother, December 10, 1820, to the Electors of Adams
County [1832], and to J. Fenwick Brent, March 22, 1845, in Claiborne, *Quitman*, I,
56, 125, 127–28; Quitman to Eliza Quitman, September 16, October 2, 12, 1832, in
Quitman Family Papers, SHC; May, *Quitman*, 53–55.

leadership of South Carolinians in this struggle for liberty, Quitman warned a friend, "we may as well prepare our necks also for the yoke of colonial bondage." Quitman believed a consolidated government with unlimited powers would become "an engine of the most grievous oppression upon the South. I wish I were in the Legislature," he explained. Even if he failed in his efforts to lead the resistance movement in Mississippi, "I would glory in martyrdom in such a cause."[9]

The next year Quitman tried to lead the states'-rights movement in Mississippi in an unofficial capacity. Although the nullification crisis had passed, Quitman continued to fear consolidation of federal power. In January, 1834, he participated in a states'-rights meeting in Jackson. As one of five authors of the official address, Quitman called for the creation of an independent states'-rights party to fight the president's "unlimited, consolidated despotism." Although he did not yet believe that secession was the only way to secure southern rights, he clearly affirmed the right of secession and like other fire-eaters denied that any state was "the subject of the United States government." Regarding both nullification and secession, Quitman echoed the thought of Beverley Tucker when he claimed that if "the State government is not the final judge of the powers and rights reserved to it," then it "is therefore not a government." He vehemently denied that a president could use military force or federal money to coerce a state or to punish its citizens for obeying state laws. "Such power," he concluded, "reduces the State government to a corporation, to a mere subdivision or province of one great empire." Quitman had a leading role in a later states'-rights gathering in Jackson. He called on Mississippians to oppose the president's "threat to enforce with the the bayonets" a law he believed contrary to the spirit of the Constitution, "impolitic and oppressive in its operation in the Southern States." He claimed that President Jackson had planned to use the army to invade South Carolina "and butcher its citizens before their own altars, before their wives and their children." Before it adjourned, the convention formed the State Rights Association of Mississippi and instructed its members to correspond with similar committees in other states and to publish tracts to promote their cause. Quitman also led by example. Now associating himself with John C. Cal-

---

9. Quitman to Nathan G. Howard, January 14, 1833, in Nathan G. Howard Papers, MDAH; May, *Quitman*, 46–48, 60–62.

houn, Quitman declared himself "a pure Nullifier" and promised to "maintain and support the doctrine of State Sovereignty and state interposition against all the world." He also pledged to fight efforts at consolidating federal power whether they came from Democrats or from Whigs.[10]

Quitman's duties as chancellor conflicted with his campaign to resist federal power and drained his energy. His wife begged him to resign his office and spend more time at home. Quitman decided to step down by the first of October, 1834. He admitted that he had neglected Eliza both emotionally and financially and assured her that he felt "light hearted" since resolving to retire from public life. To his son, however, he remarked, "I consider it the solemn duty of every lover of his country, in times like the present to step forth and raise his voice against misrule & corruption." Only a month after he returned to his family in Natchez, his relentless ambition led him back into state politics. When a vacancy suddenly opened in the state senate, Quitman quickly declared himself available for election. Local Whigs, though uncomfortable with Quitman's out-spoken views on nullification, cautiously endorsed his candidacy and helped him obtain a narrow victory.[11]

Then, an unusual series of events elevated Quitman to the governor's chair. The incoming governor, Charles Lynch, was unable to assume office until January, 1836, and Governor Hiram C. Runnels' term expired in November, 1835. The secretary of state called for a special legislative session to choose a president *pro tempore* of the state senate, who, by provisions of the state constitution, would serve as acting governor. Although Democratic strength was building rapidly in Mississippi, Democratic senators failed to unite behind one man. Whigs and others who opposed the Democrats coalesced around Quitman.

"I hope my dearest wife," Quitman wrote from Jackson, "that instead of repining at my absence you will feel an interest in the character and reputation of your husband which will give you happiness instead of sorrow." With only a few weeks to serve, Quitman worked feverishly to leave his mark on the state and to provide a

10. Jackson *State Rights Banner*, January 24, 1834; Woodville *Republican*, June 7, 1834; Quitman to F. S. Claiborne, September 5, 1834, copy in Quitman Family Papers, SHC.

11. Eliza Quitman to John Quitman, July 12, 1834, Quitman to Eliza Quitman, July 16, 22, 1834, to F. Henry Quitman, September 25, 1834, in Quitman Family Papers, SHC; May, *Quitman*, 64.

model of leadership for the entire South. "My friends properly insist that I should set an example to the country of what a *Nullifier* can do," he told Eliza. He assured her that his election had "animated our party" with new vitality, and he moved quickly to capitalize on it. In his message to the legislature Quitman set forth both domestic and federal objectives. Anticipating many of the ideas that William Yancey would later propose in Alabama, Quitman urged the legislature to continue reforms of the state's penal institutions, called for the establishment of an extensive public school system, and argued for state support of banks and railroads. When he shifted to national issues, he repeated the views on state and federal relations that he had enunciated in states'-rights meetings a year before. Quitman explained that if northern abolitionists grew strong enough to pass federal laws that tampered with slavery, southern states must protect themselves by nullifying those laws. If abolitionist assaults continued, southern states should act in concert to protect their rights. For the first time, Quitman hinted at secession.[12]

When his brief term expired, Quitman realized that his call for resistance to federal power had drawn little support. Unwilling to admit that public opinion was against him, Quitman felt that some other force had worked to foil him. He quickly concluded, "The power & patronage of the Federal Government are carrying everything before them." He accused Jackson's successor, Martin Van Buren, of bribing Mississippi politicians with the promise of federal jobs and positions of influence in the Democratic party. "I am quite disgusted with the miserable corruption I see about me," he told his wife. "My disposition induces me to make open war against it, or to retire from its influence." If this perceived corruption continued unabated, Quitman might go "to the wilds of Texas, where at least Honor & honesty may be appreciated." He was so certain he was destined for greatness that throughout his life he attributed personal setbacks not to a rejection of himself but to the mischief of others and the "corruption" he imagined around him.

Even before his brief term as governor, Quitman had taken great interest in events in Texas. He preferred to help "freemen who are struggling for their violated rights" rather than remain in Mississippi with his family. He had promised Eliza that he would

12. Quitman to Eliza Quitman, December 3, 9, 1835, in Quitman Family Papers, SHC; May, *Quitman*, 70–71.

not leave her again after his duties in the legislature ended, but only a few weeks later Sam Houston wrote to Quitman and asked for his help in the Texas Revolution. Ambition triumphed over love and Eliza's strenuous objections; Quitman began preparations to lead a militia unit into Texas.[13]

Early in April, Quitman left Natchez with forty-five men—most of them members of the Natchez Fencibles—and worked his way west to the Sabine River. A band of Virginia volunteers joined him as he led his men over the Texas border and into the town of Nacogdoches. There, several fleeing Americans told him of an impending Mexican attack. Seventy more men joined Quitman's unit, and his force remained in Nacogdoches until he could accurately determine the size and location of the enemy. Discovering that rumors had exaggerated both the strength and proximity of the Mexicans, he led his band westward into the Texas interior, where he received news of Houston's stunning victory at San Jacinto. Two days later, Quitman arrived at the battle site and met with General Houston. The field was still "literally strewed with dead Mexicans," and the Texans held their commander, Santa Anna, prisoner. Though awe-struck by the boldness and heroism of the Texas soldiers, Quitman must have been disappointed that he arrived too late to share in the glory.[14]

The Texas adventure was anything but a loss for Quitman. "The country is truly beautiful," he reported to Eliza. "The eye cannot behold anything more so." Early in the expedition he had expressed a desire to purchase land in Texas if he "could be . . . fully assured of the acquisition of this country" by the United States. Before his return to Natchez in May, he received all the assurance he needed. For fifteen cents an acre, he bought twenty thousand acres of land, which he believed would be worth twenty dollars an acre after the United States annexed Texas. Recalling his disgust with Mississippi politics, Quitman told his brother that he might soon move to Texas. He investigated the purchase of additional land on Galveston Bay and promised his wife that it would make an ideal site for a new home. When Quitman returned to Natchez, he was

13. Quitman to his brother, October 17, 1835, in Claiborne, *Quitman*, I, 139; Quitman to Eliza Quitman, January 16, February 5, 1836, Eliza to John Quitman, April 11, 1836, in Quitman Family Papers, SHC; Sam Houston to Quitman, February 12, 1836, in Claiborne, *Quitman*, I, 139–40.

14. Quitman to Eliza Quitman, April 29, 1839, to F. Henry Quitman, July 31, 1836, in Quitman Family Papers, SHC; May, *Quitman*, 85.

greatly surprised to find that local newspapers had dubbed him a hero even though he never participated in battle. In a rare moment of modesty he admitted: "I belong to the fortunate class of men. Whatever I undertake, prospers and while some are laboring and toiling for reputation and fame without success, I obtain it without seeking or meriting it."[15]

Hoping to capitalize on his popularity, Quitman ran for Congress in 1836 as a Whig. Although he had the support of most of the state's old nullifiers, he lost to his opponent in a close race. Democrats assailed him for his political inconsistencies—switching his support from John Quincy Adams and nationalism to John C. Calhoun and nullification yet remaining a Whig and supporting as a presidential candidate Hugh L. White, a Tennessean who opposed nullification. Quitman professed to be content with the election results and pleased to return his attention to personal matters. In the same breath, however, he blamed the unintelligent, brute masses for his defeat. Perhaps trying to convince himself more than his son, Quitman told the young Henry that his supporters, though few, "combined 19/20ths the intelligence of the state." Before he withdrew from the public stage, Quitman received a vote of confidence and gratitude when he was elected major general of the Mississippi militia. Through this military capacity, he would soon return to the public spotlight.[16]

His forced retirement gave Quitman time to reassess his political views. He now unequivocally pronounced himself a disciple of Calhoun and attacked the Whig positions on tariffs and internal improvements as "a system of legal robbery." As cavalier as any fire-eater in his views of organized parties and more utilitarian than most, Quitman joined the Democrats. They welcomed him; Whigs felt dismayed at his apparent betrayal of them.[17]

Before Quitman could resume an active role in politics, financial disaster struck. By 1840, he had accumulated debts totaling $95,000, primarily by endorsing loans for friends who defaulted in the aftermath of the Panic of 1837. His insistence on caring for the widows and orphans of Natchez Fencible members further drained his

15. Quitman to Eliza Quitman, April 13, 15, 29, May 7, 1836, to his brother, May 28, July 31, 1836, in Quitman Family Papers, SHC.
16. May, *Quitman*, 92–94; Quitman to F. Henry Quitman, December 7, 1836, in Quitman Family Papers, SHC.
17. May, *Quitman*, 98; Quitman to T. Bole and S. Shackleford, December 13, 1838, in Claiborne, *Quitman*, I, 165–68.

resources. Despite an income of $45,000 in 1839 from his flour-ishing cotton and sugar plantations, Quitman's fiscal obligations forced him to cancel all unnecessary expenditures. "My pockets are empty," he complained to a friend, and when he encountered people he owed money to, "if I can conveniently dodge them I do." He resumed practicing law early in 1840 and intensified his efforts to solve his economic woes. "There are more than 2,000 suits on the docket," he told Eliza in the spring. Quitman maintained this incredible pace for the remainder of the year and let nothing im-pede his work. When business took him to Jackson in December, he refused to return to Natchez either for his anniversary or for Christmas, much to his family's dismay. As the next year began, Quitman wrote his wife that "in a few years by close attention to the disordered state of the affairs, and by rigid economy we shall be enabled to wipe out the debts and then shall have one of the finest estates on the [Mississippi] river." Not even politics could distract him from this goal. He explained to a friend, "I have neither the time nor inclination to embark in a political cause however good." [18]

During the early 1840s, Quitman paid closer attention to the management of his plantations. Just as his financial problems seemed under control, he and his brother-in-law bought the large Palmyra plantation in March, 1842. In making this purchase, Quit-man incurred a portion of a $75,000 debt that took him until 1857 to pay off. He transferred many of the slaves from his Springfield plantation to augment the work force of 230 at Palmyra and real-ized sizable profits in 1842 and 1843. Because he continued to buy land, he was forced to practice law to earn an income. To Eliza he grumbled, "My task is like that of a galley slave, I am as closely chained." He scolded his wife for not "encouraging, sustaining & supporting me" in his efforts to rebuild the family fortune. Finally, by 1844, Quitman believed that he had his financial problems under control and he could afford to renew his career in politics. [19]

Quitman's friend and former law student John F. H. Claiborne

18. Quitman to Claiborne, January 27, February 26, 1840, in Claiborne, *Quit-man*, I, 186–89; Quitman to Eliza Quitman, May 6, 1840, Eliza Quitman to Quitman, December 20, 1840, Quitman to Louisa Quitman, December 20, 1840, and to Eliza Quitman, January 3, 1841, in Quitman Family Papers, SHC; May, *Quitman*, 108–109; Quitman to Robert J. Walker, February 14, 1842, in Robert J. Walker Papers, MDAH.

19. Quitman to his brother, January 16, 1842, in Claiborne, *Quitman*, I, 191; Quitman to Eliza Quitman, January 18, 1843, in Quitman Family Papers, SHC; May, *Quitman*, 111–12.

began to promote Quitman for a seat in the United States Senate in 1845. For the past year Quitman had added his voice to the popular call for the annexation of Texas. He had supported Democrat James K. Polk for president on a pro-annexation platform. When asked by Mississippi Democrats to run for office, he gladly accepted. Although eager to enter the political contest, Quitman adhered to an old philosophy that senatorial candidates lost their dignity by engaging in stump speaking. He asked Henry S. Foote, an attorney from Jackson, to speak on his behalf. State legislators, not the state's electorate, chose senators, but Quitman underestimated the importance of standing before the public. His long-standing distaste for popular politics cost him dearly. Ironically, he not only lost the election, but legislators chose Henry Foote instead.[20]

State politics had not ceased to annoy Quitman since the 1830s. He was so distressed at the results of the 1843 elections that he claimed, "I would almost as soon have seen our house burned down." Again he complained, "The state will scarcely be fit [to] live in." Eliza's desire that her husband spend less time in politics and more at home never diminished. Just before the legislature elected Foote, she told him, "I almost hope that you may not be elected on account of the children."[21]

Just as Texas distracted Quitman from his worries in 1836, the renewal of tension between Texas and Mexico in the 1840s "roused me from my lethargy." Quitman described the impending struggle in the most graphic terms. As his political protégé John F. H. Claiborne recalled, "He regarded . . . the great bulk of the Mexicans as a bastard and robber race, incapable of self-government, and fit only for servitude and military rule." Quitman assured a friend in Texas that southerners "will never permit an Indian and negro colony to be planted on the frontier. Come what will, that must not happen." Regardless of whether the United States government helped Texans in a conflict with Mexico, Quitman continued, "the *people* of the South will cheer you on and aid you."[22]

20. May, *Quitman*, 120–23, 126–29. Although May correctly demonstrates that Quitman's attitude about campaigning betrayed ineptitude in the era of Jacksonian politics, see also Kenneth S. Greenberg, *Masters and Statesmen: The Political Culture of American Slavery* (Baltimore, 1985), 3–22, for the extent of this antidemocratic practice in the Old South.

21. Quitman to Eliza Quitman, November 17, 1843, Eliza Quitman to Quitman, January 7, 1846, in Quitman Family Papers, SHC.

22. Claiborne, *Quitman*, I, 192–93; Quitman to [unidentified], March 19, 1842, *ibid.*, I, 271.

Quitman believed that war with Mexico would provide both a crusade to vindicate the South from antislavery attacks and an opportunity for personal triumph. In 1845, he asked his governor to allow him to recruit and command Mississippi volunteers should war break out; as a major general in the militia, he demanded a prominent position in any contribution Mississippi might make. He petitioned the Mississippi congressional delegation on behalf of the South, his state, and himself. He offered to raise five thousand men "to confer honor on their much-abused state, and win laurels for themselves." Quitman called for the conquest of all Mexico, which, he argued, would also be a victory over northern critics. "We desire no aid from the Abolitionists," he explained. "The Northern States question our strength in war. Then let this war be the test. Let President Polk give us an opportunity of showing our spirit, muscle, and resources, and of repelling the slanders upon our institutions." Quitman went to Washington to ask Polk for an army commission. In the summer of 1846, he was commissioned as brigadier general and ordered to report to the Texas-Mexico border. His ambition left him bitterly disappointed with a rank he considered low. When he entered Mexico a few weeks later, Quitman told Claiborne that his goal was "a major general's baton, fairly won on the field of battle, or a Mexican grave!"[23]

Quitman's determination to achieve distinction in Mexico did not escape the notice of his troops or his family. One of his men reported that "in Genl Quitman I have no confidence at all. He is a weak, vain, ambitious man, who is anxious to do something to distinguish himself, and I believe would not care at what sacrifice." Predictably, Quitman threw himself into the crucible of battle at his first opportunity. He described his boldness at the Battle of Monterrey to Eliza: "In the several actions my Brigade has gained the highest distinction & honor. It has suffered more severely than any other. I was necessarily much exposed, but was fortunate enough to escape injury. I had three horses shot and killed under me. My horse Messenger alone escaped. One ball passed through my hat, and a piece of a shell struck me on the thigh. A kind Providence watched over me, for no man was more exposed." He called this battle "one of the greatest victories ever achieved by American soldiers" and took great pride in his own leadership. Intoxicated by

23. Quitman to Governor Albert G. Brown, September 6, 1845, to Congressmen Davis, Adams, Thompson, and Roberts, May 22, 1846, to Claiborne, May 20, September 15, 1846, in Claiborne, *Quitman*, I, 223–28, 241; May, *Quitman*, 148–49.

this early victory, Quitman insisted that American troops must penetrate deeper into Mexico or risk the "contempt of our national character." Although disease ravaged his troops the next winter, Quitman "never felt better" and eagerly awaited another battle.[24]

Over the next several months, Quitman began to worry that he might not get the official recognition he believed his actions had earned. In his fellow Mississippian Jefferson Davis, who served under him at Monterrey, Quitman saw "an envious disposition & a selfishness which I have rarely witnessed." He asked his family if there were any truth to the story that, on a trip to Vicksburg, Colonel Davis had claimed "the merit of having done every thing." If this were true, Quitman feared, Davis might replace him in the minds of Mississippians both as the outstanding military hero from the state and as a leader in the state Democratic party. Even after President Polk appointed Quitman major general in April, 1847, he was not content. His commander, General Winfield Scott, denied Quitman an independent command until reinforcements arrived. Quitman protested that he would not "submit to the humiliating position assigned me," but he reluctantly accepted Scott's order that he "cheerfully bend to circumstances."[25]

When the American army approached Mexico City in September, Scott selected Quitman to lead one of the assaults on the city's stronghold, Chapultepec castle. Believing older officers like Scott too cautious and sensing his chance for glory, Quitman ordered his men to advance despite Scott's call for restraint. Quitman was unharmed in the initial assault, but again his men drew heavy casualties. Undaunted, Quitman ordered them to continue. After more heavy fighting, Quitman's men entered the city. Early the next morning, the Mexican forces surrendered. Scott ordered Quitman's troops to occupy the Grand Plaza and raise the American flag over the ancient capital; he then named Quitman civil and military governor of the city.[26]

Quitman's ego swelled as never before. "Here I am Governor of

24. William B. Campbell to Frances Campbell, January 2, 1847, in Campbell Family Papers, WPL; Quitman to Eliza Quitman, September 25, October 7, 1846, in Quitman Family Papers, SHC; Quitman to Robert J. Walker, November 12, 1846, in Claiborne, *Quitman*, I, 272; Quitman to F. Henry Quitman, January 11, 1847, MDAH.

25. Quitman to Eliza Quitman, February 20, 1847, in Quitman Family Papers, SHC; Quitman to General Scott, May 30, June 3, 1847, Scott to Quitman, May 3, 1847, in Claiborne, *Quitman*, I, 302–307; May, *Quitman*, 180–82.

26. May, *Quitman*, 189–94.

Mexico and chief in the Halls of Montezuma," he wrote to Eliza from the National Palace. "Since the days of Cortes we are the first invaders of this country & the people look upon us with astonishment." Providence, he explained, had again turned bullets from him as others fell by his side. "So far as the credit of the thing is concerned, my honors sit very easy upon me." In Mexico, the ambitious Quitman had realized the fulfillment of his dreams: "I posses absolute powers."[27]

While diplomats negotiated a formal settlement, Quitman enunciated his own views on Mexico. The beauty of Mexico captivated him, but he thought the Mexican people "are unworthy of such a paradise." He was a proponent of Manifest Destiny and declared: "I am satisfied that we are but the instruments of a benevolent Providence to improve this country and its condition. Our invasion will result in the establishment of some good government and in conferring blessings upon the people." After only a month as governor, Quitman regally concluded, "My subjects consist of the most infamous population with which any great city was ever cursed." Like those fire-eaters who professed that only Caucasians were capable of self-government, Quitman clearly believed that the multiracial population of Mexico was unable to rule itself well. He wished to import American institutions, including African slavery, to this conquered province.[28]

General Scott sent Quitman to Washington late in 1847 to receive new orders directly from the secretary of war. As he awaited his instructions, a treaty with Mexico ended remaining hostilities. Simultaneously the presidential election of 1848 heated up. Many spoke of Quitman as a possible candidate for president or vice-president. He received a great deal of support from Democrats who approved of his "all Mexico" position. Henry Foote rallied Mississippi Democrats behind him. In the national party convention, Quitman finished a strong second on the first ballot for vice-president, but William O. Butler of Kentucky won the nomination. Again refusing to accept a personal rebuff, Quitman accused Jefferson Davis and other Mississippians of conspiring against him. Realizing that his political future depended on cooperation with his

27. Quitman to Eliza Quitman, May 21, September 18, 19, 1847, to Louisa Quitman, October 5, 1847, in Quitman Family Papers, SHC.

28. Quitman to Louisa Quitman, November 28, 1846, to Eliza Quitman, December 30, 1846, January 6, 27, February 15, April 23, June 3, October 11, 1847, *ibid.;* Quitman to F. Henry Quitman, May 25, 1847, in John A. Quitman Papers, HSP.

party, he resigned himself to his fate and dutifully supported the ticket of Lewis Cass and Butler.[29]

While military governor of Mexico, Quitman had correctly observed, "The effects of the taking of Mexico have not yet been felt, and no correct speculation can be made as to immediate results." One immediate result, however, was the renewal of the national debate over the expansion of slavery into the territories. Many southerners had hoped that the new president, Zachary Taylor, a slaveholding southerner, would engineer a solution favorable to southern interests. When Taylor's administration supported the initiative of Californians to form a free state, southern indignation intensified. In Mississippi, 1849 was an election year; Democrats asked Quitman to run for governor and lead the fight to extend slavery into the territories that he had recently helped conquer. Quitman could hardly restrain his enthusiasm. "I will be easily elected," he predicted, and "by a large majority." He was right. Choosing to rely on his fame as a war hero and his reputation as a states'-rights man, Quitman won by a wide margin without making a single speech. He considered his election a "severe rebuke to the imbecile and anti-southern administration of Genl Taylor." Before the election that November, Quitman attended a southern rights meeting in Jackson. The assembly declared that any attempt by the federal government to tamper with slavery would be unconstitutional. Delegates then called for representatives of slave states to meet at Nashville, Tennessee, in June, 1850, to discuss strategies of southern resistance to anticipated northern aggression against slavery.[30]

Believing that the sentiments expressed in this meeting accurately reflected the popular mood of his state, Quitman prepared a radical southern rights message for the state legislature. He began by asserting that every state in the Union retained sovereign powers, and he reminded legislators that the Constitution left all control over slavery to the individual states. In the South, he stated, slavery "is entwined in our political system, and cannot be sepa-

29. Quitman to Eliza Quitman, May 21, June 6, 1848, in Quitman Family Papers, SHC; Quitman to Gen. Shields, September 9, 1848, in Claiborne, *Quitman*, II, 15–16; May, *Quitman*, 196–98, 205–209. For Quitman's position on Mexico, see Quitman to John O. Knox, March 8, 1848, in Claiborne, *Quitman*, II, 13–14.

30. Quitman to Eliza Quitman, September 19, 1847, in Quitman Family Papers, SHC; Quitman to F. Henry Quitman, July 2, September 7, November 11, 1849, in Quitman Papers, HSP; May, *Quitman*, 224.

rated from it, without destruction to our social fabric." Although some northerners condemned slavery, Quitman argued, "We do not regard it as an evil, on the contrary, we think our prosperity, our happiness, our very political existence, is inseparably connected with it." The right to own slaves "is one of those essential rights which cannot be yielded up without dishonor and self-degradation. None who believes that we have inherited the free spirit of our fathers," the governor continued, "can doubt our determination at all hazards to maintain these positions essential to our security." The South had already submitted to too many federal usurpations of power, and he warned, "Dishonor, degradation and ruin await her, if she submits further." He charged that "a systematic and deliberate crusade against our sacred rights is now in progress" and that Congress was "the theatre of this war against slavery." Only two results were possible from this confrontation: "the ultimate destruction of our domestic institutions, or the dissolution of the Union."[31]

In 1850, congressmen searched for a compromise solution to all outstanding sectional disputes, and southern radicals began to campaign for secession. Quitman believed that northerners would not yield in their efforts to ban slavery from the federal territories, and therefore the Union "is on the verge of dissolution." Viewing the crisis as another link in his destiny, as an honorable means to promote his own fame by defending the South, Quitman determined to take charge of events in Mississippi. As governor, he ordered an inventory taken of the state's military supplies in case secession led to war. As a private citizen, he chaired a meeting in July that called for the creation of Southern Rights associations in every county. Although the Nashville Convention failed to promote secession, Quitman continued to believe that "the South will not submit to be robbed of the territory acquired from Mexico." If California were admitted as a free state, "we should secede from the Union." Quitman suddenly became the most prominent secessionist outside South Carolina.[32]

Quitman offered his leadership to any state that resisted compromise efforts. When Congress included federal assumption of

31. *Inaugural Address of Governor John A. Quitman, Delibered Before Both Houses of the Mississippi Legislature, January 10, 1850* (N.p., n.d.), in John A. Quitman Papers, LSU.

32. Quitman to F. Henry Quitman, March 2, 1850, in Quitman Papers, HSP; May, *Quitman*, 234, 241–42.

the state debt of Texas as part of the Compromise of 1850, he urged his friends there not to "sell their sovereignty" and promised to head a military expedition to Texas if resistance to the national government led to war. He responded enthusiastically when Governor Whitemarsh Seabrook of South Carolina tried to rally other states to oppose the compromise. Seabrook feared that South Carolina still bore the odium of its radicalism in the 1830s and desperately hoped some other state would lead the fight for southern rights. Quitman gladly volunteered. He told Seabrook that if Congress tampered with slavery in any way, he would call a special session of the Mississippi legislature "to take into consideration our Federal relations, with full powers to annul the Federal compact, establish new relations with other States, and adapt our organic laws to such new relations." As for himself, Quitman explained, "Having no hope of an effectual remedy for existing and prospective evils, but in separation from the Northern states, my views of state action will look to secession." The people of Mississippi, he assured Seabrook, would do the same.[33]

When Congress admitted California as a free state and adopted the Compromise of 1850 in September, Governor Quitman called a special session of the legislature to meet in November. Although he professed to have "not a selfish motive connected with these questions," the intensely personal nature of the conflict was evident. He blamed "conspirators" for using a "widely extended scheme of fraud & deception" to foil his efforts to achieve secession. Quitman told his son, "I defy these assaults from the miserable submissionists who would lick the hand that smote them." He promised a friend in Louisiana that, "so far as it depends on me," Mississippi would not "quietly submit to be robbed of her share in the broad harbours of the Pacific coast, and the vast territories," which southerners had given their lives to help win. Such submission would be tantamount to accepting a brand of inferiority, and, he vowed, "I will not be the instrument of surrendering our birthright of liberty and equality."[34]

33. Quitman to General J. Pinckney Henderson, August 18, 1850, Whitemarsh Seabrook to Quitman, September 20, 1850, in Claiborne Collection, MDAH; Quitman to Seabrook, September 29, 1850, in Whitemarsh B. Seabrook Papers, LC. Seabrook had sent a circular letter to all southern governors. See Seabrook to [Governor Henry W. Collier], September 20, 1850, *ibid.*

34. Quitman to F. Henry Quitman, August 26, November 16, 1850, in Quitman Papers, HSP; Quitman to Eliza Quitman, September 21, 1850, to Louisa T. Quit-

Quitman knew that his message to the legislature "will no doubt excite great interest and produce much sensation both here and at the North." Governor Seabrook assured him that South Carolina would secede as soon as any other southern state or a second Nashville Convention called for secession. In his message, Quitman stated that the most southerners could concede was an extension of the Missouri Compromise line of 36°30′ through all remaining territories. He argued, however, that southerners could no longer seek equal treatment in the Union and recommended "secession in preference to submission." The most extreme step the legislature was prepared to take, though, was to schedule elections in September, 1851, to elect delegates for a state convention in November to consider secession. Although Quitman wished the convention would be held earlier, Unionist strength had increased so much that he considered the delay a triumph for the radicals. After the special session, Quitman asked the leader of the secession movement in South Carolina, Robert Barnwell Rhett, for suggestions "in relation to the proper course to be pursued by the South" in the upcoming year. When Governor Seabrook again assured Quitman that South Carolina would follow Mississippi out of the Union, Quitman believed that he had successfully set the South on the road to independence.[35]

Writing from New York, Quitman's sister Louisa proclaimed, "I care not how soon the word of secession is spoken." His daughter told him, "I am a *terribly hot Southern rights* advocate—a perfect *fire-eater* of the most voracious kind." Other southerners, however, did not share the convictions of these women. John Quitman remained hopeful that his state would secede but began to worry that his ambitious schemes might falter. "The imaginary evils" of secession, he feared, might cause some to "recoil and pause a long time in doubt and uncertainty." The border states might never secede unless "forced to choose between a Northern and Southern confederacy." Even though he argued that "great political movements must be bold, and must present practical and simple issues," Quitman wished that South Carolina would act first "and force the other

man, October 1, 1850, in Quitman Family Papers, SHC; Quitman to Samuel A. Cartwright, October 2, 1850, in Samuel A. Cartwright and Family Papers, LSU.

35. Quitman to F. Henry Quitman, August 26, November 16, 1850, in Quitman Papers, HSP; Seabrook to Quitman, October 23, December 3, 1850, in Claiborne Colleciton, MDAH; May, *Quitman*, 247; Quitman to Robert Barnwell Rhett, November 30, 1850, in Seabrook Papers, LC.

states to meet the issue plainly." He pleaded his case to Seabrook. Mississippi was "unarmed, in debt, seriously divided and have [*sic*] no sea ports, nor commercial outlets." Throughout the South, the people had sunk into apathy "under the greatest aggressions, merely because they are distant and indirect. Our equality is already lost, and our rights and domestic institutions endangered, and yet the people of the South are not aroused." The destiny of the South, he told Seabrook, "now depends upon the bold and prompt action of your noble state."[36]

As signs of southern vacillation grew, Quitman's friends in South Carolina feared that their state would be left to challenge federal power unaided, just as it had done back in 1832. Secessionist Maxcy Gregg cautioned Quitman that Mississippi's failure to support secession "might cause some fatal defection" in South Carolina. Seabrook warned him that failure to resist the national government would lead to "oblivion" for both states. Rhett echoed the report of the newly elected governor, John Means, that secession sentiment in South Carolina continued to grow. Rhett asked Quitman if foes of immediate secession had written to him "to draw from you some support of their policy." If so, Rhett said, "the[ir] design is to use you, to overthrow the Secession party of this State." Gregg wrote again and struck at Quitman's most sensitive nerves by appealing to his ambition and ego. "In this great struggle, the South wants a great leader, with the mind and the nerve to impel and guide revolution. Be that leader," Gregg urged, "and your place in history will remain conspicuous for the admiration of all ages to come."[37]

In the midst of this crisis, Quitman's obsessive desire to lead a great movement jeopardized his influence in Mississippi and the South. Narciso López, a Cuban expatriate, planned to launch a private expedition in 1850, which he hoped would spark a revolution in Cuba. Basing his operations in New Orleans, López appealed to many American expansionists by promising that a free Cuba would apply for annexation to the United States. López correctly supposed that Quitman would be interested in the affair and asked the

36. Louisa S. Quitman to Quitman, December 18, 1850; Louisa T. Quitman to Quitman, July 25, 1851, in Quitman Family Papers, SHC; Quitman to John S. Preston, March 29, 1851, in Claiborne, *Quitman*, II, 123–27; Quitman to [Seabrook], January 26, 1851, in Seabrook Papers, LC.

37. Maxcy Gregg to Quitman, May 9, 15, 1851, Seabrook to Quitman, June 9, 1851, Rhett to Quitman, July 22, 1851, in Claiborne Collection, MDAH; John Means to Quitman, May 12, 1851, in Claiborne, *Quitman*, II, 133–34.

general if he would consider commanding the assault. With great reluctance, Quitman refused, but he did put López's agents in contact with others who might supply money and arms. After an abortive landing on Cuba soil, López was arrested in New Orleans on June 7 for violating American neutrality laws. When a United States District Court grand jury concluded its investigation, it indicted, among others, Governor Quitman.[38]

Quitman was in a dilemma. His initial response was to resist arrest. Because he considered himself the head of a sovereign state, he believed that no other authority, not even the federal government, could either arrest him or force him to stand trial. But resisting arrest, he conceded, might entice federal authorities to remove him forcibly from office. After consulting with friends and lawyers, he chose a "middle course" between submitting to federal authority and "bringing about a collision of arms between this state and the general government *prematurely*." He decided to face trial, but as a private citizen. He resigned from office on February 3, 1851.[39]

Quitman's resignation did not mean that he would not fight. In fact, he pledged that his trial would be a contest against federal power. Quitman proclaimed, "I shall feel honored with being the first subject of the experiment." He would either defeat the federal prosecutors or "fall in the breach" and become a martyr for the cause of states' rights. He asked Barnwell Rhett, who had recently been selected as a United States senator, to unleash "a vigorous assault upon the judicial encroachments of the federal courts." He told Rhett that the neutrality laws were "so vague as to furnish a suitable cloak for the boldest tyrant." In his letter of resignation, he tried to heighten southern indignation by suggesting that the federal government seemed more concerned with removing a governor from office than with retrieving fugitive slaves from the North. Quitman's boldness was grounded in his confidence that he had violated no law. "I would not hesitate to publish to the world, whatever connection I may have had with the [López] matter," he said. Quitman saw Cuba's struggle as identical to that of Texas in 1836. As an American, he believed, he could take part in the revolution

38. May, *Quitman*, 237–40.
39. *Ibid.*, 237–41, 248–49; Jacob Thompson to Quitman, September 2, 1850, in Claiborne, *Quitman*, II, 62–65; Quitman to Rhett, January 24, 1851, in Claiborne Collection, MDAH. The emphasis in the quotation is added. Also see Ambrosio J. Gonzales to Quitman, April 5, March 20, 1850, John Henderson to Quitman, May 2, 25, 27, 1850, in Quitman Papers, MDAH.

only "if invited to by the people of Cuba after they should have erected the standard of independence."[40]

Before Quitman's trial began, he found evidence that his strategy of challenging federal authority was achieving the ends he desired. From all over the South, supporters urged him on. Enthusiasts in Tennessee and Missouri offered to raise military units if Quitman wished to invade Cuba, regardless of federal laws. "You can defy a 'world in arms,'" said one Mississippian. Another promised Quitman that "the people are beginning to look to secession as the only effectual remedy" against federal power. A newspaper editor in Savannah assured him of sympathy in Georgia but asked for a delay in the acquisition of Cuba until after the formation of a southern confederacy. It appeared to Quitman that all of New Orleans had rallied behind him. "My room is sometimes crowded for hours. All approve of my course." With great satisfaction, he reported to Eliza, "I now believe that my message & letter of resignation have given me more reputation than the Mexican war."[41]

After federal prosecutors failed to convict others involved in the López expedition, they dropped their charges against Quitman. Suddenly he was free to resume his campaign for southern rights in a more conventional manner. He decided to run for governor again in 1851. "We claim redress for the past, and guarantees for the future," he told Seabrook. He insisted that the North either extend the Missouri Compromise line or repeal all laws that prohibited slavery from the territories. "If our just demands are refused, we propose to prepare ourselves to unite with other dissatisfied states in a new confederacy." Quitman announced his political creed in a letter to a Southern Rights Association in March:

> The political equality of the states is the vital principle of the Constitution. Upon its strict maintenance depends our liberties. We are not permitted to surrender it even to purchase temporary peace for ourselves. It is a sacred inheritance, bequeathed by our sires, which it is our duty to transmit unimpaired to our children. If assailed, we must defend it,

40. Quitman to Jacob Thompson, August 15, 1850, in Claiborne, *Quitman*, II, 62; Quitman to Rhett, January 24, 1851, in Claiborne Collection, MDAH; Claiborne, *Quitman*, II, 66, for Quitman's message to the people of Mississippi upon his resignation; Quitman to E. T. Griffith, July 22, 1850, in Quitman Papers, MDAH.

41. George Muncy to Quitman, May 24, 1850, J. H. Sims to Quitman, February 19, 1851, T. J. Wharton to Quitman, July 9, 1851, J. McDonald to Quitman, March 9, 1851, Thomas Jones [Pope] to Quitman, May 5, 1851, in Quitman Papers, MDAH; Quitman to Eliza Quitman, February 22, 1851, in Quitman Family Papers, SHC.

even though the Union perish in the contest. But firmly and inflexibly to insist upon all our constitutional rights, and to maintain them at all hazards, is the only mode of preserving the Union of the Constitution. All that we ask is justice and equal rights. If they have been extended, we have no right to complain. If not, we should demand them, insist upon them with confidence and without fear of consequences.[42]

Quitman's opponent was his once-loyal lieutenant Henry S. Foote. After a period of indecisiveness, Foote had become a devout Unionist. Quitman felt betrayed. He sickened at all "hosannas to the 'glorious Union,'" and agreed to a series of debates against the "wily and adroit" Foote. Never a good public speaker, Quitman was at a distinct disadvantage against Foote, who was among the best stump speakers in the state. Exasperated by Foote's forensic displays, which often included cutting personal remarks, Quitman assaulted Foote during one of their encounters. After the brawl, Quitman canceled the remainder of his engagements. Foote, however, adhered to the schedule and spoke throughout the state without opposition. Quitman received a debilitating blow when elections for the legislature that summer showed that Mississippians overwhelmingly rejected secessionist candidates and voted instead for Unionists. "I bow in respectful submission to the will of the people," he told a group of Democrats in September. Rather than face certain defeat in November, Quitman withdrew from the race. Foote excitedly announced, "Quitman and Quitmanism are *dead* in Mississippi forever."[43]

Quitman, of course, disagreed. Still convinced that he was destined to lead a southern crusade, Quitman acknowledged only the defeat of secession, not of southern rights, and set to work on a new strategy. After making loud and ominous threats to secede, Quitman knew that "wishy-washy resolutions" would convince no one that southerners still insisted upon certain rights. Instead, he advo-

42. Quitman to Seabrook, January 26, 1851, in Seabrook Papers, LC; Quitman to C. S. Tarpley, G. T. Swann, and E. Barksdale, March 31, 1851, in Claiborne, *Quitman,* II, 131. Clearly, Quitman was not, as Robert May claimed, a "reluctant secessionist" (May, *Quitman,* 228).

43. Quitman to Tarpley *et al.,* March 31, 1851, to the Democratic State-rights Party of Mississippi, September 6, 1851, in Claiborne, *Quitman,* II, 129, 146–47; Quitman to Seabrook, January 26, 1851, in Seabrook Papers, LC; May, *Quitman,* 261–63; Henry S. Foote, *Casket of Reminiscences* (1874; rpr. New York, 1968), 354–55; Henry Foote to Howell Cobb, July 8, 1851, in U. B. Phillips, ed., *The Correspondence of Robert Toombs, Alexander H. Stephens, and Howell Cobb* (Washington, D.C., 1913), 242.

cated voting against all southerners who supported the Compromise of 1850, "who assisted to rob us of our equality, and to cheat us out of the public domain." Replacing these men with ones who insisted on recognition of southern rights would allow the South to maintain "an armed neutrality." Southern politicians would either "assume positions consistent with our equality and safety in the Union" or, one day, lead them out of it.[44]

Quitman's first opportunity to test his new policy came during the presidential election of 1852. At the beginning of the year, Quitman recommended that advocates of states' rights continue to work within the Democratic party "because I know not where else to look . . . for effective help in this day of tribulation to the South." He planned to support the Democratic presidential candidate unless the party chose a southerner who had supported the Compromise of 1850. "I may pardon the advocacy of the measures by a Northern man," he explained, "because, in the struggle for supremacy, he but sided with his section; but the Southern man who deserted us in the hour of need I can never trust." He recalled that when he ran for governor the previous summer, "the contest was noble and sublime," but he had no personal stake in the presidential election and took "but little interest in the struggle." Hoping the "Old Guard" of secessionists would adopt his plan of "armed neutrality," the general was distressed to see many former radicals abandon principles the way "a deserter casts off his uniform." If radicals would remain prepared to stand for states' rights, "We may succeed in securing our equality in the Union, or our independence out of it, or at least fall gloriously" in the attempt.[45]

As the election neared, Quitman decided that the only glimmer of hope for southern rights in 1852 came from "the movement in Alabama in favor of a separate states' right ticket." A group of radicals held a convention in Montgomery in the summer of 1852 and nominated George M. Troup of Georgia, an old nullifier, for president, and Quitman for vice-president. Anticipating that the new party would offer him a nomination, Quitman wrote to his son, "I should regret this, but whenever & wherever the flag of state's rights is unfurled, I shall be under it." In November, the Southern

44. Quitman to W. D. Chapman, December 29, 1851, in Claiborne, *Quitman*, II, 152–55.

45. Quitman's address at the Democratic State Rights Convention, January 8, 1852, in Claiborne, *Quitman*, II, 156–61; Quitman to B. F. Dill, February 20, 1852, and to W. D. Chapman, June 9, 1852, *ibid.*, 161–67.

Rights party drew votes only from Alabama and Georgia. It received less than 5 percent of the votes cast in Alabama and a pathetic 126 votes in Georgia.[46] Not even Quitman could blame a conspiracy for so complete a repudiation. Stung by the election results, he realized that if he were to lead any southern crusade, at least at the present time, it could not be a political one.

Only a few months after the disheartening defeat of the Southern Rights ticket, Cuba again grabbed Quitman's attention. A group calling itself the Cuban Junta solicited Quitman's help in attempting to wrest Cuba from Spanish domination. Rumors that Spanish officials intended to abolish slavery on the island made many southern expansionists—including Quitman—fearful that this might be their last opportunity to acquire new slave territory. Publicly, Quitman described Cuba as the "battle ground" that would decide European or American ascendancy in North America. Cuba, he said, must fall under American control or become "a strong negro or mongrel empire" that "would forever put a stop to American progress and expansion on this continent." After the Compromise of 1850, Quitman knew that the federal government would do little to help southerners obtain Cuba as a new slave territory, and he asked, "Would I perform my duty to God, to my country, to humanity, and to civil freedom, were I to refuse to devote a portion of my life to such a cause?" Undeterred by his previous experience with Cuba, Quitman jumped at the junta's offer. He insisted upon full and exclusive control of the expedition, and the junta gladly complied, appointing him commander in chief and offering him "all the powers and attributes of dictatorship" once they landed in Cuba. If that were not enough, the junta promised him "the compensation of one million dollars" for his efforts.[47] Cuba provided an irresistible combination of opportunity for personal distinction and the expansion of southern territorial and political power; it was another vehicle for both honorable and useful ambition.

Quitman carefully began planning his "great & glorious" project. Offers of help poured in from all over the country, not just the

46. Quitman to F. Henry Quitman, September 12, 1852, in Quitman Papers, HSP; May, *Quitman*, 268.

47. Quitman to Thomas Reed, August 23, 1854, the Cuban Junta to Quitman, April 29, 1853, Quitman to the Cuban Junta, April 30, 1853, in Claiborne, *Quitman*, II, 206–208, 386–88. For the agreements between Quitman and the junta see *ibid.*, 389–90. For a full discussion of the expedition, see May, *Quitman*, 270–95.

South. By the middle of 1854, he coordinated the recruitment of men and arms from San Francisco to Mobile and New York to Savannah. As they had done a few years before, volunteers offered their services and advice. From New Orleans, John Quitman Moore petitioned his namesake for a part in the expedition. One of Quitman's associates wrote from Vera Cruz to ask the general to expand his operations to include a conquest of Mexico. If both Cuba and Mexico were captured, he suggested, southern rights would no longer be "at the mercy of fanatical Northern demagogues, or entrusted to the feeble hands of our compromising, vacillating brethren." The filibustering expedition proved too unwieldy for Quitman. After failing to raise enough money and being investigated again by federal authorities, Quitman's operation collapsed in 1855.[48]

Quitman's certainty that destiny awaited him helped him to rebound quickly from the Cuban affair. He had always pursued several interests simultaneously, and he did so throughout his involvement in the Cuba project. As early as 1853, he contemplated running for Congress. Two years later, he made a concerted effort to run for office. Basing his campaign on a defense of all aspects of slavery, he blamed a "violent and strained construction of the neutrality laws" for preventing enterprising southerners from spreading slavery to Cuba. He therefore promised to eradicate all federal impediments to the expansion of slavery. Quitman warned, "The hosts of anti-slavery are everywhere rallying their forces, for a final assault upon our institutions." Anticipating the sentiments of William L. Yancey's Slaughter letter, Quitman claimed that "no national party organization will fully protect us." He vowed to work with congressmen who "concur with me on the slavery question," regardless of party affiliation. He fully expected other representatives to turn to him for leadership because, as he told a friend, "I feel that I have the nerve to meet the onslaught of our foes."[49]

48. Quitman to F. R. Witter, February 11, 1855, in John A. Quitman Papers, LC; Quitman to L. Norvell Walker, August 24, 1854, C. R. Wheat to Quitman, June 15, 1854, John A. Winston to Quitman, June 2, 1854, Louis Schlessinger to Quitman, November 7, 1853, J. Quitman Moore to Quitman, December 28, 1854, J. T. Picket to Quitman, March 20, 1854, in Quitman Papers, MDAH; Quitman to F. Henry Quitman, July 1, 1854; in Quitman Papers, HSP; Claiborne, *Quitman*, II, 392; May, *Quitman*, 292–95.

49. Quitman to C. R. Clifton, November 18, 1853, in Claiborne Collection, MDAH; Quitman to B. F. Dill, July 14, 1855, in Quitman Papers, MDAH; Quitman to W. A. Stone, July 19, 1855, in Claiborne, *Quitman*, II, 210–12.

Although he had hoped for a seat in the Senate, Quitman gladly accepted a nomination to the House of Representatives in the summer of 1855. He believed "the destiny of the South" might be decided in the next session of Congress and promised to remain "a sleepless sentinel" for southern interests. When he received a clear majority in the general election, Quitman vowed to act "as boldly as if I had been unanimously elected."[50] In language that recalled his quest for glory in Mexico, Quitman told his son, "My destiny is action, and I will prostrate all opposition or die in [the] harness." At least one southerner was overjoyed that the valiant Quitman was prepared to wage war upon the abolitionist menace. Describing himself as a "*Strict construction State Rights Secession democrat out & out,* in fact a *Red Southern rights man,*" R. O. Love thanked God that the South had "one man in Congress that we can depend on."[51]

Upon his arrival in Washington, Quitman acted much as he had as a freshman legislator in 1828. "I find myself in high consideration here," he boasted to his son. He told his children that President Franklin Pierce often requested his company for walks and that rumors abounded that he would receive a vice-presidential nomination in 1856. "Of course the old politicians are a little jealous," he smugly reported, because "no man receives more attention than I do."[52]

Quitman's sense of self-importance quickly gave way to one of frustration. He made few speeches and seldom took part in debates. He found that his duties as chair of the Military Affairs Committee brought him "a formidable pile of papers" but no glory. Most southerners were concerned over the fate of slavery in Kansas Territory, but Quitman was obsessed with the neutrality laws and expansion into Latin America. He called for the acquisition of Mexico, Nicaragua, and especially Cuba. Quitman insisted that Congress repeal all laws that prevented individuals from launching private efforts at territorial acquisition. Obviously recalling his own frustrated ambitions, he claimed that the neutrality laws prevented a citizen from availing himself "of the rewards of his skill, his inge-

50. Quitman to Dill, July 14, 1855, Quitman to Edward Pickett, H. L. Van Eaton, and James McDonald, July 29, 1855, in Quitman Papers, MDAH; Quitman to Claiborne, November 18, 1855, in Claiborne, *Quitman,* II, 215–16. Quitman defeated his opponent, Giles M. Hillyer, by a vote of 6,558 to 4,543.

51. Quitman to F. Henry Quitman, October 28, 1855, in Quitman Papers, HSP; R. O. Love to Quitman, December 2, 1855, in Quitman Papers, MDAH.

52. Quitman to F. Henry Quitman, January 26, 1856, in Quitman Papers, HSP; Quitman to Rosalie Quitman, January 2, 1855, in Quitman Family Papers, SHC.

nuity, or his labor." He argued that the federal government had no specific grant of power to circumscribe this entrepreneurial spirit and therefore concluded that filibustering must be recognized as one of the many "reserved rights" of each state.[53]

Soon after his reelection in 1857, Quitman realized that Kansas was the most crucial issue facing Congress. Referring to the debates over the Lecompton constitution, which proposed to make Kansas a slave state, Quitman told his new young friend Congressman Laurence Keitt: "The test struggle is before us. . . . It will soon be seen whether we will maintain our equality, or sink into a degrading subserviency to political masters." Quitman warned that if southerners compromised again, they would "become the willing slave of an insatiable master." The South, he now believed, must "finally and irrevocably" insist upon spreading slavery to Kansas and stand or fall on Lecompton. If Congress admitted Kansas as a free state, the southern states would have no alternative but to secede. "I am sick to death of compromises, and will not bend an inch to dodge the naked question," Quitman thundered. The growing militance of his remarks paralleled a rapid decline in health. Weakened after eating contaminated food in 1857, Quitman died from a fever on July 17, 1858, at his home in Natchez.[54]

Throughout his life, John Quitman strove for distinction. As a young man, he paid homage to the Founding Fathers not only for their gift of liberty but also for leaving "ambition uncontrolled." His political, military, and financial success stand as testimony to his lifelong drive to achieve fame. From the Mexican countryside, Quitman tried to inspire his young son to follow his example. He told young Henry to "give your utmost attention to those studies which are to fit you for a life of usefullness & reputation." Although he also told the boy, "I trust in all things your conduct will be high-toned, honorable and respectful," Quitman's own actions often betrayed a greater concern for personal renown than for "high-toned" principles. Henry S. Foote remembered Quitman as a

53. Quitman to F. Henry Quitman, January 26, 1856, in Quitman Papers, HSP; Quitman to Rosalie Quitman, March 24, 1856, and to Eliza Quitman, January 6, [1857], in Quitman Family Papers, SHC; *Speech of John A. Quitman, of Mississippi, on the Subject of the Neutrality Laws* (Washington, D.C., 1856), in Southern Filibusters Collection, LSU.

54. Quitman to Laurence Keitt, July 23, 1857, in Quitman Family Papers, SHC; Quitman to John Marshall, February 2, 5, 1858, and to William W. W. Wood, April 3, 1858, in Claiborne Collection, MDAH; Quitman to F. Henry Quitman, February 27, 1858, in Quitman Papers, HSP; May, *Quitman*, 328–29, 349.

truthful, honest, and brave man. But Foote also recalled, "He was over ambitious, fond of taking the lead in all things, [and] somewhat given to selfishness." Concerned that Quitman had lost sight of principle in the closing days of the secession crisis in 1852, E. C. Wilkinson warned him: "You are expected to carry out your creed in all its severity, and not to flinch in the least from its conclusions . . . for when the State-rights party is formed again . . . it will naturally turn at once to you, who have stood, and stand now, like old Torquil in the romance of [Sir Walter] Scott, all alone, battered, but not beaten, while every living soul has fallen around you. But, to be perfectly frank with you . . . this must be what you wish." [55]

Expansion of slavery to the Southwest and a persistent concern with states' rights enabled Quitman's ambition to take root in his adopted society and propel him to prominence. Like many others, he believed the continued extension of slavery was essential for the survival of the institution and his society and soon came to see such expansion as likely only after the slave states seceded from the Union. Although surely there were disgruntled and maladjusted southerners who took up the crusade for disunion in an effort to start afresh or find personal advancement, to Quitman it appeared the only means of preserving the status and rank he had already achieved. [56]

55. Quitman to his brother, March 29, 1820, in Claiborne, *Quitman*, I, 44–45; Quitman to F. Henry Quitman, March 2, 1847, August 26, 1850, in Quitman Papers, HSP; Foote, *Reminiscences*, 356; E. C. Wilkinson to Quitman, August 18, 1852, in Claiborne, *Quitman*, II, 176–77.

56. William J. Cooper, Jr., *Liberty and Slavery: Southern Politics to 1860* (New York, 1983), 220–21; John McCardell, *The Idea of a Southern Nation: Southern Nationalists and Southern Nationalism, 1830–1860* (New York, 1978), 75, 227–73; Robert E. May, *The Southern Dream of a Caribbean Empire, 1854–1861* (1973; rpr. Athens, Ga., 1989), esp. 206–44; James Oakes, *The Ruling Race: A History of American Slaveholders* (New York, 1982), 74–78, 129, 134, 147.

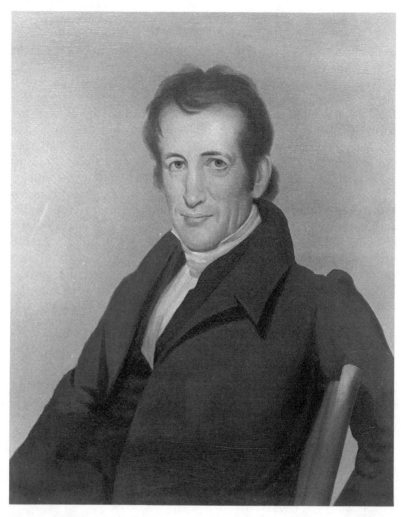

Nathaniel Beverley Tucker

From a portrait by Bethuel Moore copied from an original portrait by Joseph Wood. Reproduced courtesy College of William and Mary in Virginia, gift of Janet Coleman Kimbrough and Cynthia Coleman Moorehead.

William Lowndes Yancey
Courtesy Southern Historical Collection, Library of the University of North Carolina at Chapel Hill

John Anthony Quitman
Courtesy Archives, University of the South, Sewanee, Tenn.

Robert Barnwell Rhett
Courtesy South Caroliniana Library, University of South Carolina

Laurence M. Keitt
From *Harper's Weekly*, IV (December 22, 1860). Courtesy Special Collections, Hill Memorial
Library, Louisiana State University Library.

Louis T. Wigfall
Courtesy Library of Congress

James D. B. De Bow

From *De Bow's Review,* After the War Series, III (June, 1867). Courtesy Special Collections Department, Duke University Library, Durham, N.C.

Edmund Ruffin
Courtesy Southern Historical Collection, Library of the University of North Carolina at
Chapel Hill

William Porcher Miles

From Mrs. D. Giraud Wright, *A Southern Girl in '61: The War-Time Memories of a Confederate Senator's Daughter* (New York, 1905). Courtesy Special Collections, Hill Memorial Library, Louisiana State University Libraries.

FOUR

How Best to Controul and Use Man
Robert Barnwell Rhett

The most powerful politician in antebellum South Carolina, John C. Calhoun, died in March, 1850. Carolinians mourned his passing for months. In eulogizing Calhoun, Robert Barnwell Rhett listed his accomplishments, extolled his virtues, and praised his leadership. But he also criticized. In his characteristically blunt manner, Rhett told the South Carolina legislature that Calhoun's "great defect was, that he pursued principles too exclusively." Principles, Rhett said, were unerring; to apply them, however, "we have to deal with erring man." Too rigid an adherence to principle, therefore, endangered political effectiveness. Again referring to Calhoun, Rhett explained: "He understood principles—he understood how they should be enforced—but he did not understand how best to controul [sic] and use, for their enforcement, that compound of truth and error—reason and prejudice—passion and weakness—man."[1] Although Rhett never claimed to achieve control over either men or politics, he strove throughout his life to do both. Even more doctrinaire than Calhoun when he entered the political stage, Rhett learned the futility of unadulterated idealism and the need for political pragmatism. More than any other fire-eater, Rhett became an adroit political tactician.

Even his name showed his awareness of political realities. Born Robert Barnwell Smith on December 21, 1800, in Beaufort, South Carolina, he changed his name in 1837 when he embarked on his congressional career. Though proud of his father, James Smith, who had fought in the American Revolution, he preferred the name of his ancestor Colonel William Rhett, who once served as governor general of the Bahamas. Realizing that a name of distinction would fetch attention in aristocratic South Carolina, Rhett

1. *The Death and Funeral Ceremonies of John Caldwell Calhoun, Containing Speeches, Reports, and Other Documents Connected Therewith, the Oration of the Hon. R. B. Rhett Before the Legislature, &c. &c.* (Columbia, S.C., 1850), 164.

also eschewed his first name and preferred instead to be called Barnwell.[2]

Before Robert Smith became Barnwell Rhett, he had already overcome a poor education and begun a promising career in law and politics. His grandmother taught him to read and write on his family's plantation in North Carolina, and his formal studies at Beaufort College ended abruptly when his father needed help on the plantation. He began his legal training at age nineteen in Charleston under the direction of Thomas Grimké and was admitted to the bar in South Carolina two years later. At first he established a law practice in Beaufort District but in 1823 entered a partnership with his cousin Robert W. Barnwell in Colleton District. There he developed both a lucrative practice and a reputation for oratorical prowess. In 1826, the people of St. Bartholomew's Parish in Colleton District elected the impressive young lawyer to the lower house of the South Carolina legislature. Soon after taking his seat, he married Elizabeth Washington Burnet. Her calm and even temper helped sustain him through one of the stormiest political careers in American history.[3]

Rhett entered state politics just as the tariff issue began to shake the political foundations of his state. Radicals like Thomas Cooper, president of South Carolina College, advised Carolinians to consider seriously the value of remaining in the Union. Rhett was most impressed by the series of essays entitled *The Crisis* written by Robert J. Turnbull. Taking to heart the positions of these men, the young, enthusiastic Rhett quickly became the most radical politician in his state.[4]

Rhett's address to his constituents in Colleton became the opening salvo in the nullification crisis. A protective tariff, he argued, was unconstitutional because the Constitution gave Congress no clear authority to administer one. Furthermore, if Carolinians permitted a northern majority in Congress to tax them against their will, they would be consenting to a dangerous precedent. "All the property we possess," he explained, "we hold by their boon; and a

2. Laura White, *Robert Barnwell Rhett: Father of Secession* (1931; rpr. New York, 1965), 4–9. Rhett's brothers also changed their names at the same time.

3. *Ibid.*, 10–13.

4. *Ibid.*, 10–13; Lacy K. Ford, *Origins of Southern Radicalism: The South Carolina Upcountry, 1800–1860* (Oxford, 1988), 113–19. For a complete account of the nullification crisis, see William W. Freehling, *Prelude to Civil War: The Nullification Controversy in South Carolina, 1816–1836* (New York, 1966).

majority in Congress, may, at any moment, deprive us of it and transfer it northward." He warned that the federal government had already grown too powerful, that time would only augment that power and simultaneously weaken the power of individual states. Rhett therefore called for a state convention to take decisive action. The task was difficult, he acknowledged, "But if you are doubtful of yourselves—if you are not prepared to follow up your principles wherever they may lead, to their very last consequence— if you love life better than honor,—prefer ease to perilous liberty and glory; awake not! stir not!—Impotent resistance will add vengeance to your ruin. Live in smiling peace with your insatiable Oppressors, and die with the noble consolation, that your submissive patience will survive triumphant your beggary and despair."[5]

While Calhoun searched for a mechanism to save both states' rights and the Union, Rhett became more radical. After being returned to the legislature by his faithful supporters in Colleton, Rhett led a states'-rights meeting at the capital in the fall of 1830. With shrill rhetoric, he asserted that Carolinians faced two political alternatives: resistance to the federal government or absolute submission. If they submitted to federal power, Rhett said, "yo[u] are the vassals and slaves of a consolidated empire." He would give his life to save the Union if it were one "of equal liberties and equal rights" that respected the interests of each state. But rather than submit to a union of unlimited powers, Rhett preferred secession: "Aye—disunion, rather, into a thousand fragments. And why, gentlemen! would I prefer disunion to such a Government? Because under such a Government I would be a slave—a fearful slave, ruled despotically by those who do not represent me, & whose sectional interests are not mine . . . with every base and destructive passion of man bearing upon my shieldless destiny." Rhett knew that many would consider such sentiments treasonable, but he refused to "tremble at epithets, or shake when a tongue rails." He claimed that the true friend of the Union would struggle to preserve its principles, and the best way to do that was to nullify the tariff. "If to think, to speak, to feel such sentiments as these, constitute me a disunionist and a traitor . . . then, gentlemen, I am a Disunionist!—I am a Traitor!"[6]

The more thoughtful and mature Calhoun urged Rhett to aban-

5. Charleston *Mercury,* June 18, 1828.
6. *Ibid.*, October 19, 1830.

don his inflammatory, extreme political rhetoric and work instead for a peaceful, constitutional settlement of the tariff conflict. In the legislature, Rhett dutifully obeyed Calhoun by calling for a state convention to consider nullifying the tariff. For a while, Rhett tempered his language, but when Congress passed a new tariff in 1832, he again exploded.

Rhett used the occasion of a Fourth of July address at Walterborough to heighten Carolinians' spirit of resistance. "Revolution! Sir, I feel no chilling fears, no appalling terrors come over me at the sound: on the contrary, I feel my mind elate, and my spirits rise. . . . What, sir, has the people ever gained, but by Revolution? What have Tyrants ever conceded, but by Revolution? From the beginning of time, Liberty has been acquired but at the price of blood, and that blood shed in Revolution. . . . What, sir, has Carolina ever obtained great or free, but by Revolution?" Rhett warned his listeners that an oppressed people who dared not resist tyranny faced "one evil, worse, far worse in its existence and consequences, than Revolution—Slavery." This prospect was particularly horrible for "those who own our *peculiar property.*" In South Carolina, where slaves outnumbered whites, complete control over black slaves was viewed as the only way to maintain peaceful relations between the races, especially in Rhett's Tidewater parishes. Furthermore, like many other planters and all other fire-eaters, Rhett believed that only a slaveholding people truly knew what it was "to be the creature of the will of others." Again he vowed to support a Union of equal rights and laws, but rather than becoming political slaves to the North, he called on the assembly to "let our free spirits wing the glorious way in the death of freemen."[7]

Rhett's speech sent other nullifiers scrambling to "counteract the recklessness of their too honest subordinate." The Charleston *Mercury,* Calhoun's political organ, retreated from its previous unqualified support for Rhett. Rhett's cousin Robert W. Barnwell told residents of St. Bartholomew's Parish that it was ridiculous to link nullification with war. Calhoun himself assured Carolinians that state interposition would be peaceful. Nullification, Calhoun said, was not the bloody resistance that Rhett spoke of but merely a referendum on a disputed issue to be settled by the states.[8]

Whether they listened to Calhoun or to Rhett, most Carolinians

7. White, *Rhett,* 20; Charleston *Mercury,* July 14, 1832.
8. White, *Rhett,* 24–25.

supported nullification by the fall of 1832. Its success, however, was short-lived. Even before President Andrew Jackson, armed by Congress with the Force Bill, threatened to send federal troops into Charleston to collect tariff revenue, Calhoun, true to his word, began to work for a peaceful resolution. He worked with Congressman Henry Clay to construct a compromise tariff. At Columbia, Carolinians met in convention to determine their response. The promise of a lower tariff, Jackson's constant threats to invade the state, and the dubiousness of joint resistance by other southern states all combined to convince even Rhett that the convention must repeal nullification.

Even in defeat, Rhett refused to temper his beliefs. He was elected as attorney general by the legislature in December, 1832, and used his new stature to salvage a measure of resistance to federal power. Nullification, he insisted, must be repealed in the same spirit in which it was passed. When the convention proposed to term the compromise tariff a "triumph," Rhett's hackles rose. "Let us . . . unsay nothing of what we have already said, so nobly and so well," he argued. He moved to strike the words "congratulations" and "triumph" from the official repeal message. South Carolina was forced to bow to political realities, and "I will not praise that which, under the abused names of Union and Liberty, attempts to inflict upon us every thing that can curse and enslave the land." The enemy—consolidated federal power—had been beaten back with the compromise tariff, but, according to Rhett, it would return to menace the state someday, "with thicker numbers, and redoubled fury." Before the convention adjourned, it struck the word "triumph" from its official message.[9]

Rhett was determined to set his personal views on record. "Once indeed, my pulse beat high for this Union," he explained, but the American flag "no longer waves in triumph and glory for me." He told a gathering at Columbia, "I fear, that there is no longer any hope or liberty for the South, under a Union, by which all self-government is taken away." Although in later years Rhett would give 1844 as the year of his conversion to secessionism, in March, 1833, he proclaimed, "If a Confederacy of the Southern States could now be obtained, should we not deem it a happy termination—happy beyond expectation, of our long struggle for our rights against oppression?" He summarized why he believed ex-

9. Charleston *Mercury*, March 20, 1833; Freehling, *Prelude to Civil War*, 296.

treme resistance so necessary in what became his political watch-words: "A people, owning slaves, are mad, or worse than mad, who do not hold their destinies in their own hands." Every instance of consolidation of power, he believed, brought the federal govern-ment ever nearer to the South's peculiar institution; unless they re-sisted quickly and effectually, Rhett feared, southerners would lose all power over slavery.[10] For the moment, Rhett admitted defeat. For the rest of his life, however, he would adhere to the principles of strictly limited federal power and exclusive southern control of slavery; he would spend over a quarter-century searching for ways to enforce them.

Rhett involved himself in a variety of interests for several years while he recovered from the defeat of nullification. He continued to serve as attorney general until 1835, but the remainder of his tenure was uneventful. He devoted time to his law practice and to a new plantation in St. Bartholomew's Parish. Always a devout Chris-tian, he became active in the Charleston Bible Society and the Charleston Port Society for promoting the gospel among seamen. He lent his aid to the Young Men's Temperance Society and the South Carolina Society for the Advancement of Learning. Politics, however, continued to attract Rhett's attention. When friends sug-gested that he run for Congress in 1836, he leaped at the oppor-tunity. In a close race, Rhett was elected to represent the third con-gressional district of South Carolina.[11]

Rhett entered the House of Representatives in the midst of the gag rule controversy. Southern representatives grew alarmed when increasing numbers of northerners sent abolitionist petitions to Congress, and none more so than Barnwell Rhett. Insisting that only slave states could legislate on the institution and that Congress had no business entertaining petitions for things it could not do constitutionally, Rhett searched for a strategy to control the discus-sion of slavery in the capital. First, he called for constitutional amendments. He proposed one that specifically denied Congress the power to tamper with slavery in the District of Columbia and the federal territories, another to extend and make permanent the Missouri Compromise line, and a third to prohibit congressional debate on all matters connected with slavery. When lack of support killed the young parliamentarian's elaborate scheme, he turned to

10. Charleston *Mercury*, March 26, 1833.
11. White, *Rhett*, 32–33; Robert Barnwell Rhett to Col. John Stapleton, January 16, 1841, in Robert B. Rhett Papers, SHC.

an alternate plan. He insisted that the South Carolina legislature should withdraw its congressional delegation if abolitionist "fanatics" continued their agitation in Congress. Rhett hoped this would show northerners that Carolinians earnestly believed only slaveholders could deliberate over slavery. If all else failed, Rhett called for disunion "rather than suffer the discussion of the Abolition question in Congress." If other slave states continued their "apathy and lukewarmness," South Carolina should proceed alone. Rhett's ire was spared. In a procedural move called the twenty-first rule, Congress resolved to table all antislavery petitions without discussion.[12]

His spirited entry into national politics earned Rhett the accolades of many Carolinians. The citizens of Beaufort District dined and feted him during the summer of 1838. His constituents cheered long and loud every time Rhett condemned the "venality and corruption of their rulers" in Washington. One of Rhett's supporters in St. Luke's Parish hailed the "disunionist and traitor" who battled fearlessly on their behalf. Although unable to attend one of these gatherings, John C. Calhoun wrote to its organizers to express "my very high regard for one, who, on the great question of the day, has so nobly stood up for the cause of the people and the Constitution." Calhoun said that he had already come to respect Rhett, but lately his admiration for the young congressman had grown immensely. As a mark of his friendship and support, Calhoun instructed that this letter be published in newspapers in Charleston, Columbia, and Washington, D.C.[13]

With the essential support of Calhoun, Rhett's influence and power in South Carolina grew rapidly. From 1837 to 1844, Rhett shared the leadership of a powerful political clique with former nullifier Franklin H. Elmore. They served together in Congress from 1837 to 1838, and even while in Washington they continued to wield tremendous influence at home. Elmore controlled the Columbia *South Carolinian,* and his brother served in the legislature. Rhett's brother-in-law John A. Stuart was editor of the Charleston *Mercury.* Although that newspaper was ostensibly Calhoun's mouthpiece,

12. Charleston *Mercury,* September 6, 10, 1838; White, *Rhett,* 38–43. One of Rhett's greatest adversaries during these congressional debates was John Quincy Adams, a distant cousin of his through the Smith family and Adams' mother, Abigail Smith Adams.

13. Charleston *Mercury,* August 23, 27, September 6, 10, 1838; John C. Calhoun to G. P. Elliott and others, August 19, 1838, in Clyde N. Wilson, ed., *The Papers of John C. Calhoun* (18 vols. to date; Columbia, S.C., 1959–), XIV, 402–403 and 403n.

Calhoun often needed Rhett to put Stuart "on his guard." Rhett's brothers Albert and James represented Colleton and Charleston in the legislature. Elmore left Congress in 1839 to become president of the Bank of South Carolina; one of the bank directors was Benjamin Rhett, another brother.[14]

The Rhett-Elmore faction, variously called "the clique" and "the Regency," acquired power; "Rhett arrogance" brought it many enemies. One friend of Calhoun, perhaps not realizing that the senator backed Rhett, charged that Barnwell Rhett was "*entirely* selfish" and because of financial troubles "is now looking solely to office." "I know *the respect* in which your talents *are* held by your Colleagues— but I also *know* that some of them have little love for you," Elmore reported to Rhett. When James H. Hammond ran for governor in 1840 without the clique's support, he lost to John P. Richardson, the Regency's candidate. When he ran again in 1842, Hammond grudgingly accepted Rhett's support. Rhett-Elmore backing was instrumental in his narrow victory; the power Rhett held, and Hammond's awareness of it, caused Hammond to worry about Rhett for the rest of his career.[15]

Personalities began to factionalize South Carolina politics. As Albert Rhett explained, his family began to "resemble the 'Bunch of Sticks,' we are something of *Lucifers*—dipped one end in Sulphur, and extremely apt, if any one or two ignite from severe [friction], the whole to flame up in sympathetic conflagration." In the fall of 1842, Albert reported that during his campaign for the legislature, "*Down with the Rhetts* was the war-cry" among his opponents. Although his victory was narrow, he noted with satisfaction that another brother, Edmund Rhett, had also won election in Beaufort "so that, after all, the Anti-Rhett cry, instead of putting *one* Rhett *down,* only put *two* up." Governor Richardson trusted Barnwell Rhett implicitly. He once told Rhett, "I must depend on some one to *think* for me on matters not pertaining to Office—and there is no

14. White, *Rhett,* 41–42, 56; Calhoun to R. B. Rhett, September 13, 1838, in Wilson, ed., *Papers of Calhoun,* XIV, 425–26. For more on the control of the *Mercury,* see John S. Coussons, "Thirty Years with Calhoun, Rhett, and the Charleston *Mercury:* A Chapter in South Carolina Politics" (Ph.D. dissertation, Louisiana State University, 1971), and for an examination of the Rhett-Elmore faction from a different vantage point see Ford, *Origins of Southern Radicalism,* 145–82.

15. Drew Gilpin Faust, *James Henry Hammond and the Old South: A Design for Mastery* (Baton Rouge, 1982), 222–23, 232–33, 235; Francis W. Pickens to Calhoun, November 8, 1842, in Wilson, ed., *Papers of Calhoun,* XV, 535; Franklin H. Elmore to Rhett, November 18, 1844, in Rhett Papers, SHC; Albert Rhett to Hammond, February 6, 26, 1842, in James H. Hammond Papers, LC.

one I am sure that I would sooner depend on than yourself."
Robert W. Barnwell, though not always in agreement with his cousin, also turned to Rhett for "your counsel & your sympathy in . . . important things." [16]

The Rhett-Elmore faction overextended itself in 1842 while trying to tighten its control of the state. Because of his political acumen and personal loyalty, Rhett won a special closeness to Calhoun. In 1842, Calhoun planned to resign from the United States Senate to focus his attention on the presidential contest of 1844; he wanted Rhett to succeed him in the Senate. The Rhetts prepared an elaborate plan to capitalize on this opportunity. Albert would run for Barnwell's seat in Congress, James would run for Congress from Charleston, and Edmund would enter the legislature from St. Helena's Parish. This time, however, "Rhett arrogance" caused a backlash. In the legislature, Barnwell lost the senatorial election by a vote of 82 to 71. James lost his bid for Congress, Albert withdrew from his campaign, and Barnwell scrambled to retain his seat in the House of Representatives. Elmore's brother had died a year before, and Albert died suddenly in 1843. The clique was crippled, but it sputtered on with Calhoun's support. As late as 1846—two years after Barnwell challenged Calhoun's control of the state—the envious Hammond reported, "Rhett is stronger than many think." [17]

In 1843, Rhett received a renewed vote of confidence from Calhoun when the senator chose him to manage his presidential campaign for 1844. To be a successful manager, Rhett first had to test the power of Martin Van Buren, the leader of the Democratic party. In September Rhett traveled to New York to gauge electoral support for Calhoun in the Northeast. "You are daily encreasing [sic] in popularity," he told Calhoun, perhaps optimistically. He found Massachusetts Democrats unwilling to support Van Buren and received news of support for Calhoun from Rhode Island and Connecticut. In Van Buren's home state, New York, Rhett believed that Calhoun might win the backing of Tammany Hall. Rhett's sources stated that Van Buren "is out of the question" in Pennsylvania. He concluded that Calhoun would carry the South and run well in the West and, in imperial tones, prophesied: "On the whole,

16. Albert Rhett to R. B. Rhett, June 18, October 2, 1842, John P. Richardson to Rhett, January 21, 1842, Robert W. Barnwell to Rhett, May 15, 1841, in Rhett Papers, SHC.

17. White, *Rhett*, 58–59; Calhoun to James H. Hammond, January 23, 1843, in Wilson, ed., *Papers of Calhoun*, XV, 628; Hammond to William Gilmore Simms, November 10, 1846, in Hammond Papers, LC.

our prospects are bright and growing brighter; and judging from the past, we have only to keep matters as they are, and we must control the next presidential election."[18]

Rhett's faith in Calhoun's chances of victory matched his own rising self-confidence. He began to assert his strategy more aggressively. When Calhoun hinted that he might return to the Senate, Rhett sternly (but politely) told him to remain out of Congress and avoid "the cross fire of your enemies." While claiming to respect Calhoun's other advisers, Rhett boldly suggested, "I may be a far better judge of the effect of political questions, and the temper of the People of the Union." So sure was Rhett that he had the situation under control that in September, 1842, he began writing editorials attacking Henry Clay, the most likely Whig nominee in 1844.[19]

Despite his confidence in popular support for Calhoun, Rhett worried about Van Buren's influence among party regulars. In 1843, therefore, Rhett began a campaign to wrest control of the Democratic nomination process from the New Yorker. As matters stood, state party conventions chose delegates for the national convention, where they voted in state units. Rhett feared that this method favored Van Buren. In his pamphlet *An Appeal to the Democratic Party*, Rhett proposed that popular elections be held to choose delegates in each state. Although he hoped this plan would capitalize on his perceived grass-roots support for Calhoun, he couched his appeal in the language of Jacksonian democracy. The president, he said, represented all the people; all the people, therefore, not just a few professional politicians, "ought to have the power of choosing him." Never before had Rhett encouraged mass participation in politics. During the nullification crisis he had believed that the state legislature must lead the people. But now, with the underlying motive of securing a presidential nomination for Calhoun, he taunted Van Burenites by asking: "Do you dread the voice of the people? Or would you have them to be mute, either from an incapacity of having an opinion, or a slavish fear of expressing it?"[20]

18. Rhett to Calhoun, October 3, 13, 1842, in Wilson, ed., *Papers of Calhoun*, XV, 485–87, 493–96.

19. *Ibid.*, and 487n.

20. *An Appeal to the Democratic Party, on the Principles of a National Convention for the Nomination of President and Vice President of the United States*, published in pamphlet form and in Charleston *Mercury*, January 25, 1843, and New York *Herald*, January 26, 1843. See Wilson, ed., *Papers of Calhoun*, XV, 584–85.

The *Appeal* drew an enthusiastic response from Calhoun and his followers. To a supporter in northwest South Carolina, Calhoun explained that Rhett's pamphlet "will show the ground we assume." He regally suggested, "It would be well to have it published in the [Pendleton] Messenger, with proper remarks." Former congressman R. M. T. Hunter of Virginia called on Calhoun men in his state to support "the principles of Rhett's pamphlet." Democrats wrote from New York, New Jersey, and Indiana to Rhett pledging their support for the principles expressed in the *Appeal*.[21]

During the next year, however, several events undermined Rhett's attempt to control the party. Van Burenites committed one state after another to the old convention system. Calhoun tried to pump life into his dying campaign in September, 1843, by making Rhett editor of the Washington *Spectator,* a newspaper the senator had begun in 1842 to promote his candidacy. But as the convention drew closer, Democrats turned away from both Van Buren and Calhoun, favoring instead James K. Polk of Tennessee. Running on a platform of vigorous territorial expansion, Polk not only captured the nomination but also swept into the presidency.[22]

In the months before Polk's nomination, political developments in Congress attracted Rhett's attention. From December, 1843, to May, 1844, he had worked stoically but futilely to fight a new tariff. Simultaneously, he opposed new federal appropriations for internal improvements, but again his efforts were in vain. These revenue measures, he insisted, would "sink the government into a hopeless corruption and imbecility," transform it into "a mighty machine of oppression," and make its citizens "political slaves." Rhett wrote directly to Van Buren and threatened to bolt the Democratic party and launch a movement to nominate Calhoun as an independent presidential candidate unless Van Buren used his influence to oppose the tariff. In the same session of Congress, Rhett also threatened disunion. When Congress abolished the gag rule, Rhett warned that southerners would defend their right to be the exclusive judges and arbiters of slavery "in the Union or out of the Union."[23] When the issue of Texas annexation emerged, Rhett lost

21. Calhoun to T. G. Clemson, February 6, 1843, Hunter to [?], February 20, 1843, both in Wilson, ed., *Papers of Calhoun*, XV, 660, 681; B. Bates to Rhett, January 26, 1843, Peter C. Manning to Rhett, January 26, 1843, Tilgham A. Howard to Rhett, January 28, 1843, in Rhett Papers, SHC.

22. White, *Rhett*, 57, 62–67.

23. *Congressional Globe*, 28th Cong., 1st Sess., 44, 98, App., 174–75, 656–59, 775–77; Rhett to Van Buren, February 26, 1844, in Martin Van Buren Papers, LC.

his faith that the Democratic party could or would protect southern interests. Calhoun reconciled himself to work with the party and angle for the presidency in 1848, but Rhett decided to leave it.

When Congress adjourned, Rhett returned to South Carolina to warn his constituents that their liberty was under attack. A northern majority, he explained, was plotting the destruction of African slavery. The tariff and the abolition of the gag rule exposed the northern strategy. "The tariff takes the revenue of our [slave] property, but our property itself, is not left to us unmolested." Once southern institutions became ordinary topics of discussion in Congress, Rhett asked, could federal legislation on slavery be far behind? And why did so many northerners object to Texas annexation? "It is because Texas is in the South," Rhett insisted, "and may aid in protecting your institutions from the open assaults and meditated overthrow of internal . . . enemies."[24]

His indignation aroused, his self-confidence high from seventeen years of experience in state and national politics, Rhett launched a daring effort to seize control of South Carolina. "I am sick and disgusted with the meanness and falsehood of the Democratic Party, whilst I detest the open, impudent despotism of the other [party]," he told a friend. Rhett would not allow "Polk born, equivocating letters" to restore his trust in the Democrats, nor "have I any hope in the South generally." Fully aware that he risked isolation and again being labeled "Disunionist, Mischief-maker Traitor etc.," on July 31, at the town of Bluffton in St. Luke's Parish, Rhett challenged Calhoun's leadership in South Carolina and threatened the nation with disunion.[25]

At Bluffton, Rhett brought the ever-present resistance spirit of his faithful constituents to a fever pitch. He repeated his accusations that Democratic deceit had encouraged abolitionism and protective tariffs and might cost the South the acquisition of Texas. He denied that either the election of Polk or a southern convention could return the government to its proper course. He therefore demanded nullification, secession, "or any thing else" but "base and cowardly submission." The Bluffton movement had begun.[26]

24. Charleston *Mercury*, June 27, 1844.

25. Rhett to R. M. T. Hunter, August 30, 1844, in Charles H. Ambler, ed., *Correspondence of Robert M. T. Hunter, 1826–1876* (Washington, D.C., 1918), 70–71; Charleston *Mercury*, July 27, August 8, 1844.

26. Charleston *Mercury*, August 8, 1844. See Chauncey S. Boucher, "The Annexation of Texas and the Bluffton Movement in South Carolina," *Mississippi Valley Historical Review*, VI (1919), 3–33, and White, *Rhett*, 68–84.

In Beaufort, Colleton, Orangeburg, and Barnwell districts, the movement gathered momentum. A resident of St. Luke's Parish said of Rhett, "We not only admire him, but we go with him." Rhett's supporters began a series of dinners and rallies even more numerous than similar meetings six years before. Noting this rising public support, John Stuart wrote in the *Mercury*, "The ball seems to be moving on." Stuart himself gave the ball a shove by siding with Rhett and against Calhoun. Throughout the state, Rhett's supporters proudly referred to themselves as "Bluffton Boys."[27]

As Rhett had expected, opposition quickly arose. An anonymous correspondent to the *Mercury* warned, "In all time past, no public man in this state has ever pitted himself in direct *hostility* to JOHN C. CALHOUN, who has not fallen for it." Rhett tried to minimize his conflict with Calhoun by writing in the *Mercury* that the two differed merely "as to the course the State should now pursue" and that he had no intention of replacing Calhoun's leadership after the crisis ended. Calhoun, however, was unwilling to accept even a temporary challenge. Rhett soon discovered that his longtime associate Franklin Elmore "is not in the movement"; he opted to remain in Calhoun's camp. Rhett found fellow Congressman Armistead Burt, whom he had counted on for support, unwilling to join the movement for fear of Calhoun's wrath. "By your silence," Rhett complained, "you are all supposed to be opposed to any State action at any time. My constituents have marched out into the open field, and placed themselves and me, in open line for battle. You and your Constituents are back in the woods, and lying so still and concealed that they are claimed as a post of our enemies." Rhett understood the freshman congressman's reluctance to defy Calhoun but complained, "Your silence had nearly killed our Party in Charleston." Indeed, Rhett could not fault Burt, for he himself realized that Calhoun aimed "to crush me."[28]

At this point, Rhett was almost ready to admit defeat. Stuart returned the *Mercury*'s support to Calhoun in September, and Rhett returned to Washington. Thinking that Rhett had learned his lesson and eager to repair internal divisions in South Carolina, Calhoun treated Rhett like a prodigal son, allowing him back into his camp and even letting him resume the editorship of the *Spectator*.

27. Charleston *Mercury*, August 10, 12, 28, September 5, 10, 19, 1844; Coussons, "Thirty Years with Calhoun," 168.

28. Charleston *Mercury*, August 12, September 3, 1844; Rhett to R. M. T. Hunter, August 30, 1844, in Ambler, ed., *Correspondence of Hunter*, 70; Rhett to Armistead Burt, September 9, 1844, in Armistead Burt Papers, WPL.

But in Rhett's absence, the movement gathered a second wind. The widely respected former congressman Langdon Cheves, though opposed to Rhett's call for separate state action, lent his support to united southern resistance and even a southern confederacy. Senator George McDuffie also supported the spirit of Bluffton, though he wished for "no noise, no excitement" from the volatile Rhett. James Rhett spread the word of Bluffton to the citizens of Georgia in a stirring speech in Macon. Again choosing to defy Calhoun, Rhett resigned from the *Spectator* and returned to South Carolina.[29]

Rhett knew he faced powerful opposition when he resumed leadership of the movement. His language became more confrontational. He concluded one speech by quoting Scripture; "I call Heaven and Earth to record this day against you, that I have set before you life and death, blessing and cursing; therefore choose life that both you and your seed may live." Again Rhett dismissed the possibility of cooperation from other southern states. In a letter published in the *Mercury* he explained cynically that "it will be very easy to obtain their aid and cooperation . . . *after the proper issue is made by the conduct of a single State.*" In other words, South Carolina must act alone and force other slave states to join her or remain in the Union. Within six weeks, however, the Bluffton movement collapsed. A Unionist defeated Blufftonite candidate Whitemarsh B. Seabrook in the gubernatorial election. Polk captured the presidency, and Calhoun made known his determination to work with the new administration. Rhett realized that no one could set a new political course for South Carolina while Calhoun remained in control.[30]

One anonymous Carolinian suggested that "none but an idiot would . . . risk incurring odium with the great majority of South Carolinians" by defying Calhoun. Barnwell Rhett had challenged him twice; but he was no idiot. Rhett could bank on support from his congressional district. In the midst of the Bluffton conflict, his constituents reelected him without opposition. Rhett indeed incurred a healthy dose of odium, and this condition plagued him the rest of his life. Many Carolinians never forgave the man who could so impudently say no to Calhoun. Many more found Rhett's periodic calls for unilateral, forceful resistance to federal power

---

29. Coussons, "Thirty Years with Calhoun," 173–74; White, *Rhett*, 79–82; Charleston *Mercury*, September 10, 27, 1844.

30. Charleston *Mercury*, September 12, 20, 1844; White, *Rhett*, 83–84; Coussons, "Thirty Years with Calhoun," 182–83.

disquieting and worrisome. But the vast majority of voters in south-
eastern South Carolina did not. Rhett knew this, and so did Calhoun. Even after Rhett's second effort against him, Calhoun took
his old lieutenant back into the fold. Although the two would never
be as close as they had been before Bluffton, Calhoun continued to
respect Rhett's organizational abilities and political adroitness. Calhoun needed Rhett to keep the third congressional district under
control and depended on the Rhett-Elmore faction to enforce his
agenda in the state while he remained concerned with national
politics. Neither Rhett nor his allies suffered from their breach with
Calhoun.[31]

Not only did Rhett avoid personal disaster, but he also laid the
foundation for future secession movements. His Bluffton Boys, as
the name indicated, were relatively young. In the fall of 1844, Calhoun was sixty-two years old. Rhett, almost twenty years younger,
attracted to his movement many young men who had had little or
no previous political experience. The oldest prominent Bluffton
Boy was Whitemarsh Seabrook at age fifty-one. Although he lost
his bid for the governorship in 1844, he won several years later and
played a critical role in the sectional contest of 1850. John Mc-
Queen, a forty-year-old lawyer from Marlboro District, launched
his political career by running for Congress on a pro-Bluffton platform. During the 1850s Congressman McQueen would keep Rhett
abreast of political developments in Washington. David Flavel Jamison, thirty-three years old in 1844, would serve as president of the
South Carolina secession convention in 1860 and influence a younger fire-eater, Laurence Keitt. These and countless other, less distinguished men entered politics with a baptism of resistance and a
benediction of secession. They also shared a reverence for the political leadership of Barnwell Rhett.[32]

Rhett's political proficiency extended beyond the borders of
South Carolina. Although he had defied both Calhoun and Polk
during the Bluffton summer, once he returned to Washington
Rhett began to court the favor of both. He met with his brother
James, Franklin Elmore, and several other Carolinians in the spring
of 1845 to discuss the best strategy for Calhoun's next presidential
campaign. During the course of the Mexican War, Rhett won for

31. Charleston *Mercury,* September 3, 1844; Coussons, "Thirty Years with Calhoun," 182–83; Ford, *Origins of Southern Radicalism,* 191, 290; John B. Edmunds, Jr.,
Francis W. Pickens and the Politics of Destruction (Chapel Hill, 1986), 50–53, 55–58, 98.
32. Charleston *Mercury,* August 8, 16, 22; White, *Rhett,* 84.

himself a place of great influence with President Polk. "I suppose it is the result of a personal respect for me" and not a partisan matter, Rhett postulated, because he had voted against Polk's assertion that Mexico had started the war. By the end of 1847, the artful Carolinian had become one of the few congressional leaders to whom Polk turned for advice.[33]

Despite Rhett's tenuous return to the Democratic party, his passionate desire for resistance never abated. He explained his situation in a parable. He remembered once seeing a master whipping a slave for some offense, "and after giving him more [lashes] than I thought he deserved, I went to interceed [sic] for him; Oh says the Master, I am now only flogging him because he hollers! So it is with us. We are not allowed to holler." Silently, therefore, Rhett resolved, "I will keep up the fire [of resistance], if like the lost hunter in a Priarie [sic] I have to kindle it slow, with my flint, and watch by the blaze, rifle in hand, to keep off the wolves." Rhett told Congressman Burt that if South Carolina resisted federal power again, "it will be the impulse of your constituents & mine. Mine are ready," he promised.[34]

After 1844, Rhett's alliance with Calhoun remained precarious. Beverley Tucker put it best when he described "that mischievious faction of which C[alhoun] is the head, and Rhett the tail (it is you know a sort of political amphisbeana and sometimes goes tail foremost)." During these years, Rhett showed no remorse for Bluffton. In fact, he often opposed or ignored Calhoun. In 1846, he argued against an internal improvements bill for the Mississippi River that Calhoun supported. In the summer of 1848, Rhett contemplated backing John A. Quitman for the Democratic presidential nomination. According to Burt, Rhett had not consulted with Calhoun about that or "about anything this session."[35]

The presidential campaign of 1848 brought yet another disagreement between Rhett and Calhoun. Quietly and unenthusiasti-

33. D. H. Lewis to Calhoun, May 9, 1845, in Chauncey S. Boucher and Robert P. Brooks, eds., *Correspondence Addressed to John C. Calhoun, 1837–1849* (Washington, D.C., 1930), 293; Rhett to Hammond, September 11, 1847, in Hammond Papers, LC; Milo M. Quaife, ed., *The Diary of James K. Polk During His Presidency, 1845–1849* (4 vols.; Chicago, 1910), III, 236.

34. Rhett to Burt, June 24, 1845, in Burt Papers, WPL.

35. Nathaniel Beverley Tucker to Hammond, December 6, 1848, in Hammond Papers, LC; *Congressional Globe*, 29th Cong., 1st Sess., 529, App., 447–49; White, *Rhett*, 88; Burt to H. W. Connor, July 4, 1848, in Armistead Burt Papers, SCHS.

cally, Calhoun threw his support to the Whig nominee, Zachary Taylor. Rhett considered Taylor and his party unsound on all questions of interest to the South and instead supported Democrat Lewis Cass. Speaking in Charleston, Rhett admitted that the Democrats had proven themselves inconsistent on tariffs, internal improvements, and slavery, but he argued that the Whigs were avowed enemies. Rhett denied Calhoun's contention that Taylor, a southern slaveholder, would protect the peculiar institution. Without an unambiguous promise to veto the Wilmot Proviso, Rhett insisted that southerners should not trust Taylor.

Rhett spoke of the election of 1848 as a turning point for the South. For years southerners had talked of resisting federal usurpations of power but had done nothing to stop it. "You must act, and act decisively," he demanded. "You have talked and threatened until you were despised." Like other fire-eaters, Rhett warned southerners that they could not rely on political parties to save them. "The South must protect itself," he said, and repeated his old warning that "no slaveholding communities can be safe but by their own energies." If others were allowed to tamper with slavery, it would provide "proof conclusive of your imbecility, and prove also that the Constitution has failed in affording you that 'domestic tranquillity' which on its face it was established to secure." If Southerners could no longer protect their rights within the Union, particularly "this great question of slavery," they must dissolve it. "Gentlemen!" he cried, "I long for the union of the South for the sake of the South. I care not what may be the measure that produces it." As he had said many times before, if other southern states would not act, South Carolina must, and force the rest to choose sides.[36]

When Taylor captured the presidency—and a substantial portion of the southern vote—Rhett grew despondent. He worked with Calhoun, who tried to rally southern unity by sponsoring a bipartisan Southern Address which declared that Congress could not interfere with slavery in the territories. Despite the efforts of the two Carolinians, less than half of all southern congressmen signed the address. Rhett became convinced that the South had grown weaker and more divided than ever. He looked desperately for any new strategy to restore southern unity and power. "On this account," he told Calhoun, "I am sorry to come to the conviction that

36. Charleston *Mercury*, September 29, 1848.

there is no chance for the Wilmot Proviso, or the abolition of slavery in the District of Columbia at the approaching Congress. Would to God, they would do both, and let us have the contest, and end it once and forever. It would then accomplish our emancipation, instead of that of our slaves."[37] When he ended his seventh and final term in Congress in 1849, the dejected Rhett felt that the South could not count on northerners to commit such a blunder.

Only a few months passed, however, before measures proposed in Congress to settle the territorial question suddenly brought about the conflict Rhett had wished for. In March, 1850, the single greatest obstacle to Rhett's political ascendancy disappeared with the death of John C. Calhoun. The impending congressional compromise and Calhoun's death presented Rhett with the most difficult but also the most promising challenge he had yet faced; he now had an opportunity to control his state and through it lead the South to secession. Events over the next two years would test his political acumen and try his organizational agility. Although he fixed his sights firmly on secession, he began to modify his tactics to capitalize on each opportunity that presented itself.

The first such opportunity was the Nashville Convention. Rhett had never believed cooperative southern resistance was possible. Instead, he had feared that southern conventions would compromise principle for the sake of partisan harmony and political office.[38] When the call for Nashville was met with enthusiasm and apparent earnestness, however, Rhett decided to give cooperation a try. He remained silent during most of the proceedings. The rest of the Carolina delegation—Elmore, Hammond, Langdon Cheves, and Robert W. Barnwell—eclipsed their more radical colleague. Even when the assembly resolved only to insist upon an extension of the 36°30′ line, Rhett did not speak out. He did, however, write the official "Address of the Convention" to the people of the Union.

The "Address" was filled with familiar Rhett verbiage. For fourteen years, it began, the North had tried to meddle with slavery through Congress. It did so "not from a mere lust of power," but also "to assail and destroy slavery in the South." Yet the South had done nothing to defend itself. Rhett argued that southerners should have met the issue boldly in 1844 either by forcing the North to maintain the gag rule or by seceding. Instead, he la-

---

37. William J. Cooper, Jr., *The South and the Politics of Slavery, 1828–1856* (Baton Rouge, 1978), 253, 266–68; White, *Rhett*, 99–100; Rhett to Calhoun, July 19, 1849, in Boucher and Brooks, eds., *Correspondence to Calhoun*, 517–18.

38. See, for example, Charleston *Mercury*, June 27, August 8, 1844.

mented, southerners did neither, "and their forbearance has had the effect of inspiring the Northern people with the belief that we value a union with them more than we value the institution of slavery." He concluded with his old warning that a slaveholding people "must rule themselves or perish."[39]

The extremism of Rhett's "Address" in no way matched the mood of the convention, but it did illustrate how Rhett interpreted cooperation. He issued the "Address" less to cooperate with the convention than to use and control it. By having the final word at Nashville, Rhett was able to impose his views on others by sheer assertion. He insisted that Nashville marked "the beginning of mighty changes" when he reported on the convention's actions to the people of Charleston. Rhett's boldness succeeded to a certain degree. Newspapers in Mississippi and Georgia hailed his "Address" and joined his call for resistance. In South Carolina, Rhett's actions left some of his opponents baffled. None showed greater confusion than Hammond. In a single letter he said: "Although I concur on every sentiment of Rhetts . . . I regret extremely that he gave utterance to them just now," "Such men [as Rhett] spoil all movements," and "I must not object to anything from Rhett."[40]

Rhett did not, however, use cooperation exclusively to manipulate others. Two months after the convention, he participated in a genuine act of cooperation. In August, 1850, Rhett made his first and only public address outside South Carolina. He joined William Lowndes Yancey of Alabama and others at a secession rally in Macon, Georgia. His message and his presence marked his honest support for united southern action. Wherever there was "a Southern heart to beat with indignation at Southern wrongs," Rhett announced, all southerners should confer together and offer counsel to each other.[41]

The failure of cooperative efforts like those at Nashville and Macon to result in effective political resistance led Rhett back to the conclusion that South Carolina must act alone and force other southern states to choose sides. Over the next year, as South Carolinians formed secessionist and cooperationist parties, Rhett spared no effort to attack cooperationism and vilify its advocates. But even while Rhett tried to convince Carolinians they had nothing to fear

39. *Ibid.*, June 20, 1850.
40. *Ibid.*, July 2, 3, 20, 1850; Hammond to William Gilmore Simms, June 27, 1850, in Hammond Papers, LC.
41. "Speech of the Honorable R. B. Rhett Delivered at the Mass Meeting at Macon, Georgia, on the 22 Aug 1850" (Fragment in Rhett Papers, SHC).

if they seceded first, his exchange of letters with John A. Quitman suggests that Rhett also worked covertly to foster cooperative resistance with Mississippi. If he could help push another state out of the Union, Rhett no doubt realized that he would eliminate forever the question of separate state action versus cooperation and would achieve his goal of a southern confederacy. No wonder that both he and Quitman, who also ostensibly favored separate state action, lied about their correspondence.[42]

Rhett's few attempts at cooperation did not reduce the need he felt for South Carolina to force other states into action; they merely demonstrated his awareness that many Carolinians were reluctant to risk repeating the embarrassment, alienation, and odium they had incurred by acting alone in 1832.[43] These efforts to promote southern unity, however, never distracted him from his more immediate goal, the secession of his own state. He would have gladly let any other state lead the secession movement, and he gave others the opportunity to try. But in his heart he believed everything depended on the action of South Carolina. He therefore expended most of his energies in attempting to achieve separate state action.

The first step in Rhett's effort to control his state involved Southern Rights associations. Many of these organizations arose spontaneously out of popular indignation over the compromise measures pending in Congress. Rhett determined to tap this popular energy. His call for the immediate secession of South Carolina at the meeting of a Charleston association drew the overwhelming approval of most of its members, including Hammond's closest friend, William Gilmore Simms. Rhett made similar appearances and remarks at Southern Rights meetings throughout the tidewater region; many of the Bluffton Boys reemerged to do the same further inland. Everywhere the message of Rhett and his lieutenants was the same. As Laurence Keitt said, South Carolina "should withdraw alone from the Union."[44] Rhett's determination to control his state also led him into a confrontation with James Ham-

42. Rhett to Quitman, July 22, 1851, in J. F. H. Claiborne Collection, MDAH; Quitman to Rhett, November 30, 1850, in Whitemarsh B. Seabrook Papers, LC; Robert E. May, *John A. Quitman: Old South Crusader* (Baton Rouge, 1985), 260; John Barnwell, *Love of Order: South Carolina's First Secession Crisis* (Chapel Hill, 1982), 178–79.

43. For example, see D. Wallace to Whitemarsh Seabrook, November 7, 1849, in Seabrook Papers, LC.

44. Charleston *Mercury*, October 4, 12, 1850, April 8, 12, August 8, 27, September 4, 18, 20, 1851.

mond. After Calhoun died, these two were the obvious contenders to replace him in the United States Senate and, presumably, as political master of the state. The legislature would not select a new senator until December, 1850; in the intervening months Rhett proved that he possessed both a greater awareness of the political mood of his state and more cunning than his often-confused opponent.

Rhett correctly perceived that Carolinians continued to wish for united southern resistance even after the Nashville Convention failed to produce concrete results. Hammond, disgusted at how ineffective Nashville was, chose not to attend a second convention there later in 1850. Rhett went. As Simms later pointed out, these developments gave many Carolinians the impression that Hammond lacked commitment to resistance. Rhett's attendance proved his willingness to seek redress either alone or with a united South.[45]

The competition between Rhett and Hammond continued into autumn, literally over the bones of Calhoun. The citizens of Charleston selected Hammond to give the city's official funeral oration for Calhoun; Governor Seabrook chose Rhett to do the same in the legislature. Both speakers traced Calhoun's illustrious career and lauded his accomplishments. But Hammond spoke of Calhoun's death as a crippling blow to the South, whereas Rhett invoked the senator's name to further his own objectives. In the same speech in which Rhett criticized Calhoun for his failure "to use and controul . . . man," Rhett attempted to do just that. He boldly put words in Calhoun's mouth and, through a singular interpretation of Calhoun's actions, promoted secession.

After Calhoun collapsed in the lobby of the Senate shortly before his death, Rhett claimed, he extended his hand and said: "Ah! Mr. Rhett, my career is nearly done. The great battle must be fought by you younger men." What was the "great battle" Calhoun spoke of? Rhett claimed to know: "Had his mighty spirit devised some way to save the Union, consistent with the liberties of the South? Or did he wish to utter there that word which all his lifetime he could not speak, although wrong and oppression tortured him— that word, which dying despair could alone wring from his aching heart—disunion!!" Whether Calhoun came to believe that the South must secede is arguable; that he hand-picked Rhett as his

45. White, *Rhett*, 115; William Gilmore Simms to Hammond, January 30, 1851, in Mary C. Oliphant, Alfred Taylor Odell, and T. C. Duncan Eaves, eds., *The Letters of William Gilmore Simms* (5 vols.; Columbia, S.C., 1955), III, 88.

successor, after years of friction between them, is improbable. Nevertheless, that was the picture that Rhett presented to the legislature. He also designed his closing remarks to force lawmakers to commit themselves to secession. If they truly mourned the passing of Calhoun, he said, "we cannot but hate the tyranny that hurried him to his grave,—and love the liberty for which he lived, and wasted, and died. Cherishing his memory, we dare not be slaves."[46]

In December, the legislature selected Rhett for the Senate seat over Hammond by a vote of 97 to 46. Furious over this roadblock to fulfilling his ambition, Hammond lashed out at Rhett, calling him a Robespierre and saying that he possessed no statesmanship whatsoever. He told his friend Edmund Ruffin, "I have long thought he was not sincere in his Revolutionary tactics. They were too wild & *insured defeat*." At its calmest, Hammond's anger amounted to a smoldering jealousy. To Simms he lamented that Rhett was the new master of South Carolina, that the political elite of the State had "anointed him leader."[47]

When Hammond discovered that Simms had asked their friend Beverley Tucker to review Rhett's and his own orations for Calhoun together in the *Southern Quarterly Review*, he erupted. "Do I belong to Rhett?" he demanded of Simms. "He has crushed me it is true so far [as] my present & future political prospects & moral character are concerned." But, he protested, "Am I, soul & body, to be blasted by him? . . . What is there between us & associating us but that he has been my conqueror and destroyer?" To Tucker, Hammond said that he could "never comprehend the necessity of placing Rhetts oration & mine in the same caption, nor why he should thus be gratuitously & by my friends be made to neutralize me in literature after destroying me in politics."[48] Not even Simms's saying he wished "the Rhetts & Co may be decapitated" consoled Hammond. After straining his relationship with the aged and dying Tucker, Hammond resigned himself to his fate.[49]

46. Faust, *Hammond*, 300–301; *Death and Funeral Ceremonies of Calhoun*, 117–68, esp. 162–65, 168.

47. Charleston *Mercury*, December 19, 1850; Hammond to Simms, February 14, May 24, 1851, in Hammond Papers, LC; Hammond to Edmund Ruffin, November 21, 1851, in Edmund Ruffin Papers, SHC.

48. William Gilmore Simms to Beverley Tucker, March 2, [1851], in Oliphant, Odell, and Eaves, eds., *Letters of William Gilmore Simms*, III, 93–94; Hammond to Simms, May 29, 1851 in Hammond Papers, LC; Hammond to Tucker, June 13, 1851, in Tucker-Coleman Collection, ESL.

49. Tucker to Hammond, May 25, June 23, 1851, Hammond to Simms, July 1, 7, 1851, in Hammond Papers, LC; Hammond to Tucker, April 8, 1851, in Tucker-

Neutralizing Hammond, however, was only part of Rhett's strategy. He had to convince the voters of South Carolina that they had no alternative but secession. To do this, Rhett tried a variety of rhetorical devices. The first was his standard approach—allusions to the gallantry of the Founding Fathers and exhortations to emulate their heroism. As he had done during the nullification crisis, Rhett loudly proclaimed in 1850, "I am a Traitor," a "Traitor in the great cause of liberty, fighting against tyranny and oppression." While speaking to a gathering in Charleston, he explained, "To meet death a little sooner or a little later, can be of consequence to very few of us."[50] The prosperous businessmen and merchants of the city, however, were no more eager to embrace Rhett's call to risk their lives and fortunes than were most people in the state. By the next summer, Rhett realized that his clarion call for a southern revolution had cost him more support than it attracted.

With this realization came a determination to stand his message on its head. Henceforth, Rhett would not only deny that the South entertained revolutionary intentions but would accuse the North of overthrowing the Constitution and waging an aggressive, methodical campaign against the conservative and passive South.

Rhett had already begun to adapt his language in 1850. If southerners allowed the North to prevent them from expanding slavery into the federal territories, he said, all new states would be free and, in time, the North would be able to abolish slavery constitutionally through the amendment process. Rhett warned of an evil, menacing conspiracy growing in the North which plotted to "degrade and ruin the South." He claimed that abolitionists designed to "place upon your front, the brand of inferiority." For the innocent, law-abiding slave states, liberty, honor, and "existence itself" hung in the balance. If Congress could prohibit the spread of slavery or tax the southern people against their will, Rhett explained, "you are ruled by the North." If the North ruled the South, he asked Carolinians, "are you a free people?"[51]

Coleman Collection, ESL; Simms to Tucker, June 26, 1851, in Oliphant, Odell, and Eaves, eds., *Letters of William Gilmore Simms*, III, 132–34. His defeat by Rhett aggravated Hammond's sense of political powerlessness. Seven years earlier, Hammond's brother-in-law Wade Hampton II, a prominent South Carolina planter and politician, discovered Hammond's sexual liaison with Hampton's daughters. Hampton used his considerable influence to impede Hammond's political career. Rhett's victory in 1850, therefore, compounded Hammond's frustrations. See Faust, *Hammond*, 241–45.

50. Charleston *Mercury*, July 20, 1850, April 21, 1851.
51. *Ibid.*, June 20, July 20, 1850.

Not merely a Cassandra, Rhett offered a solution. Just as Beverley Tucker had done at Nashville and Yancey and other fire-eaters would do increasingly, Rhett began to emphasize that secession would bring redemption and honor, liberty and prosperity to the South. Nowhere was this shift in rhetoric more apparent than in his address at Macon. After another long recitation of northern trespasses against the South, Rhett focused on the supposed benefits of secession. The South, he predicted, would have a free hand in the West after secession. "New Mexico and Utah, contiguous to us, will be easily ours; and how long will California keep out of a Southern Confederacy?" he asked. Californians, he was sure, joined southerners in their desire for lower tariffs and required slaves to work in their gold mines "—need them more than any people in the world;—the South alone can supply her with them." A southern nation would soon absorb all of Mexico. With "so glorious a destiny before them," Rhett said that southerners would prove "the most stupendous instance of imbecility, folly and cowardice, the world has ever seen" if they did not form their own nation. Later, in South Carolina, Rhett repeated his vision of territorial glories and added that secession would bring a new age of commercial prosperity. Free trade would increase European commerce with the South, cripple northern business, and thus preclude the possibility of a northern naval blockade or civil war. According to Rhett, the South had much to lose by remaining in the Union and much to gain by seceding.[52]

Senator Rhett's initial confidence that his many-layered strategy would work diminished as the year 1851 progressed. In February he felt certain that the nation would split apart over the slavery question. His wife reported from South Carolina that "the prospects of the State are brightening, the country is coming out bravely for secession," although she noted that the residents of Charleston demonstrated "a craven spirit of doubt & fear." Despite the activities of Southern Rights associations all summer, the people of South Carolina began to shy away from separate state action. Rhett panicked. In July he urged Governor John Means to seize federal forts in the state so as to precipitate an armed conflict and force southerners to unite. Means refused. "Although I see

52. "Speech of the Hon. R. B. Rhett delivered at the Mass Meeting, at Macon, Ga., on the 22d August, 1850," in Abraham Watkins Venable Scrapbook, WPL; Charleston *Mercury*, April 21, 1851.

much force in the reasons you give, as to the Union of the South in case of success," the governor calmly responded, "yet were it to *fail*, I should look upon it as a *death blow* to our cause."[53]

In an October election for delegates to a state convention, the voters of South Carolina backed cooperationists over secessionists by an aggregate of 25,045 to 17,710. The Rhetts grew sullen. The "submissionists" had triumphed, Elizabeth told her husband. She could not believe that sentiment for secession had collapsed so quickly after he had helped raise it to a peak only months before. She lashed out at "this ungrateful, cowardly, stupid State" in which politicians, made aware of their duty by Rhett, refused to act like men. "My heart actually sickens, at the prospect before us— what abject humiliation, what deep degradation is ours," Elizabeth moaned. "I think death preferable to dishonor."[54]

As influence over the state slipped from his grasp, so did Rhett's self-control. After the fall elections presented secessionists through-out the South with a fait accompli, formerly avid secessionists in Congress scrambled toward Unionism. All except Rhett. "I am a se-cessionist—I am a disunionist," he trumpeted on the Senate floor. When a colleague challenged Rhett's claim that he had been a se-cessionist for only a few years, he snapped, "I do not care whether you say twenty or one hundred years, if I was so old." The Com-promise of 1850, he said, effectively dissolved the Union by violat-ing the equality and rights of southerners in the territories. "Others may submit: I will not," he announced defiantly. "I will secede, if I can, from this Union. I will test, for myself and for my children, whether South Carolina is a State or an humbled and degraded province, existing only at the mercy of an unscrupulous and fanati-cal tyranny."[55]

In April, 1852, a state convention resolved, by a vote of 136 to 19, that South Carolina "has good cause to secede from the Union, and forbears to do so only from motives of expediency." A few days later, Rhett resigned from the Senate. His action surprised many who, like Hammond, had assumed that Rhett's ambition centered on political office rather than secession. In a letter to Governor

53. Rhett to N. Foster, February 1, 1851, Elizabeth Rhett to R. B. Rhett, Febru-ary 5, [1851], in Rhett Papers, SCHS; John H. Means to Rhett, July 30, 1851, in Rhett Papers, SHC.

54. Barnwell, *Love of Order*, 177–81; Elizabeth Rhett to R. B. Rhett, October 17, [1851], in Rhett Papers, SCHS.

55. *Congressional Globe*, 32nd Cong., 1st Sess., 655, App., 43–48, 57.

Means, Rhett explained that even after the October elections he could not believe his countrymen would opt for "absolute submission" until he received news of the recent convention. Rhett said that he could not honorably represent a state that had so completely repudiated his extreme political positions.[56]

"Mr. Rhett is the most consistent of politicians," an editorial in a Virginia newspaper stated. "He pushes his doctrines to their legitimate conclusions. He is rigidly logical, but remarkably impracticable. He is something of a fanatic withal." This accurate assessment pointed to a great irony: while working for his political objectives, Rhett had committed many of the same tactical errors that he had criticized Calhoun for only a few months before. Although it is doubtful that any individual could have maneuvered South Carolina out of the Union in 1851 or 1852, Rhett's experiences in this crisis taught him much about both principles and political effectiveness. Appeals to reason, it seemed, had proved futile; consistency and personal integrity had not resulted in action. Certain that another sectional conflict was inevitable, Rhett waited for a new opportunity to exploit both this new knowledge and "that compound of . . . reason and prejudice, passion and weakness—man."[57]

While Rhett waited, fate tested the fortitude of his entire family. In December, 1852, Elizabeth died after giving birth to their twelfth child. Their eldest son, Robert Barnwell Rhett, Jr., suffered a series of bad crops on his plantation. To one of his brothers, the junior Rhett quipped, the only way out of his financial troubles was if "one of you loafers marries a rich girl quick and lends me some money." The elder Rhett had problems of his own. In 1855 he sailed to Paris to see a doctor about a growth on the side of his nose which had plagued him for years. He was relieved to hear "that it is a lesion of the skin merely and not at all dangerous."[58] Unfortunately, the physician misdiagnosed the symptoms. After the Civil War, Rhett's cancer would spread, horribly disfigure his face, and cause his death.

The early 1850s, however, were not entirely bad for Rhett. He married Catherine Herbert Dent, who brought cheerfulness and

56. Charleston *Mercury*, May 1, 10, 1852; Rhett to Means, May 5, 1852, *ibid.*, May 10, 1852. For an example of Hammond's attitude, see Hammond to Simms, January 21, 1851, in Hammond Papers, LC.

57. Petersburg *Democrat*, reprinted in Charleston *Mercury*, May 15, 1852.

58. White, *Rhett*, 133–34; Robert Barnwell Rhett, Jr., to A. Burnet Rhett, July 17, 1854; Barnwell Rhett to R. B. Rhett, Jr., August 15, 1855, in Rhett Papers, SCHS.

happiness back into his life. He devoted his time to his law practice in Charleston and to his plantations. Rhett already owned a plantation on the Ashepoo River, and during the 1850s he purchased a rice plantation in the Altamaha district of Georgia; 190 slaves worked Rhett's properties.[59]

Although refusing to take a public role, Rhett kept his hand in politics. He published anonymously a "Tract on Government" in the April, 1854, issue of the *Southern Quarterly Review*. Although he carefully avoided the issue of secession, he filled the piece with his concepts of limited governmental powers, the perpetual struggle of liberty against tyranny, and the necessity for a slaveholding people to rule themselves. Through former Bluffton Boy John McQueen, then serving on the House Territorial Committee, Rhett gathered information about goings-on in the capital. McQueen told Rhett of the status of the Kansas-Nebraska bill. Although both men favored its passage, the wrangling over the bill in Congress made McQueen agree with Rhett that "we are at the mercy of the plundering unscrupulous North and are not freemen."[60]

Sentiments such as McQueen's convinced Rhett that he had not been wrong in his political strategy, but only that "I have been ahead of the times, and have fallen." In 1856, after the surprisingly strong electoral performance of the new Republican party, Rhett believed it time to renew his work for secession. He began his campaign with an open letter to Governor James H. Adams. After a generation of northern agitation on the tariff and slavery, he stated, a "complete revolution" had transformed a once free government into "a sheer despotism." Southerners were ruled by a hostile northern majority in Congress, "vulgar and fanatical, hating us and hating our institutions." Secession was the only solution to this problem. Rhett then tipped his hand concerning what he would do over the next few years to promote secession. "To induce any people to desist from any policy," he explained, "you must place before them an alternative, which presents to them the impossibility of their policy being carried out, or that greater evils are to result from its continuance than its abandonment." Rhett then presented just such a set of choices. The evil was Unionism, manifested in the humiliation of southern congressmen forced "to sit in

59. White, *Rhett*, 134–35.
60. "Tract on Government," *SQR*, IX (April, 1854), 486–520; R. B. Rhett to Daniel London, n.d., in Daniel H. London Papers, VHS; John McQueen to Rhett, February 3, 1854, in Rhett Papers, SCHS.

a legislative body controlled by Abolitionists" and by the murder of southerners in Kansas Territory. The alternative that he suggested was secession. "If we are true to ourselves," Rhett held, "a glorious destiny awaits us, and the South will be a great, free and independent people!"[61]

To facilitate the propagation of his message, Rhett acquired control of the *Mercury*. His son R. B. Rhett, Jr., bought out William R. Taber early in 1857 and jointly edited the paper for a time with John Heart. The younger Rhett remained steadfastly loyal to his father, whom he often left in charge while he was out of town. Indeed, one cannot separate the two in the tenor, style, or substance of their editorials. "If we could only now get a great sectional issue like that of 1850," said the young editor, "the Union would not last a month." And yet Rhett's son knew that he had to exercise extreme caution in setting an editorial tone because of the odium his family "incurred by the controversy of '51." For the next three years, therefore, as Barnwell Rhett's biographer stated, the two set a "devious course."[62]

Their first step was to infiltrate the enemy camp. By feigning a tone of moderation and conciliation, the Rhetts tried to prove that they had renounced their radicalism and were once again willing to work within the Democratic party. Whether secession or cooperation was preferable, they now said, was a dead issue. "The Mercury has long abandoned the separate action of the state, and seeks *bona fide* the union of the South for action on any proper occasion," they claimed. If southerners united behind such leaders as Jefferson Davis and James Hammond (who was finally elected to the Senate in 1857), the *Mercury* believed southern rights would be safe.[63]

To many, the Rhetts' new policy seemed genuine. For example, they abandoned their editorial support for the revival of the African slave trade after controversy over the issue threatened southern unity. They even denied other fire-eaters access to the *Mercury*.

61. Rhett to Henry Wise, November 7, 1856, in Autograph Collection of Simon Gratz, HSP; Rhett to James H. Adams, November 7, 1856, in Charleston *Mercury*, November 10, 1856.

62. Charleston *Mercury*, February 5, 1857; Simms to Hammond, April 12, 1858, in Oliphant, Odell, and Eaves, eds., *Letters of William Gilmore Simms*, IV, 49; R. B. Rhett, Jr., to William Branch, May 23, 1857, in William H. Branch Papers, SHC; R. B. Rhett, Jr., to Edmund Ruffin, April 5, 1860, in Ruffin Papers, SHC; White, *Rhett*, 140, 149.

63. Charleston *Mercury*, November 27, December 1, 5, 1857, June 28, July 5, 15, 1858.

To one radical, this treatment constituted nearly "the greatest mortification which I have ever suffered in political affairs." A supporter of the Rhetts commended the editor for balancing firmness and moderation and for defending himself "ably & triumphantly" from critics' attacks. The junior Rhett easily convinced Hammond that he and his father completely backed the new senator. Kind treatment in the *Mercury*'s columns convinced the gullible Hammond to support his old nemesis. Hammond now told Simms, "I rather like the Rhetts."[64]

The Rhetts' public policy, however, was a charade. Occasionally their real intentions found their way into print. For example, at the same time they decided to retract their call for the reopening of the African slave trade, they suggested that southerners should reconsider the issue later—after secession. Their endorsement of Yancey's League of United Southerners proved that they, like Yancey, believed in working within existing parties only to control them. The Rhetts clearly betrayed their true policy in the summer of 1858. "Absolute union in the South to resist any of its aggressions is impossible," they said. It would require only a few states, however, to "force the issue of protection in the Union or independence out of it."[65]

A careful and critical reading of the *Mercury*, therefore, shows that Barnwell Rhett held exactly the same position he did in 1852. With this insight, one observant reader accurately predicted what the coming years would decide. In a letter to Hammond he said: "I think Mr Rhett the logical consequence of Mr Calhoun. I think you the logical correction of Mr Calhoun. But then there is a logic also of facts and the question is whether the facts of the last few years have so developed that either you or he can square the logic of your theories with living, voting realities."[66]

The growth of the Republican party provided Rhett with a great opportunity to "square the logic" of his theories with the voters of South Carolina. He renewed his effort to control the state, not through the *Mercury* but in his first public address in seven years.

64. Charleston *Mercury*, June 25, 1857; Maxcy Gregg to Barnwell Rhett, September 14, 1858, in Rhett Papers, SCHS; William H. Branch to R. B. Rhett, Jr., August 26, 1858, in Robert Barnwell Rhett Papers, WPL; R. B. Rhett, Jr., to Hammond, August 2, November 5, 1858, Hammond to Simms, October 2, 1858, in Hammond Papers, LC.

65. Charleston *Mercury*, June 25, 1857, July 26, August 10, 1858.

66. William H. Trescot to Hammond, December 5, 1858, in Hammond Papers, LC.

At a Fourth of July celebration at Grahamville he dramatized the perils of remaining in the Union and proclaimed the advantages of secession. Since his retirement from politics, Rhett said, compromises had failed to leave the South in peace. Sectionalism "is no longer a spasmodic evil" but a permanent feature of American politics. Because they had refused to act decisively, southerners were now a helpless, defenseless minority, ruled by an antagonistic North and threatened by a party pledged to the eventual extinction of slavery. Rhett predicted that soon northerners would incite slave insurrections in the South and, even more insidiously, might use the pretense of these insurrections to impose military rule and use emergency war powers to emancipate slaves.[67]

After carefully describing the threat, Rhett offered an alternative. An independent South, he claimed, would be invincible. Eight million whites, holding 4 million slaves, "are too mighty in their strength to trust any other people to shape their destiny," Rhett argued. "They must be independent and free in the high station for which they are designed amongst the great nations of the earth." Furthermore, southerners had a "high mission" imposed upon them: they had a duty to show the world a slaveholding republic could not only exist but thrive. A thriving future, he said, was inevitable. Freed from the restraints of Yankee domination, he pledged, "Expansion shall be the law of the South." In his incredible picture of the future, a southern nation would consume all potential plantation regions in the Western Hemisphere, reaching thirty degrees north and south of the equator (roughly from Virginia to the southern tip of Brazil). Southern institutions would thus remain safe for centuries, southern economic power would dominate the world, and liberty for white southerners would never again be in jeopardy. If northerners joined southerners to elect a Democrat president in 1860, the South might choose to remain in the Union a while longer. But if a Republican were elected southerners must choose between a dangerous Union and a "glorious Southern Confederacy."[68]

A few months after this speech, John Brown's raid on Harpers Ferry made Rhett's warnings seem prophetic. In relatively restrained language, the *Mercury* explained that the raid was "the legitimate fruit of the Union" and that southerners could expect

67. Charleston *Mercury*, July 7, 1859.
68. *Ibid.*

more such acts of "hostility and insurrection." Only secession, it argued, could prevent the recurrence of such raids. The Rhetts claimed that the South could better protect itself out of the Union than in it. "If we had a separate government of our own, the post office, all the avenues of intercourse, the police and the military of our country, would be under our exclusive control." After John Brown's raid, when Rhett said, "The South must control her own destinies or perish," more and more southerners agreed.[69]

Before the excitement over Brown's raid faded, the Rhetts began their drive to influence the upcoming Democratic national convention in Charleston. They had already proposed a virtual copy of the Alabama Platform, declaring that if nominees for president or vice-president would not clearly endorse the expansion of slavery into the territories, southern states should withdraw their delegations. The Rhetts then began taunting and threatening southerners in an attempt to stifle the influence of national Democrats. Southerners, they demanded, must rid themselves of the "brood of Southern toadies to Northern opinion, whose statesmanship consists in periodically saving the Union by compromising the rights and safety of their section." If the South permitted Stephen Douglas' faction to dominate at the convention, "it will establish the enemy in her midst and paralyze her for any efforts at extrication and redemption."[70]

Ultimately, the Rhetts hoped to see the Democratic party destroyed. They believed that would ensure a Republican victory and provide southerners with the impetus for secession. The younger Rhett traced their strategy for fire-eating Congressman William Porcher Miles. "The South must dissever itself from the rotten Northern element," he began. He knew that there was no chance for states'-rights men to gain control of the entire party and therefore pinned his hopes on disrupting the convention. "Hence the importance of attaining the secession of the Alabama and Mississippi delegations. . . . If they will do it . . . the game will be ours." As far as attaining united action by southerners at the convention, the junior Rhett explained, "the idea is as absurd, as it is unnecessary." If only two states acted together, it would be enough to "break down the spoils Democracy and, on the election of a Black Republican, to dissolve the Union." "Rhett arrogance" surfaced

---

69. *Ibid.*, October 31, November 1, 1859.
70. *Ibid.*, October 13, 1859, January 13, 14, 19, 23, February 28, April 18, 1860.

once again: "Those who are not prepared to face opposition at home are not fit for the crisis. The South must go through a trying ordeal before she will ever achieve her deliverance, and men having both nerve and self sacrificing patriotism must head the movement and shape its course, controlling and compelling their inferior contemporaries."[71]

In April, when Yancey led the bolt of southerners from the convention, the Rhetts were overjoyed and hailed Yancey as the champion of southern rights. When they discovered, however, that Yancey entertained the notion of reunion with the national Democrats, the Rhetts determined to do everything in their power to keep the party splintered. When Carolinians assembled in a state convention to elect delegates to the southern Democratic convention in Richmond, Rhett influence asserted itself again. Barnwell Rhett, his brother Edmund, and R. B. Rhett, Jr., were all selected to go to Richmond.[72]

Speaking in the capital of Virginia, Rhett echoed the message Yancey had given at Charleston. "I have never been an enemy of the constitutional Union," he proclaimed. "I am not now." Southerners, he later explained in the *Mercury*, were the true conservatives; Republicans "are the practical revolutionists and hatchers of trouble." In the early 1850s, Rhett won few converts with this language. John Brown's raid and Republican pledges eventually to eliminate slavery, however, gave him new credibility, as both he and his son were well aware. Therefore, throughout the summer of 1860 the *Mercury* continually asserted that the southern Democrats were committed to perpetuating the Union and that the menacing, meddling Republicans plotted to destroy slavery, the Constitution, and the South.[73]

A befuddled Hammond actually believed Rhett "has come [out] for the Union." A wiser William Porcher Miles, admitting his surprise at Rhett's latest tactic, understood it as "ingenious." In 1851, he recalled, "Secessionists certainly would have indignantly repudiated the title of 'Union-savers.'" But because Rhett found "that his ultra course has not given him the control of the State [he] is now

71. R. B. Rhett, Jr., to William Porcher Miles, January 29, 1860, in William P. Miles Papers, SHC.

72. Charleston *Mercury*, April 30, 1860; R. B. Rhett, Jr., to Miles, May 10 (letter and telegram), 12, 1860, in Miles Papers, SHC; White, *Rhett*, 165–66.

73. Charleston *Mercury*, June 7 (Rhett's remarks), July 11, 18, 19, 20, 27, August 13, 15, 20, 21, 25, September 3, 7, 12, 1860.

bidding for the suffrages or at least the approbation of the more moderate States Rights men."[74]

While depicting themselves as good Unionists, the Rhetts continued their campaign to prove how the "terrors" of a Republican regime "are ten-fold greater even than the supposed terrors of secession."[75] To dramatize this idea, they flooded the *Mercury* with editorials designed to show how Republicans would degrade, plunder, and destroy the South, and other editorials showing the supposed advantages of a southern confederacy.

"No people degraded," the Rhetts reminded their honor-conscious readers, "can be free." According to the Rhetts, Republican rule promised degradation. New Yorkers might soon enfranchise free blacks. The "fugitive slaves of the South" would then achieve political equality with their former masters. The Rhetts speculated wildly that Republicans might place Frederick Douglass, a former slave, in the cabinet. Aiming at the most base emotions of southerners, the Rhetts claimed that Hannibal Hamlin, the Republican vice-presidential candidate, was a mulatto, "to which fact he probably owes his nomination." The Rhetts knew that southerners could not accept the idea of a mulatto presiding over their senators in Congress.[76]

Republican insidiousness, said the Rhetts, extended even further. Republicans, representing a sectional majority, would create a despotic government, one "totally irresponsible to the people of the South, without check, restraint, or limitation." Republicans, therefore, threatened "a total annihilation of all self-government or liberty in the South." Republicans "will plunder us before destroying us" through protective tariffs and other discriminatory taxes. Once looted and degraded, the South would watch helplessly as Republicans abolished slavery and "an ignorant, semi-barbarous race, urged to madness by the licentious teachings of our northern brethren," either amalgamated with whites or launched bloody racial warfare.[77]

Simultaneously, the Rhetts maintained that "the South, in the

74. Hammond to I. W. Hayne, September 19, 1860, Miles to Hammond, August 5, 1860, in Hammond Papers, LC.

75. Charleston *Mercury*, October 4, 11, 1860.

76. *Ibid.*, July 13, 27, September 13, October 4, 23, November 8, December 13, 1860.

77. *Ibid.*, September 3, October 3, 23, 31, 1860. For similar editorials, see *ibid.*, July 19, 20, August 20, September 28, 1860.

control of her own commerce and destiny, will bound forward in a career of prosperity and power, unsurpassed in the history of nations." Cotton and other staple crops would supply a southern nation with economic might unattainable within the Union. Unencumbered by protective tariffs, a southern confederacy would attract more trade than the United States ever had. Southern port cities such as New Orleans, Charleston, Mobile, and Savannah would quickly supplant northern commercial centers. Increased foreign trade would spur a boom in railroad construction and thereby promote economic development in the interior. If the border between the North and South became an international frontier, the Rhetts explained, civil and military forces, once purged of Yankees, would be able to stop the escape of fugitive slaves to the North. Furthermore, the *Mercury* stated that the North would never attack a southern nation. Eight million southerners, trained "from boyhood to the horse and gun . . . are unconquerable by any power on this continent," the Rhetts boasted.[78]

When Abraham Lincoln was elected in November, the *Mercury* proclaimed, "The tea has been thrown overboard—the revolution of 1860 has been initiated." Their message was "ACT—ACT." They announced that Carolinians were finally prepared to secede and warned that "they do not expect their representatives to be behind them." They endorsed the actions of private citizens who formed "Minute Men" organizations throughout the state. They called for the immediate resignation of southerners from service in the United States military forces and urged the governor to obtain weapons for the state by sending commissioners to Europe—even though the state had yet to secede. The Rhetts appealed to passion and emotion by telling Carolinians that northerners considered them "a blustering, weak, timid people—demoralized and paralyzed by your institutions, just fit to serve or to be tortured and destroyed." When the governor called a special session of the legislature to consider secession, the Rhetts were ecstatic. "The long weary night of our humiliation, oppression and danger is passing away," Barnwell Rhett told a crowd in Charleston, "and the glorious dawn of a Southern Confederacy breaks on our view."[79]

On the eve of his victory, Rhett again lost his self-control. After years of defending himself as a conservative and blaming north-

---

78. *Ibid.,* July 28, 30, August 7, 8, September 25, October 2, 6, 19, 25, 27, 1860.
79. *Ibid.,* October 15, 19, November 8, 9, 12, 21, 29, 30, December 3, 1860.

erners for revolutionizing the country, he proved that he had changed not at all since 1828. In December, he congratulated Carolinians for "the great revolution you have inaugurated." Although he had recently promised that secession would bring only good for the South, he now warned, "Be prepared to meet all the usual troubles and sacrifices of revolutions." Entirely unable to restrain himself, he said: "For thirty-two years, have I followed the quarry. Behold! it at last, in sight! A few more bounds, and it falls—the Union falls; and with it falls, its faithless oppressions—its insulting agitations—its vulgar tyrannies and fanaticism. The bugle blast of our victory and redemption is on the wind; and the South will be safe and free."[80]

At last, the people of South Carolina matched Rhett's enthusiasm for secession. On December 20, the state convention unanimously adopted an ordinance of secession. One southerner recalled the "thrilling scene" when Rhett joined his fellow delegates to sign the document. "As he approached the desk he sunk upon his knees and uplifted his hands to heaven, and for a moment bowed his head in prayer. Naturally," this observer concluded, "the proceeding was electric."[81]

With the secession of South Carolina, Rhett's work had only begun. Selected by his colleagues to write *The Address of the People of South Carolina . . . to the People of the Slaveholding States,* Rhett turned his attention to nation building. His *Address* repeated his accusations of northern aggression against southern rights and his maxim that a slaveholding people must rule themselves. He called on all slave states to send representatives to Montgomery and form a "great, free, and prosperous" southern confederacy.[82]

Once again chosen to represent the people of Beaufort and Colleton, Rhett played a prominent role in the Provisional Congress of the Confederate States of America when it assembled in February, 1861. He served on the foreign affairs committee and chaired the committee to draft a permanent constitution. For his work on the latter, he had "prepared a Book containing certain amendments to the Constitution of the United States" that he hoped fellow delegates would support. Rhett's model included prohibitions on protective tariffs and internal improvements, an article that enabled

80. *Ibid.,* November 28, December 10, 1860.
81. George S. Bernard Scrapbook, 195, WPL.
82. *The Address of the People of South Carolina, Assembled in Convention, to the People of the Slaveholding States of the United States* (Charleston, 1860).

any three states (through state conventions) to summon a constitutional convention, and limiting the president to a single six-year term. So much of his plan was adopted that his son heralded the Confederate Constitution as "the best constitution, we believe, ever devised by man."[83] Although other fire-eaters, according to one rumor, wanted Rhett to be president, Rhett himself followed the advice of Louis Wigfall and Robert W. Barnwell and backed Jefferson Davis. The *Mercury* followed suit. It hailed Davis' selection and enthusiastically endorsed all of his cabinet selections.[84]

By exciting the emotions of Carolinians, Rhett had finally discovered a way to influence his state and, through it, the South. Even his critics acknowledged that secession was a personal triumph for "King Barnwell the first." Diarist Mary Chesnut conceded that Rhett had "exasperated and heated" Carolinians into such a state "that only bloodletting could ever cure [them]—it was the inevitable remedy." A petulant Hammond said of Rhett and the fire-eaters: "It is certain that these men brought on this great movement. They were instruments in the hands of God (as Judas was,—though it was denied me to see it)."[85]

Rhett's mastery of South Carolina, however, was fleeting. By the summer of 1861 he again proved himself better at alienating his countrymen than at winning their hearts. The stubborn independence that characterized his early career resurfaced with a vengeance. The *Mercury*, Mary Chesnut noted, "calls everyone a submissionist but R. B. Rhett." William Gilmore Simms reported that "the Mercury has been making itself very odious" because of its sudden criticism of President Davis and the war effort. Rhett blamed the administration for the chaos exhibited in the army during and after the Battle of Bull Run. Even a direct appeal from General P. G. T. Beauregard could not dissuade the junior Rhett from printing military intelligence in the *Mercury*. By fall, when Rhett considered running for the Senate, his son realized that the

83. *Journal of the Congress of the Confederate States of America* (7 vols.; Washington, D.C., 1904), I, 42, 44; Rhett to Stuart Rhett, April 13, 1868, in Rhett Papers, SCHS; Charleston *Mercury*, February 12, 16, March 15, 1861.

84. C. Vann Woodward, ed., *Mary Chesnut's Civil War* (New Haven, 1981), 6; Rhett to Louis Wigfall, April 15, 1864, in Wigfall Family Papers, LC; Charleston *Mercury*, February 5, 21, 23, March 7, 1861.

85. David S. Fraley to Andrew Johnson, February 17, 1861, in Leroy P. Graf and Ralph W. Haskins, eds., *The Papers of Andrew Johnson* (7 vols. to date; Knoxville, 1967–), IV, 302–303; Woodward, ed., *Mary Chesnut's Civil War*, 4; Hammond to John Ashmore, April 2, 8, 1861, in Hammond Papers, LC.

anti-Rhett backlash would defeat him. Though other fire-eaters enjoyed years of service in the Confederate government, when Barnwell Rhett's term in Congress ended in June, 1862, so did his political career.[86]

The Rhetts' sudden disillusionment with the Confederate government stemmed from their unrealistic belief that the act of secession would purge southern politics of all undesirable characteristics. Only months before, the Rhetts had predicted that "the better parts of our nature will appear" after secession and relieve a southern nation of the discord caused by party politics. In a southern confederacy, they believed, unity and harmony would prevail. They had thought that secession would enable southerners to "make the welfare of the South the welfare of their representatives." When politicians were no longer tempted to yield their section's interests to northern demands, the public good in the South would become their only "road to distinction and official preferment." The Rhetts also deluded themselves into believing that, without the distractions of political parties or "toadies to Northern opinion," all southerners would embrace the Rhetts' ideals, philosophy of government, and devotion to the South.[87] Naturally, they were mistaken. Their dreams frustrated so soon after their initial triumph, the Rhetts began to lash out at the very government they had just helped to create.

The Rhetts focused their wrath on the most visible symbol of the government, President Jefferson Davis. They condemned Davis' military strategy. They opposed conscription. They censured Davis for allegedly usurping power in an "unchecked career of mischief." Their indignation climaxed when Davis and General Robert E. Lee proposed arming slaves for service in the Confederate army and rewarding them later with emancipation. "The freemen of the Confederate States," they trumpeted, "must work out their own redemption, or they must be the slaves of their own slaves." If the Confederate government could claim the power to emancipate slaves, the Rhetts said, the Confederacy "is stone dead." In 1865,

86. Woodward, ed., *Mary Chesnut's Civil War,* 12; William Gilmore Simms to Hammond, November 18, 1861, in Oliphant, Odell, and Eaves, eds., *Letters of William Gilmore Simms,* IV, 385; Rhett to R. B. Rhett, Jr., July 25, 1861, in Civil War Collection, HL; R. B. Rhett, Jr., to P. G. T. Beauregard, July 13, 1861, in Pierre Gustave Toutant Beauregard Papers, WPL; R. B. Rhett, Jr., to Edmund Rhett, October 29, 1861, in Rhett Papers, SHC; White, *Rhett,* 223.

87. Charleston *Mercury,* January 23, October 15, November 13, 14, 15, December 20, 1860, February 9, 26, 1861.

they began equating Davis with the devil and lashed out at Lee for supporting "this scheme of nigger soldiers and emancipation."[88]

War brought a crushing personal defeat to Rhett as well as devastation to the South. Until the end of his life, Rhett strove to vindicate his career. He made at least three different attempts at writing history; all failed. The first was an abortive attempt at fiction. Only thirteen handwritten pages exist of Rhett's "A Conversation Concerning the Late War in the United States," told in the form of a dialogue between an Englishman and a southerner. In it, Rhett speaks of state sovereignty and the right of secession. The fact was, "Southerner" claimed, the South did not rebel against the North; rather, the North waged a war of aggression on the South in "the grand crime of the century." Rhett then shifted to slightly more factual accounts. Because his own library had been destroyed by the Union army, Rhett asked his son and former congressman Miles for help in gathering documents upon which to base his writing. The proposed title of this project left nothing to the imagination: "The Last Decade, seen in the extinction of Free Government in the United States, and the Downfall of the Southern Confederacy, in connexion with political Life and Services of the Honorable Robert Barnwell Rhett." This and a subsequent "Autobiography" each totaled over one hundred pages; presumably, he never finished either one.[89]

In the preface of his "Life and Services," Rhett explained that "if you tell a man a lie, every Day in the year, at the end of the year, he will believe it." The purpose of his writings, therefore, was to refute the alleged lies told recently by two northern authors. Horace Greeley's *American Conflict: A History of the Great Rebellion in the United States of America* and John W. Draper's *History of the American Civil War* were, according to Rhett, filled with "misrepresentations and falsehoods . . . repeated with a boldness and ingenuity." Rhett could not sit idly by in this contest for the control of men's minds; through his writing, he vowed, "the South will yet be heard." Since

88. Charleston *Mercury*, November 6, 1861, February 27, 1862, November 3, 12, 1864, January 13, 16, 17, February 3, 1865; Rhett to Wigfall, April 15, 1864, in Wigfall Family Papers, LC. Also see Charles E. Cauthen, *South Carolina Goes to War, 1860–1865* (Chapel Hill, 1950), chap. 15.

89. "A Conversation Concerning the Late War in the United States," in Rhett Papers, SHC; Rhett to Miles, March 22, 1871, in Miles Papers, SHC; R. B. Rhett, Jr., to Rhett, January 7, 1876, "Life and Services," and "Autobiography," all in Rhett Papers, SCHS.

the War of 1812, he wrote, the North had engaged in a systematic effort to restrain and destroy slavery. The South had always reacted defensively and eventually fought "for conservatism and political liberty, against the revolutionary violence and despotism of sectional Numbers." Rhett held Abraham Lincoln responsible for the final assault on slavery and therefore believed the president deserved to be assassinated. After the war, with the South desolated, the Constitution "all rags," and the Union "a mockery," Rhett sought to absolve himself of any blame for the failure of secession. In his autobiography, he concluded that the history of the Confederacy proved only that the "greatest blunder" of the South "was in not seceding from the Northern States long before." Ironically, to Rhett, defeat in 1865 was vindication for his calls for secession decades before.[90]

While he wrote, his health declined. In 1872 he moved to the plantation of a son-in-law in St. James Parish, Louisiana. The cancer on his face was spreading, and a series of operations in New Orleans only made his appearance more alarming. Soon he was warning all but those closest to him not to expose themselves to his hideous deformities. He managed to publish one last outburst at northern society. In a book view for the *Southern Magazine*, Rhett warned that the "money power" which he alleged was propping up the administration of President Ulysses S. Grant would lead the United States to communism. His wrath and much of his credibility spent, Rhett died on September 14, 1876. His body was returned to Charleston and buried in an unmarked grave.[91]

90. Rhett, "Life and Services" and "Autobiography," esp. 117, 120, in Rhett Papers, SCHS.

91. Rhett to Catherine Rhett, n.d., and R. B. Rhett, Jr., to Rhett, January 7, 1876, in Rhett Papers, SCHS; Rhett, "Fears for Democracy," *Southern Magazine*, September, 1875, pp. 306–32, esp. 328; White, *Rhett*, 242–43.

Palmetto Recklessness and Daring

Laurence M. Keitt and Louis T. Wigfall

A s Confederate batteries fired on Fort Sumter on April 13, 1861, a tall, powerfully built man with "wild masses of black hair, tinged with grey," appeared suddenly at a Confederate installation on Morris Island. Dressed in a blue coat, a red silk sash tied around his waist and a silk handkerchief tied around his thick neck, wearing "formidable brass spurs," Louis Trezevant Wigfall, a United States senator from Texas, made a memorable return to his native South Carolina. An English observer, enthralled by Wigfall's face, noted that his hair rose up "like the vegetation on a riverbank." His coarse, black eyebrows, his square jaw, his scrubby mustache and beard contrasted with eyes "of wonderful depth and light, such as I have never seen before but in the head of a wild beast." Wigfall's face "was flashing, fierce, yet calm—with a well of fire burning behind and spouting through it, an eye pitiless in anger, which now and then tried to conceal its expression beneath half-closed lids, and then burst out with an angry glare, as if disdaining concealment."[1]

When a shot knocked down the American flag that had been flying over Fort Sumter, Wigfall felt his moment had come. While cannon fire continued to rage in Charleston Harbor, he commandeered a small boat and ordered his two black oarsmen to row toward the walls of Sumter, despite the shouts from his comrades to return. Shots splashed all around, but the defiant Wigfall made it safely to a wharf and, with a white handkerchief tied to the end of his sword, climbed through an embrasure and into the fort. Encountering a startled Union soldier, he insisted upon meeting with his commanding officer. After terms of surrender were agreed upon, Wigfall returned to his boat and set off triumphantly for shore. Carolinians thrilled to the gallantry of their home-bred hero. A northern newspaper described his actions as an example of "Palmetto recklessness and daring."[2]

1. William Howard Russell, *My Diary North and South* (1863; rpr. Gloucester, Mass., 1969), 62–63.
2. Journal of engineer, Capt. J. G. Foster, April 13, 1861, and Brig. Gen. James

During the 1850s, a South Carolina Unionist described secessionists as "a set of young enthusiasts inspired with notions of personal honor to be defended and individual glory, fame and military
laurels to be acquired."[3] His observations suited perfectly both
Louis Wigfall and a fellow Carolina fire-eater, Laurence Massilon
Keitt. The lives and thoughts of these two reflected some of the
most powerful forces of their society and the secession movement—
romance, militance, and honor—yet often manifested themselves
in different and important ways. Each man had gained a reputation as an inflexible secessionist and eloquent, though rash, spokes-
man for the South. Their youth lent vitality to the secession movement. When the Confederacy was formed, Wigfall was forty-five
years old and Keitt only thirty-six, yet each had already worked for
disunion for over a decade. To contemporaries, Keitt represented
the personification of the southern gentleman. His gallantry and
daring in both politics and war gave him the reputation of a "chivalrous knight," whose "proud spirit rebelled against Yankee domination."[4] Wigfall, however, achieved ignoble notoriety. Although
he professed adherence to a code of gentlemanly conduct, Wigfall's
behavior frequently demonstrated crass selfishness and wanton
violence, and his fearlessness often mocked the honorable values
both he and Keitt had sworn to uphold. For both men, the idealism
and vigor that set them apart from their peers led them alter-
natively to glorious triumphs and stupendous failures.

A proclivity for violence and disruptiveness, unmatched even by
the young William L. Yancey, marked Louis Wigfall's youth. He
was born on a plantation near Edgefield, in western South Carolina, on April 21, 1816. Both his parents died by the time he turned
thirteen, leaving him to the care of a guardian, Allen B. Addison,
with more than $13,000 to provide for his needs. Addison tutored
Louis at home until 1834, when the youth left for Rice Creek
Springs School, a military academy near Columbia. After a year,
Wigfall enrolled at the University of Virginia. There, his fiery temper and immature sense of honor surfaced at a dance given by a
professor. A woman Wigfall had been dancing with thought him

Simons to Brig. Gen. Beauregard, April 23, 1861, in *The War of the Rebellion: A Compilation of the Official Records of the Union and Confederate Armies* (130 vols.; Washington, D.C., 1880–1901), Ser. I, Vol. I, 23–24, 38, hereinafter cited as *OR;* D. Girard
Wright, *A Southern Girl in '61: The War-Time Memories of a Confederate Senator's Daughter* (New York, 1905), 41–46.

3. Benjamin Perry, quoted in John Barnwell, *Love of Order: South Carolina's First
Secession Crisis* (Chapel Hill, 1982), 150.

4. *DBR,* XXXV (July–August, 1864), 103.

drunk and walked off on the arm of another man. As the couple departed, the woman's escort said something to Wigfall to which he took exception. Wigfall promptly challenged the offender to a duel. College authorities interposed and convened a court of honor to resolve the situation. The woman in question testified that she had been mistaken about Wigfall's condition at the dance; the court concluded that the entire episode had arisen out of a misconception and that no point of honor had been involved.[5]

Wigfall returned to the Palmetto State in 1836 to complete his education at South Carolina College. His behavior, however, became more disruptive. He found the orations sponsored by the college Euphradian Society more to his liking than classes; his attendance was erratic, and he often excused himself for days at a time. He developed an interest in law and used his native talent to write petitions and expositions regarding student rights. He was fond of visiting taverns off campus and throwing food in the commons on campus. In his first year there, he and a few other students left college for three months to fight in Florida as volunteers in the Seminole Indian War. Wigfall rose to the rank of lieutenant of volunteers; years later, he brashly called himself "colonel." Despite all these distractions, he managed to complete his studies and graduated in 1837.[6]

In many ways, Laurence Keitt's early years were similar to Wigfall's. Born in St. Matthews on October 4, 1824, Keitt grew up in Orangeburg District in the midlands. Like Wigfall, Keitt attended a private school. A childhood friend once reminisced with Keitt that while they attended St. Matthews Academy, "You were famous for foot races, the gift of gab, and for never wincing when your [sic] were flogged," implying, of course, that the youth often incurred the wrath of his teachers. Also like Wigfall, Keitt attended South Carolina College. Although Keitt found the activities of the Euphradian Society as alluring as did Wigfall, the study of history and political economy also captured his interest. He studied under Francis Lieber, professor of political economy and a devout Unionist.[7]

Keitt and Wigfall believed that they would do great things in their lives. They knew that South Carolina College served as a breeding ground for the state's leaders; throughout the antebellum

5. Alvy L. King, *Louis T. Wigfall: Southern Fire-Eater* (Baton Rouge, 1970), 8–12.

6. Daniel W. Hollis, *South Carolina College* (Columbia, S.C., 1951), 138, 253, Vol. I of Hollis, *University of South Carolina*, 2 vols.; King, *Wigfall*, 16.

7. John Holt Merchant, Jr., "Laurence M. Keitt: South Carolina Fire-Eater" (Ph.D. dissertation, University of Virginia, 1976), 11–16.

period, the college produced almost half of South Carolina's state and federal officers. Wigfall's closest friend at school was John L. Manning, who would become governor in 1852. The social status of their respective families further enhanced their sense of destiny. Wigfall's mother, Eliza Trezevant, descended from one of the state's oldest families, French Huguenots who settled in the colony in the 1690s. His father, Levi Durant Wigfall, was a successful merchant in Charleston before he moved to an up-country plantation. The sizable inheritance he left for his son seemingly guaranteed a life of success, comfort, and ease for young Lewis, as he was then called. Keitt's ancestry was equally notable. His grandfather, George Kitts, moved from Bermuda to Big Bull Swamp near Orangeburg around 1760. Three of his four sons, preferring a more unusual name, changed the spelling of theirs to Keitt. Laurence's father, also named George, owned Puritan Hall, a plantation near St. Matthews. By his death in 1861, George Keitt's holdings included twenty-five hundred acres and more than fifty slaves. Because of their background of wealthy families and an influential college, both Keitt and Wigfall left school with great expectations.[8]

Initially, both young men attempted careers in law. Wigfall soon discovered that success was far from automatic. In 1839 he returned to Edgefield, where his brother Arthur had a lucrative practice. Arthur planned to retire soon, enter the ministry, and leave his business to his younger brother. The ambitious junior partner had problems from the start. He found "mere office business" deadening. Worse, over the past several years he had not only squandered his inheritance but also accumulated debts. Even when he began to make money through his practice, he could not support himself on his earnings. He soon began a "very foolish course" of borrowing and spending. At first, he blamed his troubles on "my gentleman-blackleg friends" but after careful introspection realized that "my entire want of *common sense* damned nearly ruined me." For the present, he could only dream of a time "when juries shall hang upon my lips & courts shall bow to my decisions" and large fees would fill his pockets. When he stopped dreaming, he knew that it might take him a decade to "establish some reputation as a back-country lawyer" and earn a decent income.[9]

Wigfall's recklessness continued. Occasionally he tried to reform

8. Hollis, *South Carolina College*, 256–58; King, *Wigfall*, 8–9; Merchant, "Keitt," 10.

9. L. T. Wigfall to John L. Manning, March 23, [no year given], April, 1839, in Wigfall Family Papers, BTHC. The Wigfall papers in the Barker Texas History

himself, "to see some things 'face to face,'" in the hope that "I will not be such a damned fool as I have been." To his old college friend John Manning he once declared, "Wine, *women* & cards and your humble servant have . . . *finally shaken hands.*" The new Wigfall would be "virtuous & sensible & like other people." Either to convince Manning or himself, he repeated: "Wine & women have lost their charmes [*sic*] for me. Ambition shall be my mistress & Law my Liquor!" He admitted that the old Wigfall did not adhere to such resolves, but he now swore, "I have lost all relish for the things that once gave me pleasure." As proof, Wigfall told Manning of a trip he had just made to Augusta, Georgia. "I neither attended the race-course, houses of a certain description or got *even tipsey* at dinner," he boasted. "I am a predestined old bachelor," Wigfall added. "I have *calmly determined never to marry.*" [10]

But Wigfall was a weak as well as a passionate man. Despite his awareness that indulgence had almost ruined him, he could tolerate his new life-style for only a few months. "All my pleasures are past," he complained to Manning late in 1839. "I live now with no brighter prospect than that of being able to kill time." He grew so depressed that he briefly contemplated suicide. Because he could not both control his urges and be happy, he quickly abandoned his efforts at personal reform. Soon he was again spending beyond his means, and in 1841 he married. Even after his bride-to-be, Charlotte Cross, had loaned him some money, Wigfall owed over $1,300 to various creditors by October, 1841. His financial difficulties cost Wigfall the respect of many in Edgefield and eventually alienated him from Manning. Over the next five years Wigfall's troubles increased. A son, John Manning Wigfall, died at the age of three after a short lifetime of illness. When the Wigfalls could no longer appease their creditors, they lost their home and property in a sheriff's sale in 1844. They recovered briefly, but by the spring of 1846, the Edgefield sheriff returned. This time they lost everything: their home, their four slaves, their livestock, his books. This time the plaintiffs included his brother Arthur. [11]

For Laurence Keitt success came as easily as recklessness and ill

---

Center are typescript copies of those in the Williams-Chesnut-Manning Collection, South Caroliniana Library, Columbia, South Carolina.

10. Wigfall to Manning, n.d., and March 23, [no year given], Wigfall Papers, BTHC.

11. Wigfall to Manning, September 24, 1839, October 24, 1841, July 29, October 1, 1843, January 3, 1844, *ibid.;* King, *Wigfall*, 36, 38; Edgefield *Advertiser*, May 13, 27, 1846.

fortune did for Wigfall. After college, Keitt moved to Charleston and read law under the tutelage of James L. Petigru, one of the leading attorneys in South Carolina. Keitt passed his bar examination in 1844 and eagerly returned to Orangeburg to open his own practice.[12]

Although law occupied his time, politics captured his imagination. Early in 1846, he traveled to Washington, D.C., to observe the process of government at first hand. Initially, the United States Senate confirmed his naive and fantastic notions about American politics. He reported to his former teacher Professor Lieber that the Senate was "as august and noble a body as ever dignified the fame of old Rome." Soon, however, Keitt discovered that the political process and the nation's leaders were not so pristine as they had appeared to him in his college studies and at first glance in the capitol. He observed that debate over territorial expansion turned the House of Representatives into a den of "intrigue and corruption." After reflecting upon his visit, and with characteristic cockiness, he told Lieber, "I was astonished last winter at Washington to discover the fat and cumbrous errors of hoary headed and renowned Politicians, upon points which appeared to me lucid and obvious." To Keitt, congressmen had transformed the rather simple territorial issue into a "gordian Knot," one which they might find themselves unable to unravel without a sword.[13] Keitt's trip had a profound impact on him. Confident in his own intellect and abilities and disappointed by the quality of representation in Washington, he decided to run for public office.

When Keitt turned his attention to politics, he found that sectional issues continued to command the most attention in South Carolina. Carolinians of Keitt and Wigfall's generation could not recall a time when the relationship of state and federal governments had not been seriously questioned; Wigfall was only twelve when the tariff controversy first rocked the state in 1828, and Keitt was but eight years old when the compromise tariff of 1833 temporarily quieted it. For most of their lives men like Keitt and Wigfall heard people like Barnwell Rhett issue both ominous warnings about the danger the South faced in the Union and demands for firm resistance. As Keitt entered adulthood, he viewed the conflict

12. Merchant, "Keitt," 17. Merchant notes that any records pertaining to Keitt's law practice were destroyed by the army of General William T. Sherman on its march through the Carolinas in 1865.

13. L. M. Keitt to Francis Lieber, January 18, September 2, 1846, in Francis Lieber Papers, HL.

between North and South as "momentous" and the Union as filled
with potential "catastrophe to the South." He therefore responded
to Rhett's calls for defiance. In 1847, a year before he ran for state
office, Keitt began to build his political platform. Because several
northern states had enacted laws that interfered with the retrieval
of fugitive slaves, Keitt determined that these "forays, of such an
insolent and rapacious kind, as have been perpetrated upon us by
the North, should not pass unnoticed and unredressed." "Piracy
justifies Letters of Mark and Reprisal," he believed. Confident that
he would be elected to the legislature, he pledged to introduce a bill
to prohibit South Carolina "from extending any aid in the collection of debts, due to citizens of any State," which had circumvented
the federal fugitive slave laws.[14]

The people of Orangeburg elected Keitt to the first of three consecutive terms in the lower house of the legislature in 1848. As he
waited for sectional issues to reach the floor, he participated in a
brief surge of reform. Keitt, like Yancey and John Quitman, supported the establishment of free schools and a state penitentiary.
He also served on a committee charged with nominating trustees
for South Carolina College. The moment the legislature turned its
attention to national politics, however, Keitt seized his opportunity.
The speech that accompanied his resolution regarding fugitive
slaves drew the attention and praise of the Charleston *Mercury*.
Later, Keitt endorsed fire-eating state representative Whitemarsh
Seabrook's resolution that either passage of the Wilmot Proviso
or the abolition of slavery in the District of Columbia would be
grounds for disunion. Furthermore, Keitt moved that the South
Carolina legislature support any southern congressman who refused to vote for anyone for Speaker of the House of Representatives who was "in the slightest degree tainted with unsoundness
on the slavery question." This resolution drew the approval of Seabrook and of Benjamin C. Yancey, the brother of Alabama's pre-
mier fire-eater.[15]

As the sectional conflict intensified in 1850, Keitt grew more
strident. In March, he joined former Blufftonite David F. Jamison

14. L. M. Keitt to John C. Calhoun, October 1, 1847, in Chauncey S. Boucher
and Robert P. Brooks, eds., *Correspondence Addressed to John C. Calhoun, 1837–1849*
(Washington, D.C., 1930), 402.
15. Merchant, "Keitt," 18; Charleston *Mercury*, November 29, December 8, 10,
20, 22, 1849. For an overview of reforms and state regulations see Lacy K. Ford,
Origins of Southern Radicalism: The South Carolina Upcountry, 1800–1860 (Oxford,
1988), 308–37.

at a public meeting in Orangeburg. Keitt called for firm, resolute southern resistance to the impending congressional compromise; Jamison said that unless the forthcoming Nashville Convention could salvage southern rights, the South must dissolve the Union. After Nashville failed to satisfy southern radicals, Keitt helped Jamison create a Southern Rights Association in Orangeburg to promote secession. The *Mercury* reported that Keitt delivered "a brilliant and powerful address" at the association's first meeting, one which "rivetted the attention and kindled the feelings of his auditory into burning indignation against our oppressors and intense enthusiasm in defence of the rights of the South." If necessary, the young orator announced, South Carolina must secede alone. By 1851, Keitt had placed himself irrevocably in the camp of Barnwell Rhett and the seceders. South Carolina "must stand erect or crouch," he once explained. "I shall offer no objection to her crouching, if it be only the crouching of the lion, preparing with strained sinews and contracted muscle to spring with more deadly aim upon his foe." For the rest of the year, Keitt preached, "Loyalty to the Union is treason to liberty." He spoke throughout Orangeburg and in Charleston, appearing with Jamison, with Rhett, and alone.[16]

In October, 1851, Carolinians chose cooperationists over secessionists by an overwhelming margin in an election for delegates to a special convention to discuss secession. Keitt was stunned. He could not believe that the convention would not act; he could not believe the people had rejected secession. When he faced the reality that secession had failed, he grew sullen. For the remainder of his tenure in the statehouse he spoke infrequently and without the fire and zeal that had made him famous. His daring stand for secession, however, won him a special place in the hearts of voters in the Third Congressional District (the one Rhett had represented for over a decade). When a special election was held there to fill a vacancy, Keitt won by a large majority. He would continue to represent this district until his state seceded in 1860. When he departed for Washington in the fall of 1853, the new congressman had just turned twenty-nine.[17]

Keitt thoroughly enjoyed life in Washington. He frequently attended balls and mingled with members of the South Carolina con-

16. Charleston *Mercury*, March 27, October 16, 1850, June 19, August 8, September 4, 18, 20, 1851.

17. *Ibid.*, December 9, 1851; Merchant, "Keitt," 36–40.

gressional delegation. James H. Hammond became a close friend; the two once caroused until early in the morning and lied to their wives when they came home. Representative John McQueen recalled a "flying visit" from Keitt in which he spent "two or three hours with a fair one near us two weeks ago, & about thirty minutes at my house, & was off about as rapidly as they send word across the Atlantic by Telegraph." To Keitt, only the charms of women rivaled his love of politics. Before his marriage to Sue Sparks of South Carolina in 1859, Keitt had established quite a reputation. "We must limit Keitt as to the Belles," another colleague remarked; "he will interfere too much with the other single men." For a time Keitt turned his romantic attention to Harriet Lane, niece of President James Buchanan and acting first lady in the bachelor's White House. Politics, however, remained his true love. Keitt bragged to Sue about "the cheers of my own success," and he believed "I may fairly grasp at anything." [18]

In contrast to Keitt, Wigfall never held public office before he left South Carolina. For years he denied having any interest in a political career, though he admitted that political affairs fascinated him. His first public speech, however, gave him more satisfaction than his fledgling law practice. Although it was entirely apolitical, the Fourth of July oration he delivered in 1839 "proved more agreeable to the palates of 'my friends & fellow citizens' than I had even *hoped*." Smugly he told Manning, "I am told it has done me some credit." After this speech, Wigfall began to participate in public affairs in various unofficial capacities. When Manning's uncle John Richardson ran for governor in 1840, Wigfall and Manning acquired control of the Edgefield *Advertiser* and used it as a campaign organ for Richardson, with Wigfall serving as editor. His outspoken denunciation of Richardson's foes later resulted in a series of duels and fights that, combined with his chronic debt, would drive him from the state. [19]

Two years before he left, however, he gained his first experience in the politics of sectionalism when he joined the ranks of the

---

18. Keitt to Sue Sparks, n.d., January 20, May 9, July 11, September 11, 1855, April 30, 1856, Sue to her mother, December 26, [1859], in Laurence M. Keitt Papers, WPL; John McQueen to W. P. Miles, September 28, 1858; M. L. Bonham to Miles, January 30, 1858, in William P. Miles Papers, SHC; Merchant, "Keitt," 275–76.

19. Wigfall to Manning, March 23, [no year given], April, July 27, 1839, January 29, February 17, 1840, in Wigfall Papers, BTHC; Edgefield *Advertiser*, January 30, February 27, May 14, 1840; King, *Wigfall*, 26–27.

Bluffton Boys. A settlement of the tariff question in 1844, Wigfall said, should not "be hindered by our supposed allegiance to the Federal Government." He claimed that southerners could not trust the Democratic party on the tariff, preventing Congress from discussing slavery, or Texas annexation. Wigfall considered the latter "the paramount issue of the times." Although he believed the Democrats' presidential candidate, James K. Polk, favored Texas annexation, Wigfall asserted that Polk's party was an impotent "airy nothing." Like other Blufftonites, Wigfall called for a state convention to take appropriate action if the new administration failed to promote southern interests. "I confess my decided preference of Secession over Nullification," he announced.[20]

The Bluffton controversy waned, and Wigfall's political activity in South Carolina ended with it. Wigfall once told Manning that if he ever felt compelled to leave South Carolina, he would first run for a seat in the legislature. "I can I believe be elected & it would give a young man in a new state some reputation to be a member of the S.C. Legislature." If he did leave, Wigfall explained, he would move west, perhaps to Texas.[21] When he did depart for the Lone Star State in 1846, however, Wigfall took with him only a reputation for violence, drunkenness, and insolvency, not the prestige of having been a legislator.

Upon his arrival in Texas in the fall of 1846, Wigfall tried to put his tumultuous past behind him and once again focused his attention on law. He settled first in Nacogdoches, where he shared a practice with William B. Ochiltree, a friend of one of his cousins who had already moved to Texas. Discovering that his skills as an attorney compared favorably with those of most frontier lawyers, he established his own law office in Marshall, the seat of Harrison County in northeastern Texas. Wigfall received so much satisfaction from his new success and recognition that he seemingly ceased worrying about his continued financial problems. He borrowed money from Benjamin Yancey and from creditors in Texas, only to lose it all in bad investments.[22]

Once established as a lawyer, however, Wigfall resumed an active interest in politics. In 1848, he represented Harrison County at a Democratic meeting in Galveston. As chair of the resolutions

20. Edgefield *Advertiser*, June 5, September 11, 25, 1844.

21. Wigfall to Manning, March 23, [no year given], in Wigfall Papers, BTHC.

22. King, *Wigfall*, 49–50; Benjamin C. Franklin to Benjamin C. Yancey, November 5, 1852, William L. Yancey to Benjamin C. Yancey, February 5, 1855, in Benjamin C. Yancey Papers, SHC.

committee, he supported and presented the convention's declaration that the Wilmot Proviso was unconstitutional. The next year, Wigfall tried to put teeth into that resolution by announcing that passage of the proviso might lead to dissolution of the Union. During the summer of 1849, he boldly attacked the popular senator Sam Houston's position on the territorial question. Wigfall chastised Houston for failing to sign John C. Calhoun's Southern Address. He claimed that the former president of Texas placed "our liberties and our lives . . . upon the political gaming table" to appease northerners and enhance his chances of becoming president of the United States. Why else, Wigfall asked, would Houston "gag Texas, when her sister states are speaking?" Wigfall publicly condemned Houston for "placing himself upon the free-soil platform." [23]

The people of Harrison County rewarded Wigfall for his boldness by sending him to fill a vacant seat in the lower house of the Texas legislature. In 1850, that body in turn selected him as a delegate to the Nashville Convention. Unwilling to leave his first elective office even temporarily, he declined to go but asked another delegate, John P. Henderson, to bring his proposal for five constitutional amendments to Nashville. Wigfall thought his amendments would bring a final adjustment to the sectional conflict. The first two explicitly denied Congress the power to tamper with the interstate slave trade and slavery in the District of Columbia. The third stated that the people of the territories, and not Congress, would create all laws pertaining to their territories except those concerning slavery, which no one could prohibit during the territorial period. The fourth prohibited Congress from "receiving, discussing, referring or reporting, upon any petition upon the subject of slavery." The last was the most drastic. It called for a ban against future constitutional amendments regarding slavery, "except by the unanimous consent of all the states." Wigfall's proposals gained editorial support from De Bow's Review but had no impact at Nashville. Nevertheless, when Henderson returned from Tennessee, Wigfall joined him at a public meeting in Marshall that endorsed both Rhett's radical Nashville address and a decision to send a Texas delegation to a second Nashville Convention. [24]

23. King, Wigfall, 51–52, 55; Marshall Texas Republican, July 6, November 8, 1849, hereinafter cited as Texas Republican.

24. King, Wigfall, 55; Wigfall to J. P. Henderson, March 9, 1850, in Texas Republican, April 18, 1850; Texas Republican, April 18, July 6, 1850; DBR, IX (July, 1850), 123–24.

The Compromise of 1850 and the failure of southern resistance failed to quiet Wigfall. Returned to the legislature for the rest of the decade, he established a reputation as "a thorough going fire eater from South Carolina." Wigfall denounced both the new Know-Nothing and Republican parties as tools of abolitionism and enemies of the South. He called for a filibustering expedition to seize Nicaragua for southern expansion and argued for the re-opening of the African slave trade.[25]

During the 1850s, Wigfall campaigned against Sam Houston and Unionism in Texas. While delegates assembled at Nashville, Wigfall helped states'-rights Democrats in the Texas legislature pass a resolution condemning Houston for laxity in protecting the rights of Texas in the United States Senate. When the senator ran for reelection in 1857, he refused to engage in public debate, so Wigfall followed him throughout the state and spoke wherever Houston did. This infuriated Houston. He began to call Wigfall "Wiggletail" and said that his antagonist had come to Texas only to escape the law in South Carolina, where, as a lawyer, he had swindled his clients. Either Wigfall never heard these barbs or he decided that the effort to dethrone Houston required him to control himself because, uncharacteristically, he did not respond in kind. This campaign earned Wigfall a reputation as the only man in Texas who ever proved a match for Houston on the stump; his efforts also helped force the senator out of office that fall.[26]

Wigfall's assault on Houston captured the attention of many Texans. By 1859, some talked of sending him to the United States Senate, even though the Marshall *Texas Republican* noted that no one in the state was "more obnoxious to Houston and his followers."[27] After news of John Brown's raid into Virginia reached Texas in October, however, Wigfall emerged as a serious candidate. Many Texans, believing the Republican party responsible for

25. John E. Campbell to his brother, November 16, 1859, in John E. Campbell Papers, BTHC; *Texas Republican*, October 11, 1856; William L. Yancey to L. T. Wigfall, April 16, 1858, in Wigfall Family Papers, LC; Dallas *Herald*, June 1, 1859; King, *Wigfall*, 67–68.

26. A. W. Terrell, "Recollections of General Sam Houston," *Southwestern Historical Quarterly*, XVI (October, 1912), 118–19; Amelia W. Williams and Eugene C. Barker, eds., *The Writings of Sam Houston, 1813–1863* (8 vols.; Austin, 1942), VII, 28; C. W. Raines, ed., *Six Decades in Texas; or, Memoirs of Francis Richard Lubbock, Governor of Texas in War-Time, 1861–63* (Austin, 1900), 256–57; King, *Wigfall*, 63–64.

27. Lorenzo Sherwood to L. T. Wigfall, February 8, 1858, in Thomas B. King Papers, SHC; Dallas *Herald*, July 3, 1858; *Texas Republican*, October 8, December 10, 17, 1859.

fomenting Brown's attack on the South, decided to retaliate by sending "the most violent partisan in the state" to Congress. When the legislature convened to elect a senator in December, 1859, anti-Republican hysteria prevented consideration of Congressman John Reagan, a moderate, for reelection and kept Houston's forces from effectively opposing Wigfall. Intoxicated by his recent triumph over Houston—and, perhaps, also by alcohol—Wigfall stood in a hallway in the capitol and told a friend sarcastically, "A lot of those fellows are fine specimens of legislators to be vested with the power of electing a gentleman to the United States Senate." When his friend warned him not to voice such reckless statements, Wigfall snapped: "I don't care a d——n. The fact remains that a whole lot of 'em are copperas breeched hayseeds and have no business here." After heated debate and three ballots, the legislators chose Wigfall over six others. When Sam Houston heard of Wigfall's election, he supposedly exclaimed, "Thank God this country is so great and strong, it can bear even that."[28]

Wigfall took his seat in Congress in January, 1860, joining Keitt in the "grand and glorious field" of politics. Each believed he could alter or control public affairs through his own actions. Both exemplified the commitment to individualism, passion, and intuition so characteristic of nineteenth-century romanticism. Beginning as a philosophical reaction against the reason and rationality of the Enlightenment, romanticism emphasized internal human drives over the external laws of nature, change and dynamism over uniformity and structure. Romantics viewed institutions as malleable, and instead of trying to force government to conform to natural laws they believed that governments must reflect the changing nature of man and society. In the American South, romanticism supported the concept of honor and its emphasis on personal distinction and bold action. For the individual, romanticism meant freeing the personality and taking risks in life. To Keitt and Wigfall, it meant the more daring the better.[29]

28. Norman G. Kittrell, *Governors Who Have Been, and Other Public Men of Texas* (Houston, 1921), 150; *Texas Republican*, December 24, 1859; C. Vann Woodward, ed., *Mary Chesnut's Civil War* (New Haven, 1981), 86; King, *Wigfall*, 70–74.

29. *Congressional Globe*, 36th Cong., 1st Sess., 322. See Russel B. Nye, *The Cultural Life of the New Nation, 1776–1830* (New York, 1960), 6–9; A. O. Lovejoy, "The Meaning of Romanticism for the Historian of Ideas," *Journal of the History of Ideas*, II (1941), 257–78; and Clement Eaton, *The Mind of the Old South* (Baton Rouge, 1976), 245–48.

"Life, in the very texture of the word, means struggle, motion, purpose, object," said Keitt. Keitt believed that one attained strength and power by defining a purpose in life and focusing on it. One could win power in the political world only "by superiority, at least by haughty self-independence and assertion, and not by dexterous trimming and whining submission." To fully realize one's destiny in life, one's purpose and potential power, Keitt said, "We may not—and often, cannot—control our spirit, soul, intellect." Keitt believed that people must let their hearts lead them and follow vigorously the dictates of the spirit instead of the mind. "Power lies in the blood, in its motion," he thought. "Where it dances wildly there cannot be weakness." For Keitt, action generated by impulse was not only infallible, it was also mystical. He held that "enthusiasm is of kin to divinity and to high purpose." All persons—and particularly all politicians—therefore had a duty to remain active, to take their destinies into their own hands. One could never allow another to impede one's course in life, no matter the consequences. He pitied or despised those who allowed "grass and stubble and straw" to block their actions, those who sought "no perils and no earnestness of purpose" in life's struggles. "Audacity drew the people to me and gave me a hold upon them," Keitt boasted early in his congressional career. "Boldness," he told Sue, "is the key to success." Only once in his life did he ever fear that this daring had made him a "reckless man." [30]

The event that tested Keitt's faith in spontaneity was the assault by Preston Brooks on Charles Sumner. On May 19 and 20, 1856, Sumner, a Republican senator from Massachusetts, delivered a speech on the Senate floor that he later called "The Crime Against Kansas." In it, he singled out a senator from South Carolina, Andrew P. Butler, for embracing the "harlot slavery," ridiculed the infirm southerner for discharging "the loose expectoration of his speech," and called him a liar. Butler was absent when Sumner made these remarks, but Brooks, a representative from South Carolina and Butler's cousin, heard about the speech and decided to punish Sumner unless he apologized for dishonoring his kinsman. On May 21, Brooks told three of his closest friends—Keitt and representatives Henry Edmundson of Virginia and James L. Orr of South Carolina—of his intentions. The next day, Keitt and

30. Keitt to Sue Sparks, January 20, February 14, July 11, 1855, July 7, September 11, November 6, 1856, and n.d., in Keitt Papers, WPL.

Edmundson accompanied Brooks to the Senate chamber. There, Brooks found Sumner seated at his desk, chastised him, and beat him repeatedly with his cane. Blood gushed from Sumner's head as he lunged from his seat and collapsed to the floor. Keitt, who had hoped to witness the assault, had his view blocked when a constituent detained him behind the president's chair. When he heard the commotion, Keitt rushed out in time to see others coming to Sumner's aid. Furious that anyone would interfere with what he considered a chivalric act, Keitt himself brandished a cane and warned bystanders to stay away. He then led Brooks from the room and helped him clean a cut he had received on his head from the recoil of his cane; Sumner lay unconscious and seriously wounded.[31]

The House of Representatives formed a committee of five to investigate the affair. The committee issued two reports: a majority report by the three northern members and a minority report by the two southerners. The majority said that Brooks should be expelled from the House forthwith and Keitt and Edmundson be censured for knowing about plans for the assault but doing nothing to stop it. The minority, in characteristic southern fashion, found no specific provision in the Constitution that empowered the House to punish its own members for "alleged" assaults and therefore refused to express an official opinion. The House acted on the majority report on July 14 and voted to expel Brooks. The congressman, however, resigned first. The next day, the House voted to censure Keitt; on July 16, Keitt resigned.[32] Neither would allow Congress to impugn his honor. Both decided to seek vindication for their actions from the people of South Carolina by seeking reelection to the seats they had just vacated.

Shortly after the attack on Sumner, Keitt wrote to his fiancée that Brooks "combined in happy proportion freedom of speech and freedom of the cudgel." He reported that everyone in Washington "feels as if we are upon a volcano. I am glad of it," he explained, "for I am tired of stagnation." After a few weeks of reflection, Keitt briefly doubted the correctness of his own actions in the

---

31. Merchant, "Keitt," 99–106, is the best account of Keitt's role in this episode. Also see *Congressional Globe*, 34th Cong., 1st Sess., 1289, 1292–93, 1348–52, 1355–59, and App., 656, 886.

32. *Congressional Globe*, 34th Cong., 1st Sess., 1348–52, 1628, 1641. Although the House voted 121–95 to expel Brooks, it lacked the necessary two-thirds vote to implement expulsion. See David H. Donald, *Charles Sumner and the Coming of the Civil War* (New York, 1960), 308.

affair. After he resigned and returned to South Carolina, however, he vigorously defended himself and Brooks. Brooks acted, Keitt said, in compliance with the code of honor. Attacks upon honor could not be corrected by lawyers or courts. Southerners believed that without defense of honor "a man's person is not worth protecting." Brooks had "redressed a wrong to his blood and his State, and he did it in a fair and manly way." According to the code of honor, Keitt noted, a gentleman like Brooks could not challenge a "cur" such as Sumner to a duel but had to beat him as though he were a beast. Keitt explained his censure by claiming that abolitionists had conspired to discredit him. He told Carolinians that even though he knew of Brooks's intentions, there was no complicity in carrying out the act. His only offense was that he did not turn informer and that he believed it dishonorable to betray even a bitter enemy's confidence to one's closest friend. He therefore decided to take his fate out of the hands of those with no understanding of southern honor and place it in those "among whom honor is maintained." The people of South Carolina sustained him and Brooks in the fall; they reelected Keitt without opposition.[33]

Despite his commitment to the code of honor, Keitt worried that "rudimental notions of what is truly honorable and great" led many southerners to forsake "the intenser glories of the intellect" in favor of "the daring of the violent." Louis Wigfall shared Keitt's dedication to honor and a life of action but not the apprehension that such a life might impede intellectual enrichment. In fact, Wigfall once stated that he would rather risk his life "than possess the intellect of a Bacon or a Locke."[34] In contrast to Keitt, Wigfall saw the code of honor merely as a rationalization for violence and the unfettering of the spirit as a justification for recklessness.

From 1839 to 1841 Wigfall engaged in a series of fights and duels that gained him a reputation for bloodthirstiness. In 1839 he

33. Keitt to [Sue Sparks], May 29, July 7, 1856, in Keitt Papers, WPL; Charleston *Mercury*, July 24, 25, October 16, 1856; New York *Times*, July 17, October 14, 1856. For the importance of honor and violence in southern society see Kenneth S. Greenberg, *Masters and Statesmen: The Political Culture of American Slavery* (Baltimore, 1985), 23–41, and Greenberg, "The Nose, the Lie, and the Duel in the Antebellum South," *American Historical Review*, XCV (1990), 57–74; Bertram Wyatt-Brown, *Southern Honor: Ethics and Behavior in the Old South* (Oxford, 1982); John Hope Franklin, *The Militant South* (New York, 1956); Dickson D. Bruce, *Violence and Culture in the Antebellum South* (Austin, 1979).

34. Charleston *Mercury*, June 29, 1858; Wigfall to Manning, March 23, [no year given], in Wigfall Papers, BTHC.

served as a second for a friend in a duel with Joseph Glover of Edgefield. During this duel Wigfall risked an encounter with Glover when he shouted to his friend, "Blow the damned scoundrel's brains out." A few months later, Preston Brooks resurrected Wigfall's conflict with Glover by stating publicly that Wigfall had called the latter a coward. Wigfall denied this and called Brooks a liar. When Wigfall and Brooks confronted each other in June, 1840, a fistfight broke out. When it ended, Brooks said that he would challenge Wigfall to a duel unless Wigfall challenged him first. Some of Brooks's friends urged him to wait a few weeks and practice because Wigfall was already known to be "a *good* shot." [35]

Friends of both belligerents quickly interceded. A group of prominent men, including Franklin Elmore, Pierce Butler, and Wade Hampton, formed a board of honor in an attempt to prevent hostilities. After an investigation, the board concluded that Brooks had heard Wigfall insult Glover before a reconciliation occurred between the two and, therefore, Wigfall's charge that Brooks had lied was invalid. The findings of the board, however, only delayed a confrontation. Brooks stated publicly that Wigfall had backed down and continued to insist that Wigfall had called Glover a coward. Wigfall published his response to Brooks in the Edgefield *Advertiser*, but Brooks was out of town at the time. In his absence his father, Colonel Whitfield Brooks, published an abusive letter to Wigfall. Wigfall challenged the colonel to a duel; he refused, and in accordance with the *code duello* Wigfall began to post placards in Edgefield denouncing the colonel as a coward and a scoundrel. J. P. Carroll and Thomas Bird, both related to the Brooks family, tried to meet Wigfall and reason with him before he posted the colonel, but they were too late. When Carroll tore down a placard, Bird thought Wigfall was about to shoot Carroll, so Bird fired twice at Wigfall. He missed. Wigfall then shot at Bird, "taking cool and deliberate aim," and mortally wounded him. Carroll then approached Wigfall, "and calmly said to him that he was a cold-blooded murderous scoundrel." For this, Wigfall immediately challenged Carroll to a duel. In November, the two met on an island in the Savannah River. Both fired and missed, and their seconds arranged an end to that affair. A week later, Wigfall and Preston Brooks met on the same site. Both missed with their first shot; with the second, Brooks struck Wigfall in the thigh, and Wigfall shot Brooks

35. Wigfall to Manning, March 23, [no year given], in Wigfall Papers, BTHC; J. P. Carroll to James H. Hammond, June 30, 1840, in James H. Hammond Papers, LC; King, *Wigfall*, 21, 29–30.

through the hip. As they laid weakened from their wounds, they agreed to allow a board of honor to try again to resolve their conflict.[36]

The board's settlement seemed to favor Wigfall, yet he was not satisfied. "I can stand any thing but being told that *my honor* is as good as *Preston Brooks'*," Wigfall fumed. He still wanted to publish a statement condemning Brooks as a liar. Brooks's injury was severe, however, and he had to use a cane the rest of his life. Although later he would use this cane to assault Charles Sumner, for the time being Brooks determined to avoid violent confrontations. Carroll believed that Wigfall had learned of Brooks's resolution to reject all future challenges to duels and would continue to harass Brooks as long as he knew that his nemesis would no longer "call him to account." In March, 1841, Wigfall told Brooks, "I do not consider all matters connected with our late difficulties entirely satisfied, and I shall take the earliest opportunity practicable to vindicate myself." All Edgefield believed yet another duel would transpire, "and a feeling akin to horror is inspired by Wigfall's supposed blood-thirstiness." Others interposed again. They agreed to another board's finding, which finally laid the matter to rest.[37]

"These difficulties in which I have for the last eighteen months been engaged have ruined my [law] practice," Wigfall conceded. They also stigmatized him for life. At least one Carolinian wished that Wigfall would leave Edgefield. James H. Hammond thought him "wholly unprincipled & treacherous to the last degree." Even after he left the Palmetto State, Wigfall could not escape his notoriety. Sam Houston denounced him as a murderer. After the dissolution of the Union, the New York *Tribune* referred to him as a "brawling traitor," and *Harper's Weekly* erroneously reported that he had shot eight men in various duels. His reputation preceded him to Fort Sumter, where a Union officer worried about this "parlous man" who he had heard was "quick to settle disputed points with the pistol."[38]

36. King, *Wigfall*, 31–33; Edgefield *Advertiser*, November 5, 1840; J. P. Carroll to Hammond, November 1, 7, 8, 1840, in Hammond Papers, LC; D. C. Ray to C. W. Lord, June 9, 1925, in Wigfall Papers, BTHC.

37. Wigfall to Manning, April 25, 1841, in Wigfall Papers, BTHC; J. P. Carroll to Hammond, June 12, 19, 1841, and to J. H. Hammond, J. S. Preston, Thos. Stark, W. Hampton, *et al.*, June 15, 1841, in Hammond Papers, LC; John B. Edmunds, Jr., *Francis W. Pickens and the Politics of Destruction* (Chapel Hill, 1986), 52; Wigfall to Brooks, March 5, 1841, in Edgefield *Advertiser*, July 22, 1841.

38. Wigfall to Manning, October 17, 1841, in Wigfall Papers, BTHC; M. L. Bonham to Hammond, June 15, 1841, Hammond to Marcellus C. M. Hammond,

Wigfall once told his daughter that he believed the code of honor improved "both the morals and the manners of a community" by engendering "a most restraining tendency on the errant fancy." It certainly would in any community that included Louis T. Wigfall and his hypersensitivity to attacks on his perception of his honor. Although he never dueled again after 1840, Wigfall's commitment to other forms of violence parodied chivalric notions of gentlemanly behavior. In 1844 he based his preference for governor on the willingness of one candidate to use force against the federal government. "Seabrook is for resistance—war at once—war to the knife—*He* would *therefore* get my vote." When discussing the guerrilla warfare that led to the sobriquet "Bloody Kansas" in the 1850s, Wigfall dispassionately remarked, "Let Kansas bleed if she has a fancy for it." "Blood is a very common fluid," Senator Wigfall said while discussing the possibility of civil war. "It is worth very little. A man is killed, it does not matter much; it is really a matter of small consequence to him, to his family, or to the country."[39]

For both Wigfall and Keitt southern honor was as important as personal honor. They agreed with the Rhetts when they said, "No people degraded can be free." Keitt had believed that the Compromise of 1850 so insulted the South that its people must either dissolve the Union or be "degraded and manacled." Because southerners owned slaves, Keitt asked his northern counterparts in Congress: "Would you 'form a more perfect union' by stigmatizing and degrading us (the South) from equality with you? 'Establish justice' by excluding us from territory won by our common blood and treasure, and seizing the whole of it to yourselves, (the North?)." The South, he explained, would be "base" and "craven" to "submit to the overthrow of her honor, peace, and existence." To Keitt, such submission would "make us change places with our slaves." Rather than allow the North to dishonor the South by surrounding her with "a belt of fire," Keitt threatened that southerners would "burst the wall of fire, though the flames should shrivel our sinews

May 20, 1843, in Hammond Papers, LC; Terrell, "Recollections of General Sam Houston," 119; New York *Tribune* in *Texas Republican,* February 23, 1861; *Harper's Weekly* in *Texas Republican,* May 18, 1861; Abner Doubleday, *Reminiscences of Forts Sumter and Moultrie in 1860–61* (New York, 1876), 164.

39. Wright, *Southern Girl in '61,* 31–32; L. Wigfall to A. Burt, April 7, 1844, in Armistead Burt Papers, WPL; Wigfall to S. S. Thompson and others, August 25, 1858, in Dallas *Herald,* December 8, 1858; *Congressional Globe,* 36th Cong., 1st Sess., 1301–1302.

and blast our eyeballs, resolved to fall, if fall they must, struggling blindly it may be, but struggling like men."[40] When the Republican party emerged in the 1850s and pledged to place slavery on the road to ultimate extinction, Keitt's concern over southern honor grew. He warned southerners that if Republican John C. Frémont won the presidency in 1856, "*You have to choose between submission and dissolution.*" The South must never bow its head to "Black Republican rule," Keitt insisted. Rather than submit to the election of a Republican Speaker of the House of Representatives in 1859, Keitt announced, "I would shatter this Republic from turret to foundation stone."[41]

Wigfall agreed that the South could never honorably submit to "Black Republican rule," but he adopted more vulgar rhetoric than Keitt. In 1856, the Republican party had condemned slavery and Mormonism as "twin relics of barbarism." Would southerners allow others to compare George Washington with Brigham Young, "the pure patriot and the lecherous beast," he asked. Did southern women—"our mothers, our wives, our daughters"—fall into the same category as "vile harlots who, herded like cattle, live in their keeper's harems in promiscuous concubinage," just because they owned slaves? "It is deliberately-written libel on fair women and brave men," Wigfall said, and he insisted that no constitutional reform could prevent such insults. Like Keitt, Wigfall declared that the South would never permit the North "to belt us round with free States, to starve us out or cause us . . . like poisoned rats, to die in our holes." In the Senate Wigfall assailed northerners even more vehemently than Keitt had in the House:

> You denounce us, degrade us, deride us, tell us we shall live under a Government that we say is not tasteful to us; you tell us that we are degraded, that we are not your equals. . . . And when we say to you, if we cannot live together in peace, we will separate, you say we shall not; and then, because I do not choose to make a ninny of myself, because I do not choose to stultify myself, and vote for resolutions that mean nothing, in order that Senators may telegraph over the country that all is

40. Charleston *Mercury*, July 27, 1860, June 19, September 4, 1851; *Congressional Globe*, 33rd Cong., 1st Sess., App., 465, 467. For the impact of honor on southern politics, see William J. Cooper, Jr., *The South and the Politics of Slavery, 1828–1856* (Baton Rouge, 1978), 69–74; Bertram Wyatt-Brown, *Yankee Saints and Southern Sinners* (Baton Rouge, 1985), 183–213.

41. New York *Times*, October 14, 1856; Charleston *Mercury*, October 13, 1858; *Congressional Globe*, 35th Cong., 1st Sess., 24.

peace and quiet—because I do not choose to do that, or to be led by the nose as tenderly as asses are, I am charged with a conspiracy . . . to dissolve the Union.

Wigfall vowed that before accepting inequality and degradation he would indeed dissolve the Union: "I would burst it; I would fracture it, splinter it into more fragments than gunpowder would blow glass."[42]

Vindicating southern honor occasionally led Keitt to commit the reckless acts of violence that he had once claimed to deplore. For instance, while representatives debated what action to take after the Sumner-Brooks affair, Keitt leaped suddenly at John Hickman of Pennsylvania. A congressman from Alabama grabbed Keitt by the coattail as he rushed by and prevented a fight. A New York *Times* correspondent found the incident "a mystery." A Washington correspondent, however, had observed Keitt's "nervous gesticulation" on the House floor. He noted that Keitt moved "restlessly about as if suffering from a continual succession of electric shocks." Keitt admitted an inability to control this nervous energy. He confessed that "my nervous irritability" prevented him even from holding still long enough to have a daguerreotype made.[43]

Keitt's testiness led to the most reckless act of his political career. At two o'clock in the morning on February 6, 1858, the House of Representatives was locked in a series of debates and parliamentary maneuvers concerning Kansas. Keitt lay across two desks in a restless sleep, one shoe dangling from his toes. Galusha Grow, a Republican from Pennsylvania, had crossed over to the Democrats' side of the floor to confer briefly with his colleague John Hickman, when he objected to a motion by John Quitman. Keitt rose slightly from his improvised couch and grumbled, "What business have you over on this side, any how?" "This is a free hall," Grow replied, "and I have a right to object from any part of it, when I choose." After a further exchange of words Keitt moved toward Grow and shouted, "I'll show you, you d——d Black Republican puppy!" Grow rejoined, "You may think me what you please, Mr. Keitt; but let me tell you that no nigger-driver shall come up from his planta-

42. *Texas Republican*, October 20, 1860; Louis T. Wigfall, *Speech of Louis T. Wigfall, on the Pending Political Issues; Delivered at Tyler, Smith County, Texas, September 3, 1860* (Washington, D.C., 1860), 27–28; *Congressional Globe*, 36th Cong., 2nd Sess., 74, 667.

43. New York *Times*, July 10, 1856; Merchant, "Keitt," 113–14; Charleston *Mercury*, April 12, 1856; Keitt to Sue Sparks, June 6, 1855, in Keitt Papers, WPL.

tion to crack his lash about *my* ears!" "We'll see about that," muttered Keitt as he leaped upon Grow and grabbed his throat. At least six congressmen joined the melee. When Cadwallader Washburn of Wisconsin, in an attempt to pick up William Barksdale of Mississippi by the hair so as to punch him, found himself swinging wildly at air with one hand while the other clutched Barksdale's wig, laughter conquered anger and the brawl ended.[44]

Even Keitt realized that he had gone too far. On February 8, he apologized to the House for "violation of its order, its dignity, and its decorum." Although he accepted full responsibility for the affair and expressed his profound regret, he never apologized to Grow. Furthermore, when a report surfaced that Grow had struck him during their scuffle, Keitt denounced it as "a foul lie." Although the Charleston *Mercury* hailed Keitt for his "chivalrous and manly apology" and some Carolinians thought that, having again proven his mettle, Keitt should run for senator, most people were appalled. An anonymous writer in *Punch,* the London magazine, was moved to write:

> Sing, oh goddess, the wrath, the ontameable dander of KEITT—
> KEITT of South Carolina, the clear grit, the tall, the ondaunted—
> Him that hath wopped his own niggers till Northerners all unto KEITT
> Seem but as niggers to wop, and hills of the smallest potatoes.

One Carolinian, who expressed great admiration for Keitt's talents, felt "contempt and disgust." Another asked Keitt's colleague Congressman William Porcher Miles, "With what Kind of ammunition was Keitt's gun charged to make so furious an explosion[?]"[45]

Although Keitt often carried the defense of southern honor to ridiculous extremes, his actions resulted from a conviction he shared with Louis Wigfall that northerners' values and culture were so different from those of southerners that they could not be reasoned with, much less treated as equals. Both Keitt and Wigfall were southern nationalists; they considered the southern people unique and the Union an unnatural bond that trapped them to-

---

44. New York *Times,* February 8, 1858.
45. *Congressional Globe,* 35th Cong., 1st Sess., 623; Keitt to Ellison [Keitt], February 17, 1858, in C. C. Jones Autograph Letters, WPL; Charleston *Mercury,* February 13, July 28, 1858; "The Fight over the Body of Keitt," *Punch,* XXIV (March 6, 1858), 100; William H. Trescot to W. P. Miles, February 7, March 20, 1858, Allan Macfarlan to Miles, February 14, 1858, in Miles Papers, SHC. Also see Alfred Huger to Miles, February 18, 1858, *ibid.*

gether with a foreign North. They agreed with Beverley Tucker that neither an American nation nor an American people existed but only a union of different peoples. To Keitt and Wigfall, secession would not only vindicate southern honor and promote southern interests but also allow the South to develop fully its own nationality.

Keitt most likely derived his concept of southern nationalism from his kinsman and political confidant David Flavel Jamison. Jamison has been called "the mouthpiece of romantic Southern nationalists." As a student at South Carolina College in the days of Thomas Cooper, Jamison leaned toward southern radicalism early in life. A planter, author, and lawyer, he also represented Orangeburg in the South Carolina legislature from 1836 to 1848, when Keitt succeeded him. He was one of Rhett's Bluffton Boys in 1844 and a delegate to the Nashville Convention in 1850. During the ensuing secession movement, he led the call in Orangeburg for immediate secession. By that time he had already immersed himself in the ideas of such European writers on romantic nationalism as François Guizot, Johann Herder, François Mignet, Jules Michelet, and Alphonse Lamartine. Later, he joined the literary circle of William Gilmore Simms, the South's foremost man of letters and a firm believer in southern nationalism. In December, 1860, when a secession convention declared South Carolina a free and independent state, David F. Jamison presided over the assembly.[46]

Jamison and Keitt worked closely together in the campaign for secession in 1851, and Jamison's ideas clearly influenced his young associate. "We have now," Keitt declared in 1855, "in interest, two Confederacies, with a debauched Constitution, and a tyrannical and irresponsible Congress." Appeals to northerners would therefore be futile. "The South must organize to save herself," he stated, and South Carolina must lead that effort. Keitt asserted, "South Carolina has led the column of Southern civilization: and that civilization, peculiar and original, I believe to be now in peril." To Keitt "Southern civilization" was uniquely moral and spiritual. All other nations, he claimed, "are material." European nations and the North both suffered from "effete social forms," suffocated from dense populations, and were racked by conflicts between labor and

46. Keitt to Sue Sparks, May 9, 1855, in Keitt Papers, WPL; Rollin G. Osterweis, *Romanticism and Nationalism in the Old South* (Baton Rouge, 1971), 150–52; Charleston *Mercury*, September 16, 1844; Drew Gilpin Faust, *The Creation of Confederate Nationalism: Ideology and Identity in the Civil War South* (Baton Rouge, 1988), 10.

capital. Slavery set the South apart. "At the South we have . . . a harmonious and permanent adjustment between labor and capital," he claimed, harmonious because slave labor was a form of capital. Repeating the "mud-sill" idea formulated by Beverley Tucker and enunciated by James Hammond, Keitt remarked that individual liberty was a "rank and privilege" appreciated by southerners more than any people on earth. Concepts of states' rights, federal relations, and the morality of owning slaves differed so sharply above and below the Mason-Dixon Line that Keitt concluded that "a whole world lies between the North and the South, both upon the question of slavery, and the character of the government."[47]

Wigfall shared these convictions, but he developed them without the refinement or scholarly guidance of Keitt. Instead, Wigfall's concept of southern nationalism crudely synthesized popular contemporary truisms and dutiful loyalty to "King Cotton." An English observer found Wigfall's thoughts on the matter affected and "of logic all his own." "We are a peculiar people, sir!" Wigfall patiently explained.

> You don't understand us, and you can't understand us, because we are known to you only by Northern writers and Northern papers, who know nothing of us themselves, or misrepresent what they do know. We are an agricultural people; we are a primitive but a civilised people. We have no cities—we don't want them. We have no literature—we don't need any yet. We have no press—we are glad of it. We do not require a press because we go out and discuss all public questions from the stump with our people. We have no commercial marine—no navy—we don't want them. Your ships carry our produce, and you can protect your own vessels. We want no manufacturers: we desire no trading, no mechanical or manufacturing classes. As long as we have our rice, our sugar, our tobacco, and our cotton, we can command wealth to purchase all we want from those nations with which we are in amity, and lay up money besides.[48]

Their belief in southern nationality led Keitt and Wigfall to believe a sectional conflict inevitable. "It needs but a weak horoscope to see future events, in momentous convulsions, sweeping like a magnificent thundercloud through the sky," Keitt predicted in 1855. He believed, however, that men of fortitude and daring

---

47. Charleston *Mercury*, August 16, October 18, 1855, September 27, 1860.
48. Russell, *Diary*, 99. Also see *Congressional Globe*, 36th Cong., 2nd Sess., 73.

could direct the course of the coming storm.[49] Both he and Wigfall saw themselves as such men, politicians with unique abilities to guide the South through anticipated political convulsions and into a new national existence.

In 1859 Keitt's devotion to the South triumphed over his new commitment to his bride. While on their honeymoon in Europe, the newlyweds learned of John Brown's attempt to lead a slave insurrection at Harpers Ferry, Virginia. Keitt decided he must return to Washington. "Disappointed, disappointed," sighed Sue. "And the cause *Politics.* How I *hate* the word." When she looked beyond her own frustration, however, she must have recalled his words to her early in their courtship. He had told her that he believed South Carolina had "more weight in the federal councils than any state in the Union." And he believed that he possessed the power "to turn the tide in this state." "Sue, shall I seek the strength of the eagle," he had asked her, "or cower like the linnet?" She knew the answer.[50]

Excitement over John Brown's raid lingered in Washington when Keitt returned in December, 1859. He immediately met with Congressman Miles and others to obtain information and discuss appropriate responses. In the House Keitt declared, "There is an indissoluble connection between the principles of the Republican party . . . and their ultimate consummation in blood and rapine on the soil of Virginia." Hardly had Keitt vented his rage at Brown and Republicans when he received the alarming news that his brother Dr. William J. Keitt had been killed by his own slaves while he lay sick in bed at his plantation near Ocala, Florida. Vigilantes there hanged the slave who slit Dr. Keitt's throat; three accomplices awaited sale out of the state. Keitt had always believed that "the relationship between master and slave is one of kindness and protection" and that slaves rebelled against their masters only when incited by northerners. He refused to believe that his brother's conduct toward his slaves or the institution of slavery could drive a black to commit such a ghastly act. Three of the four slaves involved had recently been purchased from Virginia, which helped Keitt rationalize that slavery on his family's plantations was benevolent and that geographic proximity to the North and abolitionists

49. Keitt to Sue Sparks, July 11, September 19, 1855, in Keitt Papers, WPL; L. Keitt to J. Pettigrew, May 15, 1860, in Pettigrew Family Papers, NCDAH.

50. Keitt to Miles, May 18, 1859, in Miles Papers, SHC; Sue Sparks Keitt to Carrie, [1859], Keitt to Sue, n.d. [1855 or 1856], July 11, 1855, in Keitt Papers, WPL; Merchant, "Keitt," 277–80.

disrupted the kindly relationship between master and slave. For Keitt, the threat that a Republican regime would turn slave against master had become horrifyingly real.[51]

The dangers of remaining in the Union went beyond mere rhetoric for Keitt. "Our Negroes are being enlisted in politics," he complained to Hammond. "I confess this new feature alarms me, more even, than every thing in the past. If Northern men get access to our Negroes to advise poison and the torch, we must prevent it at every hazard." For northerners, Keitt explained, the election of 1860 was just another election. "Although with us," he said, "it is life or Death." Publicly and privately Keitt demanded immediate disunion if the Republicans won the presidency. When news of Lincoln's election reached South Carolina, Keitt told the citizens of Columbia, "Take your destinies in your own hands, and shatter this accursed Union." In Charleston he promised to carry Orangeburg and Beaufort districts during the forthcoming secession convention in honor of Barnwell Rhett. In language identical to Rhett's, Keitt asserted that submission to the Union was slavery. "And when I am called upon to choose whether I will be a traitor or a slave, God help me—*I am a traitor!*" Carolinians had built the United States, he said, and repeated his promise that "now we mean to pull it down from turret to foundation-stone." As a delegate to the secession convention, Keitt helped fulfill that promise.[52]

"Liberty is a serious game," Keitt once said, "to be played out . . . with knives and hatchets, and not with drawled epigrams and soft petitions." Unafraid of warfare against his northern foes, Keitt was anxious to play the game. While in Congress, he responded to "attacks upon the revolutionary history of South Carolina" with a long, detailed speech that dramatized southern military prowess and denigrated that of the North. Soon thereafter he published an article based on his speech in *De Bow's Review* in which he added a similar account of the sections' participation in the Mexican War. In the event of civil war, Keitt truly believed that southern military might would bring an easy victory over a cowardly North. Embold-

51. Sue Keitt to "Dear Mar," December 4, 1859, Keitt to Sue Keitt, January 29, 1860, in Keitt Papers, WPL; *Congressional Globe,* 36th Cong., 1st Sess., 220; R. B. Rhett, Jr., to W. P. Miles, January 24, 1860, in Miles Papers, SHC; *Congressional Globe,* 33rd Cong., 1st Sess., App., 465; Merchant, "Keitt," 302.

52. Keitt to Hammond, August 4, September 10, October 23, 1860, in Hammond Papers, LC; Keitt to Miles, October 3, 1860, in Miles Papers, SHC; *Charleston Mercury,* July 20, November 13, 21, 1860; Merchant, "Keitt," 337–40.

ened by these views, Keitt declared that he had had as much as he could stand from the North, *"except on the battle-field."* [53]

Romanticism affected Keitt's attitudes about warfare as well as politics, about death as well as life. He remained convinced that only action could make life meaningful, that without struggle and "self-sacrificing efforts" liberty would be lost. He cited John Milton's injunction that the man who would write a heroic poem must make his entire life heroic, and he believed that heroes must take risks. From his earliest days in politics Keitt proclaimed, "It is our duty to ascertain our rights," defend them, "and leave consequences to God." To accomplish his political goals, Keitt expressed his willingness to "perish in the struggle." For Keitt, risking one's life was ennobling. "Not only in the victory shout may the laurels be bound around the brow," he explained to Sue, "the kingdom of civil warfare is richer in dangers, and gives greener and more lasting laurels." Death in the struggle for a virtuous cause did not signal failure to Keitt, but rather sublime success. It would be glorious to die "with the consciousness that yours is a noble mission, and trying to the last articulately to utter the high message given you, though the death rattle stifles at half-delivered." To die while fighting for one's country, "to become intermingled with the very life, infused into the very heart, and associated with the organized existence of a great people" brought immortality. Carolinians held their liberty not only because the Founding Fathers "lived as freemen, or died as martyrs, but because we can furnish many more men to live as they lived, and die as they died." [54]

Romantic literature, particularly the works of Sir Walter Scott, also affected Keitt's views of warfare. "Epic dreamings" pervaded his thoughts and crept into his rhetoric. In 1851 he said, "South Carolina, single and alone, mailed and weaponed, can cleave her way to the falling pillar [of liberty], and uphold the sinking temple, or bravely perish in the very sanctuary of liberty." He told Sue that in one session of Congress, "I had won a crown here and a chaplet there, I had broken a sword in this fight and beaten down a castle wall in another contest." In the capitol he warned northerners that if they tampered with slavery "the South will meet you with gaunt-

53. Charleston *Mercury*, July 20, 1860; *Congressional Globe*, 34th Cong., 1st Sess., App., 833–39; Laurence M. Keitt, "Patriotic Services of the North and the South," *DBR*, XXI (November, 1856), 491–508; New York *Times*, September 29, 1856.
54. Keitt to Sue, n.d., July 29, September 19, 1855, in Keitt Papers, WPL; Charleston *Mercury*, July 20, September 27, 1860, June 19, 1951.

lets on." He believed that when the South faced its northern foe, it would "meet him with helmet on, with visor down, and lance couched." If South Carolina seceded, Keitt said in October, 1860, he would abandon politics; "I intend to take the field."[55]

Wigfall shared Keitt's views, if not his knightly imagination and demeanor. In Texas he campaigned briefly though vigorously for Breckinridge and Lane, always reminding his audiences that if Lincoln won they had no alternative but secession. Both in Texas and Washington Wigfall blamed Republican "John-Brown men" for a recent, mysterious outbreak of fires in his state. After Lincoln's election, Wigfall both defended the right of a state to secede, "whether there be cause or not," and urged South Carolina to do so immediately. Like Keitt, neither death nor the failure of southern resistance mattered to Wigfall. He said that even if northern armies made the South "a graveyard of freemen," it could never make it "the habitation of slaves."[56]

In the Senate Wigfall did all he could to encourage secession. In December, 1860, he urged South Carolina to secede and seize all federal military installations and munitions within its borders. A week before South Carolina left the Union, Wigfall and twenty-nine other southern congressmen signed the "Southern Manifesto," in which they declared that all argument had been exhausted, that no legislation or constitutional amendments could possibly satisfy the South. "We are satisfied the honor, safety, and independence of Southern people require the organization of a Southern Confederacy," they concluded. In January, 1861, when Senator John J. Crittenden of Kentucky tried desperately to save the Union with a series of compromise bills, Wigfall led the southern opposition.[57]

Although other southern congressmen returned to their respec-

55. Charleston *Mercury*, June 19, 1851; Keitt to Sue, July 29, 1855, February 17, 1856, in Keitt Papers, WPL; *Congressional Globe*, 33rd Cong., 1st Sess., App., 468; *ibid.*, 34th Cong., 1st Sess., App., 443; Keitt to Miles, October 3, 1860, in Miles Papers, SHC.

56. *Texas Republican*, August 4, 11, October 20, 1860; Wigfall, *Speech of Louis T. Wigfall*, 17–18, 24; Walter L. Buenger, *Secession and the Union in Texas* (Austin, 1984), 75, 99–100; *Congressional Globe*, 36th Cong., 2nd Sess., 12–14, 73, 86. Wigfall's son Halsey shared his father's views. He looked forward to "glorious war, with the spirit-stirring drum and ear-piercing fife" (Halsey Wigfall to Louly Wigfall, March 3, 1861, in Wigfall Family Papers, LC).

57. *Congressional Globe*, 36th Cong., 2nd Sess., 14; *Texas Republican*, January 5, 12, 1861.

tive homes when their states seceded, Wigfall remained in Washington after Texas left the Union on February 1 and stayed even after the Texas legislature elected him to the Provisional Confederate Congress. He justified his remaining by explaining that the Texas legislature had not officially advised him to leave the Senate and until it did, he would speak, debate, and vote "if it suits my convenience." Actually, Wigfall chose to stay in the enemy capital as a self-appointed "rear-guard," to antagonize his foes and to gather intelligence for Confederate officials. He excelled at the former. When Zachariah Chandler, a senator from Michigan, said that rather than listen to proponents of secession he would move west and live among the Indians, Wigfall responded: "God forbid! I hope not. They have already suffered much from their contact with whites." Wigfall concluded a debate with Unionist Senator Andrew Johnson by saying, "Now let the Senator from Tennessee put that in his pipe and smoke it." After South Carolinians chased a federal supply ship out of Charleston Harbor by firing a warning shot across its bow, Wigfall blustered: "The Star of the West swaggered into Charleston harbor, received a blow planted full in the face, and staggered out. Your flag has been insulted; redress it, if you dare. You have submitted to it for two months, you will submit to it for ever. . . . You tell us you will keep us in the Union. Try the experiment." When a friend of Wigfall's in South Carolina heard of the senator's antics he observed: "Wigfall chafes at the restraints of civil life. He likes to be where he can be as rude as he pleases, and he is indulging himself now to the fullest extent, apparently."[58]

While Wigfall remained in Washington he did more than wage a war of words. Acting in concert with the Confederate War Department, he established a recruiting station in Baltimore, Maryland, to receive volunteers and weapons for the Confederate army and arrange for their transportation to South Carolina. He also informed southern officials of northern popular opinion, about what President Buchanan might do, and about what they might anticipate from the Lincoln administration. The New York *Tribune* protested Wigfall's use of the franking privilege and the United States mails "to hatch and promote treason" while he continued to draw his pay from the federal government. Such protests were in vain. Only

58. *Congressional Globe*, 36th Cong., 2nd Sess., 1442, 1372–73, 1440; Charleston *Mercury*, April 5, 1861; Kittrell, *Governors Who Have Been*, 153; Woodward, ed., *Mary Chesnut's Civil War*, 12.

the promise of combat in Charleston could force Wigfall to leave Washington.[59]

The people of Charleston gave Wigfall an enthusiastic welcome home when he arrived in early April. "I have returned to my native land," he told a crowd that gathered to greet him at his hotel. He claimed that secession had already produced wonders. By leaving the North the Confederate States had eliminated all sources of political corruption. They had turned their backs on democracy and returned to the republican form of government the Founding Fathers had intended. The new Confederate Constitution proved "that we are wiser than our ancestors" because it ended the "miserable scramble" for the presidency by limiting tenure of office to a single six-year term. The selection of Jefferson Davis as president demonstrated the wisdom of the southern people. According to Wigfall, Davis had "great, striking, and remarkable qualities" and combined the statesmanship of John C. Calhoun with the courageous leadership of Andrew Jackson. For Wigfall, only one objective remained unfulfilled; he wanted war and an invasion of the North.[60]

Wigfall had trouble choosing between a military and a political career in the Confederacy. Initally, he pursued both. Although the Texas legislature had already selected him for the Provisional Congress in Montgomery, Wigfall decided to linger in Charleston,. where he hoped war would begin. General P. G. T. Beauregard appointed him brigadier general of volunteers on April 10, and he joined former Governor John Manning—his old friend—as an aide to Beauregard. Acting on his own authority (and, according to one witness, under the influence of alcohol), Wigfall stormed Fort Sumter during the bombardment and successfully negotiated its surrender. His daring made him a southern hero. He was greeted with cheers and adulation as he journeyed to Montgomery. In June, when the Confederate capital moved to Richmond and close to the enemy's army, the temptation to act in a military capacity

59. L. T. Wigfall to General Beauregard, March 16, 1861, to L. P. Walker, March 21, 1861, L. P. Walker to Wigfall, March 21, 1861, in *OR*, Ser. I, Vol. I, 276, 278; Wigfall to [L. P. Walker], March 17, 1861, C. K. Sherman, R. Cleary, W. N. Barker to Wigfall, March 16, 1861, *ibid.*, Ser. I, Vol. LIII, 134–35; Wigfall to Governor F. W. Pickens, March 4, 1861, *ibid.*, Vol. I, 261; Wright, *Southern Girl in '61*, 32–34; Louis Wigfall to [?], February 18, 1861, in C. C. Jones Autograph Letters, WPL; New York *Tribune* in *Texas Republican*, February 23, 1861.

60. Charleston *Mercury*, April 4, 5, 1861.

again overcame Wigfall. After the First Battle of Bull Run, Wigfall assumed command of the 1st Texas Battalion and served as a military aide to Davis while he continued to serve in the Congress. His preference for military affairs, however, did not escape notice. "Heavens! How that redoubtable Wigfall did rush those poor Texans about," observed South Carolina diarist Mary Chesnut. She noted that despite ninety-degree heat, "He maneuvered them until I was weary for their sakes." Because of his diverse and energetic services, Wigfall's fame spread quickly through his infant country. Davis turned to him as a confidant. Wigfall had never enjoyed such success.[61]

Ironically, Wigfall's passion for military affairs poisoned his relationship with Davis and largely destroyed his popularity. By 1862 Wigfall began to blame Davis for Confederate military defeats and joined with "other malcontents, in giving him what trouble they could." After the Confederate defeats at Gettysburg and Vicksburg, Wigfall's anger grew. "Has it ever occurred to you that Davis's mind is becoming unsettled?" he asked a colleague. "No sane man would do as he is doing." After Wigfall's family snubbed the Davises at a dinner party, Mary Chesnut wrote: "It seems incredible—but Edgefield and Texas combined makes one stouthearted enough for anything." In the Senate, Wigfall supported both conscription and military confiscation, a law allowing the government to take any goods it needed from the private sector and pay only what the government deemed a fair price. Even if these measures were necessary to sustain the war effort, Hammond told Wigfall, "Your acts of last Session were posatively [sic] cut-throat, all taken together. . . . You have broken all the Banks, the speculators & Manufactures."[62]

During the next decade, Wigfall's behavior mocked the gallantry and daring he had professed all his life. After Robert E. Lee surrendered in April, 1865, Wigfall tried to reach General Kirby-Smith's army in Texas. He was afraid of being captured and punished for treason and so shaved his beard and procured a private's

61. King, *Wigfall*, 119–21, 131; C[harlotte] M. Wigfall to [Halsey Wigfall], April 20, May 23, 30, 1861, in Wigfall Family Papers, LC; Russell, *Diary*, 63; Woodward, ed., *Mary Chesnut's Civil War*, 123.

62. King, *Wigfall*, 139, 150–51; Woodward, ed., *Mary Chesnut's Civil War*, 359, 433; Walter F. McCaleb, ed., *Memoirs, with Special Reference to Secession and the Civil War, by John H. Reagan* (New York, 1906), 161; Wigfall to C. C. Clay, August 13, 1863, in Clement C. Clay Collection, WPL; Hammond to Wigfall, April 15, 1864, in Hammond Papers, LC.

uniform and parole to disguise himself as Private J. A. White of Texas. He left his family near Montgomery but upon arrival in Texas learned that Kirby-Smith's army had also surrendered. Wigfall decided he could not remain in the South after his brother Arthur wrote from Edgefield that "the Parish is permanently destroyed" and "the state is ruined—& no longer a fit place to live in." Like many other former Confederates, Wigfall fled to London. By October, 1866, his family joined him there for a poverty-stricken, self-imposed exile. "They say it is as much as his wife can do to keep him out of the gutter, he is drunk all the time," wrote one acquaintance. Wigfall sent periodic dispatches to friends in the South to determine the condition "of our down-trodden conquered country." In 1872, he returned to the United States. He and his wife lived in Baltimore until 1874 and then moved to Texas. He had planned to resume his law practice in Marshall, but on February 18, 1874, he died in Galveston from an undisclosed cause.[63]

The Confederacy offered as much reason for optimism for Laurence Keitt in 1861 as it did for Wigfall but ended even more disastrously. Keitt told his old friend Jamison that the Provisional Congress acted harmoniously and wisely, created a good Constitution, and chose an able president, though he had preferred Howell Cobb of Georgia. Keitt became disenchanted with the new government sooner than most, however. Early in 1861 he feared that Davis favored reunion with the North. By summer he worried that Confederate financial policies and the lack of domestic industry provided "the most unsubstantial foundation" for a new country. Personal concerns compounded his political anxieties. Even the "pageantry—cheers, enthusiasm, and waving kerchiefs" at Montgomery did not excite him, he told his wife, because "your absence is a sad drawback to me."[64]

Keitt hoped the army might provide him with more excitement and bring him closer to his family. As colonel of a volunteer regi-

63. Wright, *Southern Girl in '61*, 242–46; Arthur Wigfall to Louis Wigfall, August 15, 1865, in Wigfall Papers, BTHC; [M. F. Maury to Richard Maury], December 15, 1866, in Richard L. Maury Papers, WPL; Wigfall to Clay, October 17, 1866, in Clay Collection, WPL; Wigfall to Simon Bolivar Buckner, October 23, 1866, in Simon Bolivar Buckner Papers, HL; King, *Wigfall*, 231.

64. Keitt to D. F. Jamison, February 9, 1861, in David F. Jamison Papers, WL; Woodward, ed., *Mary Chesnut's Civil War*, 433; Keitt to Hammond, February 13, August 20, 1861, in Hammond Papers, LC; Keitt to Sue, February 19, 1861, in Hammond Papers, LC; Keitt to Sue, February 19, 1861, in Keitt Papers, WPL.

ment, he was stationed on Sullivan's Island in Charleston, near his plantation in Orangeburg. At his barracks he could receive visits from Sue and supervise the management of his 115 slaves. His initial military experiences confirmed Keitt's romantic preconceptions of warfare. "This camp life is a stirring one," he joyously reported to Sue in January, 1862. "The men are getting into their new uniforms and they are looking famous."[65]

Like countless other southerners, Keitt became disillusioned with the administration, Congress, and the conduct of the war. "Davis has become odious," he reported to Sue in May, 1862. "It seems things are coming to this pass: to be a patriot you must hate Davis." Keitt considered the president incompetent, an imbecile, and a coward. "You cannot find a more signal failure in history," he wrote Hammond. Keitt thought the best service Davis could render the country was "to get a rope and hang himself." And Congress was no better. "Congress seems to be made up of idiots. In our government there are only dreamers and mountebanks," Keitt complained. He urged Barnwell Rhett to run for Congress in 1864 to set the Confederacy back on a proper course. By 1864, Keitt was disturbed by political divisions within the Confederacy. With a "worthless Government" and an invading army to fight, he believed liberty was threatened by both internal and external foes. He wondered whether political cohesion in the South required "the antagonism of alien interests and people," an antagonism that vanished with secession. Keitt believed that lack of virtue in the South was killing his cherished cause. "To see a great cause lost, and a great people butchered by gross and criminal incapacity," he complained to Sue, "strikes like a dagger to the heart. To see a sacred struggle moulder away day by day, and high hopes sink into the grave . . . inspires fear that our people have not risen to the height of this present crisis."[66]

Desertions, threats of mutiny, and war weariness combined to tarnish Keitt's ideal of warfare. "War in any aspect is cruel, but this war is robbed of chivalry, and is scarcely more than butchery," he complained. "It is hate, without manliness—war without generousity—cruelty without courage—rapine without greatness." By

65. Keitt to Sue, January 21, 26, 1862, in Keitt Papers, WPL.
66. Keitt to Sue, May 4, 1862, January 13, 15, 22, 24, 31, 1864, *ibid.;* Keitt to Hammond, June 14, 1862, in Hammond Papers, LC; Robert Barnwell Rhett, "Autobiography," in Robert Barnwell Rhett Papers, SCHS.

1864 war had touched most of the South and affected soldiers, civilians, and politicians, yet "nowhere has anyone risen up with a star upon his forehead." Keitt believed that he had "as much to do probably as anyone else in bringing about this Revolution" and decided that he must assume a more active role in it.[67]

Keitt had tried to secure a promotion to brigadier general—at one time enlisting the aid of Louis Wigfall—but he remained only a colonel charged with garrison duty in Charleston. In the spring of 1864, however, the army transferred him to Virginia. He eagerly anticipated the opportunity to distinguish himself and to face his northern foe. "I don't think I fear death more than a gentleman ought," he had told his wife two years before, "but I do hate to leave you." As he readied himself and his men for battle, an observer noted that Keitt had more enthusiasm than ability. Each of his men "knew that he was being led by one of the most gifted and gallant men in the South, but every old soldier felt and saw at a glance his inexperience and want of self-control." Keitt showed no lack of boldness and aggressiveness, "but he was preparing for battle like in the days of Alva or Turene, and to cut his way through like a storm center." Keitt was determined to restore chivalry to the war. At Cold Harbor on June 1, he mounted his gray horse "like a knight of old." Without even a line of skirmishers to precede him, Keitt led his men across an open field toward the Union Army of the Potomac. After advancing only a few yards, Keitt was shot in the liver. Other officers ordered his men to retreat, and comrades took the fallen colonel to a field hospital. Four days later he died and became "intermingled with the very life" of his dying country. He was only thirty-nine.[68]

James Hammond had once described Keitt as "a true man to every body but himself & sagacious where he is not concerned." Sam Houston once said of Wigfall, "I should think more of the fellow than I do, if it were not that I regard him as a little demented either from hard drink, or from the troubles of a bad conscience." Both Keitt and Wigfall believed that a life of daring would bring success and fulfillment, but both trapped themselves in a web of

67. Keitt to Sue, January 13, 17, 24, February 11, March 1, 1864, in Keitt Papers, WPL; Keitt to Hammond, December 11, 1863, in Hammond Papers, LC.

68. Keitt to Wigfall, January 16, 1863, in Wigfall Family Papers, LC; Merchant, "Keitt," 401; D. Augustus Dickert, *History of Kershaw's Brigade* (Newberry, S.C., 1899), 365, 368–70, 375; Keitt to Sue, May 1, 1862; R. S. Ripley to Sue Keitt, June 2, 1864, S. D. Hammond to Sue Keitt, June 5, 1864, in Keitt Papers, WPL.

recklessness and emptiness that helped drag thousands of like-thinking southern youths to their graves during the war. A description of Keitt's speaking style from 1860 serves equally well as a summary of his and Wigfall's lives: "As an orator, he has created more decided sensation than any one now a M[ember of] C[ongress], having a pyrotechnic style, rich in versatility, startling paradox, and copious expression. His speeches are melo-dramatically effective, made up of the entrances and exits of ideas, that sparkle vividly while they are on the stage and go off in a tumult of applause, leaving an intoxicating sense of beauty and daring, yet nothing distinct but a metaphor or bold antithesis."[69]

69. Hammond to W. G. Simms, October 23, 1860, in Hammond Papers, LC; Houston to Andrew Jackson Hamilton, March 17, 1860, in Williams and Barker, eds., *Writings of Sam Houston*, VII, 527; *Harper's Weekly*, IV (December, 1860), 802.

Ploughshares Come Before Philosophy
James D. B. De Bow

No fire-eater loved the South more than James Dunwoody Brownson De Bow, and none criticized it more. He blamed many of its problems on the ignorance and idleness of planters and on the tendency of so many southerners to look back on an idyllic, bygone era. When agricultural depression struck, he said, planters invariably accused banks and tariffs or unseen politicians for causing their woes, made their slaves produce more cotton, lowered their profits, and continued to wonder what was happening to them. De Bow said that whenever sectional tensions rocked the Union, the southern politician went to the stump to expostulate about constitutional theory or the next presidential election and harangued about northern merchants and manufacturers who had "conspired to put him down" or take away his slaves. The typical planter or politician would moan and complain but would not "for the soul of him go to work." Instead, he would cling blindly to his ideals and wait impatiently for "the 'good old times' to return again."

In dramatic contrast to most other fire-eaters, De Bow considered this nostalgic agrarian romanticism an anathema. "Why . . . should the planter above all others be permitted to pass his days and nights in listless idleness," he asked in the first volume of his *Commercial Review* in 1846. Planters must work, De Bow said, just like merchants and manufacturers. He called on planters to abandon the use of overseers and to "remember the old saying, 'the master's footsteps are manure to his land.'" Southerners should grow less cotton, he suggested, and more corn and forage and raise more livestock. Furthermore, the planter must teach his sons that "idleness is the 'road to ruin'" and his daughters that "they are not dolls or milliner girls, but that they are the future makers or marrers of this beautiful republic." In a subsequent issue De Bow complained: "That the South should be DEPENDENT upon the North for its imports, is inexplicable upon any sound principle of political economy, and evidences a state of things humiliating in the extreme. We do not want *capital*," he explained, "but most sadly want *enterprise*."[1] Whether they remained in the Union or chose to secede, De Bow insisted that all southerners must learn to provide for themselves.

The circumstances surrounding De Bow's youth made him value self-sufficiency and diligent work. He was born on July 20, 1820, in Charleston. His father, Garret De Bow, was a successful merchant in New York City before he moved to South Carolina in the early 1800s. When Garret died in 1826, however, he was broke and left his widow with no money to raise their four children. Although "weak in body," the young De Bow had to help support himself and his family. As a teenager he found a job as a clerk in a wholesale grocery store. In his off hours De Bow read extensively, and without the benefit of a formal education was able to secure a job in 1836 as an instructor in a log cabin school near Charleston. His determination to improve his education and find a better-paying job led the young teacher to enroll at Cokesbury Institute, a vocational school in Abbeville District. He studied agriculture there for a year before deciding to go to college. He could not afford to enroll at South Carolina College and had saved barely enough money to attend the less prestigious College of Charleston.[2]

De Bow always demanded more from himself than of others. He kept a journal during his youth so as to instill a sense of discipline. Its brief daily entries were not noteworthy except for those in which he chastised himself for idleness. On January 10, 1837, he wrote:

——— Laziness ———
is the only cause that I can attribute
the suspension of
this Journal
for more than six months and a half
I trust to be more regular
——— hereafter ———
1837
James D B De Bow

1. *DBR*, I (May, 1846), 434–35; II (December, 1846), 407. De Bow's journal went by a variety of names but will be referred to here as *De Bow's Review* and cited as *DBR*.

2. *DBR*, After the War Series, III (June, 1867), 497–99; Paul F. Paskoff and Daniel J. Wilson, eds., *The Cause of the South: Selections from "De Bow's Review," 1846–1867* (Baton Rouge, 1982), 1–2; Ottis Clark Skipper, *J. D. B. De Bow: Magazinist of the Old South* (Athens, Ga., 1958), 1–3.

After failing again to maintain his daily regimen, De Bow lamented, "Oh Idleness how great an Evil art thou," and vowed "hereafter we shall be at least deadly enemies." Although De Bow made only sporadic efforts to continue his journal over the next few years, he fulfilled his pledge to combat indolence.[3]

In college De Bow's study habits earned him a reputation for diligence. "We called him 'Old De Bow'—he was so earnest and untiring in his pursuit of knowledge," one classmate recalled. De Bow often studied all night and went to class disheveled but "ready for any discussion or intellectual tilt." It was at college that De Bow first showed an interest in writing and publishing. During his first term, the enthusiastic freshman gave a speech in the college chapel urging students to begin a monthly campus periodical. The frail De Bow might not have been able to lead as vigorous a life as Louis Wigfall and Laurence Keitt, but he believed that a campus publication would produce a "yearly quota of gladiators, well armed, equipped and disciplined for conquest in the glorious arenas of literature" and thereby bring honor to his "gallant state." Although De Bow's efforts to launch a campus periodical failed, his labors in the classroom did not. He graduated in 1843 at the head of his class.[4]

Like Keitt and Wigfall, De Bow turned to law immediately after college. He read for a year and passed his bar examination but was soon bored with legal matters. His friend and first biographer, the Louisiana historian Charles Gayarré, said that De Bow was not destined to be an attorney. "He was a born statistician, with a dash of the man of letters," Gayarré remembered. De Bow tried his fortunes as the latter. He submitted an article to the *Southern Quarterly Review,* the leading journal in the South, with headquarters in Charleston. Daniel K. Whitaker, editor of the *Review,* published De Bow's first piece in July, 1844, and three more over the next year. De Bow's writing, consisting of reviews of recent works on history, politics, and philosophy, was well received by readers. More important, however, Whitaker learned of De Bow's interest in the business aspects of the *Review* and by 1845 made him junior editor.[5]

Even though De Bow complained that "the whole duties of the

3. De Bow Journal, Box 5, J. D. B. De Bow Papers, WPL.

4. *DBR,* XXVII (November, 1859), 572–73; *DBR,* After the War Series, III (June, 1867), 499; De Bow Journal, October 30, 1840, Box 5, De Bow Papers, WPL.

5. *DBR,* After the War Series, III (June, 1867), 499; *SQR,* VI (July, 1844), 95–129; VII (January and April, 1845), 75–103, 479–526; VIII (July, 1845), 191–243; De Bow to J. F. H. Claiborne, September 12, 1845, in J. F. H. Claiborne Collection, MDAH.

Editorial department have developed upon me," his work consumed neither all his time nor his attention. Ever since his youthful experiences with the merchants in Charleston, De Bow was fascinated with all aspects of commerce. The world of business excited him. To De Bow, financial transactions and ledgers proved as exhilarating as military glory did for John Quitman; progress and technological advances were as romantic to De Bow as the novels of Sir Walter Scott were to Laurence Keitt. De Bow found the noise of a steam engine "an eternal melody of iron" and the seemingly boundless resources of his young country a beckoning invitation for anyone with "ability, energy, and enterprise." He predicted enthusiastically that one day "our children shall throw away the telegraph as a play-thing and a bauble."[6] At Charleston in 1839 he had attended his first southern commercial convention, an assembly of business promoters who met annually at various southern cities. From his editorial post on the *Southern Quarterly Review* De Bow solicited articles on commerce and gained a name for himself among Charleston businessmen. At a meeting in October, 1845, Charlestonians elected De Bow as a delegate to the next southern commercial convention to be held at Memphis, Tennessee.[7]

In November, before he left for the convention, De Bow wrote a series of newspaper articles on topics that would come under discussion at Memphis such as the tariff, slavery, federal aid to improve navigation on the Mississippi and Missouri rivers, and a railroad connection between Charleston and the Mississippi. As he gathered information for these articles, De Bow became convinced of the need for a southern commercial journal. In Charleston, he issued a circular calling for the creation of a merchant's review modeled after *Hunt's Merchant's Magazine*, a commercial journal published in New York. Like *Hunt's*, this new magazine would include articles on trade, commerce, manufactures, and agriculture. At Memphis, De Bow promoted this project and received much encouragement, including the best wishes of fellow delegate John C. Calhoun.

On his way to and from Memphis, De Bow passed through New Orleans. The bustling port city fascinated him. He had already

---

6. De Bow to Claiborne, September 12, 1845, in Claiborne Collection, MDAH; "Fragments of the Past," *DBR*, After the War Series, I (June, 1866), 630; *DBR*, V (February, 1848), 173.

7. *DBR*, IV (October and November, 1847), 122, 337–38; John B. O'Niell to De Bow, October 1, 1845, in De Bow Papers, WPL; Skipper, *De Bow*, 15.

considered it a promising location for a southern journal while still at his desk at the *Southern Quarterly Review*. By 1845, subscriptions to that periodical had shrunk to twenty-five hundred, which De Bow attributed to the indifference of the people of Charleston to literary ventures. When a reader in Mississippi suggested to De Bow that the journal might prosper in the expanding, thriving city of New Orleans, he responded enthusiastically. He had previously noted the success of the *Southern Medical Journal* published in the Crescent City. If printers and the public in New Orleans showed enough interest, De Bow thought the removal of the *Southern Quarterly Review* to New Orleans an outstanding idea.[8]

De Bow left the *Southern Quarterly Review* late in 1845 after a personal dispute with Whitaker. He moved to New Orleans in November and began preparations to start a monthly commercial journal. His efforts at Memphis and Charleston had yielded enough money to begin publishing in January, 1846. De Bow did not want to issue a strictly literary publication like the one he had just left. "Ploughshares come before philosophy," he explained. Intending his journal to meet "the practical wants of every-day life," he thought of calling it the *Practical Review* but realized that title offered "inelegance and no little ambiguity." De Bow decided to call the first volume the *Commercial Review of the South and West*. As he had planned, the *Review* included articles on trade, commerce, commercial policy, internal improvements, manufactures, and agriculture; only occasionally did he include literary works.[9]

De Bow knew many Americans doubted that the South could ever become a great commercial region. "The climate is uncongenial, say they—produce corrupts in your summers—you have no energy in such hot regions—slavery retards you." He claimed these were all misconceptions and dedicated his *Review* to combating them. De Bow said the only factors that inhibited southern commercial development were the blind devotion of southerners to "the once rich but now decaying results of *agriculture*, and . . . ignorance of the true nature and dignity of COMMERCE and the elevating influences it is calculated to exert." De Bow saw the southern economy as a slumbering giant. "We invoke the South to awake," he

---

8. De Bow to Claiborne, September 12, 1845, in Claiborne Collection, MDAH; *DBR*, After the War Series, II (July, 1866), 109; Skipper, *De Bow*, 21; John McCardell, *The Idea of a Southern Nation: Southern Nationalists and Southern Nationalism, 1830–1860* (New York, 1979), 119.

9. Skipper, *De Bow*, 14–15, 17; *DBR*, I (January, 1846), 2–5.

trumpeted, and "construct its railroads, extend its commerce, build up its manufactures, protect its arts, endow its universities and colleges, [and] provide its schools." De Bow recognized that agriculture would remain essential to the South but insisted "Commerce is King."[10]

From 1846 to 1849, De Bow struggled to keep his *Review* solvent. He spent almost nothing on himself. His room above his office in Exchange Alley had no furniture, and he slept on a mattress on the floor. He wrote almost one-third of the articles for the first two volumes himself while trying frantically to solicit contributions from such men as James H. Hammond and William Gilmore Simms. His brother Frank and his brother-in-law Edwin Q. Bell served as the nucleus of his small staff of correspondents and collection and subscription agents. Many of them worked on commission; none earned much. De Bow suspended the August, 1846, issue to conserve his dwindling resources. A local philanthropist, however, soon came to the aid of the struggling editor. Maunsel White had arrived in the United States a poor Irish immigrant but made a fortune as a merchant and sugar planter in south Louisiana. White lent De Bow enough money to keep the *Review* in print. New financial problems forced De Bow to suspend publication again from January to June, 1849, but by the end of the year he had paid off all his debts. With the help of two new subscription agents the list of subscribers grew steadily. By 1848 the *Review* had more than eight hundred subscribers; in two years its list of almost five thousand subscribers was one of the largest of any southern periodical.[11]

Both De Bow and his *Review* quickly achieved national renown. After 1849 he seldom had trouble soliciting articles. Many southerners, like Laurence Keitt, used the *Review* as a forum to express their views on a variety of topics to a wide audience. De Bow did not, however, limit the *Review* to southern issues or readers. "We have the broadest notions of our country," he wrote, as was customary, in the plural. "We cherish Maine and Louisiana as sisters." Although northerners constituted only a small fraction of his subscribers, many held his work in high regard. John Quincy Adams

10. *DBR*, II (September, 1846), 115; IV (October, 1847), 211; VII (September, 1849), 230–31. De Bow used the motto "Commerce is King" for the *Review*.

11. *DBR*, After the War Series, III (June, 1867), 500–501; J. H. Hammond to De Bow, May 4, 1849, in De Bow Papers, WPL; Skipper, *De Bow*, 21–26, 50; *DBR*, XXXV (July and August, 1864), 97; Clement Eaton, *The Mind of the Old South* (Baton Rouge, 1964), 54.

was an early patron, and Senator Charles Sumner once turned to De Bow for statistical information. Even Herman Hunt, proprietor of *Hunt's Magazine*, praised De Bow's work and wished his southern counterpart well.[12]

De Bow earned respect from many northerners for his professional ability, but he acquired distinction in the South for his unflinching sectionalism. Although he claimed to publish a journal with a national focus and adhere to an "active *neutrality*" regarding politics, De Bow was a vocal southern partisan. He always believed that the North had neither an understanding of southern institutions nor a right to interfere with them. Slavery, "and of course, the very existence of the South, are in constant danger," he warned. In May, 1845, the Southern Baptist Convention was organized in Augusta, Georgia, separating from northern church members over questions concerning slavery. As a delegate De Bow had voted in favor of separation, an act he later remembered as the proudest of his life. He had first tried using a journal to help promote sectional interests that same year while he was still working for the fledgling *Southern Quarterly Review*. "For the interest of Southern Letters & Southern Character & Southern *Rights* this work must not be suffered to perish," he said.[13]

As editor of the *Review*, De Bow emerged as a leading defender of slavery. When De Bow launched his journal, he stated that the debate over slavery "has long been settled, and so far as the south is concerned, should never be more mooted." In 1856 he printed an article that gave a biblical defense of the institution but complained that "the subject is growing hacknied [*sic*]." Provoked by persistent attacks on slavery by "crack-brained abolitionists," however, De Bow responded with an intricate rebuttal. He repeated the popular assertion that emancipation would prove harmful to the slaves because free blacks could not care for themselves without the constant surveillance and pressure "of a superior race." De Bow also echoed the beliefs that American economic prosperity and republican government rested on the foundation of African slavery. "Civilization itself," he said, "may almost be said to depend upon the

12. *DBR*, IV (October, 1847), 210; Skipper, *De Bow*, 26, 50; Charles Sumner to De Bow, March 1, 1854, Herman Hunt to De Bow, July 23, 1850, in De Bow Papers, WPL.

13. *DBR*, IV (October, 1847), 211; XII (May, 1852), 504–505; XXIX (August, 1860), 250; McCardell, *Idea of a Southern Nation*, 192–93; De Bow to Claiborne, September 12, 1845, in Claiborne Collection, MDAH.

continual servitude of the blacks in America." Because he believed the future of the South required territorial expansion, De Bow advocated the geographic extension of slavery. He believed that slavery would accompany southerners on their march through Mexico and into Central America. If the natural growth of the slave population failed to keep pace with the increased demands of a vast slave empire, De Bow hoped southerners would revive the African slave trade. Regarding slavery as a versatile and adaptive institution, De Bow argued that it must accompany southern economic diversification, that slaveowners must transfer some of their chattel from the fields into cotton mills and railroad construction. If "properly organized and directed," De Bow claimed, slaves would constitute a skilled industrial labor force that would last well into the twentieth century. [14]

Although De Bow shared the concern of other fire-eaters that consolidation of political power threatened slavery, "the great centralization of capital at the North" worried him more. De Bow warned that the South must emulate the industrial advances of the North either to match its "strength and weight" within the Union or to defend itself as an independent nation. "The great progress of this nation cannot and will not be confined to localities," he insisted. Because of slavery, he conceded, "The hands of all mankind seem to be against us." If their defense of slavery led southerners to secede, De Bow warned, a southern nation could not sustain itself with agriculture alone. "We want *physical* strength, the sinews of defences and war," products that only an industrial society could create. Because sectional conflict appeared to threaten the country periodically with civil war, De Bow viewed southern dependence on the North for industrial goods as economic slavery. In 1852 he beseeched fellow southerners: "Throw off this yoke of bondage, and begin to show your manhood at once. We are poor and miserable, whereas we should be great. . . . Whatever divisions exist in southern politics

14. *DBR*, III (May, 1847), 421; IX (September, 1850), 281; XV (November, 1853), 537; VII (September, 1849), 205; XI (February, 1851), 132, 146; XIII (September, 1857), 70–71, 228–29; *DBR*, VII (July, 1849), 62; XXII (June, 1857), 663–64; XXV (August, 1858), 166; XII (May, 1852), 557–59. In "The Origin, Progress and Prospects of Slavery," *DBR*, IX (July, 1850), 9–19, De Bow projected that the South would have a slave population of over 10.5 million by 1910, more than three times the number in 1850. For an interesting discussion of the industrialization of slave labor in the late antebellum period, see Fred Bateman, *A Deplorable Scarcity: The Failure of Industrialization in the Slave Economy* (Chapel Hill, 1981), 83–85.

there can be none upon this of *Southern Industrial Independence*. Fire-eater and compromiser must all meet here. . . . Here is separate state action upon which all must agree—that of the loom, and the spindle, and the locomotive." De Bow insisted that such independence was possible if only his fellow southerners would "put their shoulder[s] to the wheel, intellectually and physically."[15]

Of southerners' physical prowess De Bow had no worry; it was their intellect that required stimulation. He thought that generally southerners suffered from insufficient and inadequate education. His editorial experiences had proven to him the "painful truth" that the South lacked a large reading population. Antiquated attitudes toward agriculture, he held, had blinded southerners to the need for industrial development. He watched with dismay as hundreds of youths every year left the South to attend better colleges in the North. Like Beverley Tucker, De Bow went to the classroom and the press in an effort to reeducate southerners. Unlike the Virginian, De Bow considered practical, not philosophical, knowledge the key to southern redemption.[16]

De Bow's concern with the shortfalls of education in the South led him to advocate sweeping reforms. Sounding like Thomas Jefferson, De Bow said, "The more universally educated the people become, the more stable will become the republic." Accordingly, he called for a comprehensive system of free education. He urged city and state governments to raise taxes for the support of both common schools and universities. The former must better prepare students for college because, he asserted, primary education would be in vain "if there be nothing beyond." He insisted that ability alone should determine who attended college and suggested that poor students receive fee exemptions. Better education in the South would also prevent northern schools from luring away southern youth and, De Bow promised, would thereby fulfill an important political function. He explained, "The South should take charge of her own sons, and not trust them to the tender keeping and instructions of those who are hostile to the interests which those sons are hereafter to maintain."[17]

15. *DBR*, II (September, December, 1846), 75–76, 407; IV (October, 1847), 211; XII (May, 1852), 504–505; *DBR*, After the War Series, I (January, 1866), 4. For the escalating concerns other southerners shared regarding economic independence see McCardell, *Idea of a Southern Nation*, 91–140.

16. *DBR*, I (January, 1846), 2–3; VII (September, 1849), 228, 230–31.

17. *DBR*, V (March, 1848), 232–35.

The University of Louisiana provided De Bow with an opportunity to put his theories of education into practice. Authorized by the state constitution of 1845 and located in New Orleans, the university existed in name only when the legislature incorporated it in 1847 but provided no funding. In February of that year Maunsel White suggested, "It is high time that some efficient steps were taken to organize and set in operation the Institution." De Bow agreed. Recognizing the legislature's reluctance to raise revenue for support of the school, De Bow set forth a plan to operate it as a joint-stock company under the control of the state, the city of New Orleans, and private investors. In the *Review* De Bow proposed that the university include a department of commerce and statistical information, the only one of its kind in the world. He argued that New Orleans was uniquely suited for such a program. He cited the census of 1840 to show that one in thirteen New Orleanians was engaged in commercial activities, a greater concentration than in any other American city. De Bow pictured the university as a dispensary of practical education, one that gave preference "to the *useful* over the *ornamental.*" His goal was to "diffuse knowledge among *men,* and not among *philosophers!*" He wished to replace "antique" subjects like metaphysics, philology, and dialectics with pragmatic ones such as civil engineering, "the Philosophy of Manufactures, the Chemistry of Agriculture, the Principles and Laws of Commerce, and the mysterious and inexhaustible powers of the Steam Engine." De Bow's plan won White's wholehearted endorsement. In 1848, White offered to donate land and money to the university if it would create a chair of commerce and statistical information and place James De Bow in it.[18]

University administrators unanimously named De Bow to the Chair of Commerce, Public Economy, and Statistics in 1848 and gave him until August, 1849, to organize his department. Having anticipated his nomination, De Bow had carefully prepared for his new duties. He recommended that the university secure an endowment of $20,000 to $25,000 for the commerce department, though he offered no suggestion as to where this money should come from. This endowment, he anticipated, would yield between $2,000

18. John P. Dyer, *Tulane: The Biography of a University* (New York, 1966), 20–25; Maunsel White to De Bow, February 10, 1847, in *DBR,* III (March, 1847), 260–65; *DBR,* VI (August, 1848), 111; V (March, 1848), 237; VII (September, 1849), 226, 228–29; Maunsel White to the Board of Administrators of the University of Louisiana, January 28, 1848, in *DBR,* V (March, 1848), 240; Skipper, *De Bow,* 43–44.

and $2,500 annually in interest, which should constitute the professor's salary. He proposed also, "as a further stimulus to exertion," that the professor receive "certain moderate fees from individuals attending his classes or private Lectures." Students had to pay $50 in tuition to the university, and anyone else could attend individual lecture for $10 each, "with the exception of those whose means are limited, and who shall receive the advantages free." The state, he said, should allocate money for a hall and appropriate $500 a year to increase the collections of commercial and economic literature in the library. De Bow provided a list of almost three hundred books that he considered basic. Turning from administrative matters, De Bow discussed the syllabus. His course would consist of two parts: the theory of commerce, economy, and statistics, and practical applications. He planned to require twelve books, including Adam Smith's *Wealth of Nations* and annual economic reports from American and foreign governments. He would deliver twelve lectures, and students would take a public examination at the year's end.[19]

De Bow began his academic career optimistically. Despite small enrollment in his class and the university he anticipated hiring many professors and inviting distinguished speakers to give guest lectures. He now planned on delivering twenty-five to thirty lectures and hoped the university would publish them; he would use the work as a textbook in subsequent classes. He split his course in two, offering one class on economics and the other on commerce. After attending public examinations in 1851, Professor De Bow boasted that the University of Louisiana was the best school in the Southwest and had the potential to become "the best in the world."[20]

The realities of higher education in Louisiana, however, crushed De Bow's dreams. Enrollment in the university and in De Bow's class had not increased appreciably by the time he left the faculty in 1855. Few people matched Maunsel White's financial support for the school so the Board of Administrators could never provide an endowment for the Department of Commerce. Legislators proved more indifferent to the plight of the university than the citizens of New Orleans. During De Bow's tenure, the school received an average of less than $9,000 annually from the state,

19. *DBR*, III (June, 1847), 512–16; Skipper, *De Bow*, 44–45.
20. *DBR*, III (June, 1847), 513–14; VII (August, 1849), 188; XI (August, 1851), 220–21.

and most of this amount went to the medical school. In 1855 De Bow complained that school buildings were generally "unfinished and untenantable." The university would not prosper until after the Civil War, when, under private control, it was renamed Tulane University. As his friend Gayarré said, De Bow's professorship proved a "barren honor."[21]

De Bow continued to manage the *Review* while he worked at the university, yet he "was always craving for some additional task," Gayarré recalled, and he found many from 1847 to the early 1850s. In 1847 he helped establish the Louisiana Historical Society and remained active in the organization after it merged with the state Academy of Sciences. Gayarré, when secretary of state in Louisiana, recommended that De Bow be appointed to direct the new state Bureau of Statistics. De Bow had always had an innate curiosity about statistics and considered their accurate and reliable compilation not only fascinating but essential for economic planning and commercial development. He gladly accepted his new post.[22]

To De Bow, statistical information also became a major element in the conflict between northerners and southerners.

> The former have for a variety of reasons had the advantage of us in exhibiting their resources and strength. They have had all the statisticians to themselves and all the statistical reports. They have used them as powerful implements of aggression, and the South, having nothing to show in return, has been compelled to see her cause greatly prejudiced. Until almost the present day none of the southern states have regarded it at all important to secure records and returns of population and wealth. Not one periodical devoted itself to those subjects, though the North had many. We were taunted with our comparative weakness, poverty, insecurity, decay, and told that they were the natural results of slavery! Having no facts to oppose, we were passive, and for the most part admitted the justice of the charge. We had not studied our own strength.

De Bow maintained, however, that the South was not an economic backwater, as northern foes claimed, and that a slave society could compete with any in an industrial age. He was sure that a care-

21. Dyer, *Tulane*, 22, 335; Skipper, *De Bow*, 46; *DBR*, XIX (October, 1855), 436; *DBR*, After the War Series, III (June, 1867), 501.
22. *DBR*, After the War Series, III (June, 1867), 502; Charles Gayarré to Governor Alexander Mouton, June 19, 1847, in De Bow Papers, WPL; De Bow to Edmund Burke, n.d., in *DBR*, VIII (January, 1850), 32–39; Skipper, *De Bow*, 46–47.

ful statistical analysis would prove that "the South has nothing to blush for."[23]

In its initial promise and eventual frustration, De Bow's experience at the Bureau of Statistics resembled his work at the state university. In the *Review* he congratulated Louisiana legislators for creating the first permanent statistical bureau in the country and urged other states to follow their example. He published a sample survey in the *Review* in 1848 that provided guidelines and suggested topics of inquiry for the bureau. De Bow's elaborate questionnaire, to be completed by parish officials, asked for information on such subjects as local history, topography, demographics, ethnicity, education, and religion, descriptions of local agriculture and manufacturing, local professional societies, and literary production. After two years, however, De Bow's survey had "produced little fruit." He complained that legislative appropriations for the bureau were too small and handicapped his ability to collect information. By 1851 only three parishes had responded. Despite a multitude of other commitments, De Bow redoubled his efforts to complete his survey of the state. With sectional tension adding urgency to his labors, he insisted that southerners must stop the "unlicensed misrepresentation or widely propagated error" of northerners. If sectional conflict led to war, his survey would help show southerners "our resources of resistance."[24]

Few southerners matched De Bow's energy or shared his vision. Only a bare majority of parishes in Louisiana ever responded to his survey. By 1852 he was so discouraged that he recommended the abolition of the state Bureau of Statistics. He believed the work should continue, but under private auspices. De Bow published preliminary findings in the *Review* and still tried to convince people in other states to emulate his work. His crusade, however, ended in failure, and he was never able to publish a complete report.[25]

De Bow's work brought him into contact with officials in Washington. In 1850 he had written to the commissioner of patents in the recently established Department of Interior to ask for help in promoting the collection of statistical information in other states. The same year De Bow had also written a series of letters to Joseph

23. *DBR*, VIII (May, 1850), 441; XI (February, 1851), 152.
24. *DBR*, VI (July, October, and November, 1848), 79–80, 285; VIII (May, 1850), 442–43; IX (September, 1850), 286–87; Skipper, *De Bow*, 46.
25. Skipper, *De Bow*, 47–48; *DBR*, XIV (May, 1853), 431.

Kennedy, director of the Census Bureau, offering suggestions about administering the next census. The enlarged and more sophisticated seventh census resembled the survey De Bow had conducted in Louisiana. Kennedy was fired soon after President Franklin Pierce took office in 1853, the victim of a patronage battle. Because Democrats in Louisiana had been prominent supporters of Pierce, the president wanted to reward his backers there by selecting a Louisianian as the new superintendent of the census. De Bow was the obvious choice.[26]

De Bow was already in Washington petitioning for a different job when administration officials offered him the one at the census office. He had hoped to receive an appointment as commissioner of patents, as he had hoped he would four years earlier. At that time he had expected a fellow Louisianian, President Zachary Taylor, to make him the first commissioner ever from the South. He wanted applications for patents from southerners to receive special attention and must have been disappointed when he was not chosen. In 1853, however, when Pierce's men offered him the post at the Census Bureau—and a $3,600 annual salary—De Bow graciously accepted.[27]

When De Bow took office in March, 1853, he found the Census Bureau in disarray. Although Kennedy had supervised the collection and initial tabulation of census returns, De Bow considered the bureau's traditional procedures obsolete and inefficient. He said the bureau had printed previous censuses "in such a manner as unfitted them for general use, understanding, or reference," and much information had been inaccurate. The bureau had incomplete holdings of schedules from before 1830, and those it did possess were "unbound, and in great confusion." Shortly before he began work the Census Bureau had 160 employees, many of whom were strictly political appointees. Although De Bow also owed his job to politics, he complained that many of his staff had no previous experience and that some could not even add. He fired most of these "laggards" and maintained a staff of only 35 "*working men*."[28]

De Bow also offered a thoughtful program of reform in the hope

26. De Bow to Edmund Burke (commissioner of patents), n.d., in *DBR*, VIII (January, 1850), 32–39; Skipper, *De Bow*, 69–72.

27. Skipper, *De Bow*, 72; De Bow to Thomas Ewing, March 6, 1849, in James Dunwoody Brownson De Bow Letters, HNOC; *DBR*, XIV (May, 1853), 524.

28. *Seventh Census, 1850*, vi; J. D. B. De Bow, *Statistical View of the United States . . . Being a Compendium of the Seventh Census* (Washington, D.C., 1854), 11, 17–18; *DBR*, After the War Series, III (June, 1867), 593.

that changes would continue at the bureau after his tenure ended. As enumerators, those charged with collecting data, De Bow believed that every county or parish in the country should select someone familiar with statistical information and thoroughly acquainted with the area, such as local tax assessors. Each county, not the federal government, should pay for the services performed. Similarly, De Bow asserted that employees in the Census Bureau should receive special training and education. The bureau could not function effectively staffed by political appointees who gained and lost their jobs with every new administration. Instead, De Bow wanted the federal government to follow the example of several states, including Louisiana, by establishing a permanent bureau of statistics and hiring only properly trained personnel. It would take until 1880 for Congress to incorporate some of De Bow's recommendations.[29]

In the meantime De Bow proudly announced that the seventh census marked a new era in collection of statistical information. Its 640,000 pages of manuscript schedules constituted twice the number produced by the previous census and over four times that of the 1830 census. The census included more detail than ever on population, occupations, slaveholding, taxation, manufacturing, religion, schools, libraries, newspapers, crime, and pauperism. Although some northerners questioned whether De Bow's pro-South bias affected the compilation of his data, most Americans agreed that he was the leading statistician in the country.[30]

After completing his duties at the Census Bureau, De Bow proudly announced, "I am an American Citizen," and celebrated the bonds of Union in his *Review*. Only two years before he had declared, "In a question between the North and the South, I prefer the South," and used the *Review* to rally popular support for secession. This shift stemmed neither from hypocrisy nor opportunism, even though the fortunes of the *Review* had suffered from De Bow's inattention.[31] Instead, it betrayed De Bow's ambivalence toward the Union, an attitude that emerged periodically throughout his life.

From its outset the *Review* clearly revealed that its editor was torn between his dedication to the South and to the Union. As a

29. De Bow, *Statistical View*, 17–19; Skipper, *De Bow*, 80.

30. De Bow, *Statistical View*, 12; Skipper, *De Bow*, 79–80. Also see [F.] M. Kelley to De Bow, May 4, 1855, James Henry to De Bow, June 18, 1855, and Maunsel White to De Bow, August 11, 1860, in De Bow Papers, WPL.

31. *DBR*, XII (May, 1852), 500; XVII (August, 1854), 111–14; Skipper, *De Bow*, 79.

champion of commerce De Bow believed that the prosperity of the South was linked with that of the North. "Together they have flourished, and together they must falter and fall," he said in 1850. In part, De Bow spoke from personal interest. The *Review* had offices in New York and Boston as well as Washington, Richmond, Charleston, Mobile, and New Orleans, and he had invested in property not only in the South but also in Iowa, Kansas, and Minnesota. De Bow's political philosophy exacerbated his dilemma. At times his political discourses sounded exactly like Beverly Tucker's. De Bow once described American politics as a battle that pitted "federation against consolidation—chartered rights against cruel, inexorable majorities—liberty against power—a constitution against the omnipotence of parliament [Congress]." But on the question of sovereignty De Bow shared none of Tucker's logic or reasoning. He either could not make up his mind about sovereignty or did not understand its meaning. In September, 1846, he stated that the federal government enjoyed "full possession of all the high and essential attributes of sovereignty" but only eight months later claimed it was southerners' "sovereign right" to own slaves.[32]

Only issues of honor could force De Bow to choose consistently between his section and the nation. Although his advocacy of industrialization and modernization dramatically separated De Bow from most other fire-eaters, the editor had as acute a sense of honor as any southerner. Defense of personal honor could lead De Bow nearly to the extremes of Keitt and Wigfall. After the death of his wife, Caroline Poe De Bow, in 1848, De Bow's relationship with the Poe family became strained over the upbringing of De Bow's daughter. He visited the Poes in Virginia hoping to reach some understanding with them but found "their persecutions related chiefly to the child and my control of it" more than he could tolerate. Perhaps the Poes expressed understandable concern that the busy De Bow might not prove an attentive parent. Whatever words they exchanged, De Bow announced, "My line of duty is clear." He decided that unless "reason is restored to them" he would not allow the Poes to see his child. He explained to Gayarré, "She cannot in honor receive the caresses of those who by word & act have dishonored her father."[33]

32. *DBR*, VIII (May, 1850), 442; II (September, 1846), 75–76; III (May, 1847), 421; Skipper, *De Bow*, 64, 87, 130.

33. J. D. B. De Bow to Charles Gayarré, July 29, 1858, in Charles Gayarré Papers, HNOC; Skipper, *De Bow*, 108. Caroline Poe was a cousin of writer Edgar Allan Poe.

To De Bow southern honor required as vigilant a defense as did his young daughter. When northerners challenged the morality of slaveholders, De Bow snapped back, "As Southerners, as *Americans,* as MEN, we deny the right of being *called to account* for our institutions, our policy, our laws, or our government." For southerners, he maintained, slavery represented "country, life, death—everything." Attacks on the institution, therefore, were insulting, degrading, and intolerable. De Bow also perceived challenges to southern honor in the region's commercial dependence on the North. "Why are we for ever nerveless, in debt, and without surplus for any purpose, and must run off to the North whenever we would procure a little capital to work a mill site or dam a river?" he asked. De Bow insisted that only economic self-sufficiency could free the South of this mark of degradation and dishonor. Whatever the source of the insult, De Bow offered the same counsel. Rather than meekly accept dishonor, southerners must "act as patriots ever should act, doing and daring, and leaving the consequences to God." He believed that southerners must fight the progress of freesoilism and abolitionism without hesitation. When rights or honor came under attack, "the course of manhood against the invader ceases to be words." [34]

To De Bow the territorial issue and congressional debates of 1850 menaced southern rights, liberty, and honor. Although not yet prepared to advocate secession, De Bow insisted that the right of southerners to control their slaves "without compromise of any sort, *must be preserved,* or the Union will become a snare rather than a blessing." He warned his readers that northern political and economic power grew constantly "and soon will be *irresistible.*" The conflict between sections "must soon be settled." [35]

In July, 1850, De Bow published an editorial entitled "The Cause of the South" in which he warned southerners that they faced a precarious situation. The South had to defend itself from the "reckless fanaticism" of northerners, who, he charged, plotted to destroy slavery. The abolition of slavery could not occur without "a servile war, continued struggles of the races of whites and blacks, desolation of fields, hearths and homes, abandonment of half a score of great States entirely to Ethiopian manners, industry and civilization!" If southern resistance led to destruction of the Union—"the source of

34. *DBR,* III (May, 1847), 421; IX (November, 1850), 567; XII (May, 1852), 498–99; XV (November, 1853), 537.
35. *DBR,* VIII (May, 1850), 441; IX (November, 1850), 567; X (January, 1851), 1.

our greatness and strength"—De Bow predicted that southerners would suffer economic "impotency and ruin." He had hoped that the Nashville Convention might adopt some middle course but was disappointed that state after state "gave [the convention] the cold shoulder." When assemblies such as the Nashville Convention failed to lead to action, De Bow correctly observed that in the North, "Our protests are regarded [as] but gasconade; our earnestness, hypocrisy; our solemn declarations of rights, the silly declaration of men, without concert, whom the first federal thunders will coerce into submission—unwilling and boisterous and fretful, to be sure, but still *submissive.*" He thought that genuine salvation for the South lay not in "bandying constitutional arguments" with northerners, in congressional debates, or in blind faith in the sanctity of the Union, "but in the busy hum of mechanism, and in the thrifty operations of the hammer and the anvil." As long as northerners conducted southern commerce, built and navigated the ships that carried southern cargoes, supplied material and engineers for southern railroads, wove and spun southern cotton, dominated the region's publishing industry and the nation's literature, educated southern youth, and received millions annually from southerners traveling to northern "watering places," the South would never have the leverage required to protect its rights and interests within the Union. With so much at risk, De Bow exclaimed, "Before heaven! we have work before us now."[36]

De Bow was shocked when radical newspapers in Georgia and South Carolina objected that his editorial was too moderate. As one of the few Louisianians to support the first Nashville Convention, De Bow considered himself "a *very Hotspur* in these wars of the South." In turn, he lashed out at those who joined the struggle for southern rights "at the very eleventh hour!" De Bow assured his readers that he would continue to fight for southern interests "until the citadel is safe from every internal and foreign foe."[37]

After Congress passed the Compromise of 1850, De Bow began to sound like some of the radicals he had recently denounced. He said that northerners had failed to respect the compromises they had made with southerners in the past, and he did not anticipate that they would treat this new bargain any differently. Northern

36. *DBR,* IX (July, 1850), 120–24. Substantial excerpts from this article appear in Paskoff and Wilson, eds., *Cause of the South,* 183–88.
37. *DBR,* IX (September, October, 1850), 352, 463.

transgression had pushed southerners beyond forbearance, he exclaimed. While profiting from their business connections with the slave states, northerners had always held their southern neighbors in contempt. Northern hostility to southerners had been a "concealed and creeping worm," but it had now "crept up from the slime and filth to the topmost column of the national temple." By January, 1851, De Bow believed that the South was no longer safe within the Union.[38]

De Bow's familiar call for southern self-sufficiency now took on urgent and even desperate overtones. Southerners must cut all ties with the North, he said. De Bow estimated that northern businessmen earned $40 million a year through processing raw materials produced in the South. If southerners could mill every bale of cotton they produced, they would cease paying "tribute to Northern looms" and "hush the sound of every spindle in New-England." He estimated that fifty thousand southerners traveled north every year and spent $15 million there. He insisted that this practice must stop. In the *Review* he described "southern watering places and scenery" as being as attractive as any in the North. He also demanded that southerners cease sending their children to northern schools. Even if southern schools were inferior, De Bow explained, "better would it be for us that our sons remained in honest ignorance and at the plough-handle, than that their plastic minds be imbued with doctrines subversive of their country's [the South's] peace and honor, and at war with the very principles upon which the whole superstructure of the society they find *at home* is based." De Bow's statistical analysis showed that southerners' economic "vassalage to the North" cost them $100 million annually in money funneled to northern manufacturers, resorts, and schools. If southerners threw off "this humiliating dependence" and kept their money at home, De Bow maintained that they would have enough capital to create their own navy, build new factories and railroads, and improve their schools and cities. If southerners obeyed the dictates of self-defense, "a *separate confederation* will be formed, for which there are at the South all the resources of wealth, and power, and opulence!"[39]

De Bow's extremism increased when southern resistance waned and Unionism experienced a resurgence throughout the South.

38. *DBR*, XI (January, March, 1851), 106–107, 329; XII (May, 1851), 497, 499.
39. *DBR*, XI (January, 1851), 107–108, 160; XII (May, 1852), 499–500; XI (March, 1851), 352–57, 362; XI (February, 1851), 161.

Other fire-eaters no longer doubted his earnestness, but by the end of 1852 De Bow faced a more immediate and practical problem—the possibility of alienating moderates. If his *Review* were to survive, he too would have to stop discussing secession and accept the Compromise of 1850. Ever the pragmatist, De Bow did exactly that.

Only a year after vilifying northerners as treacherous enemies, De Bow resumed the comfortable business relationships he had shared with them before the recent crisis. Over the next few years most of the revenue for the *Review* came from northern advertisers, even though he offered better rates to southern businessmen. He worked with officials of the New York World's Fair in 1853 by screening potential exhibitors from the Southwest. When that same year De bow announced his decision to head the Census Bureau, he explained that his work in the nation's capital might make his *Review* more national in scope, though he promised that it would remain devoted to southern interests.[40]

De Bow's Unionism was contingent on a rigid enforcement of the Compromise of 1850 both in letter and spirit. He stipulated that all Americans must keep "the rough and jagged points of sectional rivalry" from disrupting the nation. In 1853 he warned northerners that abolitionism threatened to destroy the calm that resulted from the new compromise. When he reprinted articles from the *Review* in his three-volume *Industrial Resources, Etc., of the Southern and Western States,* De Bow included a substantial number on blacks and slavery. He vainly hoped that his anthology would "entirely exhaust the subject" and finally put an end to the national debate over slavery. When antislavery agitation continued, however, De Bow urged southerners to remain vigilant in the defense of slavery and watchful of the "growing wanton and arrogant" power of the North.[41]

By 1856, the growth of the Republican party, bloodshed in Kansas, and congressional debate over the territory's statehood combined to alarm De Bow. He found "no principle so clear" as the right of southerners to make Kansas a slave state, and he interpreted

40. *DBR*, XXII (May, 1857), 555–56; XIV (March, May, 1853), 300, 524.
41. *DBR*, XV (November, 1853), 486, 537; XVII (August, 1854), 111–14; J. D. B. De Bow, *The Industrial Resources, Etc., of the Southern and Western States* . . . (3 vols.; New Orleans, New York, and Charleston, 1853), I, preface; II, 196–345; III, 53–70; J. D. B. De Bow to H. W. Conner, April 5, 1854, in New York *Times,* April 14, 1854; De Bow to the governor-elect of Virginia [Henry A. Wise], October 2, 1855, in De Bow Papers, WPL.

northern opposition as a sign of another impending constitutional crisis. Believing the Kansas controversy proved that northerners had abandoned the spirit of compromise, De Bow irrevocably turned his back on Unionism and again focused exclusively on the cause of the South.[42]

De Bow launched his campaign for secession at the Knoxville Commercial Convention in 1857. In his presidential address to the Tennessee meeting, De Bow conceded that "in practical results" commercial conventions had proven a failure. They had "built no railroad, equipped no steamship, nor established a factory or college." They had, however, provided an annual forum in which southerners could express their grievances against the North. De Bow therefore recommended that henceforth southerners should use these conventions to promote political unity in the South and to teach its people that the South had sufficient resources to survive outside the Union "and to maintain the rank of a first class power wherever it should be deemed necessary, to establish a separate confederation."[43]

According to De Bow, the rise of the Republican party made secession imperative. Republicans not only planned to prevent the expansion of slavery into the territories, thereby excluding southerners "from every avenue of national growth," but also to "denounce us as cowards and robbers . . . unfitted to share with them in christian communion." This attitude, he believed, meant there could be no future compromises. Unless southerners were prepared to give up slavery, remaining in a Union that included Republicans would destroy their honor. And if southerners did yield to their northern "task masters," they jeopardized their very existence because free blacks would spread death and destruction over the land. If southerners could prevent the "overwhelming and seemingly unscrupulous power" of Republicans from transforming the country into an "open and palpable tyranny," De Bow insisted that they must do so. But if the Union could not be saved with southern rights intact, "It is to be crushed."[44]

Five years earlier De Bow had worried that the South lacked the

42. De Bow to [?], August 20, 1856, in De Bow Letters, HNOC; De Bow to [J. D. Davidson], August 20, 1856, in James D. Davidson Papers, WPL; *DBR*, XXI (October, 1856), 438.

43. *DBR*, XXIII (September, 1857), 230, 232–33, 301; McCardell, *Idea of a Southern Nation*, 129–31.

44. *DBR*, XXIII (September, 1857), 227–31.

industrial capacity to sustain itself as a separate nation, but by 1857 the erstwhile champion of commerce had joined the swelling number of southerners who believed that cotton provided them with unlimited economic power. The reasons for his shift remain unclear. De Bow certainly knew that world demand for cotton had grown throughout the decade, and he might have believed, as many southerners did, that the agricultural base of the southern economy saved it from the financial convulsions northern businessmen suffered when the Panic of 1857 began. Whatever the reason, De Bow now paid homage to the omnipotence of cotton. As a member of the resolutions committee of the Savannah Commercial Convention in 1856, De Bow called for increased agricultural productivity and the elimination of northern participation in the trade between the South and Europe. At Knoxville, De Bow attributed magical qualities to cotton. If a southern confederacy took the cotton trade away from the North, he predicted, "Great interior towns will spring up as by enchantment and great sea-cities and arteries of communication between them reticulate the whole face of the country." A nominal tariff would quickly give a southern government the funds to build "palaces and fleets and navies." Cotton would protect a southern nation from all adversaries and make its borders secure. De Bow explained that if the North failed to return fugitive slaves, a southern confederacy had but to withhold exports of cotton to cripple northern industry. "It is the cotton bale that makes the treaties of the world, and binds over the nations to keep the peace," he claimed.[45]

Few southerners were willing to consider secession in 1857. Most placed their faith in President James Buchanan and hoped for yet another compromise to settle sectional strife. When the president split with members of his own party over Kansas, his support in the South grew. But De Bow doubted that the Pennsylvania Democrat had the ability either to take control of his own party or to contain the growing Republican opposition.[46] In the face of popular opposition, De Bow continued his campaign for secession in 1858 more passionately and energetically than ever.

In the spring De Bow gave a speech to the alumni of the College of Charleston. As when he spoke at Knoxville, he used the occasion to advocate secession. De Bow professed love and devotion to the

45. *DBR*, XXI (November, 1856), 550–53; XXII (September, 1857), 234–36.
46. De Bow to W. P. Miles, September 4, 1857, in William Porcher Miles Papers, SHC; *DBR*, XXX (April, 1861), 429.

Union but told his audience that "people are easiest enslaved who, clinging to the traditions, the memories, and the fame of their country, are mindless, as to its present practical workings." The current political situation, he warned, offered only subjugation to the South. With no prospect of creating new slave states, southerners would soon be overwhelmed by the North. They would have no security or liberty in a Union in which they were outnumbered and politically powerless. Because the Republican party proclaimed hatred and hostility toward slavery, a Union in which the party participated would denigrate southern honor. De Bow asked, "Has republicanism in seventy years fitted us for concessions and degradations to which not a thousand years of monarchy or despotism have fitted the Cossak or the Briton?" Southerners had but two choices, he said: submission to the North or immediate secession. Only the latter was "above board and manly," and De Bow reminded his listeners that "if language has any meaning, we are committed by every regard to manliness and honor." Despite his own lingering attachment to the Union, De Bow declared himself "an extremist perhaps—a fire-eater, in the language of our enemies—a disunionist, when the question is between the surrender of the *substance* of rights and liberties and the maintenance of this *sentiment* of Union."[47]

Immediately after his speech at Charleston, De Bow prepared for the Montgomery Commercial Convention of 1858. He wanted to make the Alabama meeting into even more of a political forum than Knoxville had been. To do so, he prodded delegates into a discussion of one of the most volatile issues of the day, the reopening of the African slave trade. In 1857 in the *Review* he had called for discussion of the topic. Although he had declined to take a position on the issue, his mere mention of it emboldened others. "Stick to the Slave Trade," begged George Fitzhugh, one of the leading defenders of slavery in the South. De Bow found William L. Yancey another important ally. Of all the topics he might address at the convention, Yancey told De Bow, he preferred to discuss the African slave trade.[48]

De Bow played only a minor role once the convention assembled

47. De Bow to Lewis R. Gibbes, December 27, 1857, in Lewis R. Gibbes Papers, LC; *DBR*, XXX (April, 1861), 429–35.

48. *DBR*, XXII (June, 1857), 663–64; George Fitzhugh to De Bow, January 26, 1858, and William L. Yancey to De Bow, March 25, [1858 or 1859], in De Bow Papers, WPL.

in May, but he must have been pleased with its results. Yancey's impassioned orations on southern rights and the African slave trade had their desired effect and, combined with the attendance of Barnwell Rhett and Edmund Ruffin, transformed the commercial convention into a political one. De Bow's agenda promised to prevail again the following year; he, Yancey, and John Quitman (elected in absentia) were among those chosen to prepare the address calling for the next meeting at Vicksburg, Mississippi.[49]

Encouraged by the radicalization of the Montgomery convention, De Bow began to agitate for secession more openly than ever. In the *Review* he argued that the only remedy for the sectional crisis was to "make us independent of all nations, and respected by all." With the right of nullification rebuked and that of secession questioned, De Bow explained, "The right of revolution seems only to have survived—which is to say, that there is no remedy against oppression under a federated system." Those who looked for "an ark of safety from great and impending dangers," he promised, would "find it in separation."[50]

Yancey's inability to attend the Vicksburg convention forced De Bow to do much of the talking. Again he chose to focus on the African slave trade. If African slavery were "very right and very proper," De Bow wondered, how was it "immoral, irreligious, wicked, and inexpedient" to bring more Africans to the South? Repeating information supplied by Edmund Ruffin, De Bow pointed to the rise in slave prices and increased demand for their labor as reasons to renew the trade. Natural population increase, he said, could not keep up with demand, especially in the rapidly expanding Southwest. Besides, an influx of slaves would bring prices down and enable more whites to buy them and use them on less profitable land. Finally, De Bow agreed with Yancey that federal restriction of slavery in any form was an insulting "brand upon the institutions of the South."[51] Although only a small minority of

49. *DBR*, XXIV (June, 1858), 604. Although the assembly did not express an opinion on reopening the African slave trade, radicals at the Montgomery convention helped set the stage for victory the following year at Vicksburg. See William K. Scarborough, ed., *The Diary of Edmund Ruffin* (3 vols.; Baton Rouge, 1972–89), I, 188; McCardell, *Idea of a Southern Nation*, 138.

50. *DBR*, XXV (July, August, and December, 1858), 124, 127, 703.

51. *DBR*, XXVII (July, 1859), 97; Edmund Ruffin, "The Effects of High Prices of Slaves," *DBR*, XXVI (June, 1859), 647–57; De Bow to Yancey, June 3, 1859, *DBR*, XXVI (August, 1859), 232–34.

southerners wished the African slave trade reopened, De Bow convinced the delegates at Vicksburg to pass a resolution, by a vote of 44 to 19, urging the repeal of all state and federal prohibitions on the trade.[52]

Finding that most southerners refused to support the Vicksburg resolutions, De Bow shifted his attention back to the Republicans and the election of 1860. He said that the presidential election would resolve "the greatest political excitements ever known in the history of this country." He warned that the Republican party, "an active, powerful, unscrupulous organization," was prepared to destroy the South and the Constitution. De Bow had little hope for electoral victory over this foe, but he grew optimistic about southern resistance after the Democratic party split at the Charleston Convention in the spring of 1860. The actions of southern delegates, he believed, proved "that a union of the South is not so impracticable as its enemies have been taught to think." "Aroused from its lethargy and despair," the South was finally ready to confront its northern nemesis.[53]

In the summer De Bow turned his attention to presidential candidates and aspirants. He reviewed the qualifications of more than thirty men mentioned for the presidency. De Bow found most of them wanting, their only assets coming from the "doctrine of availability." John C. Breckinridge, Joseph Lane, and Jefferson Davis received positive evaluations from De Bow, and predictably, Abraham Lincoln got the worst. The "low and vulgar partisan of John Brown," claimed De Bow, owed his candidacy only to "intrigue and perfidity." Should Lincoln win, De Bow asked, "is there not enough virtue in our people to break the ignoble shackles [of Union], and proclaim themselves free?"[54]

As the election drew closer De Bow reverted to an old and familiar tactic. After printing pages of statistics in the *Review* comparing the economies, industry, and population of the North and South, he listed the amount of wealth the Union extracted annually from the South. Fishing bounties, customs, profits northern manufacturers made from southern resources and those of northern importers and shippers, money spent by southern travelers and stu-

52. *DBR*, XXVI (June, 1859), 713. At Vicksburg, De Bow was elected president of the newly formed African Labor Supply Association. This organization, however, apparently never met. See *DBR*, XXVII (July 1859), 120–21.

53. *DBR*, XXVIII (June, 1860), 742.

54. *DBR*, XXIX (July, 1860), 92–103.

dents in the North, and money paid to northerners working in the South totaled $231,500,000, according to De Bow. Again he hoped that his readers would realize that the South had ample resources to sustain itself if it seceded.[55]

In the last issue of the *Review* to appear before the election, De Bow's rhetoric reached its most extreme and intemperate level. In every previous sectional crisis, he said, the only southerners who claimed the North posed no threat to slavery were "certain hungry applicants for federal office, the more ambitious national politicians, a few of the larger holders of slaves, whose fathers were born in New-England, or graduated, themselves, at Harvard, and whom great property has made timid, some very respectable old ladies, and a batch of Yankee editors, and school-masters, throughout the land." Because of them, De Bow insisted, the South had made concession after concession to the North. If they would remain true to themselves, De Bow assured southerners, they would make the South safe and free.[56]

"All chance for the election of Breckinridge & Lane is gone, and that of Lincoln is almost certain," Frank De Bow wrote to James in late August. The De Bow brothers actually looked forward to Lincoln's election, believing that southern unity was never so great and secession never more certain. In October James assured an audience in Washington that South Carolina would secede soon after Lincoln's election and that Mississippi, Alabama, Georgia, and Texas would quickly follow. "Florida and Arkansas are but offshoots from the Carolina tree," De Bow stated, "and the governor of Louisiana agrees in the sentiment of 'Lincoln and disunion.'" De Bow said that for fifteen years he had tried to warn southerners about the growing fanaticism of the North, "and now the long-predicted revolution has come."[57]

On his way back to Louisiana, De Bow stopped in Charleston and spoke with Robert N. Gourdin, leader of the 1860 Association. This group was organized in September to promote secession by distributing literature throughout the South. Gourdin asked De Bow to write a pamphlet discussing the interests of nonslaveholders in slavery. De Bow's response, printed by the association, in the Charleston *Mercury*, and in the *Review*, marked the final chapter of

55. *DBR*, XXIX (August, 1860), 211.
56. *DBR*, XXIX (October, 1860), 534–35.
57. Frank De Bow to J. D. B. De Bow, August 21, 1860, in De Bow Papers, WPL; Charleston *Mercury*, November 6, 1860.

the antebellum proslavery argument. De Bow's reputation as an economist and statistician made his discourse a signal piece of propaganda during the secession crisis.[58]

De Bow insisted that all southerners had a vital interest in slavery. Though the census of 1850 listed 347,256 slaveowners, De Bow suggested that family members had to be added to obtain a more accurate idea of the number of southerners who relied on slavery. A revised total came to around 2 million. Almost every non-slaveholder came into contact with slavery, and, according to De Bow, many owed their livelihood to the institution. Small farmers grew corn and wheat and raised livestock for sale to planters, who often did not grow provisions for their slaves on their own plantations. De Bow asserted that slavery touched all aspects of southern agriculture, trade, and commerce. Like other fire-eaters, De Bow subscribed to the mud-sill theory. Whereas poor whites occupied the bottom of the social order in the North, De Bow maintained that slavery placed blacks irrevocably at the bottom of southern society. "No white man at the South serves another as his body-servant," he explained, "to clean his boots, wait on his table, and perform the menial services of his household!" Because they saw daily examples of slavery, all white southerners guarded and appreciated their own liberty. Slavery also provided southerners with potential social mobility. Many southerners could afford to purchase at least one slave, and if they bought a female "her children become heirlooms, and make the nucleus of an estate." Sons of nonslaveholders had already made a significant impact on southern society. De Bow noted that Andrew Jackson, Henry Clay, James H. Hammond, William L. Yancey, and Maunsel White, among others, had risen to prominence without having been raised by slaveowning families. Having recently purchased a few slaves, De Bow proudly counted himself among this group.[59]

Because of the interdependence and interaction of slaveholders and nonslaveholders, De Bow continued, no conflict existed within the South between free and slave labor. On the contrary, northern workers often left their jobs in crowded cities and sweatshops for more attractive employment opportunities in the South. He pro-

58. Charles E. Cauthen, *South Carolina Goes to War, 1860–1865* (Chapel Hill, 1950), 34–35, 41; De Bow, "The Non-Slaveholders of the South: Their Interest in the Present Sectional Controversy Identical with That of Slaveholders," *DBR*, XXX (January, 1861), 67–77; Charleston *Mercury*, December 15, 1860.

59. *DBR*, XXX (January, 1861), 67, 69–71, 73–75, 77.

vided statistics to show that white laborers in New Orleans, Charleston, and Nashville earned more than their counterparts in Chicago, Pittsburgh, and Toronto. He conceded that a few southerners opposed slavery but claimed that transplanted northerners and the "crazy, socialistic Germans in Texas" accounted for most of these.[60]

Nonslaveholders had more reason than anyone to preserve slavery, De Bow suggested. He considered it a truism that blacks "sink by emancipation in idleness, superstition, and vice." Slaveholders would have the resources to escape if the plague of black freedom ever befell the South, he said, but warned that poorer whites "*would be compelled to remain and endure the degradation.*" Considering all the benefits provided by slavery and the horrors sure to follow its extinction, De Bow was certain that the nonslaveholder would gladly "die in the trenches, in defence of the slave property of his more favored neighbor." In a southern confederacy "our rights and possessions would be secure," he concluded, and he predicted that "opulence would be diffused throughout all classes."[61]

In the two months after Lincoln's election, De Bow did everything he could to encourage secession. His speeches in New Orleans won him the praise of Henry J. Leovy, prosecession editor of the New Orleans *Delta*. He spoke in Charleston with Barnwell Rhett, wrote editorials for the Charleston *Mercury,* and joined Edmund Ruffin on December 20 in Charleston to witness the vote for secession. While Ruffin proceeded to Tallahassee in January to encourage a Florida convention to choose secession, De Bow went to Jackson, where he joyfully watched the Mississippi legislature vote to secede. His elation increased when his adopted state, Louisiana, voted to secede on January 26, 1861.[62]

After seven states left the Union, De Bow turned his attention to the creation of a southern nation. He hoped that the delegates at the Provisional Congress in Montgomery would quickly form a new government and name Jefferson Davis, whom De Bow had respected for years, as the new president. After Fort Sumter, De Bow reassured southerners that northern invaders could never conquer the South. Slaves, he said, provided "a powerful back ground of defence." He claimed that northern enemies would not disrupt the

60. *Ibid.*, 69, 71–72.
61. *Ibid.*, 69, 76–77.
62. Henry J. [Leovy] to De Bow, November 19, 1860, Frank De Bow to James De Bow, January 5, 1861, in De Bow Papers, WPL; New Orleans *Delta*, November 20, 1860; Skipper, *De Bow*, 120; *DBR*, XXX (February, 1861), 251.

relationship between master and slave any more successfully than
the British had during the Revolution and the War of 1812. And
because slaves could remain at home to raise provisions for a southern army, the South could put 10 million men in the field. Finally,
De Bow believed that the federal blockade of the South would lead
to the realization of his lifelong dream of southern industrial independence. "Every branch of manufacture is springing up," he exclaimed with more optimism than objectivity. He thought that
southerners would soon create everything they needed and bring
the war to a close by winter.[63]

On June 8, 1861, De Bow reviewed recent events with satisfaction and pride. On that day, "into this world of toil & labor," came
J. D. B. De Bow, Jr. A year after Caroline died, James had married
Martha E. Johns of Nashville. She gave birth there to their first son
the same day the Tennessee legislature voted to secede. "Thus,"
said the senior De Bow, "the young De Bow in recompense perhaps
of his fathers long services in the cause is a *born citizen* of the Southern Republic, upon whose escutcheon God willing he will make his
mark."[64]

De Bow, too, was eager to leave his mark on the new Confederacy. In February he had written to William P. Miles, an old
college friend and currently a Confederate congressman, to request a position in the government. "You know my capacity, training, & ambition," he said. When Union gunboats bombarded the
South Carolina coast later in the year, De Bow was tempted to join
the army and come to the aid of his native state. Realizing, however, that he could not serve in the military because of his frail
health, he consoled himself with the thought that "there is power in
the pen which may equal the blade."[65]

His desire to serve the Confederacy came to the attention of
Christopher G. Memminger, secretary of the treasury. Because of
De Bow's intimate knowledge of the southern economy, Memminger appointed him to the Produce Loan Bureau in August,
1861. De Bow's task was to secure revenue for the Confederate government through sales of commodities loaned to it by planters. "I

63. De Bow to Miles, February 5, 1861, in Miles Papers, SHC; *DBR*, XV (September, 1853), 322–23; XXX (May and June, 1861), 681–82; XXXI (July, 1861), 102,
329–30.

64. De Bow to Charles Gayarré, June 8, 1861, in Charles E. A. Gayarré Papers,
Grace King Collection, LSU; Skipper, *De Bow*, 108–109.

65. De Bow to Miles, February 5, 1861, in Miles Papers, SHC; De Bow to
Gayarré, December 16, 1861, in Gayarré Papers, LSU.

am delighted with the post," he told Gayarré. By the end of the year, Gayarré observed that De Bow was "buried under the mountain Load of the Produce Loan." Eventually, De Bow's relationship with Memminger soured, and charges of malfeasance against his subordinates tarnished De Bow's administration of the bureau. When similar charges were leveled at De Bow, he angrily wrote to President Davis denying any impropriety. With Davis' support—and a doubling of his salary to $6,000 a year—De Bow continued to serve in the government until the end of the war.[66]

De Bow's frustrations at the Produce Loan Bureau exacerbated other problems brought on by the war. Certain at the start of hostilities that world demand for cotton would break the northern blockade, De Bow was disheartened when he met with Yancey in the spring of 1862 and learned that the Confederacy could not expect foreign intervention. He had also been sure that New Orleans was impervious to attack, and he lashed out at the Confederate commander, General Mansfield Lovell, and the administration when northerners captured his home city without a struggle. His wife, son, daughter Carrie, and two slaves had moved from Martha's home in Nashville to New Orleans but escaped the Union advance and found refuge in Winnsboro, South Carolina. By August, 1862, wartime conditions forced De Bow to suspend publication of the *Review*. He printed one more issue in Columbia, South Carolina, two years later, but was then forced to stop again for the duration of the war. Losses on the battlefield and personal misfortune, however, did not diminish his faith in his cherished cause. Having long since forgiven Davis for the fall of New Orleans, De Bow tried in 1864 to rally his countrymen to the support of their beleaguered president. "He has stood, brave as Ajax and wise as Ulysses," De Bow declared, and would yet prove equal in ability and accomplishment to George Washington. Though De Bow mourned the loss of the "hero-martyrs of the war," each drop of their blood added to his defiance of "the hireling miscreants who invade our soil." As the war drew to a close, he desperately hoped that General Lee would find some way to save the Confederacy. He even considered fleeing to Mexico to help organize a Confederate guerrilla force.[67]

66. De Bow to Gayarré, August 7, 1861, in Gayarré Papers, LSU; Gayarré to De Bow, December 8, 1861, in De Bow Papers, WPL; Paskoff and Wilson, eds., *Cause of the South*, 6; De Bow to Jefferson Davis, August 4, 1864, in Jefferson Davis Papers, HTL (see also Davis' endorsement).

67. De Bow to Gayarré, July 4, 1861, January 8, June 22, 1862, February 3, 1865, in Gayarré Papers, LSU; *DBR*, XXXIII (May–August, 1862), 1, 86; XXXV (July

After surveying the physical destruction war had brought, however, De Bow decided to remain and help rebuild the South. He obtained a pardon from President Andrew Johnson and in 1865 revived the *Review*. With new headquarters in Nashville and regional offices in Boston, New York, Washington, Cincinnati, Charleston, and New Orleans, De Bow published the first postwar issue in January, 1866. He still promoted the development of commerce, manufacturing, and modern agricultural techniques but from a national rather than a sectional perspective. "Regarding the issues of the past as dead," De Bow planned to discuss only political questions that affected the current and future relationship between the states, "the permanency of the Union, and the *honor and prosperity of the Country*." He stated that his only regional concern was the reestablishment of southern economic prosperity. He retitled his journal *De Bow's Review, Devoted to the Restoration of the Southern States, and Development of the Wealth and Resources of the Country*. He subtitled it more succinctly the *After the War Series*.[68]

De Bow's apparent conversion to nationalism after the war was similar to the change he experienced after the collapse of the secession movement in 1852. As before, he did not abandon his beliefs or act merely opportunistically. He simply faced facts. The Union had dealt the Confederacy, secession, and slavery fatal blows. He testified before the Congressional Committee on Reconstruction that "the [southern] people, having fairly and honestly tried the experiment of secession, are satisfied with the result." They may have been satisfied, but were not regretful for having tried to leave the Union. After four years of bloodshed, southerners had lost everything, De Bow said, "but not, as they think, honor." Like duelists who had vindicated themselves on the field of honor, De Bow believed that once hostilities had ceased, southerners should command respect and trust from their adversaries for the gallantry and honor they had exhibited during the war. Furthermore, he genuinely believed that President Johnson intended southerners to carry out reconstruction themselves. No military force was needed to police the South, he told congressmen, "except what the States themselves would furnish." Although he still believed emancipa-

---

and August, 1864), 97, 102–103; De Bow to Miles, March 7, 1862, in Miles Papers, SHC; Skipper, *De Bow*, 171.

68. *DBR*, After the War Series, I (January, 1866), 2; III (June, 1867), 503; De Bow to [Frank De Bow], October 7, December 1, 3, 1865, January 18, 1866, in J. D. B. De Bow Papers, BTHC.

tion would prove disastrous for blacks, he said that white southerners, insofar as possible, were capable of helping blacks adjust from slavery to freedom. "No outside interference is necessary," he claimed.[69]

Although he could accept emancipation as a consequence of war, De Bow never changed his attitude toward blacks. He had pledged that white southerners would do everything possible "for the social, physical, and political advancement of the race," but he always considered these possibilities extremely limited. As a businessman he believed that white employers must treat their black employees decently so they would be "cheerful and reliable laborer[s]." But he did not consider blacks equal to whites. He thought them unfit for suffrage. He continued to profess that abolition would result in a stream of indolent blacks moving into crowded cities, "eking out a very uncertain subsistence." He blamed the Freedman's Bureau, a federal agency created to assist blacks make the transition to freedom, for creating hostility between the races, "which did not exist at the time of the surrender." De Bow promoted debate in the *Review* over how best to deal with free blacks, but far from striving for objectivity, he continued to solicit articles from such antebellum defenders of slavery as George Fitzhugh.[70]

Just as he had done before and during the war, De Bow busied himself with several ventures simultaneously. Although he and Martha both worked eight hours a day on the *Review*, in 1866 De Bow accepted the presidency of the Tennessee Pacific Railroad, a company with plans for regional development and a southern transcontinental route. In the *Review* he began to serialize a journal he had kept during the war. In the winter of 1867 he started to do the same with his "Memories of the Late War" when he received news from Elizabeth, New Jersey, that Frank had fallen ill while on a business trip to the North. Despite inclement weather, James made his way east to attend to his brother. Shortly after his arrival, he too became sick. On February 26 a doctor diagnosed James's illness as an "aggravated case of peritonitis." He died the next day.[71]

De Bow's widow and his associates took over the *Review*. They

69. *DBR*, After the War Series, I (January, May, 1866), 3, 555–56.

70. *Ibid.*, 2; De Bow to Governor B. F. Perry, October 12, 1865, *ibid.*, 7–8; De Bow to Frank De Bow, December 19, 1866, in De Bow Papers, BTHC.

71. De Bow to Frank De Bow, May 1, August 23, December 19, 1866, in De Bow Papers, BTHC; *DBR*, After the War Series, II (July–December, 1866), *passim;* III (January–May, 1867), 480–81 and *passim.*

continued to print "Memories of the War" but never found the rest of De Bow's journal. Without De Bow's tireless leadership the journal that bore his name began to founder. His heirs sold the *Review* in March, 1868, but its new owners had no better luck. They suspended publication in 1870, and the journal finally perished in October, 1879, after a firm in New York revived it as the *Agricultural Review* for four issues.[72]

In the year before his death De Bow had resumed his campaign for southern industrial independence. Rebuilding war-ravaged cities and replacing the railroads and factories that had been destroyed required southerners to "put their shoulder[s] to the wheel, intellectually and physically." He had warned his readers: "The South will lose the most compensatory lesson of the war . . . if she does not unlearn and discard the theory which once governed her policy, that she controlled her own prosperity in her control of cotton." The true source of wealth for the South, he had argued as he did before the war, would come from diversified industry. The South could not and should not wait for northerners to carry out this phase of Reconstruction, De Bow insisted; that would only recreate the antebellum economic situation of southern dependence on the North. "Put up little mills, spin a little cotton yarn, weave a little cotton cloth, make coarse and cheap woolens to start with," he suggested; "the finer and more profitable work will follow in time." Southerners should start with the best and most modern machinery and exploit all their natural resources. He pointed to the South's ample water power and timber, its coal and mineral reserves in the southern Appalachian mountains. He called for the development of an iron industry in northern Alabama and hoped that would spur industrialization elsewhere. "Every new furnace or factory is the nucleus of a town," he explained, one that would attract workers from all over the country. One of the staunchest defenders of the Old South, James De Bow finally became one of the first spokesmen for the New South.[73]

72. *DBR*, After the War Series, III (June, 1867), 603–604; IV, V (1867–68), *passim;* Paskoff and Wilson, eds., *Cause of the South,* 8.

73. *DBR*, After the War Series, I (January, 1866), 4; III (February, 1867), 173–77; Laurence Shore, *Southern Capitalists: The Ideological Leadership of an Elite, 1832–1885* (Chapel Hill, 1986), 118–20, 178–80.

The Great One Idea of My Life
Edmund Ruffin

I n the spring of 1865 Edmund Ruffin wanted to die. He was seventy-one years old, infirmities prevented him from working, and his growing deafness cut him off from the pleasures of conversation. Northern troops had sacked his plantations, and his slaves had fled. One of his sons had died while fighting for the cause that had given Ruffin's life meaning. "For years back I have had nothing left to make me desire to have my life extended another day," he had written in his diary early in May; only the hope of a miraculous Confederate triumph over the Union had kept him alive. But now that hope was gone. The last Confederate armies had surrendered. Ruffin feared that President Andrew Johnson would order the execution of many secessionists and southern wartime leaders. "I am not only a helpless & hopeless slave, under the irresistible oppression of the most unscrupulous, vile, & abhorred of rulers," he thought, but he believed that his presence endangered his family. Even if left unmolested by his northern conquerors, Ruffin could not face life among black freedmen. He found it astonishing that his fellow southerners accepted defeat and emancipation "so quietly & cooly, as if we were already prepared for, & in great measure, reconciled to their speedy approach & infliction." Their attitude seemed a rebuke to his life's work. He felt rejected and unappreciated by his countrymen, just as he had before secession. Unlike James De Bow, Ruffin would not seek a pardon, nor would he flee his beloved South, as did Louis Wigfall. The most fanatic fire-eater of all decided to defy his northern foes and leave southerners a legacy of resistance by taking his own life.[1]

Methodically and carefully, Ruffin prepared for his death. First he had to overcome his fears of death and of transgressing against God by committing suicide. He prayed for weeks that God would divert him from his intentions if they were sinful. He also read the

1. Ruffin Diary, April 15, 17, 20, 21, 24, 30, May 1, 2, 9, 16, 18, 1865, LC; Betty L. Mitchell, *Edmund Ruffin: A Biography* (Bloomington, 1981), 210–11, 215–18, 243–44.

Bible, searching for a specific injunction against suicide. He found none. God's commandment not to murder, Ruffin believed, did not apply to suicide. He reasoned that murder involved taking the life of another, and against his will. Furthermore, Ruffin noted that the Bible included exceptions to the seventh commandment by permitting the execution of criminals and of enemies in wartime. He found confirmation for his beliefs in the story of the Jews who killed themselves at Masada rather than face certain enslavement and death at the hands of the Romans. Turning from spiritual concerns, Ruffin considered how his death would affect his family. "My powers of both body & mind are so impaired that I am as incapable of rendering personal service to anybody," he decided. His departure could not hurt his family, and it would end the burden of his dependence on them in his old age. At peace with his decision, Ruffin had only to decide when to commit the act. He wanted to wait for his eldest son to return home; Edmund Ruffin, Jr., would have to attend to the burial. But he could not wait too long because he did not want his death to postpone or interfere with the upcoming wedding of a nephew. On the morning of Saturday, June 17, he decided that the time had come.[2]

Early that day, Ruffin joined his unsuspecting son, daughter-in-law, and granddaughters for breakfast at their home, Redmoor, in Amelia County, Virginia. He then returned upstairs to his study. Earlier, when he had contemplated his death, Ruffin had written a short note requesting that his remains be buried in South Carolina among the people "to whom I am indebted for much kindness & favorable consideration." He had hoped that his fellow Virginians would keep his memory alive and appreciate the efforts he had made on behalf of southern rights. To give his death meaning, however, Ruffin now decided to alter the tone of his final utterance. At ten o'clock in the morning he wrote in his diary:

> I here declare my unmitigated hatred to Yankee rule—to all political, social & business connection with Yankees—& to the Yankee race.

2. Ruffin Diary, June 16–18, 1865, LC. The last entry of Ruffin's diary, June 18, does not match the date of his death in a letter from his son to other family members. A case for each is made by William K. Scarborough and David Allmendinger in "The Days Ruffin Died," *Virginia Magazine of History and Biography,* XCVII (1989), 75–96. After reexamining the evidence, Scarborough agreed that Saturday, June 17, was correct, and has so noted in his edition of *The Diary of Edmund Ruffin* (3 vols.; Baton Rouge, 1972–89), III, xxxiii, 950–51. Incredibly, a third date is inscribed on Ruffin's gravestone (see photograph, Scarborough, ed., *Ruffin Diary,* III, 949).

Would that I could impress these sentiments, in their full force, on every living southerner, & bequeath them to every one yet to be born! May such sentiments be held universally in the outraged & downtrodden South, though in silence & stillness, until the now far-distant day shall arrive for just retribution for Yankee usurpation, oppression, & atrocious outrages—& for deliverance & vengeance for the now ruined, subjugated, & enslaved Southern States! May the maledictions of every victim to their malignity, press with full weight on the perfidious Yankee people & their perjured rulers—& especially on those of the invading forces who perpetrated, & their leaders & higher authorities who encouraged, directed, or permitted, the unprecedented & generally extended outrages of robbery, rapine & destruction, & house-burning, all committed contrary to the laws of war on non-combatant residents, & still worse on aged men & helpless women![3]

With the aid of a forked stick, Ruffin was ready to pull the trigger of his rifle when visitors came unexpectedly to the front door. Not wishing to put his guests through an upsetting ordeal, he waited for them to leave. When they did, he returned to his room to finish what he had begun. In the intervening two hours his determination had increased. He opened his diary for a final entry: "And now, with my latest writing & utterance, & with what will [be] near to my latest breath, I here repeat, & would willingly proclaim, my unmitigated hatred to Yankee rule—to all political, social, & business connection with Yankees, & to the perfidious, malignant, & vile Yankee race." He put the muzzle of the gun in his mouth and pulled the trigger, but the percussion cap exploded without discharging the shot. Downstairs, Jane Ruffin heard the noise and raced outside to find Edmund, Jr. Before they could get back to stop him, the old man had calmly reloaded his weapon and fired again. His children found his lifeless body still sitting upright, defiant and unyielding even in death.[4]

The manner of Ruffin's death served as the quintessential example of his life. A highly opinionated, obstinate, intransigent man, Edmund Ruffin would allow nothing to stop him when he had made a decision. Although he prided himself on his inflexibility, it was this very trait that posed a personal dilemma. Al-

3. Undated fragment, [1865], in Edmund Ruffin Papers, AL; Ruffin Diary, June 18, 1865, LC.

4. Ruffin Diary, June 18, 1865, LC; Mitchell, *Ruffin*, 255–56; Edmund Ruffin, Jr., to his children, June 20, 1865, in *Tyler's Quarterly Historical and Genealogical Magazine*, V (January, 1924), 193–95.

though he often contemptuously scorned all who opposed him, Ruffin simultaneously craved the love and appreciation of his countrymen. Extreme and unyielding even among fire-eaters, Ruffin had the misfortune of living in one of the least radical southern states. He knew that his political views often alienated him from more conservative Virginians, but he could find no way to restrain himself from expressing them except for withdrawing from society, which he could not do because he desperately sought to participate in public affairs. His entire life was an internal battle between his heart and his mind, a search for acceptance without compromising his ideals. It was a struggle unresolved even by his death.

Ruffin's upbringing and family heritage inculcated in him the idea that he would assume a position of importance in public affairs. Born on January 5, 1794, at Evergreen mansion in Prince George County, Edmund was of the seventh generation of Ruffins in Virginia. The first arrived in 1666 and immediately began to acquire land and slaves. Edmund's grandfather, also named Edmund, served four terms in the House of Delegates. When the younger Edmund was born, his father, George, owned more than 140 slaves spread out over several plantations and ranked as one of the largest slaveholders in the commonwealth. Small and sickly, Ruffin was raised and tutored at home. He quickly demonstrated a fondness for reading. He loved history and fiction and had read all of Shakespeare's plays by the time he turned eleven. His father wanted Edmund to receive a gentleman's education so in 1810 he sent his sixteen-year-old son to the College of William and Mary. In Williamsburg the young Ruffin found alcohol, the charms of Susan Travis, and literature more attractive than his schoolbooks. Doubtless, the knowledge that his father's estate promised him a comfortable living made it easier for him to neglect his studies. He inherited Coggin's Point plantation and some slaves when his father died, and seemed unconcerned about his subsequent suspension from college. Susan Travis' father, Champion, a prominent politician from Jamestown, had no objections either. He allowed Ruffin to marry his daughter, and the young couple moved to Coggin's Point.[5]

5. Mitchell, *Ruffin*, 3–6; Henry G. Ellis, "Edmund Ruffin: His Life and Times," *John P. Branch Historical Papers of Randolph-Macon College*, III (June, 1910), 101; Scarborough, ed., *Ruffin Diary*, II, 136, 604.

The outbreak of war with Great Britain in 1812 suddenly ended the Ruffins' honeymoon. Ruffin considered military service not only a patriotic duty but a social responsibility. As he explained years later, "Young people of 'gentle birth,' or used to early comforts, but also of well-ordered minds, could undergo necessary hardships with more contentment & cheerfulness than other persons of lower origin, & less accustomed to the indulgences & the training that wealth & high position afforded." The aristocratic eighteen-year-old enlisted as a private in the first regiment of volunteers called out from Virginia. Although he saw no action during his six-month service near Norfolk, he believed that he had borne himself with dignity. Over four decades later he would remember the military discipline and training he received during the War of 1812.[6]

He returned to Coggin's Point in 1813 to find the farmlands of Tidewater Virginia ruined. British armies had not ravished the soil, but generations of careless agricultural practices had. Failure to rotate tobacco with other crops had virtually depleted the land, and no contemporary fertilizing techniques could restore it. Ruffin's plantation produced eighteen bushels of corn per acre in 1813 and only eight the next year, while farms in the West yielded thirty-five or more. When the inexperienced young farmer looked to his neighbors for help, he discovered that they adhered blindly to traditional, ineffective methods. Unlike many other planters who left or planned to leave the area, Ruffin was determined to make his land profitable.[7]

Finding other farmers of little help, Ruffin turned to books. First he read John Taylor's *Arator*, a series of essays written in 1803 and reprinted in a book ten years later. Ruffin scrupulously followed Taylor's advice; he enclosed a large field, covered it with vegetable and animal manures, and plowed deeply. After four years, however, he found that Taylor's methods had helped only his initial harvest and deep plowing increased erosion. He had drained some of his most promising swamplands but after three years of cultivation was forced to abandon this acreage. Ruffin felt defeated. In 1817, while he waited for a buyer to relieve him of Coggin's Point,

6. Scarborough, ed., *Ruffin Diary*, I, 42; Mitchell, *Ruffin*, 6–7.
7. Avery O. Craven, *Edmund Ruffin, Southerner: A Study in Secession* (1932; rpr. Baton Rouge, 1982), 51–53; David F. Allmendinger, Jr., "The Early Career of Edmund Ruffin, 1810–1840," *Virginia Magazine of History and Biography*, XCIII (1985), 128, 130–32, 134.

Ruffin read Sir Humphry Davy's recent *Elements of Agricultural Chemistry*. Although as ignorant of chemistry as he had been of farming, Ruffin was intrigued by Davy's hypothesis that carbonate of lime might neutralize acidity in soil. Working from engravings in Davy's book, Ruffin reproduced the author's apparatus for testing the chemical composition of the soil and began testing his and his neighbors' farmlands. His tests showed that the fossil shells, or marl, so abundant in the region had sufficient alkalinity to correct the chemical imbalance in the fields. In February, 1818, Ruffin had some slaves dig marl from pits on his estate and haul it to a newly cleared plot. Tidewater farmers had experimented with marl before, but Ruffin was the first to combine the marling process with Taylor's method of cultivation. His first harvest yielded 40 percent more corn than his control sample. The self-trained scientist had proved skeptical neighbors wrong and discovered the key to rejuvenating the soil of the Tidewater South.[8]

After five years of struggling to save his land, Ruffin faced a greater and more protracted challenge: convincing other farmers to adopt his methods. Despite their own failures and Ruffin's proven success, most of his fellow planters were too conservative and unwilling to follow the progressive example of Edmund Ruffin, agricultural reformer. His friend and benefactor Thomas Cocke helped Ruffin found and organize the Agricultural Society of Prince George County in 1818, and the young planter first presented his findings to that group in October. Three years later he published a revised and enlarged version of his address in the *American Farmer*, an influential journal published in Baltimore. Although he received the praise of its editor, his fellow Virginians remained unconvinced. The intensive demand marling placed upon labor, Ruffin knew, made many question the efficiency of the practice. The procedure required as many as nineteen of the fifty-two slaves on Ruffin's plantation in the early 1820s. Even his friend Cocke called the operation "Ruffin's Folly" and in 1826 discouraged Ruffin from publishing his new manuscript, *An Essay on Calcarous Manures*. In 1829 Ruffin left Coggin's Point for Shellbanks, a new plantation a few miles away. Once again he turned a worthless farm into a profitable operation. His success gave him the confidence to

8. Allmendinger, "Ruffin," 136, 138, 142; Craven, *Ruffin*, 54–55; Lewis Cecil Gray, *History of Agriculture in the Southern United States to 1860* (2 vols.; Washington, D.C., 1933), II, 780–81.

publish his *Essay* in 1832. The *American Journal of Sciences and Arts* gave Ruffin's book a lengthy and positive review, and even the skeptical Thomas Cocke now praised Ruffin's achievements. But most farmers in Virginia stubbornly refused to change their ways, and no amount of self-assuredness or critical acclaim could compensate Ruffin for lack of public acceptance.[9]

To popularize his scientific agricultural practices Ruffin launched a monthly periodical, the *Farmers' Register*, in June, 1833. Published in Petersburg, Virginia, and briefly at Shellbanks, Ruffin's journal rose rapidly to prominence in the Old Dominion and beyond. Within a few months the *Register* forced the rival *Virginia Farmer* out of business. The editor of the *American Farmer* called the *Farmers' Register* the best publication of its kind in America or Europe. Ruffin sold Shellbanks and moved nearly seventy slaves to his son's plantation, Beechwood, so he would have more time to devote to the *Register*. As both editor and chief contributor, Ruffin wrote approximately half of the articles that appeared in the *Register* during its nine-year existence. He reprinted the *Arator* and his *Essays on Calcerous Manures* and, after his appointment as corresponding secretary for the new State Board of Agriculture in 1841, included its reports. By the early 1840s most Tidewater farmers had adopted Ruffin's techniques. Only his decision to devote more space in his journal to controversial political questions threatened the success of the *Farmers' Register*.[10]

Through his publishing efforts Ruffin had finally earned the respect of most Virginians, but that was not enough for the man who had spent a quarter-century trying to gain the approval of the public; he wanted their adulation. Even though he knew that his political views, especially a recent campaign against paper money, drew more popular opposition than his agricultural ideas, Ruffin perceived any rebuff or setback as a personal attack, a total rejection of him and all his accomplishments. The "niggardly support" and "contemptuous treatment" of the Board of Agriculture by the state legislature made Ruffin imagine "that the public of Virginia was wearied of me and my writings—& therefore that I would withdraw entirely from all connexions with the public in my native

9. Allmendinger, "Ruffin," 127, 130–31, 142, 146, 148–50; Craven, *Ruffin*, 54–56.

10. Mitchell, *Ruffin*, 35–36; Allmendinger, "Ruffin," 142, 148–49; Edmund Ruffin, "Incidents of My Life," II, 55, in Edmund Ruffin Papers (microfilm), SHC; Gray, *History of Agriculture in the Southern United States*, II, 855.

country." He resigned his post on the board in 1842, the same year he stopped publishing the *Farmers' Register*. Three years of retirement further exacerbated Ruffin's feelings of rejection. "My former & I will presume to say *great* services rendered to my native state, (however *praised* & *complimented*, by some of the public,) have been returned mostly by slighting neglect, ingratitude, & subjecting me to malignant persecution, because I *tried* to add to my other services to the agricultural interest that of defending it from the paper banking robbers," he complained to a friend. "Under such circumstances I confess being soured towards my countrymen. Any compliments & honors offered by them to me now, come *too late*."[11]

Ruffin rashly uttered these remarks after putting in a generation of frustrating public service. Although initially he had wanted nothing to interfere with his fanatical devotion to agricultural reform, his involvement with agricultural societies led to his first political venture. Opposition to the protectionist Tariff of 1816 had motivated several local agricultural groups to form the United Agricultural Societies of Virginia in 1818. With Ruffin as its secretary the organization sent a petition to Congress requesting the abolition of discriminatory tariffs. Thereafter, Ruffin gradually supplanted his agricultural crusade with various political ones.[12]

Like his distant cousin Beverley Tucker, Edmund Ruffin believed that the federal government had accumulated too much power by the early 1820s and feared that his own "state rights republican creed and principles will hereafter, as heretofore, be professed only by parties out of power and seeking its attainment." He had "very little respect for the general course and measures of any party" and therefore belonged to none. In 1823 the dogmatic Ruffin rejected all five likely candidates for the next presidential election. Andrew Jackson, Henry Clay, John Quincy Adams, John C. Calhoun, and William H. Crawford all, he believed, had disregarded constitutional checks on federal power through their advocacy of tariffs, internal improvements, and federal banks. Ruffin

---

11. Ruffin, "Incidents," III, 223, in Ruffin Papers, SHC; Mitchell, *Ruffin,* 57; Ruffin to James H. Hammond, July 6, 1845, in James H. Hammond Papers, LC. William M. Mathew, *Edmund Ruffin and the Crisis of Slavery in the Old South: The Failure of Agricultural Reform* (Athens, Ga., 1988), argues that Ruffin's reforms met little success, but Mathew's conclusions are often unpersuasive and rely too heavily on the voluminous complaints of a man who was never satisfied with less than unanimous popular support.

12. Mitchell, *Ruffin,* 23.

asserted his political independence by recommending that Virginians support Nathaniel Macon, a revolutionary war hero and elder statesman of North Carolina, for the presidency. As a last resort, Ruffin would even prefer John Marshall, a Federalist with consistent political views, over a candidate who advocated Federalist principles while calling himself a Republican.[13]

Ruffin's clear enunciation of states'-rights principles and limited government and his growing local celebrity as an agronomist moved many of his more influential neighbors to promote him for the state senate in 1823. He was elected to a four-year term "almost without seeking either public favor or any of its rewards—& certainly without my using any electioneering arts, which I always despised, & had not the tact to exercise, even if willing to be so aided." After three years in Richmond, however, the idealistic and inflexible junior senator had had enough of public office. Though he strove to base each vote on "the best interests of my country, & of my constituents, according to right & justice, & to decide on the claims of individuals according to their merits," he believed that every one of his colleagues did the opposite. He accused each of them of acting only "to promote the personal & private interests of his friend, his constituent, or his political supporter, even at more or less [the] sacrifice of the public interest." Ruffin considered himself the solitary representative with integrity in the legislature, just as he had perceived himself as the only source of truth in agriculture. He believed himself "too honest" and conscientious to curry popular support by compromising his convictions, and the constant demands by his constituents to promote "some private & selfish interest" made him "tired & disgusted with being 'a servant of the people.'" Ruffin resigned with a year left in his term. He never changed his attitude about the political process and never held elected public office again.[14]

For the next several years Ruffin remained at Shellbanks to continue his agricultural experiments and writings but spoke out on public issues whenever he deemed it important. One issue came in the aftermath of Nat Turner's uprising, a slave insurrection that resulted in the deaths of at least sixty white people in Southampton County, Virginia, in August, 1831. Hysteria spread among white in-

13. Drew Gilpin Faust, *A Sacred Circle: The Dilemma of the Intellectual in the Old South* (Baltimore, 1977), 5; *Bank Reformer*, I (November, 1841), 39; Mitchell, *Ruffin*, 23–24.

14. Mitchell, *Ruffin*, 25–28; Scarborough, ed., *Ruffin Diary*, II, 544–45.

habitants of the surrounding counties. "The true facts were enough to inspire terror," Ruffin recalled, but he also remembered that a "state of insanity" gripped the community. Lack of information led many to spread wild rumors and exaggerate the magnitude of the crime. Even after Turner and his conspirators were captured, the panic did not abate. Within a hundred-mile radius slaves who had never heard of the insurrection until after the fact were charged with complicity; many were executed.

Ruffin observed these developments with horror. Much of the evidence used against these innocent slaves "at any sober time would not have been deemed sufficient to convict a dog suspected of killing sheep." Worse still, Ruffin thought, the courts accepted testimony "from infamous witnesses," from men "of the lowest class & character," whose testimony Ruffin considered untrustworthy. He noted that if some "moderate or sane person" tried to defend a falsely accused slave or demanded a fair trial, "he incurred odium, if not personal danger, as a favorer, if not approver, of murderous insurgents, & midnight slayers of sleeping men, women & children." When a panel of four judges, and not "an ignorant & impassioned jury," sentenced one slave to be hanged, Ruffin could take no more. He composed a petition to Governor John Floyd demanding a pardon for this unfortunate slave. Believing the rule of law more important than his own popularity, Ruffin boldly canvassed the region for signatures. He received eleven. Unwilling to admit defeat and armed with self-righteousness, he personally presented his petition to Governor Floyd. Ruffin found, however, that the governor "did not dare, or deem it politic, to grant the petition, or to pardon in any such case." Upon Ruffin's return home, threats of personal violence increased his contempt for "fellows of the baser sort" and confirmed his elitist outlook.[15]

Ruffin repeated his habit of retreating to his plantation after suffering a popular rebuke. Because he was still smarting from the ignominy he suffered during the Turner affair, even the nullification controversy could not stir him to action. Although he supported the nullifiers, it was almost thirty years before he gave the movement his retroactive endorsement.[16] Of more immediate concern to Ruffin was the publication of his *Essay on Calcerous Manures* and the establishment of the *Farmers' Register*.

15. Scarborough, ed., *Ruffin Diary*, II, 207–209; Mitchell, *Ruffin*, 31–33.

16. [Edmund Ruffin], "A Reminiscence of the Time of Nullification," *SLM*, XXXII (April, 1861), 249–57; Scarborough, ed., *Ruffin Diary*, I, 579.

In the first issue of his journal Ruffin announced his intention to discuss "such subjects of political economy as are connected with preservation & support of the interests of agriculture," but he quickly began to offer unsolicited opinions on a variety of topics in his writings and in public. "Why should such a difference in the rewards of labor exist, and be increasing in degree, between the sexes?" he asked in the *Register*. Women, he insisted, should receive "at least as high rewards" as men for equal work. At about the same time, Ruffin fought for higher salaries for college professors during a six-year tenure on the Board of Visitors of William and Mary College. Although proud of his work on behalf of teachers and "especially in putting down gross abuses" at the college, Ruffin found yet again that through his services "I incurred odium & gained no thanks." [17]

Ruffin's crusading zeal often drew him to causes that appeared particularly difficult. One of his most ambitious projects came late in 1840 when he explained to a friend, "I am every day the more convinced that *this is the time* to raise the state-rights banner—& that if it is done properly, it will be supported by a *party* stronger than any in the country before 18 months from this time." The presidential ticket of William Henry Harrison, a Whig, and John Tyler, a Democrat and a friend of Ruffin's, led Ruffin to hope that "the better parts of the fragments of both [parties] will become in action what they now profess in words to be, *state-rights republicans*." To facilitate the growth of a new party that advocated "strict limitation on federal powers, Ruffin and his second son, Julian, established the *Southern Magazine and Monthly Review* in January, 1841. They hoped that their magazine would help organize and discipline the "moral and intellectual forces" of states'-rights men and serve as a forum "for the improvement of our own southern country, for building up our own literature and science, and for sustaining our own doctrines, principles and institutions." [18]

The first issue of Ruffin's *Southern Review* contained fiction, poetry, articles on classical history, and some previously unpublished letters of George Washington. It also had a piece that Ruffin had

17. *Farmers' Register*, III (September, 1835), 257–58; Ruffin, "Incidents," II, 52–53, in Ruffin Papers, SHC; Scarborough, ed., *Ruffin Diary*, II, 546; Faust, *Sacred Circle*, 105.

18. Ruffin to A. P. Upshur, October 24, 1840, in Tucker-Coleman Collection, ESL; Ruffin to John Tyler, June 29, 1841, in Scarborough, ed., *Ruffin Diary*, I, 613–16: *Southern Magazine and Monthly Review*, I (January, 1841), i–ii.

worked on for months, "Revolution in Disguise," in which he presented a theme commonly used by fire-eaters—"the great *changes* which have already been made in the *spirit* & working of the Constitution, without touching its *letter.*" Over the fifty years since the adoption of the Constitution, Ruffin explained, Americans had strayed from the careful proscriptions of power laid out by the Founding Fathers. The establishment of protective tariffs, for example, was a "truly revolutionary movement" because they discriminated against the more agricultural southern states. Nowhere, Ruffin asserted, did the Constitution permit discriminatory taxation. The growing electoral power of the masses alarmed the elitist Ruffin, who stated that the Founders never intended or expected the people to choose their president and vice-president "directly and in mass." He insisted that presidential electors must remain free from the impassioned and ignorant views of the people. The presidency had also assumed too much power. He believed that the Constitution clearly granted the legislative branch of government more power than the executive but argued that now Congress was "the foot-stool of the president." Patronage and party spoils increased the president's influence both in the capital and in the states. Ruffin blamed recent presidential judicial appointments with "polluting the fountain of justice with the filth of party and political servility." These and other usurpations of power had transformed "this once free and responsible republican government" into "a monarchy in disguise," Ruffin concluded. "The people have been blinded by party-spirit," he said, but added cryptically that once the people realized that they had been deceived and deluded "they will rise to the majesty of that moral power which virtue alone can give, to avenge and repair the violations and perversions of the good principles of the constitution." [19]

Before he began the *Southern Review* Ruffin had speculated that "the public cannot yet bear to hear the *truth*" about political corruption. The cold reception his periodical received convinced him that he was right. His greatest disappointment, however, came from the reaction of fellow states'-rights men. Ruffin complained to Beverley Tucker, who had encouraged his recent journalistic venture, that proponents of states' rights either met his efforts with "utter indifference" or considered the *Southern Review* a vehicle through which

19. Ruffin to Upshur, September 26, 1840, in Tucker-Coleman Collection, ESL; *Southern Magazine and Monthly Review*, I (January, 1841), 33–59.

they could "denounce & abuse each other, so as to render their quarrel permanent, & ensure . . . the utter annihilation of the state-rights party, & the degradation & contempt of their principles." Infighting and public apathy forced Ruffin to abandon the *Southern Review* after publishing only two volumes.[20]

Before Ruffin gave up on his states'-rights campaign he decided to focus his energy on just one issue—banking reform. Against "this enormous system of fraud & pillage," he vowed, "I determined to resist, if I stood alone." Believing paper money and federal banks unsound and unconstitutional, Ruffin made both the target of a multifaceted attack in the early 1840s. He began by writing articles in the *Farmers' Register* and the *Southern Review* that called for restrictions on loans and payments of hard money upon demand. In Petersburg he formed the Association for Promoting Currency and Banking Reform, an organization dedicated to deluging the state legislature with petitions demanding the replacement of bank notes with specie. Ruffin and his son Julian also edited and published the *Bank Reformer*,[21] which was less a periodical than a monthly polemical tract. Ruffin issued the *Bank Reformer* to promulgate "the correct principles and beneficial operations of honest and legitimate banking" and to expose the "wrong-doing and fraudulent practices" currently used by banks. He distributed his publication gratuitously "to known and zealous friends of the cause." Ruffin pledged to keep his publication free from the influence of political parties and to use it as a forum for the promotion of "the state rights creed and principles." The *Bank Reformer* included copious quotations on the evils of paper money from such men as George Washington, John Adams, Andrew Jackson, and Henry Clay. Ruffin reprinted editorials and articles on the subject from the New York *Herald*, the Philadelphia *Ledger*, and, of course, the *Farmers' Register*. In both these and original articles, Ruffin denounced advocates of contemporary banking practices as "servile and shameless . . . bank slaves."[22]

Ruffin's activities and diatribes were in vain. Petitions that he had included in the back of each *Bank Reformer* went unsigned; again, the public did not share his concern or sense of urgency. In desperation Ruffin turned to an unorthodox and sensational new tactic.

20. Ruffin to Upshur, September 26, 1840, to Beverley Tucker, February 5, 1841, in Tucker-Coleman Collection, ESL; Faust, *Sacred Circle*, 91.
21. Ruffin, "Incidents," II, 52, in Ruffin Papers, SHC; *Farmers' Register*, IX (January, 1841), 530–34; Mitchell, *Ruffin*, 40–41.
22. *Bank Reformer*, I (November, 1841), 33, 37–39.

Instead of endorsing bank notes with his signature, he started writing various admonishments on them and returning them to circulation. Courtesy of Edmund Ruffin, Virginia could read diatribes such as the following on their money: "The *paper* banking system is essentially and necessarily fraudulent. The very issue of paper as money is always a fraud; and must operate to rob the earnings of labor and industry, for the gain of stock-jobbing, wild speculation and knavery." Even when he realized that his cause was hopeless, Ruffin continued to deface bank notes. He even automated the process with the help of a small printing press. The hobby provided him with a catharsis for the anger and frustration he had accumulated in his various causes over the past two decades. Other men might spend their time and money hunting and fishing, he told a friend, but Ruffin chose "to amuse myself with hunting banks & bank directors, & in enjoying their anger & malignity."[23]

"I cannot expect to amuse myself free of cost," Ruffin admitted of his "game" with the banking interests. In fact, the cost was dear. Like his *Southern Review,* Ruffin's *Bank Reformer* was short-lived. He abandoned it in February, 1842, but public backlash against his political positions also hastened the suspension of the *Farmers' Register* three months later. His career as an editor cost Ruffin about $8,000 in unpaid subscriptions and seriously wounded his pride. After spending "ten of the best years" of his life on the *Farmers' Register,* Ruffin vowed to withdraw from public life in the ungrateful state of Virginia. It was a promise he would keep for almost a decade.[24]

A brief display of public appreciation immediately tested Ruffin's resolve. Acting upon resolutions of the agricultural committee of the South Carolina legislature, late in 1842 Governor James H. Hammond asked Ruffin to conduct an agricultural survey of the Palmetto State. Although Hammond warned Ruffin that the people of South Carolina might not prove receptive to his work, the Virginian decided to accept the offer. Politically, at least, South Carolina was more to Ruffin's liking, and accepting the job gave him the excuse he wanted to leave his position on the Board of Agriculture, thereby cutting his last official tie in Virginia. Early in 1843 Ruffin arrived in Charleston and began a six-month investiga-

23. *Ibid.,* 48; Mitchell, *Ruffin,* 41–42; Ruffin to Hammond, September 7, 1845, in Hammond Papers, LC; Hammond to Ruffin, October 10, 1845, in Ruffin Papers, SHC.

24. Ruffin to Hammond, September 7, 1845, in Hammond Papers, LC; Mitchell, *Ruffin,* 42–43; Ruffin, "Incidents," II, 56, in Ruffin Papers, SHC; *Farmers' Register,* X (January, 1842), 155.

tion of the state. He explored swamplands, looked for marl deposits, and studied local farming practices. By the end of the year he completed his *Report of the Commencement and Progress of the Agricultural Survey of South Carolina for 1843*.[25] Hammond greeted the *Report* with enthusiasm. "I congratulate you on being one of the few benefactors of mankind whose services have been appreciated by the world, while living," the governor said. Most people in South Carolina, however, proved as slow to adopt Ruffin's recommendations as those in Virginia. Although Hammond's flattery could not relieve the pain Ruffin felt after being spurned yet again, it did help forge an important new friendship that prevented Ruffin from withdrawing entirely from society.[26]

Ruffin wished to retreat again to the seclusion of farm life, but in 1843 he owned only a house in Petersburg, "a place which I heartily disliked & despised." With the money he received from his South Carolina survey Ruffin purchased a new plantation. In January, 1844, he found 977 acres in Hanover County, northeast of Richmond, and moved his family there from Petersburg along with thirty of his slaves from Edmund junior's plantation. The previous owner had built an impressive mansion on the site but had also worn out the soil. The challenge of turning another dilapidated farm into a showplace and, perhaps, the opportunity to prove his genius to Virginians led Ruffin to name his new home "Marlbourne."[27]

Ruffin immediately set to work. He had his slaves construct an elaborate drainage system and put all but six of them to work digging and hauling marl; the others spread marl over the land. Ruffin was so consumed by the marling operation that he forgot to fill his icehouse before the spring thaw. During a late freeze, some considerate neighbors sent carts and slaves to Marlbourne to help Ruffin, but his monomania drove him to use the extra labor for moving more marl. After this display of friendship, Ruffin decided to listen to his neighbors' ideas about farming. "But while this benefitted in some things," he quickly concluded, "in others I was more misled by erroneous opinions, than if I had followed entirely my own imperfect views, & reasoning in advance of all experience." He

25. Hammond to Ruffin, December 18, 1842, and Ruffin, "Incidents," II, 55, in Ruffin Papers, SHC; Craven, *Ruffin*, 80–82; Mitchell, *Ruffin*, 48.

26. Hammond to Ruffin, February 14, 1844, in Ruffin Papers, SHC; Faust, *Sacred Circle*, 1–3.

27. Ruffin, "Incidents," II, 161–62, in Ruffin Papers, SHC; Mitchell, *Ruffin*, 50–51.

resumed his carefully devised system of crop rotation and, contrary to local wisdom, chose to plant wheat, corn, and oats. He used the latest agricultural equipment, such as the McCormick plow and reaper and the Haw thresher. By 1848 he had doubled his initial production and that year earned almost $6,000 in profits on his wheat alone. Every year thereafter his crop yields and profits continued to climb.[28]

As a slaveowner Ruffin was emphatically paternalistic. At times he considered himself a bad master because of his failure to discipline his slaves harshly, but he usually believed that kind treatment was the best incentive for efficient and faithful labor. He housed, clothed, and fed his slaves relatively well, attended to their medical and spiritual needs, and avoided separating families whenever possible. When he did split his slave force, he sent part to his son's plantation and, whenever possible, allowed the men to visit their wives at Beechwood, miles away. Finding hired overseers ignorant and ineffectual, Ruffin used Jem Sykes, one of his own slaves, as overseer for Marlbourne. He trusted Sykes implicitly, let him live in the overseer's house, and gave him the keys to every building on the plantation. Whenever Ruffin left Marlbourne, Sykes was in charge of more than forty other slaves.[29]

Ruffin's seclusion at Marlbourne did not ease the "bitterness of my feelings for the slighting & ungrateful conduct of my countrymen in general, & the apparent forgetfulness of the agricultural public of Virginia of my services." Considering his attitude, Ruffin admitted that "I was therefore not a little astonished" when he read in the newspapers that the State Agricultural Society of Virginia had elected him president in February, 1845. Determined to stay angry, however, he turned down the honor. Later he realized that his response "was ungracious," but when this and succeeding societies dissolved he gloated that he had not associated himself with "these abortions." Five years later, the agricultural societies of the Eastern Shore of Maryland invited him to deliver their annual address. Marylanders had supported the *Farmers' Register,* Ruffin recalled, so this time he accepted. But the tone of his address belied his festering anger: "My speech had been written to condemn what I deemed the usual wrong procedure of agricultural societies, & to

28. Ruffin, "Incidents," II, 162–69, in Ruffin Papers, SHC; Craven, *Ruffin,* 84–85; Mitchell, *Ruffin,* 52, 55–57.

29. Ruffin to Hammond, December 3, 1853, in Hammond Papers, LC; Craven, *Ruffin,* 18–19; Allmendinger, "Ruffin," 149; Mitchell, *Ruffin,* 53–55.

indicate a better course." In 1851 Ruffin received a letter from J. D. B. De Bow asking for a biography and portrait for the "Gallery of Enterprise" in *De Bow's Review*. Even though he admired the *Review*, initially Ruffin did not want his name and accomplishments included among "galleries of . . . *nobodies*." Ruffin could not resist the free publicity long, however, and finally consented.[30]

As his sixtieth birthday approached, Ruffin began to realize that he was an irascible old man. His hypersensitivity to rejection, he now understood, stemmed from "my vanity & love of notoriety." If any of his public acts failed to win instant and widespread popular support, Ruffin shamefully realized, he grew vindictive. "And when my slow anger has been raised to the point of hostility & vindictiveness," he admitted, "my resentment is implacable." Even the passage of time or the death of an "offender" seldom abated his hatred. He was not proud of this trait but could not change. Recalling the cold reception that John Tyler experienced when he returned home after his presidency, Ruffin wrote, "If I had been in his place, I should never have forgiven these changed friends, & by returning neglect with interest, would have provoked general & undying hostility." Ruffin admitted, however, that Tyler "acted more wisely, & better." But no matter how diligently Ruffin worked to emulate his more gracious and magnanimous friend, he could not. He could never overcome his "habit of uttering my opinions of men & things freely & strongly, & uncautiously, as if every one I spoke before was a man of honour & my friend, instead of being, as often was the case, an enemy, a tattler & mischief-maker." Although he blamed others for repeating his confidential remarks out of context and "with false additions," he knew that his bluntness and inability to resist expressing his opinions were at the root of much of his trouble. "I have not been able to correct myself," he lamented. "The only attempt to prevent the certain delinquency, was in my general course of seclusion from the public" and avoiding conversation with everyone but his family, closest neighbors, and most intimate friends.[31]

One of these few friends was James Hammond. Ruffin found that he could share thoughts on a multitude of subjects with the Carolinian and receive understanding and even admiration. Mostly,

30. Ruffin, "Incidents," III, 221, 223–24, 228, in Ruffin Papers, SHC; *DBR*, XI (October, 1851), frontispiece and 431–36.
31. Ruffin, "Incidents," III, 222, in Ruffin Papers, SHC; Scarborough, ed., *Ruffin Diary*, II, 541–42; Ruffin to Jane M. Ruffin, March 21, 1854 (Typescript in Elizabeth Gilmer Tyler Miles Colleciton, AL).

the two exchanged long letters about farming. Hammond followed Ruffin's experiments at Marlbourne with great interest and told Ruffin of his own at Redcliffe. They agreed on politics as well. Hammond particularly admired Ruffin's scathing endorsements on bank notes. "What will it cost me to get a little press & do the same thing here?" he asked. He suggested that they could work together; Hammond would print remarks on notes from Virginia, and Ruffin could do the same on notes from South Carolina. Hammond was sympathetic to Ruffin's complaints of alienation and rejection. He also gathered a sense of Ruffin's egotism and vanity and therefore learned how not to upset his old friend. When asked to review the latest edition of *Essay on Calcerous Manures*, Hammond wisely declined because he knew that it would make Ruffin "mad as the devil if the whole article were not devoted to eulogizing him."[32]

Hammond's activities in the early 1850s eventually roused Ruffin from his political hibernation. Both preferred secession over acquiescence to the Compromise of 1850. Ruffin considered the compromise a "grievous wrong & humiliation of the South," but he remained a passive spectator when Hammond attended the Nashville Convention in June, 1850. "I should like exceedingly to see you there," Hammond told Ruffin. Beverley Tucker would attend as a delegate; Hammond hoped the three of them could meet in Tennessee. Ruffin was not yet ready to leave Marlbourne, but he shared vicariously Hammond's disappointment when the convention failed to instigate secession. After cooperationists triumphed over secessionists in South Carolina the next fall, however, Ruffin cautiously took a public stand. Under the pseudonym "A Virginian," he wrote a series of articles in the Richmond *Examiner* and the Charleston *Mercury* calling for southern resistance. He implored Carolinians to lead "in this holy war of defence of all that is worth preserving to the South." Ruffin endorsed Hammond and Tucker's "Plan for State Action," which recommended southerners withdraw their representatives from Congress, boycott presidential elections, and avoid all dealings with the federal government. Although resistance collapsed quickly throughout the South, for Ruffin there was no going back.[33]

32. Hammond to Ruffin, October 10, 1845, in Ruffin Papers, SHC; Ruffin to Hammond, July 6, September 7, 1845, November 26, 1846, and Hammond to W. G. Simms, July 8, 1853, in Hammond Papers, LC; Faust, *Sacred Circle*, 1–3.

33. Ruffin, "Incidents," III, 248, 254; Hammond to Ruffin, January 12, February 8, March 27, May 7, 1850, February 7, September 30, 1851, in Ruffin Papers, SHC; Charleston *Mercury*, November 7, 1851; Craven, *Ruffin*, 116–17.

After years of introspection at Marlbourne, greater public appreciation of his farming practices, and the intellectual stimulation caused by the recent sectional conflict, Ruffin was ready to return to public life. In November, 1851, after stopping in Charleston to deliver to the *Mercury* his article that called on South Carolina to cut her ties with the federal government, Ruffin continued to Georgia and delivered an address to the Macon Agricultural Fair on the benefits of calcareous manures. A few months later, when Virginians attempted again to organize an agricultural society, Ruffin vowed to help. When he attended the first meeting, he was pleasantly surprised to find himself the center of attention. Delegates compounded his delight by organizing the society exactly along the lines Ruffin suggested, and for good measure they elected him president.[34]

As Ruffin prepared his address for the new agricultural society, he realized that topics he had previously considered most important were now moot. The majority of farmers in eastern Virginia now used marl, the society operated exactly as he had wished, and political debate over the Compromise of 1850 had ceased. James Hammond, however, had introduced him to a new issue. In 1845 Ruffin had read Hammond's recent proslavery tracts, known collectively as the Clarkson letters. In 1833, when editing the *Farmers' Register,* Ruffin had believed slavery "a great and increasing evil," as had many Virginians of the time. Professor Thomas R. Dew, however, had convinced the young editor of "the utter inefficiency, or ruinous cost, of all the schemes that have been proposed for the emancipation and removal of the African race." But Ruffin's personal commitment to slavery and the growth of abolitionist agitation soon ended his ambivalence. "We shall have to defend our rights, by the strong hand, against the northern abolitionists," Ruffin decided after reading the Clarkson letters.[35] He chose to make his first contribution to the proslavery argument at the Virginia Agricultural Society.

In his address Ruffin stated that African slavery made southern society superior to that of the North. When "opposers of slavery" argued that the profit motive stimulated free laborers to work more productively than slaves and that slaveholders became "indo-

34. Charleston *Mercury,* November 11, 1851; Ruffin, "Incidents," III, 227, in Ruffin Papers, SHC; Mitchell, *Ruffin,* 81.
35. Ruffin to Hammond, September 7, 1845, in Hammond Papers, LC; *Farmers' Register,* I (June, 1833), 36.

lent and wasteful" because of their "prosperity and the ease of obtaining a living," Ruffin claimed they inadvertently proved "that the labors of the Southern slaves, in general, are lighter, and yet the profits of their owners greater" than those of northern workers and capitalists. According to Ruffin, "There exists slavery, or the subjection of man to man, in every country under the sun." Hunger and cold enslaved northern workers to any employer who offered a job. In the North, ignorant wage slaves and a growing number of immigrants "unacquainted with the principles of free government and unused to freedom in any form" could easily "be directed, governed, and enslaved by a few master-minds" and exploited "solely for the promotion of base self-interest and personal aggrandizement." He warned that enslavement of the working class in the North to a demagogue might result in "agrarianism, communism and anti-rentism—all tending to anarchy and the destruction of property." But African slavery, Ruffin asserted, protected the South from these dire possibilities. By confining "the drudgery and brutalizing effects of continued toil to the inferior races," African slavery spared white southerners from wage slavery and provided "the superior race leisure and other means to improve mind, taste, and manners." Even if slavery were less profitable than free labor—and Ruffin's experiences at Marlbourne had proven to him that it was not—he believed the institution essential for maintaining the unique "mental and moral qualities" of white southerners.[36]

Virginians' enthusiastic response to Ruffin's speech encouraged him to continue infusing his agricultural addresses with political messages. When in 1852 he returned to South Carolina to deliver a paper at an agricultural fair in Charleston, he explained that over the past decade improved farming techniques had helped raise land values and tax revenue in Virginia. Ruffin claimed that rejuvenating the exhausted soil of the Tidewater South guaranteed not only the continuation of slavery in the region but also its future expansion. Slavery had to grow following passage of the Compromise of 1850 if southerners were to preserve "their yet remaining rights and always vital interests." He called on southerners to im- prove production on their own land so that their children would not move to other states with more fertile land. This would give the

---

36. Edmund Ruffin, *Address to the Virginia State Agricultural Society, on the Effects of Domestic Slavery on the Manners, Habits and Welfare of the Southern States; and the Slavery of Class to Class in the Northern States* (Richmond, 1853), 5–8, 12, 14, 16.

South enough population for sufficient representation in Congress to check "the plunderings and oppressions of tariffs, to protect Northern interests—compromises, so called, to swell Northern power . . . and all such acts to the injury of the South." Ruffin warned his audience that the growing power of the North forced them to choose between "wealth and general prosperity" and "ruin, destitution, and the lowest degradation to which the country of a free and noble-minded people can possibly be subjected."

Privately Ruffin worried that expressing these "*extreme* opinions as to southern wrongs & rights" might have been improper "even in Charleston." In fact, compared to diatribes by Barnwell Rhett, Ruffin's speech was mild. A few months later Ruffin learned that James De Bow, who had attended his address in Charleston, had persuaded the commissioner of patents to reprint Ruffin's paper in the federal agricultural report for 1852. Ruffin was flattered and amused that the federal government would pay for the printing and distribution of his attack on northerners.[37]

Ruffin had finally achieved popularity in the South. Late in 1853 he was the center of attention at a state fair in Richmond also attended by former President Tyler and General Winfield Scott, hero of the Mexican War. "It was a glorious scene," he boasted to Hammond, and smugly described the gathering as "truly an assembly of gentlemen." Ruffin's recent renown caused many changes in his life "and in nothing a greater change than in my own happiness & feelings." With renewed confidence, Ruffin completed his return to public life in 1854 when he accepted an appointment as agricultural commissioner of Virginia. Although a poor orator and uncomfortable speaking before an audience, Ruffin overcame his nervousness and spoke throughout the state on both agriculture and politics. He also continued writing and in 1855 published *Essays and Notes on Agriculture*, fourteen essays describing his work at Marlbourne.[38]

37. Edmund Ruffin, "Southern Agricultural Exhaustion and Its Remedy," in *Report of the Commissioner of Patents for the Year 1852, Part II: Agriculture* (Washington, D.C., 1853), 373, 375, 378, 380–82, 386–87, 389; Ruffin, "Incidents," III, 247, in Ruffin Papers, SHC. By 1850 more than 180,000 natives of Virginia lived in other southern states and 155,978 had moved north of the Ohio River. See Clement Eaton, *A History of the Old South* (1954; rpr. New York, 1968), 195.

38. Ruffin to Hammond, December 3, 1853, February 26, 1854, in Hammond Papers, LC; Craven, *Ruffin*, 92; Mitchell, *Ruffin*, 86–87. Although Ruffin complained vigorously whenever he felt alienated from southern society, his growing popularity, as noted by David F. Allmendinger, *Ruffin: Family and Reform in the Old*

Although Ruffin enjoyed a resurgence in his public career, privately he experienced a series of profound crises. While preparing his address for the Charleston agricultural fair in 1852, he made the unsettling discovery that he could not remember what he had written just a few days before. The next winter he wrote, "The decay of my memory had continued to increase, (as it still has since,) so as to alarm me lest I should have greatly impaired other mental powers, without my knowing it." His mental faculties continued to deteriorate until he could remember vividly only events long past. "My mind," he complained, "has lost most of its former ability to retain recent impressions, or to receive new ones." At the same time, physical infirmities "much greater than even suited my age" forced the sixty-year-old Ruffin to limit his activities at Marlbourne. He worried that he was dying.[39]

Death often visited the Ruffin family during these years but spared its patriarch. Two of Ruffin's children had died in infancy, three grandchildren followed by 1853, and his wife died in 1846. Ruffin's greatest jolt, however, came in 1855, when three of his adult daughters died unexpectedly within a few months. Their father poured out his grief and love for his eldest daughter, Jane, in a private thirty-one-page eulogy. He composed a similar piece a month later when Ella Ruffin died. By the time Rebecca Ruffin Bland passed away, Edmund could write no longer. Less than two years later Mary Ruffin, the wife of Edmund, Jr., also died. Edmund Ruffin had considered her "a daughter to me & a sister to my children, in love & by family." When Ruffin's own health improved, James Hammond tried to console his friend with the thought that he might live to be eighty. "I would not have it," Ruffin answered. "How many more of beloved children or grandchildren might I lose by death in the next 17 years, if my life were so extended!"[40]

A strict but loving man, Ruffin had always found security and happiness among his family, even when he felt most ostracized by the public. He delighted in reading stories to his grandchildren in an Irish brogue and teaching them how to use sticks to roll wooden

---

South (Oxford, 1990), 125–31, belies any such alienation, a distinction not addressed by Faust, *Sacred Circle*.

39. Ruffin, "Incidents," III, 245–46, in Ruffin Papers, SHC; Scarborough, ed., *Ruffin Diary*, II, 541; Ruffin, "Southern Agricultural Exhaustion," 389.

40. Scarborough, ed., *Ruffin Diary*, I, 109–10; II, xxiii–xxvi; Edmund Ruffin, "In Remembrance of Jane Dupuy, Formerly Ruffin," and "In Remembrance of Ella Ruffin," both in Ruffin Papers, SHC.

hoops. Every successive death shook Ruffin more deeply than the last, and sadly his fears of the future came true. Before he took his own life, Ruffin witnessed the deaths of eight of his eleven children and eight grandchildren. After learning that his son Julian had died in battle in 1864, Ruffin was numb. "My mind cannot take in the momentous fact, nor my perceptions approach to the measure of the reality." Previously he had worried that time had decayed his memory; now he wondered if "age & decay have withered & dried up my affections & sensibilities, & hardened my heart, so that I can neither love as formerly, nor feel grief for the death of the most beloved."[41]

By 1854 Ruffin's increasing public activities had replaced his interest in farming, and the deaths of his daughters the next year left him "still less inclined to bear the labors & perplexities of conducting any regular business." He decided to sell Marlbourne and his slaves to his sons Edmund, Julian, and Charles, his daughter Mildred, and her husband, William Sayre. The Sayres lived at and managed Marlbourne. Ruffin liquidated his assets, kept $25,000 for himself, and distributed the remaining money—approximately $115,000—among his children and grandchildren. In 1856 he moved to Beechwood to live with his son, but not in idle retirement. He continued to read extensively and wrote occasional articles on agriculture. He enjoyed nothing more than writing. "When so employed, I can with pleasure write rapidly for 12 or more hours in the day & night—& until it is necessary to rest my cramped right hand." Because he found it difficult to write well after stopping for any length of time, he decided to begin a diary, both to capture random thoughts and to prevent his writing skills from deteriorating. He also decided to travel, "to visit distant friends & distant scenes, for which there had been no time in my previous busy life."[42]

One of his first trips was to White Sulphur Springs, a popular resort in western Virginia. There he spoke about politics with other vacationing southerners. Over the past two years the Kansas-Nebraska Act and the rise of the Republican party had renewed sectional tensions. Ruffin and others contemplated the best southern response in the event that a Republican were ever elected president. Ruffin vigorously promoted secession and the creation of a

41. Scarborough, ed., *Ruffin Diary,* I, 218, 293, 355, 409; II, xxiii–xxvi; Ruffin Diary, May 23, 1864, LC.

42. Scarborough, ed., *Ruffin Diary,* I, 5–7, 15–16, 43–45.

southern confederacy as the only sound policy. "I was surprised to find how many concurred with me, in the general proposition," he noted, "though scarcely one of them would have dared to utter the opinions, at first, & as openly as I did."[43]

Although he had never stopped wishing for disunion since 1850, Ruffin found that only the rise of the Republican party had convinced other southerners that perpetuation of the Union posed a real threat to their liberties, interests, and very existence. Ruffin had spent his entire life trying to save the South by rehabilitating its agriculture and defending its rights. But now Ruffin discovered his ultimate crusade: saving the South itself. The failures and rebuffs he had suffered earlier and his recent painful private misfortunes had calloused Ruffin but had also given the old reformer the resilience necessary to take on a difficult and dubious mission. No matter how encouraging he found the confidential conversations at White Sulphur Springs, Ruffin knew that "no one in Va had yet advocated such extreme measures." Aware that few others in his state had the boldness to begin the campaign for secession, Ruffin decided he was "willing to risk incurring the odium of opinions so unpopular still with many." The self-proclaimed leader of disunion in Virginia had but one reservation—that he would prove "a worthy & efficient advocate of the cause." His fanatical efforts over the next five years left no doubt of his unique abilities.[44]

Among Ruffin's most enthusiastic supporters that summer of 1856 was Roger A. Pryor, an editor at the Richmond *Enquirer.* Pryor promised to publish any editorials Ruffin wrote that promoted secession, no matter how extreme. Ruffin set to work immediately and soon completed a series of articles entitled "On the Consequences of Abolition Agitation and the Separation of the Union," which Pryor published in December.[45] He began by warning southerners that even though Republicans had lost the presidential election a month before, they had done so by the narrowest of margins; had they managed their campaign better, Ruffin said,

---

43. *Ibid.,* 16; Mitchell, *Ruffin,* 92.

44. Scarborough, ed., *Ruffin Diary,* I, 16. David Allmendinger, in *Ruffin,* places greater emphasis on the Virginian's efforts to achieve competency through his family than on his campaign for secession. In so doing, however, he incorrectly implies that Ruffin would not have worked so vigorously for southern independence had he not first achieved economic independence.

45. Scarborough, ed., *Ruffin Diary,* I, 17–19. Ruffin's essay was published under the name "Senex" in the Richmond *Enquirer* December 19 and 23, 1856.

they would have won. The rapid growth of the northern population, however, ensured the election of a Republican in 1860. Then, Ruffin explained, Republicans would destroy slavery, the South, and the Constitution without violating a letter of the law. The president would distribute patronage positions to abolitionists and send them to post offices and customshouses all over the South. Then he would replace military officers in southern forts and arsenals with more abolitionists, thus transforming all federal property into centers for abolitionist operations and havens for runaway slaves. A Republican Congress would end slavery in the District of Columbia and thereby make the nation's capital into the largest center for abolitionism in the South. By preventing the admission of new slave states—as had been done successfully so far with Kansas—admitting only free ones, and even permitting existing free states to divide themselves, a Republican Congress would allow the North to create the three-fourths majority needed to pass constitutional amendments. Then, Ruffin stated, Congress would legally abolish slavery. If the South had resisted the first assault by abolitionists against slavery, the Missouri Compromise, its foes might have been crushed in the bud. By yielding to antislavery forces in 1820 and compromising again in 1850, however, southerners had allowed abolitionism to grow too strong. Now it was too late to stop it within the Union. Ruffin asserted that the only safety for the South lay in secession. By acting promptly, he assured his readers, southerners could escape the tyrannical Union without fear of reprisal. Even if northerners were foolish enough to invade the South, he promised that southern armies would crush them quickly and decisively.

During a visit to Washington in February, 1857, Ruffin continued his campaign for secession by meeting individually with various southern congressmen. He had hoped to find support from R. M. T. Hunter, a senator from Virginia, but interpreted his reluctance to speak out on controversial issues as a sign that he had presidential aspirations and feared offending northern Democrats. In a meeting with Robert Toombs of Georgia, Ruffin expressed his approval of the senator's plan to tax northern commodities before their sale in the South, even though he doubted the constitutionality of such a scheme. Ruffin met with various other congressmen, but he also saw James De Bow. De Bow offered to publish some of Ruffin's agricultural essays in his *Review* and suggested after only a cursory glance at the manuscript that Ruffin's article on abolition and secession be reprinted. "I was surprised that he should so consent," Ruffin thought, but he was pleased to find De Bow a willing ally.[46]

A few months later Ruffin found another influential supporter. On a trip to Charleston he visited Barnwell Rhett and his son and talked at length about disunion. Ruffin cautioned them that Virginia would never be the first to secede, but if five or six states in the deep South seceded, then Virginia, Maryland, and all other slave states "would be *forced* to join their southern brethren." He wrote an article to that effect for the *Mercury*, and the Rhetts published it on May 13. That day Barnwell Rhett called on Ruffin so the two secessionists could continue their conversation. They commiserated that the South lacked "proper leaders—men who have the will & the ability, & also the necessary influence with their people" to foment secession. Some of the best politicians, they thought, were "seekers of high federal offices, & aspirants for higher, & therefore are self-bribed to a course of inactivity, or submission." To Ruffin, at least, Rhett had proved his commitment to secession for years. Because of Rhett's eagerness to publish Ruffin's editorials, in 1858 the Virginian vowed to make the *Mercury* "my channel of communication."[47]

Encouraged by the help of De Bow and Rhett, Ruffin tried to broaden his network of secessionists even further. He had long considered former governor Hammond "one of the ablest men in S[outh] C[arolina]" and the possessor of "unquestionably the most powerful mind in the southern states." Now, however, Ruffin saw his friend "rusting in solitude." In July Ruffin wrote to Hammond saying, "A leader is wanting for the south," and suggesting that Hammond was that man. "Show that you are not dead for all useful action," Ruffin urged, and begged him to attend the Knoxville Commercial Convention in August. Previous conventions, Ruffin explained, had been dominated by delegates who were "agents of northern merchants, or otherwise intimately connected with northern trade, & the keeping the south tributary to the north." Ruffin believed that the proper leader could transform these conventions into forums for the advancement of southern interests, commercial and otherwise. Because Hammond declined Ruffin's advice and did not attend the convention, Ruffin also failed to attend. After

46. Scarborough, ed., *Ruffin Diary*, I, 35–39; *DBR*, XXII (June, 1857), 583–93; XXIII (September–December, 1857), 266–72, 385–90, 546–52, 596–607.

47. Scarborough, ed., *Ruffin Diary*, I, 65–66, 225; Charleston *Mercury*, May 13, 1857.

learning how James De Bow successfully politicized the affair, however, Ruffin decided to pursue the same results at the next year's meeting.[48]

In the meantime, Ruffin continued to coax other southerners as he searched for a catalyst for secession. At the end of 1857 he paid De Bow to reprint his disunion essay in pamphlet form. Ruffin mailed copies of it to various public figures in the South, including each governor, and on another trip to Washington early in 1858 he distributed over a hundred more. While in the capital, Ruffin observed some of the tense congressional debates over the statehood of Kansas. He was not surprised, therefore, when he returned to Virginia and learned about the fight between Laurence Keitt and Galusha Grow. Although he considered such brawls disgraceful, he thought this incident "as probable a manner of the beginning of a separation of the states as any other."[49]

Perhaps animated by this belief, Ruffin composed another essay, "The Political Economy of Slavery," in which he repeated and elaborated upon standard proslavery assertions that slave labor was cheaper than free labor and that, because of the paternalism of white owners, African slavery precluded the development of pauperism in the South. With the encouragement and cooperation of William O. Goode, a congressman from Virginia, Ruffin had five thousand copies of the essay printed while on a visit to Washington in the spring of 1858. Ruffin paid for half the printing expenses, and Goode collected the rest from southern congressmen. With the help of sympathetic legislators, Ruffin placed a copy of his pamphlet on the desk of every southerner in Congress—and a few northerners as well. Over the next several days he mailed most of the rest free of charge, thanks to the franking privilege of Congressmen Goode and Thomas Ruffin of North Carolina (no relation), newly elected Senator Hammond, and Senator James M. Mason of Virginia.[50]

As he mailed his essays early in May, Ruffin learned that he had been elected as a delegate to the upcoming southern commercial convention in Montgomery. Despite De Bow's powerful disunion speech at Knoxville, Ruffin did not believe such conventions of

48. Scarborough, ed., *Ruffin Diary*, I, 75; Ruffin to Hammond, July 4, 1857, in Hammond Papers, LC.

49. Scarborough, ed., *Ruffin Diary*, I, 138, 148–49, 152, 155, 174.

50. Edmund Ruffin, "The Political Economy of Slavery," in Eric L. McKitrick, ed., *Slavery Defended: The Views of the Old South* (Englewood Cliffs, N.J., 1963), 69–85; Scarborough, ed., *Ruffin Diary*, I, 174, 180–82.

"*direct* use" for secession. But he recognized the opportunity they presented for discussing political topics with men from all over the South "& for the possible chance of forwarding the union & welfare of the southern states, & in my private capacity, instigating secession from the northern states."[51]

On his train ride to Montgomery the evangelist of disunion pressed copies of his slavery and disunion essays into the hands of all sympathetic listeners and upon his arrival began immediately talking to Rhett, William L. Yancey, and others about secession. "There seems in many a strong feeling of disunion," he noted optimistically. The proceedings of the convention did not disappoint him. Yancey's impassioned orations in favor of renewing the African slave trade impressed the old Virginian, though Ruffin believed Yancey "so fluent that he does not know when to stop." Ruffin himself was moved to make a brief speech. He suggested that future conventions should no longer address strictly commercial issues but instead "report upon each of the great questions of public policy, in which the most important interests of the South are involved." He explained that these assemblies provided a unique opportunity to avoid the influences of "unprincipled demagogues and greedy and interested office seekers" that plagued party conventions.[52]

The politicization of the Montgomery convention and the inspirational speeches by Yancey gave Ruffin the encouragement he needed for one of his "schemes for the operating on the public mind of the South." A few days after the convention, Ruffin met with Yancey to discuss the organization of associations designed to promote secession through discussion, public speeches, and publications. Ruffin asked Yancey if he would begin the effort on the next Fourth of July by giving an oration "directed to southern independence—& making use of the examples of the disunionists who declared independence of our mother country." Yancey agreed to do it and also supported Ruffin's "Declaration & League," a statement of southern grievances and appropriate responses. Yancey enthusiastically commenced the formation of the League of United Southerners in Alabama; Ruffin departed for home, where he would help form a similar group called the Association of Southerners.[53]

51. Scarborough, ed., *Ruffin Diary*, I, 183.
52. *Ibid.*, 183–85, 187–88; *DBR*, XXV (October, 1858), 459–60.
53. Scarborough, ed., *Ruffin Diary*, I, 195–97, 220.

Ruffin did not wait until he returned to Virginia to promote his association. In North Carolina he tried in vain to convince his friend and kinsman Judge Thomas Ruffin to support his endeavor. "He is too cautious—perhaps too wise—to go with me," Ruffin contemplated. Once back at Beechwood, however, his doubts evaporated when a friend agreed that "separation from the northern & oppressing states" was the only way to save the South. Ruffin immediately sent this friend a copy of the "Declaration & League" and wrote a letter of encouragement to Yancey. Roger Pryor, now editor of the Richmond *South*, published two articles by Ruffin about the association in early June. At the end of the month Ruffin read of Yancey's successful initiation of their scheme in Alabama. When Ruffin learned that a committee in Clinton, Louisiana, had recently created a similar organization, he quickly mailed it his "Declaration" and "Plan of Association." The initial success of these organizations only made Ruffin impatient for future growth. "I am not content to wait for the slow actions of other persons," he told Hammond when asking for the senator's help in franking more pamphlets that, again, Ruffin had paid for.[54]

In August, however, Ruffin's project began to unravel. Although Hammond cooperated with Ruffin, his heart was not in it; contrary to his old friend, he believed southerners were already well informed "& up to the matter" of secession. For Ruffin, worse than Hammond's lukewarm support was the publication of Yancey's Slaughter letter and the ensuing distress caused by the Alabama fire-eater's promise to "precipitate the cotton States into a Revolution." Ironically, Yancey's most vocal critic was Roger Pryor. In the *South* he denounced Yancey and his league as menaces to the national Democratic party. Ruffin claimed that the hope of retaining northern political support for R. M. T. Hunter's presidential campaign, and not a lack of faith in "the cause of the South," motivated his attack. Still, Ruffin could not forget that "Pryor knew that the scheme, of association, & the general policy recommended were *mine*," and promptly terminated his friendship with the editor. Although Yancey continued to fight for the league in editorial columns, Ruffin decided to abandon the project.[55]

54. *Ibid.*, 53 and note, 197, 200, 205, 209; Ruffin to Hammond, July 23, 1858, in Hammond Papers, LC.

55. Ruffin to Hammond, August 9, 1858, in Hammond Papers, LC; Scarborough, ed., *Ruffin Diary*, I, 220–23, 228, 263, 343.

At present, he believed, "not one in 100 of those who think with us, will dare to avow their opinions, & to commit themselves by such open action." Throughout Virginia, Ruffin observed, "any public man would destroy his political prospects by advocating the separation of the Union." Only men like himself, who neither sought public office nor had one to lose, could utter such sentiments with impunity. Ruffin believed that with a presidential election only two years away, "every man who hopes to gain anything from the continuance of the Union, will be loud & active in shouting for its integrity & permanence" and, like Pryor, call for the unity of the Democratic party. But for the time, Ruffin thought no one could "rouse the South." Personally he hoped for a sectional division of the Democratic party and the election of a Republican president "so that the dishonest & timid southern men may then be as strongly *bribed* by their selfish views to stand up for the South, as now to stoop & truckle to the North." In the meantime, Ruffin vowed to wait.[56]

Patience, however, was a quality Ruffin lacked. He knew that he could not tolerate inactivity, and he thrived on his energetic, fanatic labors for secession. In fact, his efforts over the past few years improved his health. His loss of memory continued, but he noted that since he had begun his great crusade, "I have been as contented & happy as my other circumstances permitted." He occupied his time by writing a flurry of new essays. Between 1858 and 1859 he wrote four articles for *De Bow's Review* and one for the *Mercury,* all of them arguing that emancipation would devastate blacks as well as whites.[57]

While Ruffin worked feverishly to convince southerners of the danger that would accompany a Republican administration, he found the actions of others wanting. He complained that a speech delivered by Laurence Keitt in August, 1858, was too moderate, and even a letter from Hammond could not convince Ruffin that his old friend could resist the temptation to tie his fortunes with the

56. Scarborough, ed., *Ruffin Diary,* I, 205, 223, 226–27, 444.

57. Edmund Ruffin, "Equality of the Races—Haytien and British Experiments," *DBR,* XXV (July, 1858), 27–36; "The Effects of High Prices of Slaves," *DBR,* XXVI (June, 1859), 647–57; "The Colonization Society and Liberia," *DBR,* XXVII (July, September–November, 1859), 55–73, 336–44, 392–402, 583–94; "African Colonization Unveiled," *DBR,* XIX (November, 1860), 638–649; Ruffin to De Bow, February 9, 1859, in James D. B. De Bow Papers, WPL; "Slavery and Free Labor Defined and Compared," Charleston *Mercury,* June 21, 22, 24, 28, 30, July 1, 4, 1859.

national Democracy. When De Bow failed to print Ruffin's latest contributions as quickly as their author desired, Ruffin grumbled, "These delays & long intermissions are vexatious." The Vicksburg Commercial Convention of 1859 resolved to repeal federal prohibitions on the African slave trade, but Ruffin had hoped it would do much more. All the while the Republican party grew, as did Ruffin's sense of imminent danger for the South.[58]

In October, 1859, Ruffin read about John Brown's attempt to lead a slave insurrection at Harpers Ferry, Virginia. When he learned that many northerners considered Brown's efforts heroic, Ruffin exclaimed, "It is astonishing even to me, & also very gratifying to me, that there should be so *general* an excitement & avowed sympathy among the people of the North for the late atrocious conspiracy." Surely, he thought, "This must open the eyes of the people of the south." Now even those who had feared disunion must recognize that course as "the only safeguard from the insane hostility of the north to southern institutions & interests."[59]

When he learned that Brown had been condemned to death in late November, Ruffin hurried to the "seat of war." Brown's execution promised to be the dramatic sectional confrontation that Ruffin hoped would trigger secession. "For my part, I wish that the abolitionists of the north may attempt a rescue. If it is done, & defeated, every one engaged will be put to death like wolves." Even if such an attempt succeeded, Ruffin believed, "it will be a certain cause of separation." Ruffin's excitement was heightened upon his arrival in Harpers Ferry when he walked through the town with local dignitaries and "many young men . . . saluted me as we passed, though I did not know them. It is a stirring time." Ruffin felt the reawakening of his "youthful military fervor" that had been dormant since his service in the War of 1812. He persuaded the commander of cadets from the Virginia Military Institute to let him join their ranks in the guard detail at Brown's hanging in nearby Charlestown. The old, gray-haired Ruffin realized, "I shall occupy the somewhat ludicrous position of being the youngest member (or recruit,) of this company of boyish soldiers," but he could not resist the opportunity to witness either a daring rescue attempt or the execution of the villainous Brown.[60]

58. Scarborough, ed., *Ruffin Diary*, I, 223–24, 304–305.
59. *Ibid.*, 348–51, 354, 356–57.
60. *Ibid.*, 361–63, 366–68.

As the aged soldier joined the cadets on the morning of December 2, he saw that his young comrades had to use "all the constraint of their good manners to hide their merriment." After chatting with them briefly to break their tense amusement, Ruffin marched with them to the gallows and waited for Brown's arrival. Brown was brought on a wagon, sitting on his own coffin. He said nothing as he climbed to the scaffold, and Ruffin thought his movements "gave no evidence of his being either terrified or concerned." A rope was placed around his neck, a hood put over his head. Confusion among his military escorts caused a delay of at least five minutes, during which time Brown stood motionless. This "awful state of suspense," Ruffin believed, seemed "cruel & most trying . . . notwithstanding his atrocious crimes, & worse intentions." Finally, Brown was hanged; his hands convulsed slightly after a minute, then a warm southern breeze rocked his body gently "like a pendulum."[61]

After all the anticipation, Brown's death was a strangely melancholy affair for Ruffin. "It is impossible for me not to respect his thorough devotion to his bad cause, & the undaunted courage with which he has sustained it, through all losses & hazards," Ruffin noted sympathetically. The southern fanatic gave due credit to his northern counterpart: "The villain whose life has thus been forfeited, possessed but one virtue (if it should be so called,) or one quality that is more highly esteemed by the world than the most rare & perfect virtues. This is physical or animal courage, or the most complete fearlessness of & insensibility to danger & death."[62]

Ruffin did not mourn Brown's death. Instead, he quickly developed a dramatic new scheme to keep alive both the memory of Brown's raid and the fear it caused throughout the South. The day before the execution Ruffin had procured one of the many pikes that Brown and his accomplices had brought to Virginia with the intention of arming slaves. He pasted a label on its handle that read *"Samples of the favors designed for us by our Northern Brethren."* He carried the pike with him to Washington, naturally causing quite a stir along the way. Once in the capital, he displayed his prize to various southern congressmen and the startled and curious guests at his hotel. The reaction he received made him decide to expand on his

61. *Ibid.*, 369–71; James M. Oliver *et al.* to Edmund Ruffin, January 18, 1860, in Ruffin Papers, SHC.

62. Scarborough, ed., *Ruffin Diary*, I, 350, 371.

project by sending a labeled pike to the governor of each slave state. Ruffin asked the superintendent of the armory at Harpers Ferry to send the pikes to him in Washington. In the meantime he had written labels and made arrangements with Senator Clement C. Clay of Alabama to distribute the pikes on his behalf after he returned to Virginia. Ruffin continued to display his own pike upon his arrival in Richmond and carried it on many subsequent travels, transforming himself into the symbol of secession incarnate.[63]

Early in 1860 Ruffin stumbled upon yet another new tactic to promote disunion. He read a recently published novel that forecasted the results of secession. Ruffin thought it "a very foolish book" but believed "the subject promised something, & the idea might be carried out to good purpose." He began writing his own version on the last day of February. Ruffin's novel took the form of a series of dispatches from an English correspondent in America to the London *Times* from 1864 to 1870, when civil war raged during the second administration of Republican President William Seward. Ruffin's *Anticipations of the Future* vaguely resembled Beverley Tucker's *Partisan Leader*, but as Ruffin explained, "I suppose every incident of danger, damage, or disaster to the South, which is predicted by northerners, or southern submissionists—as war, blockade, invasion, servile insurrection—(which I do not believe in my self,) & supposing these, as premises, I thence follow through what I suppose to be the legitimate consequences," that is, a southern victory.[64]

Ruffin worked intensely, but his fictional destruction of the Union and slaughter of Yankee troops "were alike amusing to my mind, & . . . conducive to immediate pleasure." By the end of April he had written over 270 pages and arranged for serializing his work in the *Mercury* under the title "Glimpses of the Future." After agreeing to cover two-thirds of the cost, Ruffin sent the complete manuscript—over 400 pages—to a publisher in June. Not even the unexpected Republican nomination of Abraham Lincoln could

---

63. *Ibid.*, 368, 375–76, 378–83, 392, 402, 431, 438–39, 442–43; C. C. Clay to Ruffin, June 21, 1860, in Ruffin Papers, SHC; Charleston *Mercury*, November 28, 1860. Later, Ruffin must have acquired more pikes. Diarist Mary Chesnut noted in July, 1861, "Old Ruffin has promised me a John Brown pike" (C. Vann Woodward, ed., *Mary Chesnut's Civil War* [New Haven, 1981], 114).

64. Scarborough, ed., *Ruffin Diary*, I, 407–408; Ruffin to Hammond, May 4, 1860, in Hammond Papers, LC. For Ruffin's own comparison between *Anticipations* and Tucker's *Partisan Leader*, see Scarborough, ed., *Ruffin Diary*, III, 592–93.

faze the author; just before sending his book to the printer he simply changed the scenario so that Seward succeeded Lincoln in 1864.[65]

Ruffin continued a variety of other activities while he wrote *Anticipations of the Future*. He obtained a cloth suit made entirely in Virginia and wore it as he paraded with his pike to promote both southern manufacturing and a boycott of northern goods. Robert Barnwell Rhett, Jr., asked Ruffin's aid in finding copies of Beverley Tucker's speech at the Nashville Convention and Ruffin's "Consequences of Abolition Agitation" for republication in the *Mercury*. Ruffin gladly complied and also sent a new article in which he attacked Governor Henry A. Wise of Virginia as "a political liar of the first magnitude." He intended all these actions to capitalize on the outrage John Brown had created in the South. By April, 1860, however, Ruffin noticed that "the violent agitation & impulse caused by the Harper's Ferry affair seem to have completely subsided."[66]

Before Ruffin grew too despondent, he received a heartening letter from Hammond. The senator believed "the end" was fast approaching in Washington and suggested that Ruffin "come & see the fun." Ruffin chose to stay in Virginia to work on his novel, but he read gleefully in local papers that an end had come to the national Democratic party at its convention in Charleston. Ruffin rejoiced on two counts: first, "that the south will be henceforth separated from & relieved of the insatiable vampyre, the northern democracy," and second, that a split in the Democratic majority would "forward the election of Seward, or any other abolitionist," and thereby hasten secession. After the events at Charleston, Hammond's "promised inducement of 'fun'" in the capital proved irresistible. Ruffin would wait a few weeks before going to Washington, when he believed "'the end' shall be more nearly approached."[67]

Before leaving for Washington, Ruffin went to South Carolina to

65. Scarborough, ed., *Ruffin Diary*, I, 413, 415–16, 428–29, 437–38; Charleston *Mercury*, April 18, 21, May 9, 11, 16, 19, 31, June, *passim*, 1860; Edmund Ruffin, *Anticipations of the Future to Serve as Lessons for the Present Time: In the Form of Extracts from an English Resident in the United States, to the London Times, from 1864 to 1870, with an Appendix, on the Causes and Consequences of the Independence of the South* (Richmond, 1860), viii, 7–8.

66. Scarborough, ed., *Ruffin Diary*, I, 384–85, 402, 404–406, 410, 415; R. B. Rhett, Jr., to Ruffin, March 1, 1860, in Ruffin Papers, SHC.

67. Scarborough, ed., *Ruffin Diary*, I, 415–18; Hammond to Ruffin, April 16, 1860, in Ruffin Papers, SHC; Ruffin to Hammond, May 4, 21, 1860, in Hammond Papers, LC.

attend the special convention for the election of delegates to the southern Democratic convention in Richmond and "to see what is the disposition as to secession of the cotton states (or any of them) from the Union." When he arrived in Columbia, he conferred with the Rhetts and others. He warned them not to expect Virginia or any border state to secede first or even simultaneously with those of the deep South but assured the Carolinians that other states would follow eventually, "after having served . . . as an impregnable barrier of defence against any attack from the north."[68]

Armed with his "usual travelling supply of pamphlets," Ruffin proceeded to Washington. He had a brief conversation with Senator Mason and Laurence Keitt, with whom Ruffin now saw eye to eye. On a short visit to Baltimore, Ruffin met Louis Wigfall. Ruffin found the senator's "oddity of speech & opinions, & their extravagance of [express]ion" amusing but had no quarrel with the Texan's views on disunion. Ruffin proudly saw his pikes in a Senate committee room, all "beautifully labelled" under the direction of Senator Clay. Meetings with others—sometimes in Ruffin's hotel room with his own pike in sight—confirmed Hammond's report that Washington was buzzing with anticipation over secession.[69]

The rapid changes in events and public attitudes made Ruffin more impatient than ever. Despite the cooperation he received from the Rhetts, Ruffin pressured them to publish his contributions faster than they were capable of doing. When De Bow could not keep up with Ruffin's writings, the Virginian denounced the quality of the *Review* and berated its editor as "a crafty & mean Yankee in conduct & principle." Having already spread the gospel of disunion along the eastern seaboard and into the Gulf South, Ruffin turned westward to Kentucky late in the summer of 1860. He knew Unionism was strong in the Bluegrass State and that "I must be deemed a sort of speculative Benedict Arnold" by many of its people. When he discussed politics, therefore, he did so "in jocular manner, & sometimes with exaggerated expressions," which left his "most odious doctrines to be inferred & understood." When he became certain that some states in the deep South would secede if a Republican were elected president, Ruffin decided that he would not wait for Virginia to join them. He vowed to leave his beloved state and "move southward, where resistance, & safety for slave property, may be hoped for—& which are hopeless in Va."[70]

68. Scarborough, ed., *Ruffin Diary*, I, 423–25.
69. *Ibid.*, 429–34, 447.
70. R. B. Rhett, Jr., to Ruffin, April 5, 1860, in Ruffin Papers, SHC; Ruffin to

In the last two months before the election, Ruffin sent another series of articles to the *Mercury*. These promised Carolinians that no amount of federal power, not even an invasion by the entire U.S. military force of less than nineteen thousand, could subjugate a single southern state. At the first drop of blood, all other slave states would join any that had already seceded. Ruffin claimed that the southern coastline was too large to blockade effectively and that the British would stop any such attempt soon after it began.[71]

Ruffin also followed the news from the North with great interest. He was elated when state elections in Pennsylvania resulted in a strong Republican triumph and believed that Republicans would also carry Pennsylvania in November, ensuring the victory of Lincoln and forcing southerners "to choose between secession & submission to abolition domination." He also read about Yancey's daring speaking tour through the North and urged his young colleague to devote "your time, your labor, & your great power as a popular orator, to speaking to assemblages of the people in every southern state," to become "another Patrick Henry."[72]

On November 6, election day, Ruffin voted. The day, he believed, would "serve to show whether these southern states are to remain free, or to be politically enslaved—whether the institution of negro slavery, on which the social & political existence of the south rests, is to be secured by our resistance, or to be abolished in a short time, as the certain result of our present submission to northern domination." He decided to vote for the southern Democrat, John C. Breckinridge, then go immediately to South Carolina, "where I hope that even my feeble aid may be worth something to forward the secession of the state & consequently of the whole South."[73]

Ruffin reached the South Carolina border the next day and discovered that a "universal secession feeling appeared." "Minute men," wearing the distinctive blue cockade, joined him at every stop on the train to Columbia. The capital was bustling with state and local officials and cadets from the South Carolina Military Academy. Soon after reaching his hotel, Ruffin heard the sound of

James De Bow, July 19, 1860, Frank De Bow to James De Bow, August 21, 1860, in De Bow Papers, WPL; Scarborough, ed., *Ruffin Diary*, I, 426, 443, 459–61.

71. Scarborough, ed., *Ruffin Diary*, I, 459, 466, 470, 477–78, 480; Charleston *Mercury*, November 6, 7, 1860.

72. Scarborough, ed., *Ruffin Diary*, I, 473, 476, 479–80; Ruffin to Yancey, October 29, 1860, *ibid.*, 633–35.

73. *Ibid.*, 481–83.

music and voices calling him out to make a speech. He responded, "*Fellow-citizens:* I have thought and studied upon this question for years. It has been literally the great one idea of my life, the independence of the South, which I verily believe can only be accomplished through the action of South Carolina." Ruffin urged Carolinians to act quickly, to "give encouragement to the timid" and to "frighten your enemies."[74]

The crowd greeted each of his brief utterances with loud cheers and applause that warmed the old man's heart. To his sons Ruffin wrote: "The time since I have been here has been the happiest of my life. . . . The public events are as gratifying to me as they are glorious & momentous. And there has been much to gratify any individual & selfish feelings. I have always heretofore been treated most kindly & respectfully by the people of S.C. But all previous did not compare with the present time." Ruffin thought the laudatory words of many "mere compliment, & in cases flattery. But even in the latter case it is gratifying to me." Only one thought dampened his enthusiasm: "Oh! if I may see such a time in Va.!"[75]

A few nights later, in Charleston, another crowd called for Ruffin. "My friends, brother disunionists," he said, if Virginia remained in the Union "under the domination of this infamous, low, vulgar tyranny of Black Republicanism" and any other state seceded, "I will seek my domicil[e] in that State and abandon Virginia forever." The next morning he participated in the raising of the Palmetto Flag on a newly erected, ninety-foot "secession pole." He then joined Barnwell Rhett on a trip to Georgia to determine that state's willingness to secede. When they learned that Georgians would not discuss disunion until they met in a special convention on January 16, the two fire-eaters returned to their respective homes.[76]

Ruffin reached Beechwood early in December, but not even the death of another daughter, Elizabeth Ruffin Sayre, could shake his attention from secession. A few days after her funeral he set out again for Charleston, where he had been invited to sit with dele-

74. *Ibid.*, 483–85; Charleston *Mercury*, November 8, 1860.

75. Charleston *Mercury*, November 8, 1860; Ruffin to Edmund Ruffin, Jr., and Julian C. Ruffin, November 11, 1860, in Ruffin Papers, SHC. Also see Elizabeth [Ruffin] Sayre to Ruffin, November 16, 1860, Julian C. Ruffin to Ruffin, November 17, 1860, and Mildred [Ruffin] Sayre to Ruffin, December 4, 1860, in Ruffin Papers, SHC.

76. Charleston *Mercury*, November 17, 1860; Scarborough, ed., *Ruffin Diary*, I, 499–501.

gates at a state convention and watch disunion become reality. After obtaining one of the pens used to sign the ordinance of secession, which he kept "as a valued memento of the occasion," Ruffin made arrangements to attend the secession convention in Florida on January 5. In Tallahassee, on his sixty-seventh birthday, Floridians invited Ruffin to join their proceedings and two days later asked him to speak. He did so, but very briefly and simply to urge them to act quickly. On January 10 news arrived that Mississippi had seceded the day before, and Floridians joined them by a vote of sixty-two to seven.[77]

Ruffin returned to Beechwood later that month, where he anxiously followed the news of last-ditch efforts in Congress to save the Union and the increasing tension between state and federal forces in Charleston Harbor. "The interest I feel for public affairs, & the Southern Confederacy, absorbs every other." News from the Provisional Confederate Congress at Montgomery could not come quickly enough for Ruffin. When he learned that Jefferson Davis and Alexander H. Stephens had been selected as president and vice-president, Ruffin hailed the new administration for having greater "intellectual ability & moral worth" than any since James Madison's. With the establishment of the Confederate States of America, Ruffin decided to leave Virginia before Lincoln's inauguration, to "avoid being, as a Virginian, under his government even for an hour." He left his state on March 2, determined never to return except to visit his family or after Virginia had joined him in the Southern Confederacy.[78]

"I fear that some of the Hot heads of the South will come into unnecessary conflict with the Fed. troops," Elizabeth had written to her father shortly before her death. No one, however, was more eager for war than Ruffin. Believing that bloodshed would force the remaining southern states to join the Confederacy, Ruffin even hoped personally to draw fire from the Union forces at Fort Sumter while he sailed with local officials to inspect Confederate fortifications in Charleston Harbor. As tensions increased, he added the insignia of the Palmetto Guards to his homespun suit and joined the Iron Brigade on Morris Island. The commander of the Confederate forces had designated the Palmetto Guards to fire the first shot at Sumter before dawn on April 12, and that company,

77. Scarborough, ed., *Ruffin Diary*, I, 503–505, 508, 510–11, 513, 515–23, 525–29; Charles Campbell to Ruffin, November 22, 1860, in Ruffin Papers, SHC.

78. Scarborough, ed., *Ruffin Diary*, I, 524, 529–31, 545, 548–51, 557, 559; Ruffin to J. Perkins, March 2, 1861, in John Perkins Papers, SHC.

in turn, gave the honor to Ruffin. After a generation of wishing someone else would strike the first blow against the federal government, South Carolinians had found their man. Ruffin was "highly gratified by the compliment, & delighted to perform the service— which I did." His shell struck the fort, and the Civil War began.[79]

"Accept my best wishes and grateful acknowledgement of your heroic devotion to the cause of the South," President Davis wrote to Private Ruffin. Julian Ruffin gave his father an even greater reward; a week after the victory in Charleston, he named his newborn son Edmund Sumter Ruffin. The same week Ruffin learned that Virginia had seceded. Proudly, Ruffin headed for home.[80]

When he returned to Virginia, however, Ruffin was alarmed at his state's lack of preparedness for war. He sent advice to Colonel Robert E. Lee about fortifications and the defense of the state. He implored President Davis to revoke the military appointments of those who recently were among "the most thorough & abject submissionists to Northern oppression & to Lincoln & abolition." He recommended that all those even suspected of being spies "be either driven out of the C[onfederate] S[tates] or treated as enemies & prisoners." For that matter, Ruffin wanted all native northerners currently in the South to be treated as enemies unless they gave "full evidence of being southern in principle & in acts."[81]

Ruffin turned his attention from imagined enemies to real ones in July when the Union army invaded his state. After the Palmetto Guards arrived from South Carolina, Ruffin rejoined his old company as it headed for Manassas Junction. Forced to march for miles in hot, muggy weather, the old man tired quickly. A Virginia militia captain came to Ruffin's rescue by allowing the venerable fire-eater to ride to battle on a caisson. During the confusing opening skirmishes of July 21, Ruffin briefly became separated from his unit; this time a sympathetic sergeant gave Ruffin a seat on a cannon as his artillerymen rushed past the Palmettos and toward Union troops who jammed the Suspension Bridge over Cub Run in their panicked retreat from Bull Run. Ruffin was allowed to fire the first shot at the bridge, and his shell struck with deadly accuracy.

The next day Ruffin returned to the bridge "to learn the num-

<hr />

79. Elizabeth Sayre to Ruffin, November 16, 1860, in Ruffin Papers, SHC; Scarborough, ed., *Ruffin Diary*, I, 566, 573–74, 581–86, 588–93.

80. Jefferson Davis to Ruffin, April 22, 1861, in Ruffin Papers, SHC; Scarborough, ed., *Ruffin Diary*, I, 606, 610; II, xxv, 18.

81. Ruffin to Robert E. Lee, May 14, 1861, Ruffin to Jefferson Davis, June 26, 1861, in Ruffin Papers, SHC.

ber . . . killed by our cannonade." He saw but three corpses, and
because two lay in a wagon, he surmised that they had been
wounded or killed already and were simply being evacuated when
his shot struck them. "This was a great disappointment to me," he
grumbled to himself. "I should have liked not only to have killed
the greatest possible number—but also to know, if possible, *which* I
had killed, & to see & count the bodies." Months later, however, his
morbid curiosity and his ego were mollified when he learned that at
least six Yankees had died at his hands.[82]

Like most southerners, Ruffin had expected the federal invasion
to be crushed swiftly and decisively; the inability of Confederate
forces to achieve a quick victory, therefore, left him frustrated. He
was sure that bunglers in the army and the government had hindered the Confederate war effort, and he joined Barnwell Rhett
and others in criticizing the administration. Ruffin was upset that
after secession "many of the earliest & staunchest movers of secession, & defenders of southern rights & interests" had been bypassed for "the honors & rewards of office" in favor of "eleventh
hour laborers," some of whom Ruffin believed "were submissionists
to the last moment of free choice." Ruffin claimed that frustrated
ambition underlay Rhett's particularly sharp denunciations of
Davis, but Congressman Rhett had not actively sought high public
office in the Confederacy. Ruffin had. In 1861 he petitioned a
friend in the Confederate Congress to help him obtain "any respectable & honorable position, civil or military," and even suggested the improbable one of special commissioner to Washington,
D.C., to engage in negotiations for recognition of the Confederacy.
After achieving success in his long struggle for secession, Ruffin's
frustrated personal ambition heralded the collapse of his dreams.[83]

Physical destruction compounded Ruffin's woes during the
heavy fighting in eastern Virginia in 1862. Union troops drove him
and his family from their plantations; after the enemy withdrew,
the Ruffins returned to scenes of wanton destruction. At Beechwood, Yankees had taken food and stolen or destroyed most of the
household contents and scattered wreckage across the front yard.
Federal soldiers let Ruffin know they knew whose house they had
sacked. In charcoal and in tobacco juice they had written on interior walls, "This house belonged to a Ruffinly son of a bitch," and
"You did fire the first gun on Sumter, you traitor son of a bitch." A

82. Scarborough, ed., *Ruffin Diary*, II, 78–95; Mitchell, *Ruffin*, 191–96.

83. Scarborough, ed., *Ruffin Diary*, II, 229; Ruffin to Perkins, March 2, 1861, in
Perkins Papers, SHC.

Pennsylvanian wrote in one of Ruffin's books, "Owned by Old Ruffin, the basest old traitor rebel in the United States. You old cuss, it is a pity you go unhanged." Marlbourne fared little better.[84]

Most of the slaves on these plantations had fled in advance of the Union army or had joined it on its retreat. After spending so many years arguing that slavery was benevolent and slaves loyal to their paternalistic masters, Ruffin was shocked by the flight of his slaves. At first he decided that they had left Marlbourne because of the negligent treatment they received from his son-in-law William Sayre. Runaways were just as common at Beechwood, however, where Ruffin believed slave management was excellent. Even after a dwarf and two handicapped slaves escaped—people from whom Ruffin never expected labor—the old man was unable to understand how desperately these people wanted to be free.[85]

Ruffin's reaction to the destruction of his property was twofold. Initially he sought vengeance. He called for a massive invasion of the North and, "justified by Yankee examples," demanded that southern armies leave "every village & town . . . in ashes" as they stormed through Pennsylvania, Ohio, and beyond. When he looked beyond his own misfortunes, however, his sympathy for other victims of the war overrode his anger. He contributed generously to the relief established late in 1862 for the victims of the Union attack on Fredericksburg. Eventually, the survival of Ruffin's beloved Confederacy took precedence over all other considerations. By 1864 he contributed hundreds of dollars to the Confederate treasury, hoping others would follow his example. He even urged the secretary of the treasury to make taxes "as heavy as our people will bear" for the duration of the war. And by the closing months of the war—in a surprising and sharp departure from the views of other fire-eaters—Ruffin declared his readiness "not only to enlist negro soldiers, but to give up the institution of slavery itself," if that might provide a means of saving his cherished Confederacy.[86]

Although he clung tenaciously to the hope of victory, his realization that the demise of the Confederacy was imminent made Ruffin long for his own death. The embittered old man wrote in his diary that death and even decomposition "cannot occur too soon." After

84. Scarborough, ed., *Ruffin Diary*, II, 323, 337–38, 345–46, 368, 416–22, 425–26, 471–72.

85. Mitchell, *Ruffin*, 211–13, 227–28.

86. Ruffin to Perkins, August 16, 24, 1862, in Perkins Papers, SHC; R. R. Howison to Ruffin, January 3, 24, 1863, in Ruffin Papers, AL; Scarborough, ed., *Ruffin Diary*, III, 748–49.

the defeat of the Confederacy in 1865, Ruffin could "foresee nothing but failure." When he learned that Yankees had stolen the coat he had made of Virginia cloth, his heart sank. He had worn it to Fort Sumter and to Bull Run and "valued [it] as a relic & memorial." With few material possessions left and believing he had nothing to live for, he found the decision to kill himself an easy one.[87]

When he reflected on his life, Ruffin found some consolation that other southerners recognized and appreciated his various accomplishments. But in Virginia, he complained, "my long continued literary labor[s] in behalf of the southern cause have been received with mortifying neglect," and "the great benefits conferred by me on the agricultural improvement & wealth of my country" had never received the attention he believed they deserved. He grumbled that his only fame in Virginia resulted from "the accident of my having fired the first gun against Fort Sumter." He did not want to die with his years of labor for the South eclipsed by "the accident at Fort Sumter." Because he felt "almost forgotten in my own country, & by the generation which I have so zealously & effectively labored to serve," he decided to entrust future generations with the remembrance and appreciation of his devotion to the South.[88] With the last act of his life, the fanatical Ruffin hoped to make his cherished cause transcend his own death.

Four months after his suicide, Emma Holmes of South Carolina noticed that almost everybody was trying to forget the agony of four long years of war. She, however, chose to remember. As she looked over photographs of Jefferson Davis, Robert E. Lee, and Edmund Ruffin, a friend of hers came by. Miss Holmes called her friend's attention to the picture of Ruffin. The friend derided the Virginian as a fool for shooting himself just because the Confederacy was vanquished. "It hurt me deeply as well as greatly shocked me to hear such a dreadful event announced in such flippant language," she responded. "I had always loved & honored the heroic old man, an aged grandfather fired with zeal for freedom & love for his native South." Miss Holmes perceived his death the same way that Ruffin's son had. When Edmund Ruffin, Jr., told his children about the suicide, he concluded, "The Yankees have . . . killed your Grandfather."[89]

87. Ruffin Diary, May 17, 1864, April 17, May 2, 9, 17, June 18, 1865, LC.

88. Scarborough, ed., *Ruffin Diary,* II, 548–49.

89. John F. Marszalek, ed., *The Diary of Miss Emma Holmes, 1861–1866* (Baton Rouge, 1979), 478; Edmund Ruffin, Jr., to his children, June 20, 1865, in *Tyler's Quarterly,* V (January, 1924), 194.

Abstractions
William Porcher Miles

A friend of William Porcher Miles's once told him that "revolutions are [not] effected on abstractions. There must be a *pinch* of some sort, & with cotton at 10c & negroes at $1000 the South will know no *pinch*." Miles disagreed. He believed, "The world is governed by 'abstractions'—the American Revolution was fought upon an 'abstraction'—honor was an 'abstraction'—all science was built upon 'abstractions.'"[1] Other southerners, living in a society in which slavery provided a constant reminder of degradation, might have viewed honor as a more concrete commodity, but Miles won the respect of southern radicals and moderates alike through a rigid adherence to his own abstract notions of honor and integrity. Because he owned no slaves himself, Miles's arguments on behalf of the peculiar institution were based more on abstractions than self-interest.[2] As an academician and as mayor of Charleston, he received plaudits for putting into practice abstract ideas of education and civic government. As a United States congressman during the late 1850s, as a Confederate congressman throughout the Civil War, and as a businessman after the war, however, Miles found the problem of reconciling abstract principles with political realities a vexing one.

In his youth Miles learned to value the abstract idea of liberty above all else. The second son of Sarah Bond Warley and James Saunders Miles, William was born on the anniversary of American independence, July 4, 1822, in Walterboro, South Carolina. His ancestors, French Huguenots, had come to South Carolina because that colony offered them the freedom to choose and practice their

1. James H. Hammond to W. P. Miles, November 23, 1858, in William Porcher Miles Papers, SHC; Charleston *Mercury,* May 21, 1860; William Porcher Miles, *Oration Delivered Before the Fourth of July Association* (Charleston, 1849), 21.

2. Thomas D. Alexander and Richard E. Beringer, *The Anatomy of the Confederate Congress* (Nashville, 1972), 376–77. For interpretations of honor quite different from Miles's, see William J. Cooper, Jr., *The South and the Politics of Slavery, 1828–1856* (Baton Rouge, 1978), 69–74, and Kenneth S. Greenberg, *Masters and Statesmen: The Political Culture of American Slavery* (Baltimore, 1985), 146.

own religion. The young Miles learned that his grandfather Major Felix Warley had fought to create a free, republican government during the Revolution. During Miles's youth, his native Colleton District was the storm center of the nullification crisis; like Laurence Keitt, Louis Wigfall, and James De Bow, Miles grew up in a time of tension between state and federal authorities, in a place where Barnwell Rhett warned that liberty was under attack by northerners. After receiving his primary education at Southworth School, Miles attended Willington Academy, the institution that a generation before had produced the leading defender of southern liberty, John C. Calhoun.[3]

Although his background was similar to those of other young fire-eaters, Miles exhibited no political propensities during or immediately after his college years. In 1838 he enrolled at the College of Charleston. His early experiences there were those of a young man unconcerned with lofty principles, abstractions, or even education. Instead of studying, Miles honed his skills at practical jokes and took particular delight when one of his victims responded to a prank with "tragic gravity." Some of his friends spent their summers continuing their studies, but Miles passed his time in the leisurely indulgence of peaches and watermelons and in pursuing a mysterious "Miss A." A friend warned him, "Oh Miles, thou hast fallen indeed, and coupling your accounts of fruit and ladies, I might suppose that your fall has been some what like father Adam's." Nothing came of Miles's first romance, but he found male companionship in a circle of friends that included James De Bow and the future historian and diplomat William Henry Trescot. At the beginning of the school year in the fall of 1840, another member of this circle, Joseph Toomer, committed suicide. His death jolted his young friends, and none more so than Miles. Perhaps shaken by this loss, after Toomer's death Miles abandoned much of his earlier frivolity (except for an occasional practical joke) and concentrated on his studies. In 1842 he graduated at the head of his class.[4]

Academia continued to absorb Miles's interest after graduation.

---

3. Ruth McCaskill Daniel, "William Porcher Miles: Champion of Southern Interests" (M.A. thesis, University of North Carolina, Chapel Hill, 1943), 1–2; W. P. Miles to Charles Lanman, October 26, 1859, in William Porcher Miles Papers, SCL.

4. William H. Trescot to W. P. Miles, August 4, 21, September 11, 1840, July 26, 1842, Samuel I. Legare to Miles, August 14, October 1, 1840, J. Maxwell Pringle to Miles, August 27, 1840, in Miles Papers, SHC.

He began to study law in 1843 under the instruction of an attorney in Charleston but abandoned it to take a job as a math tutor and, by the end of the year, accepted a job as professor of mathematics at his alma mater. As a member of the small faculty at the College of Charleston, Miles enjoyed prestige as an intellectual in his adopted city. The academic community recognized his knowledge not only of mathematics but of literature, history, and classical languages. After a few years, however, the young assistant professor grumbled that his salary was inadequate. Miles hoped that the city council, which controlled the budget of the college, would increase tuition and use the revenue for faculty raises. He capitulated, however, when he learned that the council opposed salary increases.[5]

During his first few years on the faculty, Miles showed no interest in politics. No record remains to suggest that he had the slightest concern with the Bluffton movement of 1844, and his brief bout with the city council had no immediate impact on his activity in city government. In 1846, however, national politics commanded his attention. The Wilmot Proviso challenged Miles's notions of southern rights, the equality of the states under the Constitution, and the honor of a slaveholding people. With the renewal of sectional tensions and the approach of Independence Day in the summer of 1849, Miles turned his thoughts to the lessons he had learned about the Revolution, the Constitution, and America's struggle for freedom. He believed that the North now threatened southern liberty, just as the British once had. When the Fourth of July Association of Charleston invited Miles to give its annual oration in 1849, he decided "that as a Southern man I was bound, on such an occasion, in honor and conscience, to express myself in the strongest and fullest manner."[6]

Miles began his speech with the customary discussion of the meaning of Independence Day and a brief discourse about the Revolution, with special emphasis on the contributions of Carolinians.[7] The occasion, Miles said, should not only serve as a celebration

5. Daniel, "Miles," 3; C. Vann Woodward, ed., *Mary Chesnut's Civil War* (New Haven, 1981), 536; *Dictionary of American Biography*, XII, 617; Mitchell King to Miles, March 24, 1848, in Miles Papers, SHC. Biographical information on Miles is scarce. Francis Butler Simkins' sketch in the *Dictionary of American Biography* provides the most accessible outline of his life.

6. Wm. Porcher Miles to George S. Bryan, Henry C. King, and R. W. Bacot, July 14, 1849, in Miles, *Oration*, 3.

7. A. V. Huff, "The Eagle and the Vulture: Changing Attitudes Toward Nationalism in Fourth of July Orations Delivered in Charleston, 1778–1860," *South At-*

of conservative American liberty but also as a time to review the nation's past, examine the present, and contemplate the future.[8]

Did Americans still adhere to the principles of liberty, or had they strayed from the course set for them by the Founding Fathers? According to Miles, preserving the letter and the spirit of the Constitution was the key to protecting America's inheritance of liberty. Like the fire-eaters, Miles argued that the spirit of the Constitution—specifically, the equality of the states—could be destroyed without violating the letter of the law. Americans must vigilantly defend the Constitution, he warned, "lest it be insidiously undermined while we stand supinely by, refusing to see, or seeing refusing to counteract the subtle designs of those who seek to overthrow it!"[9]

Miles then argued that the Wilmot Proviso and all attempts to prohibit the expansion of slavery threatened the equality of the states, the Constitution, and liberty. That some northerners considered slavery sinful did not bother Miles. Although he believed slavery was both the foundation of southern society and "of Divine institution," Miles could tolerate differences of opinion on the subject as long as all Americans acknowledged that the Constitution "recognized and countenanced" African slavery and left it under the exclusive jurisdiction of the states. Miles protested, however, that legislation such as the Wilmot Proviso was an unconstitutional attempt to wrest slavery from the control of southerners. By refusing to let southerners take their slave property into the federal territories, northerners tried to deny southerners an equal opportunity to move into lands they held in common with the North, lands they had helped acquire for the United States during the Mexican War. To deny the free and legal movement of slaveholders, Miles argued, was to revoke southern liberty.[10]

"So far we have considered the Wilmot Proviso as a mere abstract question of Constitutional right," Miles continued. Northern friends of the South promised that restricting the expansion of slavery posed no tangible threat to the South. These people argued that the forces of nature—aridity and cold—excluded slavery from the territories more effectively than any legislation. If that were so, Miles countered, then why did so many northerners continue to

lantic Quarterly, XII (1972), 10–22; Joseph R. James, Jr., "The Transformation of the Fourth of July in South Carolina, 1850–1919" (M.A. thesis, Louisiana State University, 1987).

    8. Miles, Oration, 5–7, 9–14.

    9. Ibid., 7, 8, 14, 27–28.

    10. Ibid., 16–17, 19, 22–24.

advocate a legislative solution to the problem and threaten the stability of the country in the process? Miles answered his own question: "They are not contending for an abstract principle—they are not influenced by a mere spirit of fanatical opposition to slavery . . . they are deliberately, intentionally and advisedly aiming a deadly blow at the South. It is intended as a blow. It is intended to repress her energies—to check her development—to diminish and eventually destroy her political weight and influence in this confederacy." [11]

Miles then lectured his audience that they, not northerners, were the ones "contending for an abstract principle." Miles considered African slavery inextricably intertwined with every facet of southern society, culture, and economy. It was "a part of ourselves." He claimed that to exclude slavery from the territories was to exclude white southerners. "We must be fumigated and purified from every Southern taint—must pass through a sort of moral quarantine, before we can be allowed to enter the precincts of the free-soil paradise!" Northerners could harbor their feelings about slavery, he said, but when they excluded southerners from the territories by declaring slavery immoral, they effectively denied that southerners were "equal members of this confederacy." If northerners could deny southerners equality in the territories because of slavery, Miles warned, they would set "the seal of inferiority" on southerners and mark them "as those who from perverse moral obliquity are not entitled to the enjoyment of full participation in the common goods and property of the Republic." To Miles this was an attack on southern liberty and an insult to southern honor. "Fellow-citizens," he cried, "are you willing to submit to such monstrous injustice—to so glaring a violation of the spirit of the Constitution?" [12]

Miles rejected compromise as a satisfactory solution to this conflict. He stated that in the past, "Every concession has but emboldened our adversaries to more unscrupulous aggression." Miles insisted that southerners emulate the Founding Fathers and resist. He reminded his audience that their ancestors would have found it easier to submit to unjust taxation than to launch a revolution and that the Founders' critics derided them as hotspurs and abstractionists. Nevertheless, Miles went on, the Founders had united behind abstract principles and triumphed over a powerful foe. Would

11. *Ibid.*, 22–23.
12. *Ibid.*, 17, 19–20, 29–30.

southerners do less, he asked, now that northerners vilified them
and sought to tamper with their slavery property?

> Carolinians! will you consent to this? Will you quietly and without a de-
> termined struggle allow this seal of infamy to be set upon you? Will you
> allow this stab to be made at the great principle of constitutional liberty,
> for which our fathers struggled so hard . . . and not throw your whole
> moral weight and force as a guard before it? Or is that principle no
> longer as dear to us as it was to the men of the revolution? Or in this
> utilitarian age is all principle to be sneered at as a "metaphysical abstrac-
> tion"—and the profoundest questions in politics and constitutional law
> to be settled solely on the basis of dollars and cents? If so, let us pause
> and reflect; for all our institutions, our liberties, nay, our very existence
> are endangered. If so let us pause and reflect for we are already degen-
> erating from the spirit of '76![13]

Like many Carolinians, Miles sided with John C. Calhoun during the conflict over the impending Compromise of 1850. After
Calhoun died in March of that year, however, Miles could only
guess what action the late senator would have counseled. In 1849
Miles had believed southerners must "act and feel as one man,"
avoid internal divisions, and use their "political weight and power
in the confederacy" to resolve the sectional conflict. He had
thought that Calhoun's calls for southern unity made sense and believed that Calhoun would have supported disunion over submission to the compromise. Miles also worried that rashness might
place Carolinians on "untenable ground from which we may be
forced to retreat." He therefore supported the cooperationists,
those who favored secession only in concert with other states, because he believed their position more nearly approximated Calhoun's ideal than did that of the immediate secessionists, led by
Barnwell Rhett.[14]

While secessionists and cooperationists formed parties and debated throughout the state in 1850 and 1851, Miles remained aloof.
As a college teacher he had no role to play in the drama other than
that of an interested and concerned citizen. Considering the convictions he expressed in 1849 and his later political career, Miles
was conspicuous for his lack of involvement in the myriad Southern Rights associations' and rallies that pervaded South Carolina.

13. *Ibid.,* 21–22, 26, 29–30.
14. *Ibid.,* 25–27; William H. Trescot to Miles, May 30, 1858, in Miles Papers,
SHC; W. P. Miles to C. G. Memminger, February 3, 1860, in Christopher G. Memminger Papers, SHC.

Perhaps he grew disgusted at the bitter infighting and factionalism that rocked his state, creating divisions he had hoped would be avoided. Perhaps the twenty-nine-year-old professor found the realities of southern unity more perplexing than they had seemed in theory. At any rate, when cooperationists defeated secessionists late in 1851, they did so without the help of Porcher Miles. And when cooperationism failed to alter the Compromise of 1850 or lead to secession, a disillusioned and despondent Professor Miles again began to contemplate the intricate and frustrating problems of self-government.

An invitation to deliver an address to the Alumni Society of the College of Charleston in 1852 gave Miles an opportunity to discuss two "Political and Social Errors which seem to be gaining ground in the World," contemporary notions about the nature of republican government, and the belief that liberty was a birthright of all humanity. According to Miles, a republican government could exist only among people who possessed "the highest Moral and Intellectual Development," self-control, virtue, and patriotism. *"Naked and Absolute Freedom"* could not be permitted because one person's freedom must not interfere with the freedom of others. *"All cannot have every thing,"* he said; in a republic, people had to learn to live with restraints on their freedom. Miles explained that the Founding Fathers had institutionalized restraint within the Constitution and had regarded it as "the essential frame-work of our Government" that even a numerical majority could never possess absolute power over others. The function of government in a republic was to prevent anyone or any group from achieving absolute freedom, to enforce "Rational Freedom—Freedom within the bounds of Law." In the 1850s, Miles asserted, Americans had lost sight of these principles. The idea of restraint had decayed so thoroughly that "Freedom of Thought, Freedom of Action, and Freedom of the Press run riot" and produced doctrines and theories that threatened to undermine "all that is venerable and time-honored in Politics—all that is conservative in Society—all that is pure in Morals." [15]

Miles stated that chief among these false doctrines was the idea that liberty was a birthright at all. He maintained that liberty was an *"Acquired Privilege,"* not an inalienable right. Asserting that indi-

15. William Porcher Miles, *An Address Delivered Before the Alumni Society of the College of Charleston, on Commencement Day, March 30th, 1852* (Charleston, 1852), 9–15, 22–23, 25.

viduals and societies must prove themselves worthy of liberty, he maintained that not every person or society could do so. Those who believed otherwise subscribed to the "monstrous and dangerous fallacy of Thomas Jefferson," which proclaimed that all men were created equal. *"Men are born neither Free nor Equal,"* Miles insisted. Like all fire-eaters, Miles categorically rejected any faith in natural equality, thereby fitting African slavery comfortably within American republicanism. Some men, he believed, were born with the capacity to earn liberty, others were not. Miles stipulated that governments must allow people the freedom to develop their natural abilities but could not "make a Statesmen of him who God intended should be a Ploughman" or "bind down forever to the plough him to whom God has given a mind capable of shaping the destinies of a People."[16]

Except for a passing reference to free-soilers and abolitionists, Miles omitted all references to northerners, and nowhere in his speech did he mention African slavery or the Compromise of 1850. And yet the issues and events of the past few years had brought a profound change in his personal temperament and political philosophy and lurked behind the ideas he presented to his audience. Obviously, for Miles to defend African slavery he had to reject the idea of fundamental human equality and argue that blacks lacked the capacity for self-government. But more important, the Compromise of 1850 had proved to Miles that some northerners were unfit for republican government. He thought their attempt to meddle with slavery a violation of "Rational Freedom" and "constitutional liberty," a failure to restrain the legislative power of a majority at the cost of the rights and liberty of a minority. In 1849 Miles had at least granted his foes the freedom to think, but since northerners had put some of their thoughts into practice, Miles believed that he could not tolerate even that. With this speech, Miles excommunicated abolitionists and free-soilers from participation in national politics. Henceforth, he would meet all threats of interference with slavery with a call for immediate secession. This speech, then, marked Miles's transformation into a fire-eater.

James De Bow gave Miles's speeches unqualified praise in his *Review* and urged his friend to take a more active role in public af-

---

16. *Ibid.,* 21–25. Years later, as a congressman, Miles denied that freedom of speech countenanced nothern attacks on slavery. See *Congressional Globe,* 36th Cong., 1st Sess., App. 205.

fairs. But Miles was content to remain quietly on the faculty of the College of Charleston, writing only infrequent expositions on local issues.[17] His complacency ended suddenly, however, during an otherwise dull summer vacation in 1855. While Miles idled away his time in the mountains of Virginia, on the coast a horrible yellow fever epidemic ravaged the city of Norfolk. Six thousand people fled, and most of the remaining ten thousand contracted the disease. Of these, about two thousand eventually died. Nearly half the local doctors died in their futile effort to stop an affliction about which they had no scientific knowledge. The call for help went out, particularly to the lower South, where long contact with the disease had given some a certain immunity. Miles decided that after all the idealistic talk of southern unity earlier in the decade, "if our great Southern talk about 'Southern men standing by each other in time of trial' meant anything, it meant that we ought to go to the side of Old Virginia when in such distress."[18]

For several weeks Miles worked as a nurse in beleaguered Norfolk, offering comfort to the sick and dying until the epidemic ended. The people of Charleston greeted the news of their local hero with a groundswell of support, coincidentally at the very time that local Democrats began to search for a candidate for mayor. Miles's friends informed him that the Southern Rights party wanted him to run and that his fame made him the most available candidate. Trescot told him, "If ever there was a case in which the office sought the man and not the man the office, here it is." Furthermore, Trescot suggested that Miles continue his labors in Norfolk while his friends carried on his campaign. Miles had some reservations about serving as mayor, but Trescot helped convince him to run. He returned to Charleston to make just one public speech but won by a vote of 1,260 to 837.[19]

By the time Miles entered office in November, 1855, he had de-

17. DBR, VII (November, 1849), 466; XI (April, 1851), 697; E. J. Pringle to Miles, January 23, 1853, in Miles Papers, SHC.

18. Virginius Dabney, Virginia: The New Dominion (Garden City, N.Y., 1972), 260; Cyclopedia of Eminent and Representative Men of the Carolinas of the Nineteenth Century (2 vols., 1892; rpr. Spartanburg, S.C., 1972–73), I, 659; Miles to L. L. Brickhouse, October 7, 1855, in Miles Papers, SHC.

19. Trescot to Miles, September 6, 16, 1855, I. W. Hayne to Miles, September 7, 1855, in Miles Papers, SHC; Clarence McKitrick Smith, Jr., "William Porcher Miles, Progressive Mayor of Charleston, 1855–1857," in The Proceedings of the South Carolina Historical Association (N.p., 1942), 30; Daniel, "Miles," 18.

veloped an interest in reform. In the local elections two years before, Miles had witnessed widespread corruption among office-holders and passive acquiescence among the citizenry. This lack of virtue in city politics challenged Miles's ideals of self-government and honor. In a letter to the editor of the Charleston *Mercury*, he accused local officials of recording the votes of the deceased and of driving a "wretched drove . . . from poll to poll like oxen." When these men defended themselves by claiming that they engaged in nefarious activities solely to do good once in power, Miles became irate. Instead of rationalizing, Miles proposed that it would "be more straight-forward and manly—far less degrading" to dispense with elections and sell public offices to the highest bidders. The current situation, he lamented, disgraced the entire city and required the efforts of everyone to change the image of the community.[20]

When a friend learned of Miles's election, he suggested sarcastically to the honorable, idealistic new mayor that he "spend all the money you can lay your hands on. . . . Charter steamboats and send ship loads of the populace away to liberalise their minds." Author William Gilmore Simms, a frequent visitor to Charleston, offered similar though less jocular advice. "Go on fearlessly; only do not be too virtuous," he said. "A people for so long a time corrupt and in corrupt hands, can't stand extreme virtue." Despite this friendly warning, the inexperienced Miles immediately began a sweeping program of reform based on his own abstract principles of good government.[21]

The first item on Miles's agenda was police reform. When he entered office, only an inefficient night watch existed in Charleston. Miles corresponded with other mayors to learn about their police systems and sent his chief of police on a fact-finding mission to Savannah and New Orleans, which Miles considered similar to Charleston. After careful analysis, Miles presented his plan of reorganization to the city council. His bill, which passed with a reduction in funding, made the police chief, rather than the highly partisan city council, responsible for appointing sergeants and privates. The

20. Charleston *Mercury*, October 18, 19, 20, 21, 1854. Also see E. J. Pringle to Miles, January 23, 1853, Miles to the Editors of the Mercury, October 21, 1854, in Miles Papers, SHC.

21. F. A. Porcher to Miles, November 9, 1855, E. J. Pringle to Miles, November 3, 1855, in Miles Papers, SHC; W. G. Simms to Miles, January 5, 1856, in Mary C. Simms Oliphant, Alfred Taylor Odell, and T. C. Duncan Eaves, eds., *The Letters of William Gilmore Simms* (5 vols.; Columbia, S.C., 1955), III, 417.

mayor would now appoint the chief, captains, and lieutenants, subject to approval from the council. Miles doubled the number of mounted police, laid out a more rational plan for patrols, and expanded police activities to around the clock. His plan brought swift results. Increased police surveillance helped in the early detection and eradication of fires and thereby allowed him to cut the budget of the fire department. His police force cracked down on "habitual violators" who had had "pretty much their own way" under previous administrations, especially tavern keepers who sold liquor illegally to slaves. Those who had once prospered under the corrupt system gave testimony to Miles's effectiveness by dubbing the vigilant new policemen "Paddy Miles's Bull Dogs."[22]

Miles had as much concern for social progress as he did for law enforcement. Under his guidance, in 1856 the city council created a house of corrections for juveniles that stressed reformative training rather than punishment. His administration allocated $40,000 for an almshouse, an orphanage, an asylum, and the juvenile facility, a large appropriation at the time for a city of Charleston's size. Miles obtained $7,000 annually from the state to help care for the transient poor and worked to increase municipal support for free black paupers. After his recent experiences in Norfolk, Miles paid close attention to public health. Working from the conventional wisdom that "a wet soil is provocative of disease, and a dry one conducive to health," he inaugurated a badly needed system of drainage and sewerage and tried to replace "the present scavenger system" of street cleaning with either a municipal sanitation service or a private, contracted one.[23]

When Miles entered office he inherited an enormous municipal debt, which was aggravated by his expansion of services. And yet, Miles believed, "'Pay as you go' is the true rule, whether for cities, or for men." Although he encouraged a variety of means to increase revenue, he decided that the only way to set the city on a sound financial footing was to increase property taxes. Miles persuaded the city council both to raise taxes and to adopt a plan that would extinguish the city's debt in thirty-five years.[24]

22. William Porcher Miles, *Mayor's Report on City Affairs* (Charleston, 1857), 15–17, 20, 22; Miles to L. R. Gibbes, May 15, 1856, in Lewis R. Gibbes Papers, LC; Smith, "Miles," 33.

23. Daniel, "Miles," 30–31, 43; Miles, *Mayor's Report,* 27, 29; Miles to Gibbes, January 20, 29, 1856, in Gibbes Papers, LC.

24. Miles, *Mayor's Report,* 10–15.

Although Miles did not eradicate every problem in his two-year term, his accomplishments were impressive. Not only did he greatly expand worthwhile services, but also, as the city council acknowledged, "both by precept and example," he brought an end to the corrupt practices of previous administrations. His success as mayor and the constant prodding of his friends, most notably Trescot, encouraged Miles to become more involved in politics and to look beyond the city limits of Charleston. When Congressman William Aiken chose not to seek reelection in 1856, Miles decided to run for his seat.[25]

Sectional issues dominated the campaign, fueled by the recent emergence of the Republican party and the heated debates over expansion of slavery into Kansas. Although other fire-eaters resorted to their standard harangues and long, bellicose orations, Miles did not. He refused to rehash southern allegations of northern wrongs or the southern view of the state of the Union; everyone knew these positions already, Miles believed, and he was tired of hearing them. He declared that the time to deliberate had passed, and the time to act had arrived. If John C. Frémont, the Republican candidate, won the presidency or if Congress prevented Kansas from adopting slavery, southerners should react, perhaps by refusing to send their representatives to Congress, or, preferably by calling for a convention of all southern states to determine some other form of protest. Whatever the immediate response, Miles argued that southerners would find lasting safety and liberty only in a southern confederacy.[26]

Miles was elected that October with a majority in a three-way race, receiving 1,852 votes to 1,521 and 323 for his respective opponents. When he took his seat in Washington in 1857, however, he was baffled by the situation that faced him. Although Frémont had lost the presidential election, the Republican party continued to grow and send more members to Congress. The debate over Kansas dragged on, causing fissures within the Democratic ranks. The

25. Smith, "Miles," 39. See W. P. Miles to J. Johnson Pettigrew, September 26, 1856, in Pettigrew Family Papers, NCDAH, and Miles to Alfred Huger, November 10, 1857, in Robert N. Gourdin Papers, RWL; James De Bow to Gibbes, December 27, 1857, in Gibbes Papers, LC; Trescot to Miles, March 30, 1856, Robert N. Gourdin to Miles, September 8, 1856, S. G. Bailey to Miles, October 13, 1856, in Miles Papers, SHC.

26. Charleston *Mercury*, October 11, 13, 1856; S. G. Bailey to Miles, October 13, 1856, Hiram Powers to Miles, October 23, 1856, in Miles Papers, SHC.

conflicting and contradictory advice of friends and associates rendered Miles's situation even more confusing. His young colleague Laurence Keitt and his friend De Bow both warned Miles not to trust President James Buchanan, his aides, or any northern Democrats. Miles discovered, however, that the Buchanan administration knew it could count on the cooperation of southerners because of their mutual desire to check Republican power. William Gilmore Simms, with whom Miles had developed a close friendship while serving as mayor of Charleston, gave Miles impossible, amateurish advice. Simms warned him that Mississippi Congressman John A. Quitman was "an old granny, with an enormous deal of vanity," yet suggested that he would prove "efficient in conducting a charge, carrying an outpost, or making a feint or sortie." Simms insisted that Miles cultivate the friendship of James H. Hammond. "He will need the help of *honest* & *fearless* Lieutenants," Simms wrote. Above all, he demanded, "Let all your game lie in the constant recognition & assertion of a *Southern Nationality!*" But Senator Hammond had decided to pursue a southern confederacy only as a last resort and preferred to work within the Union and the Democratic party to preserve southern rights.[27]

The junior congressman groped for direction during his first year in the capital and played a passive role within the vocal South Carolina delegation. When Miles made his first major speech in 1858, he was unable to cull helpful advice from his friends and adopted the same rhetoric that he had used before entering politics. He quickly discovered that it was one thing to propound his abstract theories of republican government and southern rights and honor in Charleston and quite another to do so in Washington.

Addressing the Kansas controversy, Miles conceded that the geography of the territory effectively prohibited slavery. "But, sir, the issue has been made," he said, "the battle joined; and though it be on an abstract principle which does not at present promise to result in any practical advantage to us, I am willing to stand by the guns and fight it out." By preventing the expansion of slavery into Kan-

27. Charleston *Mercury*, October 16, 1856; Laurence M. Keitt to Miles, June 15, 1857, J. D. B. De Bow to Miles, September 4, 1857, Alfred Huger to [Miles], January 9, 1858, Hammond to Miles, November 23, 1858, in Miles Papers, SHC; Miles to Gibbes, April 9, 1860, in Gibbes Papers, LC; Simms to Miles, December 28, [1858], January 28, [1858], February 8, [1858], in Oliphant, Odell, and Eaves, eds., *Letters of Simms*, III, 517–18; IV, 20, 34. For the friendship of the two, see *ibid.*, I, cxxvi–cxxvii.

sas, Miles warned, northerners risked provoking a revolution. "The South may not dissolve the Union on the rejection of Kansas," he explained, "but such rejection would, assuredly, sever still another of the cords—rapidly becoming fewer—which the course of events has been snapping one by one." Protective tariffs, he claimed, had already enriched the North at the expense of the South. Attempts to curtail the growth of slavery had stigmatized the South's social institutions, "which constitute the essential foundations of her prosperity, the very life-blood of her existence." Should a revolution come, it would not result only from "abstract questions" of southern honor and equality. Free states, "already in a preponderance, are rapidly expanding and acquiring supreme and uncontrollable power," he stated; this growing power of abolitionists and free-soilers threatened to transform the federal government into an engine of destruction. Revolutions were terrible, Miles cried, but "tyranny and injustice are worse." He feared that northerners would soon have enough political power to deprive southerners of their liberty, to make them "hewers of wood and drawers of water." According to Miles, "The slow, undermining process by which the high spirit of a free people is sapped, their strength destroyed, their faith in themselves crushed out, their enterprise checked, their prosperity paralyzed, is more appalling to the true statesman and the patriot than the temporary, though critical, fever of revolution." [28]

Faced with this menace, Miles considered it natural for the South "to look about her; to count up her resources; to estimate her strength; to measure her capacity for care of herself." And Miles agreed with his friend De Bow and other fire-eaters that the South possessed "every element of greatness, prosperity, and strength" and that slavery imbued it with a uniquely harmonious social and economic structure and helped produce commodities that allowed the South to dominate the commerce of the world. Therefore, even if Congress rejected a slave Kansas, the South would emerge triumphant. Such an event would force southerners to face "the startling fact that they have no hope in the future of maintaining their equality in the Union. It will compel them to ponder the question whether they will choose subjugation or resistance, colonial vassalage or separate independence." [29]

28. *Congressional Globe*, 35th Cong., 1st Sess., App., 288–89.
29. *Ibid.*, 285–89.

Before Miles spoke out on Kansas, Simms had warned him to consider carefully what he could do and say that others had not said or done already. Trescot thought Miles's speech an excellent one, "clear in argument, sound in doctrine and eminently proper in tone," but he agreed with Simms. "The subject was hopeless," he told Miles. If Miles really wanted to effect a change, Trescot pleaded, "tell us what to do." Like Miles, Trescot believed that "in the plentitude and insolence of their power" the Republicans might stir southern resistance but suggested that no member of Congress could hasten secession. "Your position is a false one and whatever may be your wishes, the means by which you work, prevent your accomplishing any thing," he explained. "You can't revolutionize a nation by the rules of the House"; that would constitute "National suicide," Trescot said, "and Congress cant [sic] get its own consent to that."[30]

Although the Kansas controversy reinforced Miles's conviction that the South must secede, he realized that Trescot's evaluation of the issue, if not his own role in it, was correct. Months after Miles announced his readiness to "fight it out" in Congress, he saw that battling for the abstract right of expanding slavery to a region that admittedly was not conducive to slave labor "was a bad way . . . of preparing the Southern mind for a war to the knife." He continued to believe that the preservation of southern honor required a settlement favorable to the South, but he could not discover a feasible resolution. By the end of 1858, the idealistic young congressman was left muttering "eternal and infernal Kansas-Kansas-Kansas!"[31]

Miles's speech on Kansas at least reinforced his popularity among his constituents. When they reelected him in 1858, Miles still believed he could balance his duties as a member of Congress with promoting secession. In January, 1859, he added his voice to those of James De Bow and William L. Yancey in calling for a repeal of federal laws that prohibited the African slave trade. Like these other fire-eaters, Miles claimed that the issue should fall under state jurisdiction and insisted that stigmatizing any aspect of slavery branded the entire institution as evil and all slaveowners as dishonorable.[32]

30. Simms to Miles, [February ?, 1858], in Oliphant, Odell, and Eaves, eds., *Letters of Simms*, IV, 33; Trescot to Miles, May 2, 1858, in Miles Papers, SHC.

31. Miles to Hammond, November 10, 15, in James H. Hammond Papers, LC.

32. Evan Edwards to Miles, April 16, 1858, Trescot to Miles, February 8, 1859, in Miles Papers, SHC; Charleston *Mercury*, February 1, 1859.

The Charleston *Mercury* praised Miles's stance, and his comments marked the beginning of a close alliance with the Rhetts.[33] Trescot, however, was dismayed. Miles's perceptive friend complained that reviving the African slave trade was impossible within the Union, and if southerners were really agitating over this issue to foster secession, "Why not in God[']s name let us say so and be done with it." He reminded Miles that the administration of President James Monroe, a southerner, with the cooperation of John C. Calhoun and the entire South Carolina congressional delegation, had worked with the British forty years before to stop the international trafficking of slaves. "Who cast the stigma?" Trescot asked.

Again Trescot scolded Miles and other southern congressmen for trying to "serve two masters." Trescot argued that Miles and the others "must assume the Union as the great underlying fact of his whole political life" and serve it in good faith or scorn the Union and "make a revolution at home." Trescot did not fault Miles for his intentions; they were "honest, manly, direct." He offered his criticisms only to show his highly principled friend that "our world is so completely out of joint, that the truer you are, the harder you will find it to run smoothly—an illustration which I borrow from my cotton gin and Shakespeare."[34]

During the next year Miles's world became even more chaotic. John Brown's raid occurred in October. In December, three days after his execution, the Thirty-sixth Congress convened in Washington. Thoughts of Brown haunted southern congressmen and made them more sensitive than ever to the antislavery sentiments of their northern colleagues. Nominations for Speaker inflamed tempers and brought action in the House of Representatives to a standstill when Republicans backed a man particularly odious to southerners. This chaos made it easier for Miles to understand Trescot's warnings about splitting responsibilities as a United States congressman and a secessionist and finally made the choice between the two simple.

The man behind the speakership controversy was John Sherman, a Republican from Ohio, and the issue that compounded southerners' aggravation was Sherman's endorsement of a book by Hinton R. Helper entitled *The Impending Crisis of the South*. Helper, a nonslaveowning North Carolinian who had moved to the North,

33. See Charleston *Mercury*, February 1, 1859, and *Congressional Globe*, 36th Cong., 1st Sess., 365.
34. Trescot to Miles, February 8, 1859, in Miles Papers, SHC.

condemned slavery as an inefficient and wasteful institution and appealed to lower-class whites in the South to oppose slave labor. Southerners denounced Helper as a traitor and a renegade. The Republican party prepared to distribute one hundred thousand copies of his book in the North and added captions such as "Revolution—Peacefully if we can, Violently if we must." John Sherman and a few score congressmen publicly supported this plan.[35]

Coupled with John Brown's recent invasion of Virginia, Sherman's candidacy for Speaker mortified southerners. Balloting for the speakership dragged on endlessly. Most southerners refused to vote for any candidate who had endorsed Helper's book, and the equally tenacious Republican minority refused to yield. Deadlock led to tension and threatened to erupt in hostility on the floor of Congress even more violent than the Brooks-Sumner incident or the Keitt-Grow melee. During one particularly bitter debate a gun fell from the pocket of a congressman from New York. Senator Hammond claimed that throughout the winter the only congressmen not armed with a revolver and a knife were those who had two revolvers. Another senator reported that friends of congressmen likewise brought concealed weapons into the public galleries.[36]

Miles, too, armed himself. And yet even in the midst of the tense environment of Washington, Miles remained more calm than some Carolinians at home. Governor William Gist assured Miles that the people of the state would support the withdrawal of the entire South Carolina congressional delegation in the event Sherman were elected. Gist preferred that plan to "ejecting the speaker elect by force," but if southern congressmen chose the latter, he told Miles, "write or telegraph me, & I will have a Regiment near Washington in the shortest possible time."[37]

After dozens of ballots and protracted debates, Miles rose to speak. No one, he declared, was fit to serve as Speaker who endorsed "a book containing doctrines so vile and atrocious that no honest man can find language strong enough in which to denounce them." He cautioned his northern colleagues that because "a pro-

35. David M. Potter, *The Impending Crisis, 1848–1861*, completed and edited by Don E. Fehrenbacher (New York, 1976), 386–87.

36. Potter, *Impending Crisis*, 389; A. Huger to Miles, December 12, 1859, in Miles Papers, SHC.

37. D. H. Hamilton to Miles, December 9, 1859, William Gist to Miles, December 20, 1859, in Miles Papers, SHC.

found state of excitement" caused by John Brown still rocked the South, southerners were likely to do almost anything if Sherman won the speakership. Believing states to be sovereign and "the sole judges of what is best for their own interests, and for their own peace and security," Miles warned that whenever southerners chose to they would "take their destinies into their own hands." Miles had no quarrel with those who denied that secession was a constitutional right. "Call it then revolution," he trumpeted. "Practically it will be that." America's founders had exercised their inalienable right to alter or abolish government in 1776, and, Miles said, southerners could do the same now.[38]

Although Miles, unlike most fire-eaters, believed that a civil war would be "so bloody, so terrible, that the parallel of it has never yet blotted the page of history," he explained that southerners faced greater dangers by remaining in the Union. He maintained that antislavery forces in the North not only sought to deny southerners the right "to drink from the same constitutional stream of equal rights and equal political privileges," but also used insidious propaganda to create social unrest in the South, "to set brother against brother, class against class." Northerners who condemned slavery as evil had already invaded the South in an attempt "to apply the 'knife' and 'actual cautery' fire and sword, to what they consider 'a sore' on our body politic!" Miles exclaimed. "Can the southern people endure this without degradation and ruin?" He answered himself: "Impossible." Unless antislavery agitation stopped immediately, Miles thundered, the South would "assume her independent position among the powers of the earth."[39]

Miles's speech helped fortify southern opposition to Sherman but did nothing to break the deadlock in Congress. In South Carolina, however, Governor Gist tried to force a breakthrough. In December he appointed Christopher G. Memminger, a state representative, as a special commissioner to Virginia in an attempt to convince that state to secede and lead the South toward a southern confederacy.[40] A few days after Miles delivered his speech in Congress, when Memminger was en route to Richmond, Miles decided to take Trescot's advice and promote "a revolution at home."

38. William Porcher Miles, *Speech of Hon. W. Porcher Miles, of South Carolina, on the Organization of the House* ([Washington, D.C.], [1860]), 1, 2, 5–6.

39. *Ibid.*, 7–8.

40. Steven A. Channing, *Crisis of Fear: Secession in South Carolina* (New York, 1970), 112–27.

Miles deluged Mimminger with suggestions and encouragement and told him to bank on the fear lingering in Virginia after Brown's raid.

> If Virginia could only *now* be induced to withdraw from the Union unless every demand of the South were satisfied and some *absolute* security be given for the future, the South would have a glorious start given her on the path of *independence,* which we all so ardently desire and which *must come* sooner or later. . . . If you can only urge our Carolina views in such a manner as to imbue Virginia with it—(and at present she is in the best condition to be impregnated)—we may soon hope to see the fruit of your addresses in the sturdy and healthy offspring of whose birth we would be so justly proud—a Southern Confederacy. This would indeed be a worthy heir of the joint glories of the two commonwealths to spring from the loins of the Palmetto State!

No matter what action Virginia took, Miles believed "this Union *cannot hold together very long.*" Defeating the Republican presidential candidate in November might "stave off the issue for a little while—but come it must." Miles told Memminger that he could not press Virginians too vigorously and must promote "a Southern Confederacy as the only true and thorough means" of defending and protecting the South.[41]

On the last day of January, Memminger wrote Miles, "I am very sorry to be brought to the conclusion that Virginia is not prepared to do any thing." Before Miles received this news, Sherman withdrew his name, and William Pennington, a former Whig from New Jersey, was elected Speaker. No revolution had occurred, and the spirit of resistance in Virginia had seemingly evaporated. Yet this sudden apathy only made Miles more resolute. Independently he came to the same conclusion that Barnwell Rhett had, that if Virginia would not secede, "We *further South,* must act and 'drag her along.'" Therefore, when Robert Barnwell Rhett, Jr., suggested to Miles that splintering the Democratic party at the next national convention would help the states of the deep South control the fate of "inferior contemporaries," he won Miles's wholehearted agreement.[42]

41. Miles to C. G. Memminger, January 10, 15, 1860, in Christopher G. Memminger Papers, SHC.

42. Memminger to Miles, January 30, 1860, Trescot to Miles, February 22, 1860, R. B. Rhett, Jr., to Miles, January 29, 1860, in Miles Papers, SHC; Potter, *Impending Crisis,* 388–89; Miles to Memminger, January 18, 23, February 3, 1860, in Memminger Papers, SHC.

As the year progressed, Miles emerged as one of the leading secessionists in South Carolina. His total commitment to disunion and his sudden prominence surprised his friends, especially Trescot. While state and national party conventions met, split, and reconvened during the spring of 1860, Miles acted as a conduit of information between Washington and Charleston. In particular, he helped apprise the Rhetts of the popular mood in the North and of the potential for meaningful resistance from other southern states.[43] He returned home in May and delivered a brief speech to rally the spirit of resistance in Charleston. Both tangible and abstract rights, he explained, were in jeopardy. Again he asked Carolinians why northerners would not yield if the right to expand slavery were merely an abstraction and lectured them that an "abstract right" was a right nonetheless. Miles proclaimed that the next presidential election pitted "power against principle—the majority against the minority, regardless of all constitutional barriers." As a South Carolinian, Miles trumpeted, he owed his allegiance to no other "nation," and he called upon his countrymen to join him in resisting the election of a Republican president rather than submit to "ruin and vassalage" in the Union.[44]

As the heat of summer increased, so did the vehemence of Miles's labors and language. He joined Barnwell Rhett in Charleston at a public meeting to support the nomination of John C. Breckinridge by southern Democrats. After Rhett castigated northerners for attacking southern rights, Miles discussed strategies for the future. Southerners, he said, had erred in the past by consenting to sectional compromises, and repeating hollow proclamations of defiance made them seem like the boy who cried wolf. Believing that the South had "all the elements of wealth, prosperity and strength, to make her a first-class power among the nations of the world," Miles wondered how southerners could choose to remain in a Union that, in his view, threatened their liberty. Why the South would balk at secession, "where she would lose so little and gain so much," he said with some exaggeration, "has always been to me a matter of simple amazement." Miles insisted that the time to act had come. *"Let us 'resolve' less and do more,"* he cried. "I am sick at

43. Trescot to Miles, February 22, 1860, A. Huger to Miles, May 7, 1860, R. B. Rhett, Jr., to Miles, March 28, April 17, May 10 (telegram and letter), 12, 1860; D. H. Hamilton to Miles, April 4, 1860, in Miles Papers, SHC. See all correspondence for April, 1860, *ibid.*

44. Charleston *Mercury*, May 21, 1860.

heart of the endless talk and bluster of the South. If we are in earnest, let us *act*." Instead of trying to preserve peace and union with the North, Miles advised, southerners "ought rather to be preparing to grasp the sword."[45]

Suddenly, a serious illness struck Miles during the final, critical months before the election. Typhoid fever forced him to end all activities and, ironically, to leave the sweltering South for the summer coolness of New England. Miles moved to Newport, Rhode Island, in August, where he stayed for several weeks. His condition remained so serious that for a while both Simms and Trescot feared for his life. Miles dragged himself back home in time for the election in November, but the Rhetts noted that he was "still feeble" upon his arrival in Charleston. Although Miles's illness lingered through December, the virtually unanimous secession sentiment that swept South Carolina after Lincoln's election rallied his spirits and, perhaps, hastened his recuperation.[46]

Miles recovered sufficiently to take his seat at the state convention at Columbia on December 17. His incapacity over the past three months had made him restless. Because of an outbreak of smallpox in Columbia, a majority at the convention—including the normally impatient Keitt—decided to postpone voting for secession until they could reconvene a few days later in Charleston. Miles could not tolerate any more delays. Weary of endless resolutions and threats, he continued to demand, as he had the summer before: "Let us act if we mean to act without talking. Let it be 'a word and a blow'—but the blow first." His sense of urgency failed to accelerate secession, but his resolve earned him the renewed support of his constituents, who selected him as their representative both for the provisional and regular Confederate congresses.[47]

After South Carolina seceded, the military situation in Charleston Harbor was of primary importance to Miles. Earlier in December, through negotiations with President Buchanan, he and other officials had tried to win the transfer of federal forts in the

45. *Ibid.*, July 10, 14, 1860.
46. *Ibid.*, August 27, 28, September 13, November 3, 1860; Trescot to Miles, October 2, 1860, in Miles Papers, SHC; Simms to Miles, August 31, November 4, 12, December 5, 31, 1860, in Oliphant, Odell, and Eaves, eds., *Letters of Simms*, IV, 238, 256, 262, 281, 315. See W. P. Miles to W. Garnett, November 13, 1860, in William Garnett Chisolm Papers, VHS.
47. Miles to Hammond, August 5, 1860, Hammond Papers, LC; *Cyclopedia*, 660; Miles to R. N. Gourdin, December 10, 1860, in Gourdin Papers, RWL; Daniel, "Miles," 89.

harbor to state authorities. In return they promised to restrain the people from attacking the forts unless Buchanan tried to reinforce them.[48] In the excitement that swept Charleston after secession, however, restraining the public demand for the forts became more and more difficult. Miles argued against a seizure "with all my might," fearing that a hasty attack "would cost much time and many lives." Even after the federal supply ship *Star of the West* tried to reinforce Fort Sumter in January, Miles hoped for a peaceful separation. If, however, "special spite and malice" induced the federal government to attempt another foray into Charleston Harbor, Miles was ready "to give Uncle Sam a warm reception."[49]

Like Louis Wigfall, Miles maintained an active role in both military and civil affairs in the spring of 1861. Soon after his selection as chair of the Military Affairs Committee in the Confederate House of Representatives, Miles joined Wigfall as an aide-de-camp to General P. G. T. Beauregard at Charleston and at the first battle of Bull Run. Unlike Wigfall, however, Miles recognized his limitations. He knew that his lack of military training made him of little use on the battlefield. Although tempted to fight late in 1861 when federal gunboats attacked the Carolina coast, Miles made himself focus on his duties in Congress.[50]

Like other fire-eaters, Miles found only frustration in the Confederate Congress. Before secession he had wanted to eliminate all trade duties in a southern confederacy. Now, De Bow warned him that a sudden shift to free trade would alienate and antagonize the powerful sugar planters of the Gulf South, who had prospered under the tariff policies of the Union. Miles complained that his colleagues on congressional committees made work impossible be-

48. John McQueen, William Porcher Miles, M. L. Bonham, W. W. Boyce, and Lawrence [*sic*] M. Keitt to James Buchanan, December 9, 1860, James Buchanan to Robert W. Barnwell, James H. Adams, and James L. Orr, December 30, 1860, in *Correspondence Between Commissioners of the State of South Carolina to the Government at Washington and the President of the United States* (Charleston, 1861), 5–11.

49. Miles to M. L. Bonham, December 23, 1860, in James L. Orr Papers, SHC; W. P. Miles to Howell Cobb, January 14, 1861, in U. B. Phillips, ed., *The Correspondence of Robert Toombs, Alexander H. Stephens, and Howell Cobb* (Washington, D.C., 1913), 528–29.

50. Miles to W. W. Corcoran, August 7, 1874, G. T. Beauregard to the Board of Trustees of the Hopkins University, August 23, 1874, in *Letters and Testimonials Recommending Mr. Wm. Porcher Miles, of Virginia, for the Presidency of the Hopkins University, Baltimore, MD.* (Charleston, 1874), 5–8, 26–27; W. P. Miles to W. Ballard Preston, November 11, 1861, in Preston Family Papers, VHS; *Cyclopedia of Eminent and Representative Men of the Carolinas*, I, 660–61.

cause their habitual absences prevented a quorum, and as events began to sour in the new nation he held no higher opinion of President Davis than other fire-eaters. Late in the war, when some military officials began to discuss the efficacy of using black troops in the Confederate army, Miles was perplexed. Like Edmund Ruffin he understood the urgent demands of the army, but eventually he agreed with the Rhetts that "it is not merely a military, but a great social and political question, and the more I consider it the less is my judgment satisfied that it could really help our cause to put arms into the hands of our slaves."[51]

Despite all obstacles, Miles counted on the southern people to fight to the last. He never lost his faith in or devotion to "our great struggle for liberty, independence and even existence as a people." In January, 1865, he offered a resolution in Congress stating, "That we, the representatives of the people of the Confederate States, are firmly determined to continue the struggle in which we are involved until the United States shall acknowledge our independence."[52]

Neither resolutions nor the Confederate army could stop the steady advance of Union forces. And yet even the realities of defeat did not change Miles's abstract ideas. Watching how other southerners dealt with defeat greatly upset the highly principled Miles. "When we see the most ardent Secessionists and 'Fire eaters' now eagerly denying that they ever did more than 'yield their convictions to the voice of their State,'" and call secession a heresy and slavery a curse, Miles concluded, "it is plain that Politics must be more a trade and less a pursuit for an honourable man than it ever was before." For any secessionist to return to public office in a reconstructed Union, Miles believed, entailed a forfeiture of self-respect, consistency, and honor. For himself and other secessionists, he said, politics "for a time cannot be a path which any high-toned and sensitive—not to say honest and conscientious man—can possibly tread."[53]

51. Miles to Hammond, November 15, 1868, in Hammond Papers, LC; De Bow to Miles, February 15, 1861, in Miles Papers, SHC; Miles to W. Ballard Preston, November 11, 1861, in Preston Family Papers, VHS; Miles to Gourdin, December 16, 1863, February 28, 1864, in Gourdin Papers, RWL; Miles to G. T. Beauregard, October 9, 1882, in William Porcher Miles Papers, SCL; W. P. Miles to W. N. Pendleton, December 23, 1864, in William Nelson Pendleton Papers, SHC.

52. Miles to G. T. Beauregard, December 6, 1861, May 16, July 27, 1864, in Autograph Collection of Simon Gratz, HSP; Charleston *Mercury*, 23, 1865.

53. W. P. Miles to R. N. Gourdin, September 25, 1865, in Robert N. Gourdin Papers, WPL.

Like his old friend De Bow, Miles decided that the best way for him to continue serving the South was to engage in productive labor. Unlike De Bow, the forty-three-year-old Miles had no idea what to do. Having ruled out politics, his only option seemed to be returning to academia. But in 1863 he had married Bettie Beirne, the daughter of Oliver H. Beirne, a wealthy planter in Virginia, and the salary of a teacher was insufficient for his growing family. In 1865 he vowed, "I will for the first time in my life begin 'to try and make money.'" For a couple of years he worked for his father-in-law as a factor in New Orleans, and in 1867 he took over the management of one of Beirne's plantations, Oak Ridge, in Nelson County, Virginia.[54]

Miles's career as a tobacco and wheat planter was troublesome. Bad weather compounded his inexperience, and mounting financial problems forced him to reconsider life in academia. In 1874 the board of trustees began searching for a president for the new Hopkins University of Baltimore (later, the Johns Hopkins University). Miles eagerly applied. Along with his résumé he included more than forty letters of recommendation; the list of correspondents included some of the most prominent men of the old regime in the South. Among them were generals Beauregard, Wade Hampton, and Joseph E. Johnston, former senators James Chesnut, Robert W. Barnwell, and R. M. T. Hunter, former congressmen William Aiken and Milledge L. Bonham, and several educators, jurists, and clergymen. All spoke highly of Miles, but the preponderance of southern accents proved detrimental to his application.[55]

Rejected by Hopkins, Miles continued to live in isolation on his farm, passing his time helping friends like Beauregard and Barnwell Rhett gather material for their respective histories of the Confederacy and reminiscing about people and times buried in the past. While Miles pined away in Virginia, however, important changes occurred in South Carolina. In 1877 President Rutherford B. Hayes withdrew the federal forces that had occupied the state for twelve years to support the tenuous Republican administration. Democrats subsequently reasserted their control. In higher education, the process of redemption included removing black students from South Carolina College and sending them to a new segregated institution in Orangeburg. Charles H. Simonton, a

54. *Ibid.*; Daniel, "Miles," 111.
55. W. P. Miles to Woodhouse & Porham, March 30, 1877, in Robert Alonzo Brock Correspondence, HL; *Letters and Testimonials, passim;* Daniel, "Miles," 113.

trustee of South Carolina College, told Miles that he intended to reestablish the school as a "Southern Institution" that would preserve "our Southern notions of personal honor and truth." He explained that the war and Reconstruction had left an entire generation of Carolinians uneducated. "The honor and name of the State are to them but a dream of their fathers," he wrote. "A new class are coming into control of the State, and a sort of Red Republican agrarian spirit is abroad. The College must check and destroy this, must return the tone of public opinion." Simonton tentatively offered the position of president to Miles.[56]

The college was closed for three years, and when it reopened in 1880 Miles presided over a student body of only a few dozen. Most students enrolled for only two or three years and were more interested in agriculture and mechanics than in the political and moral philosophy Simonton and Miles hoped to teach them. Frustrated in his efforts to instill in these students his notions of "personal honor and truth," Miles decided to propagate his views on education and postwar politics in a series of public addresses. He took issue with the idea of "absolute freedom and equality" as he had thirty years before, but now, he explained, the specter of free black voters made this fallacy more menacing than ever. The former slaves had not earned freedom, citizenship, or the right to vote but had had these privileges conferred upon them. "Without the slightest previous training or the possession of any qualification for it," an undisciplined black electorate threatened to subject "the property and intelligence of the [white] community to . . . pauperism and ignorance." To prevent such a development, Miles argued, "the whole population should be truly educated, trained to the just discharge not only of the right of suffrage, but of all duties of citizenship." He supported free primary education for blacks and whites alike. Institutions that provided "the right kind of education" should expose students to "subjective ideas," the abstract concepts Miles believed made self-government possible. If people, whether black or white, did not learn these principles and learn to vote intelligently, Miles argued that they must be disfranchised.[57]

When Oliver Beirne suffered a stroke in the summer of 1882

56. See Beauregard to Miles, July 26, 1869, R. B. Rhett to Miles, March 22, 1871, William Boyce to Miles, March 23, September 22, 1875, in Miles Papers, SHC; Daniel Walker Hollis, *The University of South Carolina* (2 vols.; Columbia, S.C., 1956), II, 80–81.

57. Hollis, *University of South Carolina*, II, 94–97; Wm. Porcher Miles, *True Education: How to Make Education "the Cheap Defense of a Nation"* (Columbia, S.C., 1882),

and could no longer run his vast sugar interests in Louisiana, Miles felt obligated to leave South Carolina College and take over his father-in-law's business. In August he reluctantly resigned from the college and by autumn had moved into the grandest of Beirne's plantations, Houmas House, in Ascension Parish. From there Miles supervised the activities on twelve other plantations scattered over three parishes along the Mississippi River. None of the bad luck Miles experienced on his farm in Virginia followed him; by 1890, his lands produced around one hundred thousand tons of cane annually, which yielded more than 10 million pounds of sugar and earned him a gross income of $660,000. Two years later he and his son William P. Miles, Jr., organized the Miles Planting and Manufacturing Company of Louisiana. Their enterprise was the largest of its kind in the state.[58]

A progressive planter, Miles used the latest methods of cultivation, fertilization, and chemical analysis, and he helped found a sugar experiment station in New Orleans and a weekly periodical, the *Louisiana Planter and Sugar Manufacturer*. When he turned his attention to politics, however, Miles proved to be a reactionary. In 1893, when asked to accompany a group of sugar planters to Washington to lobby for retention of a tariff on sugar, Miles demonstrated that fire-eating was not dead. Calling himself "an old fashioned, strait out, 'strict construction' Democrat, bred in the South Carolina School of John C. Calhoun and State Rights," Miles pledged to oppose protective tariffs even though that opposition was contrary to his own financial interests. "I . . . don't believe the United States to be a 'Nation,'" he intoned, "but a 'Confe[de]racy of States' & is *constitutionally* restrained from doing things that a consolidated nation can do." Although he was a planting magnate, Miles continued to believe that honor must govern the actions of individuals, businesses, and nations. In the so-called Gilded Age, Miles protested that "Monopolists" and "Demagogues" had made a mockery of "just principles of government."[59]

7–9; Miles, *Universal Education: How to Purify the Ballot-Box* (Charleston, 1882), 4, 8–9; Miles, *Entire Education: How to Educate Body, Mind and Soul* (Charleston, 1882), 7–9.

58. Daniel, "Miles," 117–21; Miles to Beauregard, October 9, 1882, in Miles Papers, SCL; W. P. Miles, *Some Views on Sugar: By an Old-Fashioned Democrat* (N.p., [1894]), 11, 15. Miles's pamphlet is in Middleton Library, Louisiana State University, Baton Rouge.

59. Daniel, "Miles," 120, 122; Andrew Price to Miles, August 31, 1893, Miles to John Dymond, September 16, 1893, in Miles Papers, SHC; Miles, *Views on Sugar*, 13; W. P. Miles to J. L. Brent, February 15, 1888, in Joseph Lancaster Brent Papers, HL.

Although time had not altered Miles's politics, it began to take a toll on his health. Afflicted with cataracts, he turned over the management of his company to his son in 1896. He died on May 13, 1899, at the age of seventy-six. His remains were moved closer to those of the rest of the Beirne family; ironically, the final resting place for this unrepentant rebel was Union Cemetery in Union, Monroe County, West Virginia.[60]

In 1841, Beverley Tucker had observed that many Americans saw those who shared his political views as "'abstractionists'—politicians of the absurd school of poor Old Virginia, who, it seems, is one of these days, to *die of an abstraction*." Shortly before Miles's death more than half a century later, the stubborn old professor from South Carolina echoed the words of his counterpart from Virginia. "Oh Bah! with your constitutional arguments!" he exclaimed in a soliloquy: "That's just like South Carolina! She always was a cantankerous little thing—prating about 'the constitution' & 'Principles of the Government'! Well—thats so. Her enemies never tired of sneering at her therefor[e]. It is true they used to say, sarcastically, that she contended for '*Abstract* principles.' As if all principles are not more or less abstract."[61]

60. Daniel, "Miles," 128–29; *Biographical Directory of the American Congress, 1774–1971* (Washington, D.C., 1971), 1407.

61. Richmond *Enquirer*, August 17, 1841; Miles to Dymond, September 16, 1893, in Miles Papers, SHC.

Conservative Liberty Has Been Vindicated

O n July 4, 1854, an angry group of abolitionists held a meeting at Farmington, Massachusetts, to protest the fugitive slave law. Their leader, William Lloyd Garrison, stood before the crowd, held up a copy of the objectionable statute, and set it on fire. But Garrison knew that formal destruction of this law would not end slavery in the United States; slavery was both recognized and sanctioned in the organic law of the country, the Constitution. To dramatize his unwillingness to live in a nation that permitted slavery, Garrison produced a copy of the Constitution, declared it "a covenant with death and an agreement with hell," and, as he reduced it to ashes, he cried, "So perish all compromises with tyranny!"[1]

The fire-eaters had no more toleration for compromise than did Garrison. As William L. Yancey said, however, the fire-eaters thought that "the disease, which preys on the vitals of the Federal Union, does not emanate from any defect in the Federal Constitution—but from a deeper source—the hearts, heads and consciences of the Northern people." Yancey argued that northerners were taught to perceive slavery as "a religious as well as a political wrong, and consequently to hate the slaveholder." According to Yancey, no law, no constitutional amendment, could reeducate the northern people on the slavery issue or prevent them from exerting their political power to attack slavery.[2] Other fire-eaters agreed. Convinced that the hostile, irresponsible, and insurmountable political power of the North imperiled southern rights, honor, and traditional liberties, the fire-eaters counseled secession.

Yancey's complaints about how northerners interpreted the Constitution point to a crucial aspect of the secession movement, a

1. Allan Nevins, *Ordeal of the Union: A House Dividing* (New York, 1947), 150–52; Louis Filler, *The Crusade Against Slavery, 1830–1860* (New York, 1960), 213–17.

2. William R. Smith, ed., *History and Debates of the Convention of the People of Alabama . . .* (1861; rpr. Spartanburg, S.C., 1975), 142.

common link among the fire-eaters, and the key to their success. Like all Americans, southerners paid homage to the Founding Fathers and strove to preserve republican government. But southerners generally and fire-eaters in particular had a distinctly different view about what this entailed. For them, localism, the creation of government as a check on power instead of a grant of power, and the slaveholders' preoccupation with the liberty and equality of all white men reveal secessionist thinking as locked into the eighteenth-century world of their revolutionary parents and grandparents as opposed to the mid-nineteenth-century America transformed by Jacksonian democracy. The force and persistence of this "old republicanism" among slaveholders, however, was not unique to fire-eaters. Author Robert Penn Warren astutely noted that thousands of southerners perceived the Constitution as equivalent to the tablets brought down from Mount Sinai, fixed and permanent for all future generations. An ever-increasing number of studies verify that adherence to early American republican thought was one of the most persistent currents in the South both through time and across the region.[3] As historian Kenneth Greenberg suggested, fire-eaters departed from their contemporaries by maintaining that secession was the only solution to the ever-growing political and social corruption of their society.[4] Their dogmatic adherence to this idea alternately attracted dedicated converts over the years and alienated them from others, but when the political system they attacked relentlessly for so long proved unable to stop the rise of abolitionism and the Republican party, they suddenly

3. Robert Penn Warren, *Jefferson Davis Gets His Citizenship Back* (Lexington, Ky., 1980), 61–62. For manifestations of this philosophy in the early nineteenth century see Norman K. Risjord, *The Old Republicans: Southern Constitutionalism in the Age of Jefferson* (New York, 1965), and Robert E. Shalhope, "Thomas Jefferson's Republicanism and Antebellum Southern Thought," *Journal of Southern History*, XLII (1976), 529–57; among the best studies illustrating this thought in South Carolina are Pauline Maier, "The Road Not Taken: Nullification, John C. Calhoun, and the Revolutionary Tradition in South Carolina," *South Carolina Historical Magazine*, LXXXII (1981), 1–19; Mark A. Kaplanoff, "Charles Pinckney and the American Republican Tradition," in Michael O'Brien and David Moltke-Hansen, eds., *Intellectual Life in Antebellum Charleston* (Knoxville, 1986), 85–122; and Lacy K. Ford, Jr., *Origins of Southern Radicalism: The South Carolina Upcountry, 1800–1860* (Oxford, 1988). Particularly useful to illustrate how the same values occurred elsewhere in the South are John C. Inscoe, *Mountain Masters, Slavery, and the Sectional Crisis in Western North Carolina* (Knoxville, 1989); and James Oakes, *The Ruling Race: A History of American Slaveholders* (New York, 1982), 194–96.

4. Kenneth S. Greenberg, *Masters and Statesmen: The Political Culture of American Slavery* (Baltimore, 1985), 135.

seemed prophetic, conservative, and wise instead of irresponsible, radical, and rash.

Although a particular ideal of republicanism brought these men together, personally and politically they were quite different. These men were variously rich and poor, planters and city dwellers, young and old, self-made and with inherited wealth, with declining and rising fortunes, elitist and democratic, owners of many slaves, a few, or none at all. Although they were dominated by South Carolinians, northern-born Quitman and northern-bred Yancey matched the dedication and energy of Barnwell Rhett. All adhered to a code of honor, but they did not all interpret that code the same way; even the outwardly militant Quitman eschewed dueling. They cannot be dismissed—individually or collectively—as reactionaries. Keitt, Yancey, Quitman, and Miles, for example, favored a variety of progressive reforms in their respective states. And though reactionary in politics, Ruffin was in the vanguard of modernization in agriculture. Conversely, even the modernizing James De Bow acted upon the same traditional notions of honor that motivated Wigfall and eventually abandoned his faith in commerce to join Tucker in the belief that cotton was king. Anxiety over their role in society certainly motivated some of these men to help lead a crusade to vindicate that society, but this sense of alienation was often a mere illusion. For instance, Edmund Ruffin's diary reveals both a man who achieved tremendous adulation, acceptance, and recognition and a cranky man who felt unappreciated unless all his schemes were completely accepted by his entire society.

Their collective behavior reflected these differences and suggests the key to their success. Although some fire-eaters had attempted to create their own states'-rights party, no fire-eater party ever existed. None had to. The fire-eaters were issue-oriented individuals; they believed that preserving southern liberty and a truly republican society depended on forming a southern republic. Beyond that, seldom did any two agree on other issues. A pervasive distrust of party organizations doubtless inhibited them from coalescing, but each had particular concerns that did not receive the same support from others. Their appeal and ultimate success lay in their diversity and complexity. A tremendous political upheaval took place in the South and around America in the 1850s. Besides the collapse of the second party system and the persistence of sectionalism, a plethora of issues brought voters to the polls in droves, not just for national elections but for state and local contests as well.[5] This diversity of issues played into the hands of fire-eaters who could—without a hint of demagoguery or duplicity—appeal to a variety of interests simultaneously and attract support from the small but growing number of southerners who believed only a separate national identity could preserve their society and traditional liberties. Southerners who came to support secession also viewed other goals as critically important. For those who wished to promote industrialization, James De Bow's version of secession was most appealing. Louis Wigfall spoke to those who rejected modernity and hoped the South would remain almost wholly agricultural. Proponents of lower tariffs, reviving the African slave trade, and territorial expansion could find their positions represented by some fire-eaters; those who wanted to maintain tariff protection or prohibit the African slave trade could find support from other fire-eaters. This range of issues defied codification in any party platform. In the words of Yancey, the aim of the fire-eaters was to thrust before the southern people as great a variety of issues as possible: "One thing will catch our eye here and determine our hearts; another thing elsewhere; all united, may yet produce enough spirit to lead us forward, to call forth a Lexington, to fight a Bunker's Hill."[6]

Though the forms used varied, the essence of the fire-eaters' message remained the same. They believed that southerners faced an overwhelming and unconquerable political threat from the North and argued their case before the southern people with consummate skill. Liberty, independence, and honor all had special meanings to those who lived in a world of slavery, dependence, and degradation. By describing the political struggle of the South as a choice between submission to an alien people or independence, the fire-eaters struck a sensitive nerve among southerners. It was no accident that the first seven states to secede were those with the highest proportion of slaves to whites, those in which voters could most easily perceive the consequences of losing liberty. In other states, areas with the greatest number of slaves were most in favor of secession.[7]

5. Michael F. Holt, *The Political Crisis of the 1850s* (New York, 1978); also see Ford, *Southern Radicalism*, 279–80 and notes.

6. John Witherspoon DuBose, *The Life and Times of William Lowndes Yancey* (2 vols., 1892; rpr. New York, 1942), I, 362; John McCardell, *The Idea of a Southern Nation: Southern Nationalists and Southern Nationalism, 1830–1860* (New York, 1979).

7. See William J. Cooper, Jr., "The Politics of Slavery Affirmed: The South and the Secession Crisis," in *The Southern Enigma: Essays on Race, Class, and Folk Culture,*

By addressing the "ills" of their society, the fire-eaters saw themselves as preservers of basic American values. They invoked the revolutionary heritage and the ideals of the Founding Fathers. They strove to perpetuate self-government as they perceived it and to correct abuses in the political process. Their concern with expansion, corruption, industrialism, and romantic, millennial reform placed fire-eaters squarely within the mainstream of contemporary American society.[8] All fire-eaters argued that they were defending their rights and values as Americans and, whether gleefully or with regret, came to believe that these aspirations could only be protected in a southern confederacy.

On December 20, 1860, the Rhetts congratulated the people of South Carolina for toppling an "arrogant and tyrannous" nation. Just as important, they claimed, "Conservative liberty has been vindicated." By the state's leaving a union with those who had no understanding of their society, the Rhetts said, "The problem of self-government under the check-balance of slavery, has secured itself from destruction."[9] Faced with the challenge of Garrison and others opposed to slavery, the fire-eaters refused to remain in a nation where theirs was not the only interpretation of the Constitution and the only vision of America.

The role of fire-eaters in the Provisional Confederate Congress and their initial reaction to their new government illustrate their mind-set and the mark they left on the Confederacy. Contrary to the assertions of many historians, more moderate southerners did not force out the fire-eaters from the government they helped create.[10] Fire-eaters persisted in number and rank at Montgomery

---

ed. Walter J. Fraser, Jr., and Winfred Moore (Westport, Conn., 1983), 199–215; Greenberg, *Masters and Statesmen;* Bertram Wyatt-Brown, *Southern Honor: Ethics and Behavior in the Old South* (Oxford, 1982); Daniel W. Crofts, "The Union Party of 1861 and the Secession Crisis," *Perspectives in American History,* XI (1977–78), 327–76.

8. Mark Summers, *The Plundering Generation: Corruption and the Crisis of Union, 1849–1861* (New York, 1987), esp. 281–92; John L. Thomas, "Romantic Reform in America, 1815–1865," *American Quarterly,* XVII (Winter, 1965), 656–81; Ronald G. Walters, *American Reformers, 1815–1860* (New York, 1978), introduction and chap. 1. Walters excludes proslavery advocates from the body of antebellum reformers because "they did not have a distinctive organizational structure to spread their ideas and to channel the energies of the faithful" (p. 12). Fire-eaters did, however, use various political organizations (such as Southern Rights committees), newspapers, and periodicals to promote a most ambitious reform—the creation of a new nation.

9. Charleston *Mercury,* December 21, 1860.

10. Among the historians who most recently claimed the fire-eaters were displaced at Montgomery are James McGregor Burns, *The Vineyard of Liberty* (New

and were the greatest initial supporters of the new regime. These radicals, who truly believed that secession would purge the southern political landscape of corruption, totally accepted both the new Constitution and leaders such as Jefferson Davis. Ironically, though no one knew better than the fire-eaters how deep and persistent political schisms were in the South, they deluded themselves into believing their own rhetoric that secession would prove a panacea; whatever was not perfected in Montgomery, they were confident, was of little consequence because without the corruption and interference of Yankees it would be made right soon.

Just as fire-eaters converged on secession from various paths, after their goal was attained each diverged again; when their mission was accomplished, what little unity they had achieved vanished. But instead of bringing an end to problems of self-government, secession led to a series of new and vexing questions for which the fire-eaters offered no solutions. In their dedication to state sovereignty they had blinded themselves to the problem of how a nation could exist on a foundation of states' rights, especially when wartime emergencies threatened its very existence. They had no program to offer to the Confederate people that could provide guidance during the crisis of war. In fact, their long diatribes about the evils of centralized power surely helped undermine the credibility of the Confederate government. Their total devotion to their "cause" led them wrongly to project their own willingness to sacrifice onto all of the southern people. Their self-appointed task had been to convince southerners that secession was necessary and its realization possible, not to point out dangers or risks that their revolutionary course entailed. After propagandizing for so long, no doubt the fire-eaters convinced themselves of the truth of their fantastic promises and predictions, the certainty of success, and the omnipotence of King Cotton as much or more than they convinced their audiences. Ironically, the disparate visions offered by the fire-eaters before secession eventually contributed to the demise of the nation they had helped create.

York, 1982), 601; McCardell, *Idea of a Southern Nation*, 337; James M. McPherson, *Ordeal by Fire: The Civil War and Reconstruction* (New York, 1982), 137; and Emory Thomas, "Reckoning with Rebels," in *The Old South in the Crucible of War*, ed. Harry P. Owens and James J. Cooke (Jackson, Miss., 1983), 8.

Bibliographical Essay

Primary Sources

Manuscripts

Most of the leading fire-eaters are well represented in the Southern Historical Collection at the University of North Carolina, Chapel Hill. The William Porcher Miles Papers not only provide the best source of information on Miles but also constitute one of the most important sources for the study of southern politics in the years immediately preceding secession. Most prominent fire-eaters from 1858 through secession are mentioned in various letters, and several corresponded with Miles. Miles's own letters in this collection are few but enlightening. The Robert Barnwell Rhett Papers, though few, provide important letters written by and addressed to the "father of secession," as well as his first attempt at writing a history of the Confederate States of America. The papers of Benjamin C. Yancey contain correspondence with his brother William Lowndes Yancey on both personal and political matters. The Southern Historical Collection has a microfilm copy of the Edmund Ruffin Papers, which are now held at the Virginia Historical Society. This invaluable collection includes Ruffin's various attempts at autobiography and some of his extensive correspondence with James H. Hammond during the 1850s. The Quitman Family Papers are one of the largest and best sources for studying John A. Quitman.

Two other collections at Chapel Hill proved to be particularly helpful. The Christopher G. Memminger Papers include several important letters from Miles concerning the prospects of secession in Virginia after John Brown's raid, and the John Perkins Papers contain some fascinating letters from Ruffin about affairs in the Confederacy.

Several collections include scattered material by or about fire-eaters. In one letter in the William H. Branch Papers, the junior Rhett speculates on secession; the Thomas B. King Papers contain a glowing evaluation of Louis Wigfall; a letter from Miles concerning the prospect of black troops in the Confederacy appears in the William Nelson Pendleton Papers; the Tucker Family Papers include some correspondence from Beverley Tucker as well as an address to Hampden-Sidney College in 1841; and the James L. Orr Papers include a letter from Miles about the situation at Fort Sumter late in 1860.

The William R. Perkins Library at Duke University contains the papers of two major fire-eaters and valuable information about most of them in other collections. The James Dunwoody Brownson De Bow Papers constitute the largest body of De Bow's correspondence; unfortunately, the vast majority of the material concerns collection of fees for *De Bow's Review*. There are, however, many useful letters, as well as some of De Bow's college notes and journals, and letters from Yancey and Ruffin. More rewarding are the Laurence Massilon Keitt Papers. In emotional and boastful letters to his wife, the immodest Keitt left an invaluable record not only of his deeds but also of his ideas and aspirations. Pertinent correspondence covers the decade from 1855 through Keitt's death in 1864.

Also at Duke, the vast Campbell Family Papers contain an interesting description of John Quitman during the Mexican War. A few Benjamin Yancey Papers are held here, and they concern both health and family matters; the M. J. Solomons Scrapbook has information on William Yancey during the Confederate years; the Armistead Burt Papers include correspondence from both Barnwell Rhett and Louis Wigfall, mostly about politics in South Carolina. The most important of the few letters in the Robert Barnwell Rhett Papers is one written to the younger Rhett in 1858 supporting the actions of his father. The Abraham Watkins Venable Scrapbook contains in full Barnwell Rhett's remarkable oration in Macon, Georgia, in 1850. The Bernard Scrapbook includes a death notice of Rhett and provides an interesting account of the secession convention in South Carolina. A letter from Rhett, Jr., about wartime affairs is in the P. G. T. Beauregard Papers. The Maury Papers include notice of Wigfall's alcoholism after the Civil War. The Charles C. Jones Autograph Letters include a description of the Washington scene in 1861 by Senator Wigfall and a note by Keitt concerning his brawl in Congress in 1858. A letter from De Bow about Kansas is in the James D. Davidson Papers. The Clement Claiborne Clay Letters have correspondence from Wigfall and Yancey about political and military affairs in the Confederacy. The Robert N. Gourdin Papers contain a fascinating letter from Miles in which he evaluates his options after the defeat of the Confederacy in 1865.

The Library of Congress holds several important collections. The extensive James H. Hammond Papers include dozens of letters from Beverley Tucker, several from William Porcher Miles, Laurence Keitt, and Edmund Ruffin, and a few from Wigfall, R. B. Rhett, Jr., and De Bow. Like the Miles Papers at North Carolina, these papers also include remarks on various political activities in the South, by Hammond and others, especially on such topics as the Rhetts' struggle for power in South Carolina and the young Louis Wigfall's various exploits.

The single best glimpse into the mind of a fire-eater is provided by the Edmund Ruffin Diary at the Library of Congress. From 1856 until his suicide in 1865, Ruffin recorded virtually every thought that crossed his mind, encompassing almost every topic imaginable, and, of course, provided editorial opinions on almost every person and event of significance during that period.

The Wigfall Family Papers at the Library of Congress contain mostly letters written by Louis Wigfall during the Civil War and by family members before the war. Important letters from Rhett and Yancey also appear in this collection. The Lewis R. Gibbes Papers include a few letters from William Porcher Miles about civic affairs in Charleston and by De Bow about his friends from the College of Charleston. The small Whitemarsh B. Seabrook Papers contain some of the most important letters from Quitman and Rhett, illustrating the maneuvering of radicals during the secession crisis of 1850–1852. The Martin Van Buren Papers include an important letter from Barnwell Rhett about the Democratic presidential campaign of 1844.

The papers of William Lowndes Yancey at the Alabama Department of Archives and History include Yancey's correspondence but are equally important for his speeches, both in pamphlets and newspaper clippings. The John Witherspoon DuBose Correspondence contains a great deal of information on Yancey, including interesting contemporary accounts that DuBose collected for his biography in 1892. The Benjamin Franklin Perry Letters provide a picture of Yancey's family life and show his continued devotion to his old Unionist friend and mentor. Other collections that pertain to Yancey are the Henry Churchill Semple Papers, the William Phineas Brown Papers, and the Colin J. McRae Papers.

The largest volume of material on John Quitman is at the Mississippi Department of Archives and History. Besides the voluminous John A. Quitman Papers, there are a few letters in the Quitman Family Papers. J. F. H. Claiborne collected hundreds of important letters from and about Quitman for his biography, and the Claiborne Collection remains a vital source for studying Quitman. This collection also includes a letter from James De Bow discussing his life in Charleston and plans to move to New Orleans in 1845 and a valuable letter by Rhett concerning the secession crisis of 1851. Other Quitman letters in this depository may be found in the Robert J. Walker Papers and the Nathan G. Howard Papers.

The Tucker-Coleman Collection at the Earl Gregg Swem Library at the College of William and Mary constitutes the best source of letters by and about Beverley Tucker. Particularly revealing are his letters to his father and half-brother, John Randolph of Roanoke. A letter by Ruffin is here, and there are occasional references to him. In Tucker's letters to and from Hammond there are several references to Barnwell Rhett around the time of the Nashville Convention.

The South Carolina Historical Society in Charleston has a fascinating collection of Robert Barnwell Rhett Papers. These include many revealing letters written from the 1850s to his death in 1876 and Rhett's various postwar literary attempts, such as his "Autobiography" and his "Life and Services." In the latter, Rhett mentions Yancey's diplomatic assignment and Keitt's efforts to persuade Rhett to run for the Confederate Senate late in 1864. The Armistead Burt Letters include a letter describing the relationship between Rhett and John C. Calhoun in 1848.

At the Louisiana and Lower Mississippi Valley Collections at Louisiana State University there are a few small collections with material pertaining to John A. Quitman. The John A. Quitman Papers and the Southern Filibusters Collection contain a few important pamphlets relating to General Quitman, but the latter is sure to disappoint those whose focus is on expansion into Latin America. The Samuel A. Cartwright Papers also include an important letter from Quitman in which he describes his efforts to lead resistance to the federal government in 1850.

The Charles Gayarré Papers in the Grace King Collection include fascinating letters written by James De Bow during the Confederate period. The Edward Clifton Wharton and Family Papers contain an insightful letter from Robert Barnwell Rhett, Jr., concerning the politics of South Carolina at the opening of the Civil War.

The Wigfall Family Papers are at the Barker Texas History Center at the University of Texas. Many of these are typescript copies of letters from Louis Wigfall; the originals are located in the Williams-Chestnut-Manning Papers of the South Caroliniana Library at the University of South Carolina. The John E. Campbell Papers contain a letter describing Wigfall as a "fire-eater." The James D. B. De Bow Papers contain several valuable letters written by De Bow after the Civil War.

The Alderman Library at the University of Virginia contains a few letters by Beverley Tucker in the Bryan Family Papers; the most important concerns Tucker's views of Andrew Jackson. The Nathaniel Beverley Tucker Letter is a long one to Littleton W. Tazewell in 1826 about various political matters. The Edmund Ruffin Papers here mostly concern his activity during the Civil War. A letter by Ruffin in the Elizabeth Gilmer Tyler Miles Collection illustrates Ruffin's contempt of the masses and of presidential power.

A letter from Miles celebrating the spirit of resistance in South Carolina after Lincoln's election is in the William Garnett Chisolm Papers at the Virginia Historical Society in Richmond. Miles's complaints about his committee duties in the Confederate Congress are recorded in a letter in the Preston Family Papers. The Daniel London Papers contain a letter from Barnwell Rhett revealing him as the author of an anonymous article in the *Southern Quarterly Review*. The Crump Family Papers include a letter from Beverley Tucker about the nullification crisis.

The Quitman Papers in the Historical Society of Pennsylvania have dozens of letters from John Quitman to his son; these constitute the best source for the latter part of Quitman's life. The James Buchanan Papers include scattered correspondence from Yancey and Rhett regarding the Democratic party. The Ferdinand J. Dreer Autograph Collection has a letter from Yancey celebrating Lincoln's election in 1860. The Autograph Collection of Simon Gratz contains an interesting self-evaluation by Barnwell Rhett in 1856 and several letters by Miles about the Civil War and the Confederate "cause."

The Civil War Collection at the Huntington Library in San Marino,

California, includes a letter by Rhett about the Battle of Bull Run. The Joseph Lancaster Brent Papers contain an example of Miles's postwar politics. The Robert Alonzo Brock Collection also has a postwar letter by Miles, several by R. B. Rhett, Jr., and one about Yancey by his first biographer, John W. DuBose, that reveals the author's reverence for his subject. The Francis Lieber Papers include some bombastic letters from the youthful Laurence Keitt, and the Simon Bolivar Buckner Papers contain an inquiry by Wigfall from London about the condition of the South in 1866.

The manuscript section of the Historic New Orleans Collection has a few letters by James De Bow in the James Dunwoody Brownson De Bow Letters and one by De Bow about his sense of personal honor and trouble with his in-laws in the Charles Gayarré Papers.

At the Howard-Tilton Library at Tulane University in New Orleans, the extensive Jefferson Davis Papers contain a few letters to and from Yancey and De Bow written during the Civil War, as well as one by Davis to Yancey's widow in 1863.

The Robert W. Woodruff Library at Emory University has letters from Miles about civic affairs in Charleston, secession, and the Confederate government in the Robert N. Gourdin Papers.

The South Caroliniana Library at the University of South Carolina holds William Porcher Miles Papers that include a brief autobiography, his views on city politics in Charleston, and reflections on the Confederacy written in 1882.

Letters from Miles and Keitt appear in the Pettigrew Family Papers at the North Carolina Department of Archives and History in Raleigh.

Washington and Lee College has a letter from Laurence Keitt in the David F. Jamison Papers describing the atmosphere in Montgomery during the meeting of the Provisional Congress of the Confederate States of America.

Newspapers and Periodicals

The dates for which I used each newspaper are given in parentheses.

The Charleston *Mercury* (1828–1865) was the organ of the Rhetts and the mouthpiece of southern radicalism for two generations; it is not only the best source for studying the Rhetts' political careers and attitudes but also for the activities and speeches of other fire-eaters, particularly Laurence Keitt and William Porcher Miles.

The Montgomery *Advertiser* (1860–1861, 1863) was the greatest supporter of Yancey in his native state; the Montgomery *Post* (1861), one of his greatest opponents. Both provided extensive coverage of Yancey's activities during the secession winter of 1860–1861. The Wetumpka *Southern Crisis* (1840), edited by Yancey and his brother during a presidential campaign, was a vitriolic anti-Whig propaganda publication. The Richmond *Enquirer* and the New York *Herald* both printed important speeches by William L. Yancey during the presidential campaign of 1860.

Edmund Ruffin's *Farmers' Register* (1833–1842) and his *Southern Maga-*

zine and Monthly Review (1841) contained his views on a variety of non-political topics but were just as clear and vocal on political matters as Ruffin's *Bank Reformer* (1841).

Local newspapers provided good coverage of other fire-eaters. Beverley Tucker wrote editorials for the Richmond *Enquirer* (1833 and 1841) in his attempt to preach both to the southern people and to President John Tyler. The *Missouri Gazette and Public Advertiser* (1819) was Judge Tucker's mouthpiece during the debates on Missouri statehood. The Jackson *State Rights Banner* (1834) and Woodville *Republican* (1834) had important information on the career of John Quitman in Mississippi politics at a time when he irrevocably turned his back on nationalism. The Edgefield *Advertiser* (1840–1846), the Marshall *Texas Republican* (1849–1850, 1860–1861), and the Dallas *Herald* (1858–1859) provided the best newspaper sources for Louis Wigfall.

Some activities of James De Bow were reported in the New Orleans *Daily Delta* (1860) and the New York *Times* (1854). The *Delta* also provided coverage of Yancey's mass meeting in New Orleans in 1860, and the *Times* (1856, 1858) frequently reported the speeches and exploits of Keitt.

Articles and editorials by James De Bow in his *De Bow's Review* (1846–1867, including the After the War Series) provide the best information on the editor's life and thought, as well as occasional correspondence. Charles Gayarré's biographical sketch of De Bow in 1866 remains one of the best. Several articles by Edmund Ruffin and one by Laurence Keitt also appear in the *Review*. De Bow published a compilation of articles from early issues of the *Review* in *Industrial Resources, Etc., of the Southern and Western States* (3 vols.; New Orleans, New York, and Charleston, 1853). Paul F. Paskoff and Daniel J. Wilson, eds., *The Cause of the South: Selections from "De Bow's Review," 1846–1867* (Baton Rouge, 1982), includes some of De Bow's most important essays and much valuable information on the editor and his magazine.

Some of the more literary magazines printed articles by and about fire-eaters. Edmund Ruffin published a reminiscence of the nullification crisis in the *Southern Literary Messenger* (1861); Beverley Tucker had several publications in that periodical (1834–1836, 1841). The *Southern Quarterly Review* contains articles by James De Bow (1844–1845), Tucker (1851), and an anonymous one by Rhett (1854). The London magazine *Punch* printed its irreverent "The Fight over the Body of Keitt" about the melee involving Keitt and Galusha Grow, on March 6, 1858. *Harper's Weekly* (September, 1860), gave favorable coverage of Yancey's activities at the national Democratic Convention of 1860 and sketches of Keitt and Miles at the end of the year (December, 1860). Robert Barnwell Rhett's desperate "Fears for Democracy" appeared in the *Southern Magazine* (September, 1875), 306–32.

Government Documents

The *Congressional Globe* from the Twenty-eighth to the Thirty-sixth Congresses offers the best information on the congressional activities of Rhett,

Yancey, Keitt, Wigfall, Miles, and Quitman in Washington, D.C. Publications of the United States Bureau of the Census provide records of De Bow's work for the federal government. *The Seventh Census of the United States: 1850* (Washington, D.C., 1853) and De Bow's *Statistical View of the United States . . . Being a Compendium of the Seventh Census* (Washington, D.C., 1854) both include prefatory remarks by De Bow on the condition of his bureau and his proposed reforms. Because of De Bow's influence, Edmund Ruffin published "Southern Agricultural Exhaustion and Its Remedy" in the *Report to the Commissioner of Patents for the Year 1852, Part II: Agriculture* (Washington, D.C., 1853).

The War of the Rebellion: A Compilation of the Official Records of the Union and Confederate Armies (130 vols.; Washington, D.C., 1880–1901) contains detailed information on the activity at Fort Sumter, including the parts played by Wigfall and Miles. The *Journal of the Congress of the Confederate States of America* (7 vols.; Washington, D.C., 1904) includes an account of the fight between Yancey and Benjamin Hill, as well as information on Rhett, Keitt, Miles, and Wigfall.

George H. Reese, ed., *Proceedings of the Virginia State Convention of 1861, February 13–May 1* (4 vols.; Richmond, 1965) illustrates the impact some of Tucker's former students had on secession in that state.

Published Letters, Memoirs, and Diaries

Several printed sources include letters by various fire-eaters as well as reactions to them by contemporaries. Among the most useful are Ulrich B. Phillips, ed., *The Correspondence of Robert Toombs, Alexander H. Stephens, and Howell Cobb* (Washington, D.C., 1913), Chauncey S. Boucher and Robert Brooks, eds., *Correspondence Addressed to John C. Calhoun, 1837–1849* (Washington, D.C., 1930), and Charles Henry Ambler, ed., *Correspondence of Robert M. T. Hunter, 1826–1876* (Washington, D.C., 1918). Mary C. Simms Oliphant, Alfred Taylor Odell, and T. C. Duncan Eaves, eds., *The Letters of William Gilmore Simms* (5 vols.; Columbia, S.C., 1955), contains a great deal of information on Tucker, Miles, Rhett, and politics in South Carolina in general. William P. Trent's *William Gilmore Simms* (1892; rpr. New York, 1969) has some important letters from Tucker to Simms. J. F. H. Claiborne's *Life and Correspondence of John A. Quitman* (2 vols.; New York, 1860) contains dozens of letters unavailable anywhere else.

Amelia W. Williams and Eugene C. Barker, eds., *The Writings of Sam Houston, 1813–1863* (8 vols.; Austin, 1942), contains some caustic remarks about Wigfall. Similarly, Leroy P. Graf and Ralph W. Haskins, eds., *The Papers of Andrew Johnson* (7 vols. to date; Knoxville, 1967–), records some critical comments about Rhett and Yancey in 1860. Clyde N. Wilson *et al.*, eds., *The Papers of John C. Calhoun* (18 vols. to date; Columbia, S.C., 1959–), provides insight into Rhett's relationship with Calhoun. A letter from Edmund Ruffin, Jr., to his children describing the elder Ruffin's suicide is in *Tyler's Quarterly Historical and Genealogical Magazine*, V (January, 1924), 193–95.

Several contemporaries of Yancey recorded their impressions of him in reminiscences and memoirs. Richard Taylor, in *Destruction and Reconstruction: Personal Experiences of the Late War* (New York, 1879), suggests that Yancey had second thoughts after leading a split at the Democratic Convention in Charleston. William Hesseltine, ed., *Three Against Lincoln: Murat Halstead Reports on the Caucuses of 1860* (Baton Rouge, 1960), has several interesting references to Yancey, as does William R. Smith, *Reminiscences of a Long Life: Historical, Political, Personal and Literary* (1889; rpr. Louisville, 1961).

Louis Wigfall had a dramatic impact on his peers. Walter F. McCaleb, eds., *Memoirs, with Special Reference to Secession and the Civil War, by John H. Reagan* (New York, 1906); C. W. Raines, eds., *Six Decades in Texas; or, Memoirs of Francis Richard Lubbock, Governor of Texas in War-Time, 1861–63* (Austin, 1900); and A. W. Terrell, "Recollections of General Sam Houston," *Southwestern Historical Quarterly,* XVI (October, 1912), 118–19, mention Wigfall's activities in Texas and Confederate politics. Wigfall's daughter D. Girard Wright recorded her memories of her father in *A Southern Girl in '61: The War-Time Memories of a Confederate Senator's Daughter* (New York, 1905). A Union officer at Fort Sumter, Abner Doubleday, recalled Wigfall's dramatics in *Reminiscences of Forts Sumter and Moultrie in 1860–61* (New York, 1876).

William Kauffman Scarborough, ed., *The Diary of Edmund Ruffin* (3 vols.; Baton Rouge, 1972–89), provides the easiest access to the Ruffin Diary at the Library of Congress. John F. Marszalek, ed., *The Diary of Miss Emma Holmes, 1861–1866* (Baton Rouge, 1979), includes one southerner's assessment of Ruffin's life and suicide. C. Vann Woodward, ed., *Mary Chesnut's Civil War* (New Haven, 1981), contains interesting references to Yancey, Miles, Ruffin, and Tucker's book *The Partisan Leader.* William Howard Russell, *My Diary North and South* (1863; rpr. Gloucester, Mass., 1969), presents an English observer's reaction to Louis Wigfall's bluster and daring. A hint of Rhett's role in Congress and the Democratic party appears in Milo M. Quaife, ed., *The Diary of James K. Polk During His Presidency, 1845–1849* (4 vols.; Chicago, 1910).

Pamphlets and Speeches

A compilation of speeches and pamphlets by William Porcher Miles called *True Education: How to Make Education "the Cheap Defense of a Nation"* (Columbia, S.C., 1882) is held at the William R. Perkins Library at Duke University. Middleton Library at Louisiana State University has Miles's, *Some Views on Sugar: By an Old-Fashioned Democrat* (N.p., [1894]), which contains the political views of an unrepentant rebel.

Edmund Ruffin, "The Political Economy of Slavery," is published in Eric McKitrick, ed., *Slavery Defended: The Views of the Old South* (Englewood Cliffs, N.J., 1963), 69–85.

No study of William L. Yancey is complete without examining his many public addresses. The most important are *An Oration on the Life and Charac-*

ter of Andrew Jackson (Baltimore, 1846); *An Address to the People of Alabama, by W. L. Yancey, Late a Delegate, at Large, for the State of Alabama, to the National Democratic Convention, Held at Baltimore, on the 22d May, A.D. 1848* (Montgomery, 1848); *Address on the Life and Character of John Caldwell Calhoun* (Montgomery, 1850); *Speech of the Hon. W. L. Yancey, Delivered in the Democratic State Convention, of the State of Alabama, Held at Montgomery, on the 11th, 12th, 13th, & 14th January, 1860* (Montgomery, 1860); *Speech of the Hon. William L. Yancey of Alabama Delivered in the National Democratic Convention, Charleston, April 28th, 1860* (Charleston, 1860); *Speech of the Hon. William L. Yancey of Alabama at Wieting Hall, Syracuse, N.Y.* (Published by Direction of the National Democratic State Committee, 1860).

William R. Smith, *History and Debates of the Convention of the People of Alabama* (1861; rpr. Spartanburg, S.C., 1975), records Yancey's central role in the Alabama Secession Convention.

In addition, the following pamphlets show Yancey's impact on Alabama politics: *Journal of the Democratic Convention, Held in the City of Montgomery on the 14th and 15th of February, 1848* (Montgomery, 1848); and *Journal of Southern Rights Convention Held in the City of Montgomery, February 10, 1851* (Montgomery, 1851).

The Death and Funeral Ceremonies of John Caldwell Calhoun, Containing Speeches, Reports, and Other Documents Connected Therewith, the Oration of the Hon. R. B. Rhett Before the Legislature, &c. &c. (Columbia, S.C., 1850) contains a fascinating speech by Barnwell Rhett about political philosophy. *The Address of the People of South Carolina, Assembled in Convention, to the People of the Slaveholding States of the United States* (Charleston, 1860) was written largely by Rhett, inviting other slave states to secede and unite in a southern confederacy.

Nathaniel Beverley Tucker's angry, blustering, fanciful speech at the Nashville Convention was published as *Prescience: Speech Delivered by Hon. Beverley Tucker of Virginia, in the Southern Convention, Held at Nashville, Tennessee, April 13, 1850* (Richmond, 1862). Tucker's *Discourse on the Dangers That Threaten the Free Institutions of the United States* (Richmond, 1841) is valuable for understanding Tucker's views on republican society.

Two other important speeches are Louis T. Wigfall, *Speech of Louis T. Wigfall, on the Pending Political Issues; Delivered at Tyler, Smith County, Texas* (Washington, D.C., 1860), and Edmund Ruffin, *Address to the Virginia Agricultural Society, on the Effects of Domestic Slavery on the Manners, Habits and Welfare of the Southern States; and the Slavery of Class to Class in the Northern States* (Richmond, 1853).

Contemporary Publications

The wartime edition of Nathaniel Beverley Tucker, *The Partisan Leader* (New York, 1861), includes editorial comments on Yancey and secessionists in general. Tucker's *Series of Lectures on the Science of Government, Intended to Prepare the Student for the Study of the Constitution of the United States* (Philadelphia, 1845) is essential for understanding both Tucker's political philosophy and his relationship with his students. Edmund Ruffin's *Anticipations of the Future, to Serve as Lessons for the Present Times* (Richmond, 1860) is similar to his cousin's *Partisan Leader* but much more bloodthirsty and pedantic.

Secondary Sources

General Studies

There are dozens of excellent studies of the antebellum South and American politics that help place the lives of the fire-eaters in context. My most valuable sources for the South were Robert E. May, "Psychobiography and Secession: The Southern Radical as Maladjusted 'Outsider,'" *Civil War History*, XXXIV (1988), 46–69; Jesse Carpenter, *The South as a Conscious Minority, 1789–1861* (New York, 1930); William J. Cooper, Jr., *The South and the Politics of Slavery, 1828–1856* (Baton Rouge, 1978), and *Liberty and Slavery: Southern Politics to 1860* (New York, 1983); Clement Eaton, *The Mind of the Old South* (1964; rpr. Baton Rouge, 1976), and *History of the Old South* (1954; rpr. New York, 1968); James Oakes, *The Ruling Race: A History of American Slaveholders* (New York, 1982); John McCardell, *The Idea of a Southern Nation: Southern Nationalism and Southern Nationalists, 1830–1860* (New York, 1979); Daniel W. Crofts, "The Union Party of 1861 and the Secession Crisis," *Perspectives in American History*, XI (1977–78), 327–76; John B. Edmunds, Jr., *Francis W. Pickens and the Politics of Destruction* (Chapel Hill, 1986); and Thomas D. Alexander and Richard E. Beringer, *The Anatomy of the Confederate Congress* (Nashville, 1972).

For national politics, the most useful works were David M. Potter, *The Impending Crisis, 1848–1861*, completed and edited by Don E. Fehrenbacher (New York, 1976), and Allan Nevins, *Ordeal of the Union* (8 vols.; New York, 1947–71). Two valuable studies for an understanding of the tumultuous events during the 1850s are David Donald's *Charles Sumner and the Coming of the Civil War* (New York, 1960), and Michael F. Holt, *The Political Crisis of the 1850s* (New York, 1978). Of importance for my understanding of particular aspects of the Civil War were James McGregor Burns, *The Vineyard of Liberty* (New York, 1982); James M. McPherson, *Ordeal by Fire: The Civil War and Reconstruction* (New York, 1982); and Emory Thomas, "Reckoning with Rebels," in *The Old South in the Crucible of War*, ed. Harry P. Owens and James J. Cooke (Jackson, Miss., 1983).

Other works that contain special references to fire-eaters include William L. Barney, *The Road to Secession: A New Perspective on the Old South* (New York, 1972); Ulrich B. Phillips, *The Course of the South to Secession* (New York, 1939); H. Hardy Perritt, "The Fire-Eaters," in *Oratory in the Old South*, ed. Waldo W. Braden (Baton Rouge, 1970), chap. 8; Alvy L. King, "Fire-Eaters," in *Encyclopedia of Southern History*, ed. David C. Roller and Robert W. Twyman (Baton Rouge, 1979), 434–35; William J. Cooper, Jr., "The Politics of Slavery Affirmed: The South and the Secession Crisis," in *The Southern Enigma: Essays on Race, Class, and Folk Culture*, ed. Walter J.

Fraser, Jr., and Winfred B. Moore (Westport, Conn., 1983), 199–215; Kenneth S. Greenberg, *Masters and Statesmen: The Political Culture of American Slavery* (Baltimore, 1985); and David S. Heidler, "Fire-Eaters: The Radical Secessionists in Antebellum Politics" (Ph.D. dissertation, Auburn University, 1985).

Far more has been written about other contemporary political groups. These include Roy F. Nichols, *The Disruption of the American Democracy* (New York, 1948); Eric Foner, *Free Soil, Free Labor, Free Men: The Ideology of the Republican Party Before the Civil War* (Oxford, 1977); David M. Potter, *Lincoln and His Party During the Secession Crisis* (New Haven, 1942); Hans Trefousse, *The Radical Republicans: Lincoln's Vanguard for Racial Justice* (Baton Rouge, 1968); Ronald Walters, *The Antislavery Appeal: American Abolitionism After 1830* (Baltimore, 1976); Louis Filler, *The Crusade Against Slavery, 1830–1860* (New York, 1960); and Peter F. Walker, *Moral Choices: Memory, Desire, and Imagination in Nineteenth-Century American Abolitionism* (Baton Rouge, 1978). Pauline Maier, *The Old Revolutionaries: Political Lives in the Age of Samuel Adams* (New York, 1980), was useful both as a model for this study and for interesting parallels between fire-eaters and revolutionary leaders.

State Studies

There are several useful studies of politics and secession in various states. The most recent, Lacy K. Ford, Jr., *Origins of Southern Radicalism: The South Carolina Upcountry, 1800–1860* (Oxford, 1988), is crucial both for understanding secession in that state and for its convincing analysis of causes for southern radicalism. Other important studies of this volatile state are Stephen A. Channing, *Crisis of Fear: Secession in South Carolina* (New York, 1970), and Charles E. Cauthen, *South Carolina Goes to War, 1860–1865* (Chapel Hill, 1950); the latter has important information on Barnwell Rhett's feud with President Jefferson Davis as well as the 1860 Association and James De Bow. William W. Freehling, *Prelude to Civil War: The Nullification Crisis in South Carolina, 1816–1836* (New York, 1966), and John Barnwell, *Love of Order: South Carolina's First Secession Crisis* (Chapel Hill, 1982), explore political crises of lasting importance to the people of South Carolina.

For other states, among the best is J. Mills Thornton, *Politics and Power in a Slave Society: Alabama, 1800–1860* (Baton Rouge, 1978). It is essential for placing the actions of William L. Yancey in the context of state politics and replaces Clarence P. Denman, *The Secession Movement in Alabama* (Montgomery, 1933). The growing number of state studies includes William L. Barney, *The Secessionist Impulse: Alabama and Mississippi in 1860* (Princeton, 1974); Walter L. Buenger, *Secession and the Union in Texas* (Austin, 1984); and Ollinger Crenshaw, *The Slave States in the Presidential Election of 1860* (Gloucester, Mass., 1969); James M. Woods, *Rebellion and Realignment: Arkansas's Road to Secession* (Fayetteville, Ark., 1987); Michael P. Johnson, *Towards a Patriarchal Republic: The Secession of Georgia* (Baton Rouge,

1977); and David R. Goldfield, *Urban Growth in the Age of Sectionalism: Virginia, 1847–1861* (Baton Rouge, 1977). A good summary of recent works is provided by James Tice Moore, "Secession and the States: A Review Essay," *Virginia Magazine of History and Biography,* XCIV (1986), 60–76.

Biographies

Previous biographical accounts of fire-eaters range from the hero worship of their contemporaries to solid scholarly works. Among the better ones are Robert J. Brugger, *Beverley Tucker: Heart over Head in the Old South* (Baltimore, 1978), and Robert E. May, *John Anthony Quitman: Old South Crusader* (Baton Rouge, 1985), which replaces J. F. H. Claiborne's *Life and Correspondence of John A. Quitman* (1860).

John Witherspoon DuBose, *The Life and Times of William Lowndes Yancey* (2 vols., 1892; rpr. New York, 1942), is by a friend of Yancey's and a soldier in the Confederate army. Ralph B. Draughon's scholarly "William Lowndes Yancey: From Unionist to Secessionist, 1814–1852" (Ph.D. dissertation, University of North Carolina, Chapel Hill, 1968) unfortunately stops before the most important portion of Yancey's career. Draughon's "The Young William L. Yancey," *Alabama Review,* XIX (1966), 28–37, is a succinct summary of the early chapters of his dissertation. George F. Mellon, "Henry W. Hilliard and William L. Yancey," *Sewanee Review,* XVII (1909), 44–47, provides a detailed account of Yancey's confrontations with his longtime Whig opponent. Joseph Hergesheimer devoted a chapter to Yancey in his romantic *Swords and Roses* (New York, 1929), 35–64, as did Clement Eaton in *The Mind of the Old South,* 267–87.

The only biography of Rhett is Laura White's solid *Robert Barnwell Rhett: Father of Secession* (1931; rpr. New York, 1965), but several important Rhett manuscripts have surfaced since the first publication of this book. Only one biographical treatment apiece exists for Keitt, Wigfall, and De Bow: John Holt Merchant, Jr.'s, uncritical "Laurence M. Keitt: South Carolina Fire-Eater" (Ph.D. dissertation, University of Virginia, 1976); Alvy L. King, *Louis T. Wigfall: Southern Fire-eater* (Baton Rouge, 1970), which focuses on Wigfall's Confederate career and feud with Jefferson Davis; and Otis Clark Skipper, *J. D. B. De Bow: Magazinist of the Old South* (Athens, 1958), which, as the subtitle states, focuses on De Bow's journalism, not his politics.

Several historians have written about Ruffin. The first was Avery Craven, *Edmund Ruffin, Southerner: A Study in Secession* (1932; rpr. Baton Rouge, 1982). Betty L. Mitchell provided a much more critical portrayal in *Edmund Ruffin: A Biography* (Bloomington, 1981) but was not as successful as Craven in capturing her subject's character and vitality. Careful attention has been given to Ruffin's agricultural reforms in William M. Mathew, *Edmund Ruffin and the Crisis of Slavery in the Old South: The Failure of Agricultural Reform* (Athens, Ga., 1988), but the author paid scant attention to the political environment that affected Ruffin and too easily projected the Virginian's failings onto his entire society. Other works about Ruffin include

Bibliographical Essay

Henry G. Ellis, "Edmund Ruffin: His Life and Times," *John P. Branch Historical Papers of Randolph-Macon College*, III (June, 1910), 99–123; David F. Allmendinger, Jr., "The Early Career of Edmund Ruffin, 1810–1840," *Virginia Magazine of History and Biography*, XCIII (1985), 127–54; and David F. Allmendinger, Jr., and William K. Scarborough, "The Days Ruffin Died," *Virginia Magazine of History and Biography*, XCVII (1989), 75–96. Allmendinger's latest work, *Ruffin: Family and Reform in the Old South* (Oxford, 1990), provides the best examination of Ruffin's family but, like Mathew, minimizes Ruffin's commitment to secession.

There are only two brief studies of Miles: Ruth McCaskill Daniel, "William Porcher Miles: Champion of Southern Interests" (M.A. thesis, University of North Carolina, Chapel Hill, 1943), and Clarence McKitrick Smith, Jr., "William Porcher Miles, Progressive Mayor of Charleston, 1855–1857," in *The Proceedings of the South Carolina Historical Association* (N.p., 1942), 30–39.

In addition, two books by Drew Gilpin Faust add to the understanding of Rhett, Tucker, and Ruffin: *James Henry Hammond and the Old South: A Design for Mastery* (Baton Rouge, 1982) is helpful for understanding South Carolina politics, especially the rivalry between Hammond and Rhett; *A Sacred Circle: The Dilemma of the Intellectual in the Old South* (Baltimore, 1977) explores the friendship and ideas of Ruffin, Tucker, Hammond, George Frederick Holmes, and William Gilmore Simms. Robert Brugger provides additional observations about Tucker and supports Faust's social alienation theory in "The Mind of the Old South: New Views," *Virginia Quarterly Review*, LII (1980), 277–95. Some insightful comments on Beverley Tucker can be found in Vernon L. Parrington, *Main Currents in American Thought* (3 vols.; New York, 1927–30).

Biographical Directories

Because so little has been written about some of these fire-eaters, biographical directories supplied a great deal of information. Especially helpful were the *Dictionary of American Biography; Cyclopedia of Eminent and Representative Men of the Carolinas of the Nineteenth Century* (2 vols., 1892; rpr. Spartanburg, S.C., 1972–73); and *Biographical Directory of the American Congress, 1774–1971* (Washington, D.C., 1971). Norman G. Kittrell, *Governors Who Have Been, and Other Public Men of Texas* (Houston, 1921), provided important information on Louis Wigfall's contemporaries. William H. Gaines, Jr., ed., *Biographical Register of Members Virginia State Convention, 1861* (Richmond, 1969), and Willis Brewer, *Alabama: Her History, Resources, War Record, and Public Men* (1872; rpr. Tuscaloosa, 1964), helped identify several of the more influential former students of Beverley Tucker.

Special Subjects

Bernard Bailyn's *The Ideological Origins of the American Revolution* (Cambridge, Mass., 1967) and Gordon Wood's *Creation of the American Republic, 1776–1787* (Chapel Hill, 1969) are the standard works on republican ideology in America; for the power and impact of classical republicanism on southern thought the most useful studies are Edmund S. Morgan, *American Slavery, American Freedom: The Ordeal of Colonial Virginia* (New York, 1975); Norman K. Risjord, *The Old Republicans: Southern Constitutionalism in the Age of Jefferson* (New York, 1965); and Robert E. Shalhope, "Thomas Jefferson's Republicanism and Antebellum Southern Thought," *Journal of Southern History*, XLII (1976), 529–56. Also useful are Pauline Maier, "The Road Not Taken: Nullification, John C. Calhoun, and the Revolutionary Tradition in South Carolina," *South Carolina Historical Magazine*, LXXXII (1981), 1–19; Mark A. Kaplanoff, "Charles Pinckney and the American Republican Tradition," in *Intellectual Life in Antebellum Charleston*, ed. Michael O'Brien and David Moltke-Hansen (Knoxville, 1986), 85–122; and John C. Inscoe, *Mountain Masters, Slavery, and the Sectional Crisis in Western North Carolina* (Knoxville, 1989).

For an explication of the peculiarly southern interpretations of the Constitution, see Don Fehrenbacher, *Constitutions and Constitutionalism in the Slaveholding South* (Athens, Ga., 1989), and a compelling insight by Robert Penn Warren in *Jefferson Davis Gets His Citizenship Back* (Lexington, Ky., 1980).

Three works offer a good introduction to the romantic spirit as embodied by some fire-eaters: Russell B. Nye, *The Cultural Life of the New Nation, 1776–1830* (New York, 1960); A. O. Lovejoy, "The Meaning of Romanticism for the Historian," *Journal of the History of Ideas*, II (1941), 257–78; and Rollin G. Osterweis, *Romanticism and Nationalism in the Old South* (Baton Rouge, 1971).

For a deeper understanding of the concept of honor and its frequently violent manifestations, the most useful works are Bertram Wyatt-Brown, *Southern Honor: Ethics and Behavior in the Old South* (Oxford, 1982), and "Honor and Secession," in *Yankee Saints and Southern Sinners* (Baton Rouge, 1985), 183–213; and Kenneth S. Greenberg, "The Nose, the Lie, and the Duel in the Antebellum South," *American Historical Review*, XCV (1990), 57–74. Other valuable sources include John Hope Franklin, *The Militant South* (New York, 1956); Bruce D. Dickson, *Violence and Culture in the Antebellum South* (Austin, 1979); Steven M. Stowe, "The 'Touchiness' of the Gentleman Planter: The Sense of Esteem and Continuity in the Antebellum South," *Psychohistory Review*, VIII (1979), 6–17; and Elliott J. Gorn, "'Gouge and Bite, Pull Hair and Scratch': The Social Significance of Fighting in the Southern Backcountry," *American Historical Review*, XC (1985), 18–43.

Because of the special academic affiliations of Tucker, Keitt, Wigfall, and De Bow, the following three works proved very useful: *History of the College of William and Mary, from Its Foundation, in 1660, to 1874* (Richmond, 1874); Daniel Walker Hollis, *The University of South Carolina* (2 vols.; Columbia, S.C., 1951–56); and John P. Dyer, *Tulane: Biography of a University* (New York, 1966).

Bibliographical Essay

Two studies of antebellum rhetoric were particularly useful for understanding the unique qualities of William Porcher Miles's speeches: A. V. Huff, "The Eagle and the Vulture: Changing Attitudes Toward Nationalism in Fourth of July Orations Delivered in Charleston, 1778–1860," *South Atlantic Quarterly*, XII (1972), 10–22; and Joseph R. James, Jr., "The Transformation of the Fourth of July in South Carolina, 1850–1919" (M.A. thesis, Louisiana State University, 1987).

John Stanford Coussons, "Thirty Years with Calhoun, Rhett, and the Charleston Mercury: A Chapter in South Carolina Politics" (Ph.D. dissertation, Louisiana State University, 1971), and Chauncey S. Boucher, "The Annexation of Texas and the Bluffton Movement in South Carolina," *Mississippi Valley Historical Review*, VI (1919), 3–33, proved important sources of information on Barnwell Rhett.

Although neither author included fire-eaters in his study, Ronald G. Walters, *American Reformers, 1815–1860* (New York, 1978), and John L. Thomas, "Romantic Reform in America, 1815–1865," *American Quarterly*, XVII (1965), 656–81, suggest that the efforts of fire-eaters placed them within the context of antebellum reform.

Other useful works include Lewis Cecil Gray, *History of Agriculture in the Southern United States to 1860* (2 vols.; Washington, D.C., 1933), for references to Ruffin; Thelma Jennings, *The Nashville Convention: Southern Movement for Unity, 1848–1851* (Memphis, 1980); Eugene C. Harter, *The Lost Colony of the Confederacy* (Jackson, Miss., 1986), which mentions the role of Yancey's sons in establishing a Confederate colony in Brazil after the war; D. Augustus Dickert, *History of Kershaw's Brigade* (Newberry, S.C., 1899), for a detailed account of Keitt at Cold Harbor; Virginius Dabney, *Virginia: The New Dominion* (Garden City, N.Y., 1972), on relief attempts in disease-ridden Norfolk that helped Miles achieve fame in the South; and Mark Summers, *The Plundering Generation: Corruption and the Crisis of Union, 1849–1861* (Oxford, 1987). The lack of agreement by fire-eaters on southern nationalism makes all the more important Drew G. Faust's thoughtful *Creation of Confederate Nationalism* (Baton Rouge, 1989). Robert E. May, *The Southern Dream of a Caribbean Empire, 1854–1861* (Athens, Ga., 1989), provides thoughtful examination of the importance of territorial expansion to disunion and secessionists. Laurence Shore, *Southern Capitalists: The Ideological Leadership of an Elite, 1832–1885* (Chapel Hill, 1986), and Fred Bateman, *A Deplorable Scarcity: The Failure of Industrialization in the Slave Economy* (Chapel Hill, 1981), help place James De Bow's antebellum critique of the South in a broader context.

Index